Bon apetit!

Adris, Frank & Children

Helen Exum's Chattanooga Cook Book

By Helen McDonald Exum

First Printing	January 1970	2,000
Second Printing	May 1970	10,000
Third Printing	October 1973	5,000
Fourth Printing	March 1975	5,000
Fifth Printing	August 1977	2,000
Sixth Printing	March 1978	2,500
Seventh Printing	March 1979	2,500

Printed by
The Chattanooga News-Free Press
Chattanooga, Tennessee, U.S.A.

Inquiries or requests for extra copies should be addressed to:
HELEN McDONALD EXUM
Chattanooga News-Free Press
400 East 11th Street
Chattanooga, Tennessee 37401

This book is lovingly dedicated to my father, Roy McDonald. Without him, the pages that follow this introduction would still be blank.

He was the man who was determined we could print the book on equipment we already had. He was the man who, after everyone else had gone for the day, was still experimenting with different styles of type for the index, or making sure the color separations were good, or setting cutlines himself.

In short this book is dedicated to the man who made it a family project and who made it come true.

INTRODUCTION

The first edition of this Chattanooga Cookbook came off the press nearly eight years ago, in January 1970. Since no one ever knows exactly what a book will do, the adventures of this book about the people, the history, the recipes used in our Tennessee city have delighted us all and surpassed our expectations.

This book about Chattanooga cooking has gone all over the country and been featured in over fifty newspapers and full color in McCalls magazine. Yet here at home we use it more regularly than any other cookbook, and people tell us they do the same. We have reprinted, revised, reprinted, revised. Now we are reprinting again.

This is a book about Chattanooga, Tennessee, a pleasant city nestled in the valley and protected by beautiful mountains and ridges. We are at the foothills of the Appalachian Mountains, which begin just south of us and stretch all the way up to Maine.

First a trading post on the Tennessee River, this was back country much later than other sections of the South. Not until the Indians were driven west in the "Trail of Tears" in the 1830's was the land settled in small farms around what was to be Chattanooga. Chattanooga is a disputed word of Creek origin meaning "rock coming to a point" or "eagle's nest." Either is an appropriate word for the point that Lookout Mountain makes as it looks over the city.

We first came into prominence in history as a railroad center and battleground during the Civil War. The railroads brought people and later, factories and industry. This is the home of bottled Coca-Colas, Krystal hamburgers, Rock City, Ruby Falls and Confederama, three insurance companies, TVA and the Chickamauga Dam, several colleges including the University of Tennessee at Chattanooga. Our factories make nuclear boilers, nylon, stoves, textiles, chemicals and carpets. One of our biggest businesses now is touring visitors who come to enjoy our scenery and history.

In Chattanooga we seem to be a combination of many traditions. We are southern but not Deep South. The southern traits that newcomers say they find here are the friendliness, the hospitality, the unhurried conversations. We are not a sophisticated people, and anyone who has lived here two or three years is likely to speak to a dozen friends on an ordinary errand to town. We entertain mostly at home.

When I first began to think about a Chattanooga cookbook, I tried to think about what type of cuisine we really do have. As people have come to our city to make their homes, they have brought many traditions. The kind of food that Chattanooga people seem to like best though, is simple southern food: Chicken fixed in a variety of ways, beef either roasted or smothered with gravy, ham for festive occasions, hot homemade biscuits, cornbread, rolls, grits, fresh vegetables and fresh fruits, pies and cakes. This is delightful old-fashioned food. Our thousands of good cooks also keep up with the latest cookbooks and magazines, bring home recipes from their travels and exchange prize recipes. Chattanooga cuisine might be described as modern and varied with southern undertones.

Twenty years ago I began writing a weekly food column for the Chattanooga News-Free Press. This has certainly been the source of some of my best recipes. I would never have called people all over Chattanooga or gone into their kitchens to get their recipes if it had not been for the food column. Meeting wonderful southern cooks, interviewing hotel chefs, going to conferences for food editors in New York and Chicago has been a great stimulus in cooking for our family each night.

This is a cookbook about Chattanooga and contains recipes from both our old families and the newcomers we have come to think of as our own. It seemed a shame to leave out some of the recipes we have brought back from trips to the beach in South Carolina as well as many other favorites that have appeared in the food column, so they are included.

As the book began to write itself, it seemed dull not to explain how I got the recipe or how we first began to use it or a little about the friend who gave it. There have crept in many family happenings, but as we think back about how we cooked everything from biscuits to gumbo, it all revolved around my own family and the things we ate every night.

Since we sent this book out and thousands of people really did buy copies, we have had some wonderful letters from new friends. And I am very conscious that God has blessed this book and the hands that wrote it. What other explanation could there be for a simple Southern cookbook to get written up in fifty papers over the country and for orders to come in from everywhere . . ..China and Hawaii to Texas and Maine.

We have had letters that said the readers got homesick, hungry, laughed, cried, or even learned to cook. What these readers didn't know was that the book was actually printed on an antique press and assembled by my own children and their friends in the most unorthodox way. We gathered and punched and bound. Even Ellen at five put return stickers on the mailers. My father directed all the activity and kept books.

When we had gone through 12,000 books and many adventures, we did get a new press to print the books on. It is a beautiful new Miehle offset and such a dream that it was hard not to stroke it when it first arrived. It is still hard not to smile and hum a happy tune when a thousand sheets of paper whiz through so quietly.

We have not changed this edition except to bring it up to date. We now look back on the 22,000 books that were gathered by hand, punched and bound by sons, daughters, friends, assembled for mailing or carried to bookstores. This edition will be our dream—a hard back book.

Reading through this book today, I have a feeling of nostalgia. This is really the way we were in the 1950's and 1960's. This is the way our city was. This is the way our friends were. The boys wore short haircuts; the girls wore short dresses. Vietman hung over us. These were the years when my six children were growing up at home and we had big dinners every night.

Yet these same recipes are good today. Granny Smartt's pound cake still gets made regularly for birthdays. A bride can learn to make vegetable soup from the directions here. And this look at Chattanooga life in the 1950's and 1960's is still the standard Chattanooga gift for a bride, a hostess, an out of town friend.

This very personal food chronicle has seen us through good times and bad, with the kitchen our mainstay. I hope that you will use these recipes as much as we have.

Helen McDonald Exum

Chattanooga, Tennessee
June 1977

CONTENTS

COLOR PHOTOGRAPHS

Cover: *As you stand at the point of Lookout Mountain and look down, the Tennessee River makes a bend and forms the shape of a moccasin. This familiar scene, combined with the cannon from the Battle above the Clouds, is the trademark of Chattanooga. The color photo is by J.B. Collins and the cover design by Samuel A. Hunter.*

PHOTOGRAPHS

Helen Exum's Chattanooga Cook Book

Chattanooga is a river city surrounded by mountains. This scenic view from Signal Mountain looks out over Williams Island and the Tennessee River to Lookout Mountain.

CHAPTER I

Soups

Just as in other parts of the country, Chattanooga entertains less formally now than in the past. Dinner parties with a first course of soup are much more rare than buffet dinners at which the guests serve themselves. This was bound to happen with less help in the kitchen and the hostess doing all the cooking, but it is a shame, because all the delicate soups people used to think up rarely get made.

Tomato soup, celery soup, asparagus soup, corn soup are all memories of the Chattanooga at the turn of the century. Now people buy them in cans or frozen. Sometimes soup is served first in the living room before going in to dinner, but most often the soup that Chattanoogans now make is hearty enough to be the main course.

Almost everyone likes a hearty vegetable soup for a winter night's supper, and many people here make wonderful vegetable soup regularly. At Thanksgiving and Christmas oyster stew is a must. Potato and onion soup is an old standby.

I hope there will always be a few die-hards like me who think soup adds enough of a special tone when served before a meal to take the extra trouble every once in a while. The freezer has put soup making within the possibility of everyone, because it can simmer at your convenience, be frozen and await your pleasure.

Good soup stimulates the appetite, nourishes the young and old alike and comforts the soul.

In the last century during the railroad boom, whether a small town grew or didn't depended on whether the railroads had a terminal there.

Chattanooga was ideally suited as a crossroads for commerce and transportation, as was later proved during the Civil War, but in 1849 Thomas Crutchfield was mayor and was very active in promoting the affairs of the Western and Atlantic Railway. He promised to build a hotel if the railroad would establish the terminal station on West Ninth Street, then called James Street. The Crutchfield House was a very popular hotel and was succeeded by the Read House.

1

The Read House, with its handsome paneled lobby and its elegant Green Room, has enjoyed a reputation for excellent cuisine over a long period of years. They make their own breads and rolls, you can order lobster, gourmet specialties, or fine steaks, but for many lovers of good food, a cup of the soup du jour at the Read House is a must.

Chef Gunther Krupp explained how he makes soup to me one day. One reason hotels and restaurants have such good soup is that they know how to make good stock and do it regularly. To make his clam chowder, Chef Krupp boils fish bones the day before.

Even in his Spanish Style Split-Pea Soup, he includes beef or chicken stock. To his practiced eye and taste, he can tell about how soup is coming along and what it needs by sniffing the fragrant steam from the huge kettles which he stirs with big wooden paddles.

Then he poured some to taste into a small shallow bowl, and simply sipped from this to check the exact seasoning. It was perfect.

Two favorite soups are Spanish Style Yellow Split Pea Soup and Clam Chowder with mushrooms.

READ HOUSE YELLOW SPLIT PEA SOUP

Soak overnight 1 pound yellow split peas. The next day drain the peas and place in a soup pot. Add 3 quarts water or beef or chicken stock, 1 small ham hock, 2 medium-sized onions, and cook until peas get half done. Now add 4 medium-sized diced potatoes, 1 piece of celery, and season with salt and black pepper.

Let cook over slow heat for one hour or even longer until all ingredients get well done. Stir frequently. Remove from heat and strain soup through colander with wooden spatula. Place back on stove and let simmer for 15 to 20 minutes. Stir frequently.

Cook separately in a skillet 1 pound of medium diced breakfast sausage, Spanish sausage or smoked Polish sausage. Cook over medium heat until brown and done. Add sausage to pea soup. If sausage is too fat, hold back some of the grease.

Serve with bread, croutons, or cornbread crumbles on top. Serves 8 to 12.

CHEF KRUPP'S CLAM CHOWDER WITH MUSHROOMS

To prepare a good chowder or any kind of fish soup, you should have a good fish stock.

Go to the fish market and buy 1½ pounds of snapper, trout, or halibut bones and scraps. Place in a soup pot with about 3 quarts of water, 1 small onion, 1 pice of celery, 1 small carrot, 1 bay leaf, 1 teaspoon pickling spice wrapped in a little cloth bag. Bring to a boil and simmer until stock reduces to about half, strain and let cool. Stock can be put in the refrigerator until the next day if you desire to get a head start.

To make the chowder, place in a soup pot $\frac{1}{2}$ stick butter, 4 ounces fat back, diced small, 1 diced onion, 1 piece celery, 1 green bell pepper, 2 medium-sized potatoes, all diced. Let simmer for 3 to 5 minutes. Add half of an 8 ounce package of frozen clams, or 1 can of clams (No. 2 size). Simmer for 5 minutes more. Do not let it get brown. Add 4 tablespoons all-purpose flour, stir and let simmer for about 3 to 5 minutes.

Now add the fish stock ($1\frac{1}{2}$ quarts). Stir mixture until base is all dissolved, no lumps. Cook over low heat for 50 to 60 minutes so that all the flavor gets out of the vegetables and clams. Stir frequently to keep chowder from sticking to the bottom of the pot. Season with salt, white pepper, a pinch of thyme, 1 teaspoon Accent. Now add $\frac{1}{2}$ can evaporated milk, the other package of clams or 1 can clams (No. 2 size), 3 pimentos, diced small, and mushrooms.

To prepare mushrooms, slice 4 ounces fresh mushrooms and saute in 1 tablespoon butter for 5 minutes. Add to chowder. You may like to use canned mushrooms. 1 can (No. 2 size) can be added directly to the chowder without cooking. Just drain juice before adding.

Serve with bread croutons or puffed rice.

Chef Gunther Krupp
The Read House

One November day Susan and I called Mrs. Gardner Bright to see if we could come see some of the Chrismons she had been making. These are tree ornaments and she was making them for the Christmas tree at the Church of the Good Shepherd.

We had a quick lunch at home and dropped in at the Bright's. When we opened the kitchen door, we were welcomed by the most heavenly smell of fresh vegetable soup, and the cozy table in the kitchen was set with three places. Susan and I promptly decided to have a second lunch.

Gardner Bright was a Realtor who early joined the group making Lookout Mountain into a year-round residential area. It used to be a summer place with people from New Orleans coming up for the hot months along with such Chattanoogans as the Pounds, Willinghams, Chamberlains, Montagues and others.

3

In the late 20s and 30s, families moved up and built permanent ·homes and now it is heavily populated from the Point to the golf club and on out to Covenant College, formerly the Lookout Mountain Hotel.

Mrs. Bright is a charming, soft-spoken lady who does things "nicely." At summer parties, she puts slices of lemon or orange or a cherry in the ice cubes as they freeze. I hope she never gets an ice maker because she wouldn't do it anymore. At buffet suppers she makes whole wheat biscuits to have along with ham. She has a pleasant, kind laugh, knows funny stories, and having lunch with her is a delightful occasion.

She makes soup as a professional would, and while being very thin, it is hearty. She calls this "substance" and says that if a soup doesn't have strength or substance, it just isn't very good.

Along with soup, she makes some unusual croutons to serve with it. She slices some bread very thin. Then she removes the crusts and cuts the bread in narrow strips. She runs them in a slow oven long enough to completely dry out, and keeps a supply on hand in a cannister so that she always has some for soup. Why should anyone buy melba toast? This is her recipe for 2-Day Soup.

MRS. BRIGHT'S 2-DAY SOUP

The first day get some soup bones from the butcher. Knuckle bones make good soup as do shank bones with marrow in them. If you have any chicken backs or necks you can add them, too. Put in a very large kettle and cover with water. Cover and simmer several hours, seasoning with salt and pepper. Strain this and pour into a large bowl or crock. Cover and set in a cold place overnight. Either put it in the refrigerator or on the back porch.

The next day skim off all the fat from the top. Your stock should be jellied. To make the soup, chop some onions, carrots, celery, add some stew beef in small pieces, any vegetables that you might have.

Sometimes she uses a half package of frozen, mixed vegetables that you buy at the store. Add a can of tomatoes. You may add sliced okra and diced potatoes. This should simmer an hour or two, but since the main simmering has been done the day before, you can get a soup with substance very easily this way. Taste to season correctly, and serve with croutons.

Mrs. Gardner Bright

A simple tomato soup to begin a meal or to serve for lunch with a sandwich was this recipe from one of Chattanooga's earliest cookbooks. It was from the late Mrs. E.O. Wells, the mother of Mrs. Ed

4

Blake. This simple mixture of tomatoes and seasoning can now be put through the blender instead of through a sieve, but the result will be a little different from canned tomato soup.

A version I have used sometimes is to combine a can of tomato soup with consomme, season to taste and garnish with chopped parsley from the herb garden.

MRS. WELLS' TOMATO SOUP

1 can tomatoes	1 slice onion
4 cloves	2 tablespoons butter
2 teaspoons sugar	3 tablespoons flour
1 pint water	Pinch of soda

Cook together 20 minutes the tomatoes, the water, onion and bay leaf. Strain, pushing everything through sieve except the seeds and seasoning. Add sugar, salt and soda, then work flour and butter together and add to the soup. Let come to a boil and serve with croutons.

Mrs. E.O. Wells.

One week when we were all down with flu, Mrs. Paul Quick brought us some soup. Why is it that something from someone else's kitchen tastes so much better than something you fix yourself? Hers was a hearty chicken broth with tender rice and celery in it. I called to ask how she did it, and she insisted that it was just this simple:

MRS. QUICK'S CHICKEN SOUP

Strain the broth left from boiling a hen and refrigerate so that the fat can easily be removed from the top. Put the broth in a large pan with about 1 cup of celery cut very fine and 1 cup of raw rice. You may need to add water. Boil until the rice and celery are tender. Taste to correct seasoning so that there is plenty of salt and a little pepper, but not highly seasoned.

Mrs. Paul Quick.

Fehn's restaurant started back in 1938 when Joseph and Frieda Fehn came here from Texas to open a restaurant on Tremont Street. Mr. Fehn had come from Hungary just after the turn of the century, lived for a while at Fort Oglethorpe when the Post was there, and then moved to San Antonio. They brought with them to Chattanooga their children Alfred, Robert, and Dora.

The word soon spread that "whatever you order at Fehn's is always good" and the family operation had a second downtown branch on Georgia Avenue before many years. In the 50's, Alfred and Robert Fehn built their dream ... a beautiful restaurant down by the river just off the bridge.

What used to be a very nondescript area is now a complex of green landscaping with trees, shrubs and borders, the Little Theater and a lovely apartment.

Fehn's is still a family operation. Alfred's boys Bruce, Donald and Bill have all been called on when needed, and Robert's girls have taken inventory and done jobs that girls can. Some people think Fehn's shrimp salad is their specialty; businessmen come home talking about the macaroon pie they had at lunch; I asked for their potato soup.

FEHN'S POTATO SOUP

4 cups Idaho potatoes sliced thin	3 cups heated milk
¼ cup celery, sliced thin	¼ teaspoon salt
2 cups Spanish onion, diced	Dash white pepper
5 cups strong chicken	Dash cayenne pepper
or beef stock	Dash ground nutmeg
¼ cup flour	2 tablespoons minced parsley
½ stick butter or margarine	

Start the sliced potatoes in cool stock and add salt. While coming to a boil, saute the onions and celery in butter. When the onions and celery are cooked clear, add the flour and continue cooking slowly several minutes keeping well stirred.

As soon as the stock in the pot boils, add part of it to the onion and butter mixture. Let it begin to simmer and continue until tender. When the potato slices are tender, break in small pieces with either a whip or by running through a ricer.

Add the pot of simmering vegetables back to the potato mixture and simmer together a couple of minutes.

Add the heated milk at the very last and turn off the heat so it won't form a skim. Finally put in the dashes of white pepper, cayenne, nutmeg, and sprinkle with minced parsley.

Fehn's Restaurant

6

One Thanksgiving we printed an oyster stew that uses as a base a can of frozen potato soup. Our readers say it is their favorite.

HOLIDAY OYSTER STEW

2 cans (12 ounces each)
  oysters, fresh or frozen
2 slices bacon, chopped
1 can (10¼ ounces) frozen
  condensed cream of
  potato soup

Chopped parsley
4 cups oyster liquor and
  half-and-half cream
1¼ teaspoons salt
¼ cup chopped onion
Dash white pepper

Thaw frozen oysters. Drain oysters, reserving liquor. Fry bacon until crisp. Remove bacon from fat. Cook onion in bacon fat until tender. Add soup, oyster liquor, cream and seasonings; heat, stirring occasionally. Add bacon and oysters; heat for 3 to 5 minutes longer or until edges of oysters begin to curl. Sprinkle with parsley. Serves 6.

The best French onion soup we know is also the quickest. The important thing is to know when and how to use the cans of stock that the soup companies painstakingly simmer for us. By combining bought stock and fresh chopped onions and butter, you can have really wonderful onion soup.

This recipe came to us from a California friend, who served it one foggy night on the West Coast. We have since brightened up many foggy, dreary nights on the mountain with this hearty soup.

QUICK FRENCH ONION SOUP

1 can condensed beef broth
1 can condensed chicken broth
2 cups water

4 medium onions, chopped
2 tablespoons butter

Into a kettle put the butter, and saute the onions in it until they are soft. Then add the cans of broth and the water. This mixture is best when it has simmered about an hour. If you are in a hurry and must serve it in 15 minutes, you'll still have compliments. Salt and pepper to taste and serve with croutons.

Pass Parmesan cheese at the table. Sometimes I sprinkle a little chopped parsley on each serving to make it look pretty.

The Mountain City Club, until 1975 when they moved into their new quarters, was the handsome columned building on Chestnut Street between Seventh and Eighth Streets, and here for many years some of the most prominent men in town have had breakfast or lunch or dinner with privacy, dignity and convenience.

fast or lunch or dinner with privacy, dignity and convenience.

For many years ladies were invited only to the Christmas party, although they are welcome for both lunch and dinner now. One friend said recently, "No matter how delicious a meal I plan, my husband will have had it better for lunch at the Mountain City today."

Unelle Johnson, now retired, presided over the kitchen at the Mountain City Club for 18 years. He says, "I'll be glad to give you any recipe I have, but to tell the truth, the men don't like fancy food. They like soups, almost any meat, fixed the way we always have, fresh vegetables, biscuits and cornbread, just southern cooking."

He cooks simply but there is a light touch, a richness, a variety that makes the most of whatever is in season. He gave me the following recipe for old fashioned bean soup which includes stock and is a much better recipe than the one given out by the Senate Restaurant in Washington.

MOUNTAIN CITY CLUB BEAN SOUP

Soak 1 pound white navy beans overnight. Wash them good and saute in bacon drippings 1 tablespoon chopped onion, 1 tablespoon celery, and 1 tablespoon chopped carrot. Add about 1 quart good beef stock, 1 bay leaf, and season to taste. Add the beans and about 2 quarts of water. Now add a small piece of ham, if you have it, or if you don't, use some bacon plus some bacon drippings.

After all this has simmered about 30 minutes add 2 potatoes, diced very small. If you put this on about 8, it will be ready about 11 o'clock. If it cooks down and gets too thick, add a little water. Take out 1½ cups beans at the last. Run all the rest of the soup through a sieve. Bring to a boil again and add the beans. Serve with croutons.

Chef Unelle Johnson
Mountain City Club.

When we have snow on our mountains and ridges, we never know how long it will last. Sometimes it is simple . . . the day it snows and the day it melts. Sometimes it lasts several days. We all get busy hunting gloves for everybody, getting chains on the car, getting the big boys to bring in wood, and drying out the little ones when they come in from sledding. By the second day we all know that what we want more than anything is a pot of good vegetable soup.

One Sunday during a cold spell, I noticed how nice and brown the

8

electric skillet was that I had cooked steak in. I emptied the grease from the skillet and poured in boiling water to get the nice brown broth or glaze you need to make soup with. By the time I had added it to the soup pot with two sirloin steak bones, a can of tomatoes, carrots, onions, celery, and some cabbage, cut up very fine, it looked as if it were going to be a good kettle of soup.

I chopped up a little ham finely to add flavor, seasoned it and let it simmer. Potatoes were added before dinner along with a can of chicken broth to make it heartier, and we all agreed that we had never had better soup. Of course, it may have been that we were all hungry, but the hot soup, plenty of buttered hoecakes, and cold milk seemed perfect as we all gathered round the table that night, warm and safe from the winter's cold.

One of the best teachers about making soup was the late Luis Diat, the famous French chef at the Ritz, who wrote cooking articles every month for Gourmet magazine. One of his best was about the great dish of France that has stood the test of ten centuries ... the pot-au-feu.

The pot-au-feu, simple vegetable soup with boiled meat to go with it, is the traditional Sunday dinner in France. The tender boiled beef is sliced and served with the vegetables, and the soup waits until the next day to be served. This is logical, because the meat from the soup bone is the sweetest tenderest meat.

The secret that I learned from him was how to get soup with a golden brownish cast and a little richer taste. For years I had been making soup that was fairly good, but it didn't taste rich enough. At first I thought I should use more meat, but I tried, and it wasn't this. When Diat explained that to get a brown stock, brown the bones first, I did.

He suggested that you add a carrot and onion to your beef bones and run them under the broiler long enough to get them good and brown. You then transfer them to a soup kettle, pour water on them and simmer. Sure enough the water will take on that beautiful brown taste and color that you want, and it won't make any difference if you add tomatoes or not, the soup will be so pretty.

We have adapted his recipe. He recommends the beef plus root vegetables. You can add tomatoes and simmer vegetables. We found that if you sauteed your chopped onions, celery, carrots, and whatever else you add, it brings out their flavor.

Soup also seems best when made in a heavy pot that holds the heat. The big cast iron pots covered with enamel are especially good.

SOME THINGS I HAVE LEARNED ABOUT VEGETABLE SOUP

Vegetable soup can be made with a soup bone, a leftover beef roast, bones from a beef roast, or bones from steak. It is best first to brown the bones, either in the oven or on top of the stove. Pour off any fat. Now pour over boiling water so that the liquid has a rich golden look. This is the same principle of making gravy from the brown bits in the skillet.

Old-fashioned cooks, when they had no meat, sugared a slice of onion and let it carmelize in a small skillet. Water was poured over this to get a broth. You can also buy meat glaze. If all this seems foolish to you, you can put the meat in a large heavy pot and start simmering it in water. You will have a nice soup, but it will not have as hearty a taste as if you had browned the meat first.

After the meat is in the pot with water, think about your vegetables. Onions, carrots and celery are a must. Chop finely. If you have time it is better to sautee them first in the smallest amount of butter or oil to bring out the flavor. Chef John Barnes is a great believer in this principle.

I like cabbage in soup. It adds strength and character. Chop very, very fine so that everyone doesn't know, and don't put too much in, about ¼ head of cabbage for a large pot. Now add a big can of tomatoes along with the vegetables.

Begin seasoning with about 4 peppercorns, a teaspoon of salt, a teaspoon of Accent, a pinch of sugar and a bay leaf. If I have any parsley, I add about ½ cup, finely chopped.

Now look in the refrigerator. Any leftover ham or chicken is very desirable. If it is fried chicken, take the skin off and chop the chicken finely and add along with the bone. If it is ham, chop finely and add. I find myself adding about a square inch of ham chopped to any chicken dish, meatloaf and spaghetti. It helps.

Skim off any foam. After an hour or two taste the soup. If it doesn't have a hearty enough taste, you need to open a can of chicken broth and put it in. About an hour before serving, add either rice, potatoes, or cut up macaroni. We like potatoes best, cut in small cubes. I think to add all three makes a mess ... choose one.

Don't let the soup boil down so that it is too thick. Thick soup just doesn't go down the throat as well. If it boils down, add water. Also look in your refrigerator for any green beans or peas. The head of the house likes okra and corn in soup; I like it better without. Your family may like something else.

Always taste and correct the seasoning at the last. If it tastes flat, add a dash of soy sauce. It's wonderful. Or sometimes tomatoes need a little acid like a squirt of lemon juice. Be sure the salt and pepper are right. When you get it right, you will know.

Soup is always best served with hoecakes.

Mrs. Paul Kruesi told me about an unusual soup made by combining several different soups along with milk and crabmeat. You end up with a sort of curried crab bisque.

CRAB SOUP

1 can Campbell's pepper pot soup   1 large can Pet milk
1 can beef consomme   1 can (7 ounce) crabmeat
½ teaspoon curry powderd

Mix the ingredients well and simmer a few minutes in a saucepan until heated thoroughly and well blended. At the last stir in some dry sherry before serving.

Mrs. Paul Kruesi

One day the mail man brought some gumbo bowls from New Orleans. The bowls are not fancy ... they look like old-fashioned ironstone and are as wide as a plate but about an inch or so deep, so that they hold the soupy gumbo and rice.

It was the first Sunday after the bowls came that we made the first gumbo. We had gumbos before that were either too thick or too highly spiced, or too stringy with file. This gumbo we all agreed was the best we ever put in our mouths. Most of us had second helpings, because the gumbo, rice, and Cuban bread was all we had for dinner.

CREOLE GUMBO

1 pound claw crabmeat   3 sprigs parsley, diced
1½ pounds raw shrimp   1 bay leaf
   (peeled and veined)   ½ teaspoon pepper (or to taste)
½ pound cut okra   1 large onion, chopped
2 cans tomatoes (No. 2 size)   3 large pods garlic, diced
2 small cans tomato sauce   4 cups water
6 tablespoons butter or oleo   1 tablespoon salt
1 medium green pepper, chopped

Place on stove a skillet containing butter or oleo and a kettle containing the tomatoes.

Saute the garlic, onions, pepper and parsley, and add to the kettle. Now add to the kettle, water, salt, pepper, and bay leaf and cook down. Fry okra and drain; add to kettle. Add crabmeat, shrimp, and tomato sauce. Cook for 30 minutes. To serve, put a mound of rice in each soup bowl, and serve over it the gumbo. French bread or light Cuban bread is good with this.

Hausmann's Recipe

11

CHAPTER II

Eggs

It is a memorable Sunday breakfast when your two granddaughters spend Saturday night, and then get up and make your favorite breakfast menu with eggs cooked exactly right. This is what Dottie Allison and Sue Ferguson, who are cousins, did when they were thirteen and spent the night with their grandparents, the James R. Hedges.

Their grandfather liked 2 shirred eggs, 2 pieces of bacon, 2 pieces of sausage, 3 slices of broiled tomatoes, a slice of toast, and coffee with honey and cream. Dot Hedges taught the girls how to do it, and they can cook all by themselves. They served the delicious breakfast and then sat down and lent their youthful company and enthusiasm and love. Interestingly enough, it led to greater things. Dottie spent the summer of 1972 at cooking school in London.

SHIRRED EGGS

Melt butter in a small skillet. They use a small oval copper one. Put two eggs in, sprinkle with a little salt and pepper, and cook over medium low heat. When the bottom and sides are firm and the yolks still a little "gooshey", as the girls say, the eggs are ready to serve their grandfather. They cook their own eggs until firm all the way through. This is personal preference, and the main thing is to please the one you are cooking for.

BROILED TOMATOES

Slice tomatoes in half, leaving the skins on. Spread with melted butter, sprinkle with salt, pepper, and sweet basil. Put in a small casserole pan and put in a 350 oven until the tomatoes are quite hot and sizzling.

Dottie Allison and Sue Ferguson

The prettiest pair of Chattanooga cateresses is Susan Ferguson and Dottie Allison, who cooked Thursday night dinners and Sunday breakfasts for their grandparents, the James R. Hedges, to get practice. In this picture, Mrs. Hedges shows them how to season a leg of lamb.

Years ago Mac Brock (Mrs. Richard) called to say that she was running out of drawer space for all the pages of the News-Free Press cooking column, and she thought we ought to put as many as possible in a cookbook.

This was the first time I knew that anyone also had the same problem that I had....finding the recipes that people all over Chattanooga have given me. Mac is a warm hearted, friendly, enthusiastic person who loves to cook as much as I do. She is a thoughtful friend, with a jar of plum jelly from her own tree, a box of fruitcake cookies, or some special new candy for anyone who drops in for a visit. This is her recipe for German pancakes, baked in the oven. This is actually a baked omelet.

GERMAN PANCAKES

6 eggs	1 teaspoon salt
1 cup flour	1 cup milk
6 tablespoons butter	

Beat eggs until very light. Add sifted dry ingredients. Spread the bottom and sides of a 10-inch cold iron frying pan with butter. Pour in the batter and bake in a hot oven at 400 degrees for 20 to 25 minutes. Bring hot to the table. Squeeze lemon juice over it, sprinkle with powdered sugar, cinnamon, and top with applesauce.

Mrs. Richard A. Brock

A cheese souffle that doesn't fall, that can be either a main dish or a side dish on a big buffet with ham, that can be made way ahead of time, and a souffle that even the children will eat, is what we are all looking for.

This one is actually a cheese casserole. Made by spreading bread slices with soft butter and cheese, cubing them, and putting them in a casserole with eggs and milk, this souffle mellows and seasons before baking. The children call it cheese sandwich souffle because under all the puffy glamor, there is the familiar taste of their favorite grilled cheese sandwich. If you are having it for supper, have a molded fruit salad with it.

"CHEESE SANDWICH" SOUFFLE

Cream together ¼ pound butter and ½ pound cheddar cheese, grated. Take 9 slices of regular bread and de-crust. (I use Pepperidge Farm type bread but you don't have to.) Spread each slice with butter and cheese and then cut in cubes. Place in baking dish lightly. Beat well 2 eggs and 2 cups milk. Add salt, pepper, and a dash of Worcestershire. Pour lightly into baking dish. Turn bread so that it is all wet.

14

The baking dish may be a cast iron casserole. It may set overnight or a few hours in the refrigerator. Let get to room temperature before baking, and fluff it up again. Bake at 350 degrees for 1 hour. Don't let it burn.

Way before Christmas one year, Franklin, the champion present giver of the family, began giving hints about all the wonderful things he was planning to give us for Christmas. I knew that he had been ordering from a catalog that specialized in free monogramming, and we were fascinated with all the dollar presents our nine-year-old had ordered with other people's names on them....engraved keyrings, personalized pencils, and door knockers. He began hinting about my present by saying, "This will change one thing about your life. Things will never be the same again."

Then he would say, "My present is going to make you the most modern cook." Several days later he would come up with, "You will like my present better than anyone else's, because it will put you in such a good humor every morning."

As Christmas came closer, he gave another hint. "The key word is 'stick'." I can't even remember all his ingenious hints, but I got the idea that it was something for the kitchen that he had had put up at the hardware store until he got all the money.

I did suggest that he go in with one of the other children so it wouldn't cost him so much. He wouldn't consider this. He says when you go in with someone else, they get half the credit even if it was your idea. When I am thanking him every morning the rest of my life, he doesn't want to share the glory.

On Christmas morning I unwrapped the Teflon skillet that he had been planning so long. He was so excited and pleased he was giggling, and I was so pleased I was smiling and said I would have never guessed. We immediately washed it and scrambled eggs that very morning, being very careful to use the special spoon he provided so we wouldn't scratch the finish.

In the weeks since, we certainly enjoyed the skillet, not just for scrambled eggs, but for omelets. I had never had trouble with omelets sticking, because I begin with a generous hunk of butter, but with the new skillet, the omelet fairly rolls out.

The omelet has been shrouded in mystery for so long, with all sorts of do's and don'ts, that many people have been discouraged from even trying. For many years I didn't try, because once I had made a tough, rubbery thing and figured I just didn't have the touch.

15

Then one of the French cooking schools here had a lesson in omelets. The teacher said you had to have a proper pan, use it for nothing else, never wash it, just wipe it out. Then she explained that as the omelet cooked very quickly, with your left hand hold the pan and shake it back and forth, and with your right hand, gently stir the omelet with a fork, and pull the omelet toward the center of the pan.

I came home to practice. I took a deep breath and got a grim look on my face as I started to shake the pan and stir the eggs at the same time. I must have looked very awkward.

I think the reason my omelets began to be good after a while was that I just kept on trying. It's that old principle of trying something over and over until you get the knack of it.

I now think omelet making is simple, that you can use almost any skillet as long as it is the right shape with rounded sides that flare out, and although it helps to keep several things in mind, there are no rigid rules. To know how to make an omelet is the greatest advantage. Omelets as a luncheon or even supper dish are better than for breakfast.

I don't know how many times I have asked people to stay for lunch when we really didn't have lunch fixed. I have made omelets filled with leftover chicken or grated cheese, or chopped mushrooms. Either a fruit salad or a green salad is quick and goes with this. And for bread have some toast or quick biscuits with ready mix. This is a very elegant meal, I think.

Omelets are perfect when you are eating alone or with little children. Susan is always the first one to notice when the chive start coming up in the herb garden, and then we have a chive omelet for lunch one day. Since Ellen and I are the only ones at home for lunch now, we have omelets with a leftover potato cut up and browned in butter or leftover bacon or ham. She eats as heartily as I do. The boys like omelets for supper along with fried potatoes. And then we have two boys who wouldn't touch an omelet if their lives depended upon it.

If your first omelets are not perfect, don't be discouraged. Just keep trying. Pretty soon they will be delicious.

ONE WAY TO MAKE OMELETS

Turn the eye of your stove to very high. This is the only time you ever cook eggs on very high heat. Into a bowl break 2 or 3 eggs. A 3-egg omelet is easiest, a 5-egg omelet very hard to manage. Salt and pepper the eggs and add 1 teaspoon water for each egg. With a fork, beat til light and frothy, about half a minute. In the meantime heat about 1 tablespoon real butter in a skillet. The Teflon skillet is about 8 inches across and the sides round and flare out just right.

When the butter is sizzling on the hot eye, it is time to add the eggs. Shake gently back and forth from time to time to prevent sticking, and with a fork or spatula, work the cooked egg as it begins to get solid, toward the middle so that the uncooked runny part comes to the outside. You want the omelet to be moist but not raw or runny. You can figure this out.

About this time, the envelope or outer covering will begin to get solid and slightly brown. When it does this, stop moving the eggs and just let it set on the hot eye about half a minute. When it is just golden, lift the outer half over the half toward you, give it about 3 more seconds, and slide out on the plate.

Overcooking an omelet on this high heat will make it tough, so don't cook too long. And remember that you can add any number of fillings just before you fold it over. Serve immediately.

A luncheon specialty is a congealed egg salad. Alice (Mrs. John) Stout made this once in a ring mold with the center filled with cold boiled shrimp.

MOLDED EGG SALAD

2 tablespoons unflavored gelatin
½ cup cold water
10 hard cooked eggs, grated
½ cup chili sauce
½ cup mayonnaise
¼ teaspoon pepper
1 cup hot chicken broth
1 teaspoon salt
1 tablespoon grated onion

Soften gelatin in cold water, then dissolve in hot broth. Allow to cool. Combine remaining ingredients and add to gelatin mixture. Pour into oiled mold. Chill until firm. Serve on lettuce with a dressing.

Mrs. John Stout

Casseroles of hard boiled eggs are very complementary to add to a buffet featuring ham or turkey, or to have as luncheon or supper dishes. One of the best is the version that Peg Brock makes for Christmas brunch.

EGG CASSEROLE

Hard boil 6 eggs. Make a cream sauce using 1½ tablespoons butter, 1½ tablespoons flour, and 1 cup milk. Season with salt and paprika.

When Jean Spears and Borden Hallowes were married, the seated wedding brunch afterward was one of the prettiest anyone remembers. The tables were covered with apricot satin and net, the gold cherub compotes held tulips, daisies, roses and boxwood, the elaborate menu featured Eggs Benedict.

Now grate ¼ pound (or more) New York cheese. Take a buttered casserole and make a layer in the bottom of rolled out Ritz crackers. Now make a layer of sliced eggs, then the sauce, then a heavy sprinkling of cheese. Repeat so that you have two or three layers depending on the size of the casserole. Top with more of the rolled out crackers and dot with butter. Sprinkle with paprika and if you have any parsley on hand, it would look nice on top.

Mrs. W. E. Brock Jr.

No one who was there will ever forget the wedding brunch following Jean Spears' wedding to Borden Hallowes. Apricot satin cloths covered with apricot net had been made for each table, and the centerpieces were golden cherub compotes filled with red and pink tulips, boxwood, daisies, ranuncalus. The feast was a menu featuring eggs Benedict. The ballroom at Fairyland Club was never more beautiful, and it was a very happy occasion.

At Fairyland Club, they say that they have found the secret to Eggs Benedict is to serve them very hot and very quickly. The recipe is a simple one.

EGGS BENEDICT

Toast an English muffin half. Top with a slice of ham. On this put a poached egg, and over it all spoon on Hollandaise sauce. This can be run in a very hot oven a minute before serving. I still do not know how they poached 200 eggs for this brunch, but they were very delicious.

Fairyland Club

19

CHAPTER III

Meats .

Chattanooga, being an inland city, grew up eating the meats that were the easiest to get. In the very early days before refrigeration, this meant the chicken and pork that were available all year round, with beef and lamb less frequently.

With modern transportation and a complete selection of meats from all over the country in our supermarkets, our food habits are slowly changing. Our good cooks like to try new recipes from other parts of the world, interesting casseroles. Yet, our men basically like meat and potatoes. They like meat cooked simply ... roasted, broiled, fried or smothered with gravy.

If you are invited to dinner, you are apt to have a dinner typical to the southern town that we are. It might be ham, roast beef, fried or smothered chicken, with plenty of hot biscuits or rolls. These are the things that we do best.

More and more our cooks are looking for imaginative ways to prepare meats and meat casseroles ahead of time. With more people working than ever, there is more planning ahead, freezing ahead, and convenience cooking. I have included both some old and basic ways of preparing beef, pork and lamb, and some of the newer Chattanooga favorites, too.

When Ross's Landing was organized in 1838 on the land made available by the Cherokee removal to the West, there were 53 citizens who had moved in during the two years since the Treaty of Echota. The land which is now downtown Chattanooga was divided into the Northeast Quarter section and into the Southeast Quarter Section, and six commissioners were elected ... John P. Long, Aaron Rawlings, George W. Williams, Allen Kennedy, Albert Lenoir, and Reynolds Ramsey. Their duty was to lay off the town in lots, designate certain lots for schools and churches, sell the lots and choose a new name for the town, Chattanooga. The streets parallel to the river were numbered, and the streets going east and west were named for the trees of the forest, just as in Philadelphia.

Mrs. Burton Frierson represents the first citizens of Chattanooga along with her grandson, Daniel Kennedy Frierson Jr., whose grandfather several generations back was one of the first white settlers to come across the Tennessee River to Ross's Landing, now Chattanooga.

The first public meeting place was a log school house at 5th and Lookout Street, which also served as a community hall. The Presbyterian, Baptist and Methodist churches were all organized in it.

It is interesting how many of our families have come down through these first citizens. In an age when it is not considered good taste to brag about one's ancestors, it is a good thing to see that children and children's children down to six and seven generations, having traveled the world and free to live anywhere that they choose, should choose the same pleasant hills and valleys of Chattanooga that their fathers loved. Who could name all the family branches that come down from these first commissioners. If you named the Longs, Williams, Rawlings, Luptons, Kruesis, Smartts, Brocks, Friersons, Keys, Pattens, you would still leave some out. But they have all given character, color, stability and leadership to our city.

Rowena Frierson (Mrs. Burton) comes down in the line from Allen Kennedy, and in a family full of Myras, Rowenas and Margarets, Daniels, Kennedys and Smartts, Rowena's grandson Daniel Kennedy Frierson, Jr. is the 8th generation from Colonel Daniel Kennedy, father of one of the first commissioners, Allen Kennedy.

Rowena, as the mother of five sons, knows that for any family celebration men like steak or roast beef. She says that they broil their steak just the usual way ... a good thick steak broiled in the oven and turned until it is as done or as rare as you like it. With it she serves a steak sauce that she calls Margaret Frierson Williamson's Steak Sauce. For this book we will call it Rowena's Steak Sauce and she says it makes any cut of steak delectable.

SIMPLE BROILED STEAK

Get a T-bone steak 1½ inches thick. Wipe with a clean cloth wrung out with cold water, trim off any excess fat from the steak and lubricate the broiler.

Place the steak on the broiler and cook 4½ to 5 minutes on each side for rare; 6 to 8 minutes on each side for medium. The broiler should be 3 inches from the heat.

If you use a steak sauce, no seasoning is required.

Mrs. Burton Frierson

ROWENA'S STEAK SAUCE

1 stick butter	Garlic salt
1 can mushrooms	Tabasco sauce
3 tablespoons Worcestershire sauce	Salt, pepper
	1 small onion, sliced

Melt the butter and add the other ingredients, seasoning to taste.

Mrs. Burton Frierson

22

In the years since Chickamauga Dam has made a lake from the waters of the Tennessee, thousands of Chattanoogans have built houses along the lake either for summertime use or for year-round living. There is a country feeling about living on the lake. The birds sing in the early morning, there is the fresh woodsy smell of trees and pine needles, the sun shines down on the water, and the world seems a peaceful, private place. Boating, fishing, swimming, and just relaxing is the order of the day, and people seem to relax, enjoy each other and enjoy eating.

It is only natural to invite friends to enjoy this kind of living. Over a Labor Day weekend, Mrs. Harold Cooper invited a house full of guests, and I asked what she planned for a whole weekend of cooking that she could do mostly ahead. For dinner the first night she had rib eye steaks, fried okra, stewed corn, mashed potatoes, beat fluffy and topped with cheese, blueberry muffins and lemon pie.

The next day's breakfast was bacon, sausage and grits, scrambled eggs, angel biscuits that she had made the day before, applesauce, cantaloupe, orange marmalade and coffee. She gets coarse grits from the Hemlock Inn in North Carolina.

They had a late lunch of chicken salad, curried fruit, potato chips, green beans, ice cream balls rolled in pecans and coconut, Miss Gertrude's chocolate sauce, and Fudgekins.

She fixes her steak a rather unusual way. She likes it well done, and bakes it in the oven with foil. It makes its own gravy and is so tender you cut it with a fork.

MRS. COOPER'S STEAK

Brown the steak in a skillet in a small amount of shortening. Then line a baking pan with foil and lay the steak on it. Season with salt, pepper and Accent. Put foil on top of this to seal and bake in a 300 degree oven for about a half hour, turning down to 250 for 30 minutes more.

Mrs. Harold Cooper

Town and Country Restaurant is just across the Market Street Bridge, and a favorite place for many a Chattanoogan to eat a good steak. They have other specialties, too, but we asked Bill Hall to give us their theories on charcoaling steak, and their recipe for a blue cheese dressing. (See chapter on salads.)

23

After you have been seated and have given your order, usually a green salad is served right away with a choice of three dressings. The blue cheese is our favorite.

TOWN AND COUNTRY STEAK

To have a delicious steak, always use a choice or better beef, properly aged. A good steak should also be 1 inch thick or more in order to give the best flavor.

Cooking over live charcoal can be very rewarding, but disastrous if the fire is not handled properly. "We use a hot fire and a cool fire for best results. Place the steak on the hot fire for roughly one minute, turn and cook for one minute. This method will seal the juices in the steak. Continue cooking over cool fire for the desired preparation."

Town and Country Restaurant

There is a beautiful spot at the foot of Lookout Mountain called **Reflection Riding**. This is property developed by the late John Chambliss as a peaceful sanctuary for specimen trees and wild flowers, birds, and even human beings who would like a beautiful park to refresh their souls. Pleasant roads meander through woodlands planted with trees and wild flowers that are labeled. There are meadows, a pleasant pond with ducks, a barn full of horses, rail fences, and charming log cabins.

One night we went down to the log cabin for a steak fry. I had marinated some rib-eye steaks, cut thin enough so that we could make steak sandwiches that we could eat without cutting. They were tender and smoke tasting, the coffee was strong and hot, and the evening a memorable one.

HOW TO MARINATE STEAKS FOR A COOKOUT

Steaks can be tenderized just by letting them sit in a vinegar and oil dressing, or in wine, or in lemon juice. A white wine or sauterne is best, I think, because there is no strong taste that some members of the family don't like. Next best is lemon juice. First season the steak with salt and pepper, using Accent and Lawry's seasoning salt or any other favorite seasoning you might have. Then pour over about ¼ cup or ½ cup white wine, and 2 tablespoons of oil, and let sit in a platter in the refrigerator for two or three hours.

When ready to grill, pour off the marinade, put the meat in a skillet with butter. Remember to use plenty of butter with filets or rib eyes, because there is no fat. For a family the sirloin steak is probably best,

24

because you can cut crosswise a piece to suit the appetite of each person.

Cook until the meat shows a faint pink when you cut into it with a knife.

One week we had an unexpected visitor. He was a friend of our Mexican Experimenter and he was Jost Kunzmann from Switzerland. He had made a three-month trip by bus over, down, and across the United States, and was heading home to Switzerland finally by way of New York. We asked him to stay with us while he saw Chattanooga.

We figured everyone in Switzerland must have Swiss steak about once a week, so we smothered some round steak with lots of onions, carrots, and tomatoes, and had some noodles to serve the gravy over. Imagine our surprise when he said, "This is very delicious, but I have never had it before. I had to come to America to have Swiss steak!"

OUR AMERICAN SWISS STEAK

Take about 2 pounds of round steak and season with salt, pepper and Accent. Now flour and beat it with the dull side of a knife to tenderize it. In either an electric skillet or a heavy iron one, brown the meat in a little oil.

Meantime, chop two medium onions, 2 carrots, and 2 ribs of celery. Saute in about 2 tablespoons of butter in a separate pan. Add to the browned meat along with 1 can tomatoes (300 can) and 1 small can tomato sauce. Add a handful of chopped parsley, a pinch of sugar, a bay leaf, and a pinch of thyme, and about 1 teaspoon soy sauce. Cover and cook very slowly for $1\frac{1}{2}$ hours or longer, until steak is very tender. Check liquid and add a little water if it gets too thick.

Now taste the sauce to correct the seasoning. It may need a little more salt. Serve with noodles, rice, or mashed potatoes.

We were expecting him any day, so we flew the flag in front of our house three days straight just in case that would be the day Kinch, our Marine son, came home from the war. Unless you've had one of your own in Vietnam or Korea or some place of war, you can't begin to know the thankfulness, the relief and the real happiness of welcoming our boy home.

We had asked him what he wanted for dinner that first night, and he had sent word ahead, "roast beef, rice, green salad and just the family." Since this was his second tour, we knew they never come in exactly when you think they will, and whenever they do, it's great.

We all ate hearty while he told of the faraway places. Coming home from the middle of the war is like traveling from one world to another. The life we enjoy here in Chattanooga is very precious, and we all sensed it that night in 1968.

When we went to church the first Sunday he was home and the choir sang "The Balm of Gilead", he said, "The last time I heard that was during a service at Camp Carroll. We were mortared four times and had to move the service to the bunker." Con Thien, Camp Carroll, Dong Ha, and Da Nang are far away. But as those boys we had been interested in came home, one by one, we looked at them and thought they were miracles, gifts from God.

All veterans should be fed their favorite foods, and in the next few days we had all the old favorites....roast beef, fried chicken, the Christmas specialties he missed, hash and hoecakes, soup one rainy night, pork chops grilled over charcoal with plenty of his favorite slaw. This is the way we did the roast beef that night.

ROAST BEEF

Buy a roast meant for roasting, such as a sirloin tip or a rib roast. Salt and pepper it and place in a heavy iron skillet. Also put in the skillet a peeled carrot and an onion. Roast at 350 for 25 to 30 minutes to a pound. If the roast needs fat, put 2 or 3 slices of bacon on the top and secure them with toothpicks. This will keep the roast basted.

After about a half hour, you will notice that the bottom of the skillet is getting brown. This is good because it adds flavor. Also as the carrot and onion cook, the natural sugar in them will get brown. Don't let this burn. Add about a cup of water to the skillet and baste the roast with this juice. Keep a little liquid in the skillet all the time.

What gives a roast flavor is the brown-ness in the bottom and the basting. Cook until rare, medium or well done, as your family prefers. Arrange the timing so that it comes out of the oven a half hour before serving, so the juices can absorb into the meat. About 25 or 30 minutes to the pound is about right for a 4-pound roast. The juices can be thickened for gravy with a little flour and water.

A roast beef dinner is the easiest meal to prepare and the accompaniments are fairly inexpensive, offsetting the cost of the meat. It leaves everyone with such a sense of well being that it is the ideal menu for festive occasions.

Sometimes you want to stir yourself to do something elegant . . . .maybe a dinner for 6 or 8, which is really the nicest and most civilized sort of way to entertain. Beef Wellington made the rounds one year, and not only is it handsome looking, but very delicious. This recipe uses puff pastry shells which you buy frozen and roll out yourself to make the crust.

BEEF WELLINGTON

1 package frozen patty shells	pepper, freshly ground
1 filet of beef, 2½ to 3 pounds	6 slices bacon
2 tablespoons brandy	1 cup chicken liver pate
salt	1 egg, beaten with a fork

Thaw patty shells several hours ahead. Remove beef from refrigerator several hours before roasting. Beef at room temperature takes less time to cook, shrinks less, makes more servings per pound. Place beef on rack in shallow pan and rub with brandy, salt, and pepper. Lay bacon slices over the beef. Roast in a preheated oven 325 degrees about 10 minutes a pound for rare, 20 minutes for medium. Use meat thermometer if possible.

Remove from oven and cool at room temperature before proceeding. Spread chicken liver pate over top and sides of beef. Roll thawed puff pastry until very thin. Place over beef, trimming and tucking edges but not making a double thickness anywhere. Decorate with cut out pastry pieces. Place in center of preheated hot oven......325 degrees. Bake until pastry is crisp, flaky, golden......about 30 minutes. Makes 6 servings.

Joanne Caldwell, who needlepoints, gardens, and keeps up with her friends, says that the eye of the round is almost as good a roast as a filet mignon. She marinates it, roasts it quickly, and slices it thin. It is just as good served cold with a sour cream and horseradish sauce.

JOANNE'S EYE OF THE ROUND

Get an eye of the round and marinate it in Good Seasons Italian dressing for an hour in the refrigerator. Take out and lightly salt and sprinkle with cracked pepper. Flour heavily, patting it on, because this will make a crust that will seal in the juices.

Using a shallow baking pan, sear the roast on the top of the stove in a little bacon grease. Criss-cross 2 bacon strips on top and put in a 450 oven for 20 minutes. After 20 minutes, reduce heat to 350 and roast for about 10 minutes to the pound, or about half an hour.

Lift out and scrape the drippings to make gravy. You can serve with a sour cream and horseradish sauce.

Mrs. Johnson Caldwell

Every Wednesday night between 300 and 400 members of the First Baptist Church gather at their new building on the Gateway and have a family dinner. The good food that they serve has been described in glowing reports to their many friends....roast beef, smothered chicken, turkey, ham, and all the good things that go with them.

The extraordinary food I sampled one day at lunch, and I immediately understood all the praise of Barbara Mitchell (Mrs. George), the church hostess. Whatever she prepares is perfectly seasoned and cooked with a little distinction like thinly sliced lemons to garnish the sweet potatoes.

Roast beef is her most popular dish, and people will hardly believe that she simply buys brisket and marinates it. She says large roasts are best and if your family is small, you will come out better buying a 15-pound brisket, roasting it, and then freezing half of it to thaw later. This is how she does it.

BARBARA MITCHELL'S ROAST BEEF

Buy from your butcher a boneless rolled beef brisket. The secret of a good roast is to get a large one, about 15 pounds. The night before, wash it off, dry it, and place in a baking or roasting pan. You will need 1 cup lemon juice, 4 onion slices, 1 teaspoon salt, 1 teaspoon pepper, 1 cup Worcestershire sauce and 3 teaspoons McCormick herb seasoning.

Salt and pepper the roast, take the onion slices and completely cover the roast, sticking them in with toothpicks to hold them. Take the lemon juice and pour over the onions. Next pour on the Worcestershire sauce. Lastly sprinkle with the herb seasoning. Cover the whole thing tightly with foil and put in the refrigerator.

The next morning uncover it and pour in enough water to make 1 inch in the bottom of the pan. Cover again with aluminum foil and put in

28

the oven at 400. Use a meat thermometer. Roast at 400 for 1 hour, then turn to 375 and let cook to the desired tenderness. She likes it rare.

For smaller families, after the large roast has cooked, cut in halves or thirds, wrap the part to be frozen in foil and enclose in a plastic bag. To thaw, put in a pan in a very low oven still wrapped in foil. When completely hot, it will taste fresh.

Mrs. George Mitchell

The kind of food the great majority of us eat is family food. . . . just good average food that is fairly easy to cook and satisfying to eat. The reason we don't have more formal company than we do is that there's no time to make the fancy dishes we think company will expect. And the strange thing is that almost any meat you are serving your family would be delicious to anyone you know.

A few summers ago we had some interesting spur-of-the-moment company who took pot luck with us, and helped make one of the nicest summer evenings that we can remember We were having a big pot roast that night, and about an hour before dinner, a strange car drove up to ask directions to Rock City. A rather nice looking man got out of the car, and as we were talking, we sensed that he was no ordinary tourist. Tourists are an interesting group of people. They all look so hot, tired and miserable. Maybe we look the same way when we are on a trip.

Our visitor had intelligent eyes, a nice manner and volunteered that he, his wife and daughter were from San Francisco and on a two-month tour of the country. We gave him directions and he left.

"What kind of business do you think he has that he can be away for two months?" I enviously said to the head of the house. He figured him out as a college professor. He did have a rather scholarly forehead and very good bone structure. He didn't look old enough to be retired. But somehow I didn't think he was a professor. He looked very refined, even a little continental.

One of the boys figured he must be a banker to be able to travel for two months. Finally we decided to settle this family argument, to go get him and ask him to bring his family to have dinner with us. Then we would be sure to solve the mystery. The roast would be more than enough to go around.

I got in the car with Susan, who was about 6 months old at the time, and two of the boys, and set off for Rock City to deliver the invitation. I had meant for Kinch and Roy to go in and look for them, but they came back and said they had to be accompanied by an adult. I will never forget trooping through Fat Man's Squeeze, two huge rocks so close together that with Susan on my hip, we had to ootch a little to get through, with the boys just ahead. Half way through we caught up with our mystery man.

He was a little surprised to see us, but consented to come back to our house for dinner as soon as they had finished the tour. We circled back through Rock City's short cut, came home and set three more places for dinner.

That night we sat around the table for a long time. It turned out he was a scholar but not a teacher. He was an expert on Oriental art objects, such as jade, vases, horses of the Ming dynasty and rugs. He had traveled all over China and the East as a buyer for Gumps of San Francisco. Now retired (he looked younger than he was), he owned an apartment or office building which he managed. And the occasion of his trip was the 150th anniversary of his family's coming to American up in New England.

When they left that night, we were richer because we had three more friends. He and his wife invited us to stay with them if ever we get to San Francisco, and every week or two that summer we got a card reporting their progress. If I had known they were coming, I might have thought up something more exciting than pot roast, but it was delicious and we all enjoyed it.

Pot roasts, stews, hash and meatloaf are all favorites of families and guests, and in some ways it is far more warm and personal to share a family's table and eat these things than to be invited to a fancy club and be served steak.

FAMILY POT ROAST

4 pounds beef pot roast (rump, chuck, shoulder or round)
Salt, pepper, Accent, flour
1 can chicken broth
1 can tomato sauce

Dash Tabasco
6 medium carrots, scraped
6 medium potatoes, peeled
12 small white onions, peeled

Salt, pepper and flour the meat. Sprinkle with Accent and soy sauce first to tenderize it. Brown meat thoroughly in Dutch oven or heavy pan, using about 2 tablespoons oil. Pour in the chicken broth and tomato sauce. Cover the pot closely and reduce heat. In all, it should cook in a slow oven from 2½ to 3 hours. One hour from the end of the cooking time, put in the carrots, onions and potatoes. When the meat is very tender and the vegetables can be poked with a fork, remove them to a serving platter. This is an easy dinner, because it is all in one pot and the kitchen stays clean.

Another easy way to fix and flavor a pot roast is by using one of the new dehydrated onion soup mixes. This is one you can fix and forget and still know that it will have a robust and hearty flavor.

ONION SOUP POT ROAST

3 or 4-pound beef pot roast
3 tablespoons flour
1 package (1½ ounces)
   dehydrated onion soup
1 cup water
8 medium carrots

3 tablespoons lard or
   bacon drippings
½ teaspoon salt
3 stalks celery
Flour for gravy

Preheat oven to 325 degrees. Dredge the meat in flour. Brown in lard or drippings. Pour off drippings. Combine salt, onion soup, and water, and add to pot roast. Cover tightly and cook slowly 2 hours in oven. Cut each carrot in 3 pieces, and celery in 2-inch pieces. Add to meat and continue cooking another hour or until vegetables are done. Thicken cooking liquid for gravy. This will serve 6 or 8.

The Gulas family has been prominent in restaurant circles for years. The News-Free Press staff members who have lunch at Gulas Restaurant insist that they make the best cornbread in town; others say their barbecue is best. Mike Gulas says that people are always asking him how he fixes the German pot roast he serves on Friday nights.

GERMAN POT ROAST

You will need a 10-pound chuck, shoulder or round roast. Place the roast in a deep roasting pan. Mix 1 button garlic, crushed, 1 small onion, chopped, 1 ounce whole mixed spice, 4 bay leaves, salt and pepper, ¼ cup Worcestershire sauce, ½ cup vinegar, the juice of 1 whole lemon. Pour this over the roast in the pan. Now pour enough water over it to cover the roast. Put the whole thing in the refrigerator and let stand 3 or 4 days.

Take the roast out and saute it in butter until browned nicely all over. Put it back in the roasting pan with the marinade over it and bake covered in the oven at 325 until done. When you poke it with a fork and it is tender, then it is done. Strain off the juice and thicken it with flour and cold water to make gravy

Serve this pot roast with potatoes or spaghetti.

Mike Gulas
Gulas Restaurant

HOW TO MAKE HASH FROM LEFTOVER MEAT

If you have as much as a cup of leftover chicken, beef, lamb, or ham, you can make hash. First chop coarsely equal amounts of celery and onion. We chop about 2 onions and that much celery. Sometimes we chop up a carrot very fine, too.

The important thing is to saute these vegetables slowly in a skillet to bring out the flavor. Use about a tablespoon of butter and a tablespoon of oil or bacon drippings. When they are transparent, add the leftover meat. Let cook slowly. Now add liquid, either water or a can of chicken broth.

Let cook very slowly for about 45 minutes or an hour. If it looks pale, shake in some paprika or a teaspoon of soy sauce. If you had any gravy or juices, add them, too. If you have any parsley, chop up about ½ cup. Shake in some Accent, salt and pepper. Now taste it. If it tastes bland, add tabasco and a pinch of thyme.

We don't add potatoes to hash, because the children like it served on either generous helpings of rice, grits, noodles, or creamed potatoes. It is also delicious served on cornbread or hoecakes.

Once Humberto Chavez, our Mexican friend was visiting us. After we had spent an afternoon touring the Chickamauga Battlefield, I said, "Now Humberto, we are going to show you what the South lived on after the battle of Chickamauga when we were very poor." Then we had beef hash, about 4 or 5 hoecakes each, a green salad and milk. He said it was our best meal and should be our national specialty!

Sometimes I have a great desire to do something popular here at home. I make people do so many things, and I seem always to be reminding one or another to pick up his shoes, or to take out ashes, to feed the dogs or to stop teasing each other. One night one of the boys came to dinner, looked at the squash on his plate, and said, "I knew we would have either squash, okra or cabbage tonight. This just isn't my day."

I felt so sorry for him and knew just how he felt. Someday he'll like squash the way we do, but I promised myself to have a dinner the next night that the children would all love. They are enthusiastic about either beef stew or spaghetti.

BEEF STEW

2 pounds lean stew beef,
   cut in small cubes
3 tablespoons flour
2 tablespoons tomato paste
1 teaspoon salt
1 teaspoon Accent

1 cup any other vegetable
¼ teaspoon pepper
2 tablespoons shortening
1 can chicken broth
   or consomme
3 or 4 carrots

Go over the beef and cut bit-size chunks. Trim gristle. Those big chunks aren't pretty and they have to be cut before they go in your mouth. Salt, pepper and accent the meat. Coat the pieces with flour and brown in oil or shortening.

Carrots and onions do more for beef than any other vegetables, so be sure to include them. Don't chop too finely, but don't make huge chunks either. Now remember a tip from a chef friend. Never throw vegetables into liquid before first sauteeing them a minute in a small amount of shortening. For some reason this brings out the best flavor and they can be added then to the pot. This rule is used in soup making, too, in good hotels, so saute the vegetable a minute always before adding to stew and soup.

The next thing to remember has to do with the liquid you use. The French always use wine or stock or water from vegetables. Since our stock pot is not always going on the back of the stove the way a good French wife's is, we always keep several cans of chicken broth on hand.

It is mild and good, and to our way of tasting, it is better than beef broth. The can of chicken broth goes into the meat along with a little tomato paste for body. This will give you a beef stew the family will rave about. Made with water, they will probably eat it, but not say anything.

A good stew deserves to be served on mashed potatoes, noodles, rice, or even grits. You may want to thicken it slightly with cornstarch after it has simmered two or three hours on top of the stove. At the last, taste it to correct the seasoning.

This is very important and is the difference between an excellent cook and just a good one. Promise yourself to taste every dish before it leaves the kitchen.

John Barnes

When I went to interview Mrs. E. C. Berwanger for a series on ministers' wives, she invited me to a lunch of beef curry. This is a specialty she brought back from Panama where she served two years as a Methodist missionary.

The ground beef curry is served with rice and a variety of condiments and Dr. Berwanger says this has been a favorite of young people wherever they have been, but especially a young student from India who lived with them for a couple of years, and the young people at the Hixson Methodist Church. Mrs. Berwanger also teaches at Orange Grove School.

GROUND BEEF CURRY

Brown 2 pounds of ground beef in a skillet. Add to this 4 small onions, chopped, and 3 small apples. Add salt and pepper and then curry powder to taste. You can vary this, but start with at least 1 tablespoonful. You can add more. Put in ½ teaspoon ginger. When everything is cooking nicely, add some pineapple juice and water and simmer for about 2 hours slowly. Don't let it dry out, and you may have to add liquid from time to time to keep it juicy.

Prepare plenty of rice. When time to serve, place the bowl of rice on the buffet first, then the bowl of beef curry. Finally have 8 or 9 small dishes with the condiments which you can change according to your taste. These are favorites with the Berwangers: chopped peanuts, chopped cucumbers, chutney, chopped beets, chopped hard-boiled eggs, coconut, crushed pineapple and raisins, pepper relish and green bean salad.

Mrs. E. C. Berwanger

The Southern Inn was for years one of our popular eating places, with fresh vegetables, homemade hot rolls, and good things to eat. The owners, Mr. and Mrs. Charles Gabor, occasionally try one of their own Hungarian specialties to vary the menu.

Iby and Charles escaped in the Hungarian uprising. Iby's family had owned two restaurants in Budapest, one family type where people could even bring bear or deer and have it cooked to their order, and another that was more of a supper club.

One day they made some Hungarian stuffed cabbage for their customers. This is how Iby fixed it.

SOUTHERN INN STUFFED CABBAGE

1½ pounds ground beef   1½ teaspoons salt
1 small onion, grated   1 tablespoon red Hungarian
¼ cup rice, uncooked   sweet paprika
2 eggs   ⅛ teaspoon pepper

Mix together. Boil a large head of cabbage 4 minutes in boiling water. Carefully peel off leaves, trying not to tear them. Remove tough stem on each leaf with a sharp knife. Make meatballs and put in the middle of each cabbage leaf. Roll it up and tuck both ends in the meat. Put aside.

Take 4 cups firmly packed sour kraut, and wash 3 times in cold water. You will need some small pieces of smoked ham. Now take 1 tablespoon grated onion and saute in bacon fat. Add 3 tablespoons flour to thicken. Add paprika and remove from stove. Put the washed sour kraut in this thickening, and add ham pieces. Add a little water and cook ½ hour.

Put the rolled cabbage leaves in a pot and cover with the sour kraut. Make several layers. This can be put in a pot or roasting pan. Bake in a 400 degree oven for about 1 hour. Serves 8.

In Hungary this is served with sour cream beside a roast loin of pork. In the winter this is an important dish.

Mrs. Charles Gabor
Southern Inn

One way to make meatloaf is by using an onion soup mix. The dried soup mixes have wonderful possibilities in cooking because they have seasoning and condensed broth to help whatever they are added to. One night this recipe was very good, and the boys suggested that we stop trying out any other meat loaves and stick to this.

ONION SOUP MEATLOAF

1 envelope onion soup   ½ cup catsup or
   dry mix   tomato sauce
2 eggs   1½ cups soft bread crumbs
2 pounds ground beef   ¾ cup warm water

Break eggs in a bowl; beat slightly. Stir in catsup, warm water and soup mix. Add crumbs and ground beef and mix well. Shape into loaf or pack in pan or shape into 2 loaves. Bake at 350 degrees for about an hour. Serves 6 to 8.

One of the most colorful and informal restaurants in Chattanooga is Darras East on Ashland Terrace. Sam Darras is a witty extrovert who likes to make signs for the walls, and pizza, pasta, and Italian specialties for his customers. He gave us his tomato sauce (or salsa) to be used with any kind of pasta or spaghetti.

SALSA DE DARRAS

¼ cup olive oil (no substitute)
1 cup chopped onion, very fine
6 ounce can tomato paste
1 can (2½ cups) Italian
  plum tomatoes
1½ cup water or stock
½ teaspoon salt

¼ teaspoon pepper,
  freshly ground
1 bay leaf
¼ teaspoon oregano
  (leaves or crushed)
¼ teaspoon basil

Heat oil and saute onion. Put in everything except oregano and basil. (They would be too strong if added at the first.) Simmer uncovered 1½ to 2 hours. Stir occasionally. Then add oregano and basil and cook 10 minutes longer. This makes about a quart.

After putting on the pasta, add grated cheese. This is a basic sauce that can be doctored up with diced eggplant, green pepper, or whatever you like. You may add ground beef to this and have a spaghetti sauce.

When we heard that the ladies at the Brainerd Methodist Church had found a way to make a hundred or so hamburgers all at once, have them all hot at the same time, and have no mess to clean up afterwards when feeding the young people on Sunday night, we could hardly wait to hear the secret. What they do is to mix up catsup, mustard, dried onion and seasonings in with the ground beef while raw.

They then make out individual patties to fit the bottom buns, and refrigerate until ready to bake. About 15 minutes before the hungry teen-agers are ready, the trays of hamburgers are put in a hot oven to bake, with the top part of the bun going on the last couple of minutes.

Any cook who has made hamburgers for the family knows that it is slower and messier than you would at first think. We were so fascinated with the possibilities of this new method that we had a batch of oven hamburgers the next Sunday night.

Sam Darras is a witty gourmet who specializes in pizza. He can roll out pizza dough in his kitchen and talk to customers at the same time.

The meat was so moist and the buns so hot and crisp, that I should have fixed three times as many. We have had them many times since, and I have thanked Sue Deck, who passed them on to me, for this easy dinner.

EASY OVEN HAMBURGERS

1 pound ground beef	Dash of pepper
1 tablespoon grated onion	3 tablespoons chili sauce
(fresh or dried)	or catsup
1 teaspoon salt	1 teaspoon prepared mustard

Mix together as for meat loaf. Suit your taste......the seasoning could vary. Divide into 8 equal balls. Arrange 8 small sized hamburger buns (the bottom half) on a cookie sheet. (Sue Deck lines the sheet with foil.)

Shape each ball of meat to exactly fit the bun, coming to the edges. Then shape it in a little ridge all around so that it is a little nest. This will keep all the meat juice on the meat so that it won't run off into the pan while it bakes. Bake for 20 minutes at 375. Put top half of the bun on the hamburgers and return to the oven for a couple of minutes until hot. I brushed the top half with butter once and liked it.

For large groups such as young peoples' Sunday night suppers at church, these may be made several hours ahead and refrigerated until time for the oven. They can be served with lettuce and dill pickle slices, or just as it is, which is the way we have them.

Mrs. Sanford Deck

You can almost know people by reading through their personal cookbooks. You know the foods they like, the kind of entertaining they do, a little about their friends. I never knew my husband's mother, but her recipes, hand written in a bound book, are a fascinating story of a person who loved good food, knew how it should taste, and was ever on the lookout for a new idea.

In Mississippi, hostesses put the "big pot in the little pot" when they have company. They start with a basic menu, then add three more vegetables, and extra meat, maybe a shrimp dish, piping hot home-made bread every ten minutes and even hotter coffee about that often.

All this good food leads to good talk. Just reading through her recipes is enough to make me hungry and put me in a good humor at the same time. There is much swapping about of family recipes and there are recipes from every aunt, sister, cousin and old friend.

One of her recipes that we have especially enjoyed is her spaghetti which she used to make for teen-age and college gatherings. We began using it in our student days at Stanford, and it has become a family standby. We have made it for the children's friends and for the young people at church. We have printed it in the column several times and readers say they like it as well as we do.

MISSISSIPPI SPAGHETTI

1 pound ground beef
  or ground chuck
1 clove garlic, finely minced
1 teaspoon salt
1 teaspoon Accent
1 can mushrooms
1 can tomatoes (No. 2 can)

2 cups chopped celery
2 onions, chopped
1 green pepper, chopped
1 tablespoon chili powder
  (more if you like it hot)
½ cup chopped parsley

Saute the celery, onions, and green pepper in a little butter and oil in a heavy skillet or an electric skillet. Remove from pan and put in the meat, with garlic and seasonings. Stir this around until it is brown and crumbly.

Don't just mash it and pulverize it. You want it to be coarse chunks of meat, so that you can taste them. The celery, onions, and green pepper should be chopped too, but not minced too fine. Some people make almost a paste of spaghetti sauce, but it is not as good. Now drain off any excess fat, so that the spaghetti will not be greasy.

Add tomatoes and mushrooms and chili powder along with the celery onion mixture. Simmer for about 45 minutes or an hour. You can add the handful of chopped parsley or some chopped chives if any is growing in your garden.

Check for the liquid content of this sauce. If it cooks away, add more water so that it will be saucy enough for the spaghetti. Add the mushrooms last. The sauce should simmer for about an hour. This much can be done way ahead of time, and sometimes I fix twice this recipe and freeze half of it for later use.

Now cook 8 or 10 ounces of spaghetti in boiling water that has been salted. Cook til tender to the teeth. Drain and rinse in a colander to remove the stickiness. Mix the spaghetti with the sauce and let heat a few minutes until it is all piping hot. Serve with a green salad and French bread.

People who like to cook and enjoy recipes really are kindred spirits. One of our readers sent me a Mexican casserole that she got from a restaurant in Texas. Knowing how hard tortillas and Mexican sauce are to find outside the Southwest, a Texas chef suggested an easy casserole anyone could make that would stir up pleasant memories of a trip West.

His substitute casserole calls first for a layer of Frito corn chips, then a sprinkling of raw chopped onion, then a sauce of canned chili, topped with grated cheddar cheese. Repeat these layers a second time and put in a hot oven until the sauce bubbles. The nights we serve this with a big green salad, it disappears fast. There is also a real run on milk, as happens with chili!

MRS. GWINN'S MEXICAN CASSEROLE

1 bag corn chips	½ cup chopped onions,
1 can chili with beans	more if you want
¼ can water	1 cup grated cheddar cheese

Put half the corn chips in the bottom of a casserole. Sprinkle with half the onions. Combine chili and water and pour half over the casserole. Top with half the cheese. Repeat this. Put in a 400 degree oven until it bubbles. This serves 4 or 5.

I first heard of Betty Leigh (Mrs. C. L.) by a phone call from a substitute teacher.

"I substitute in many schools," she said, "but the cafeteria at Westside is so exceptional and the food is so delicious that you must go see for yourself. Mrs. Leigh has homemade rolls coming out of the oven hot for each class, and every dish is so lovingly and beautifully prepared that it is a pleasure to eat there." I went out to see for myself, and it was true. The roll recipe can be adapted for sweet rolls or pizza.

MRS. LEIGH'S PIZZA

1 pound ground beef	1 teaspoon basil
1 medium onion	1 teaspoon oregano
1 teaspoon salt	1 can (8-ounce) tomato sauce
¼ teaspoon pepper	1 cup grated cheese,
¼ teaspoon garlic salt	cheddar or Mozarella

Brown meat in large frying pan. Add onion and cook on medium heat until onion is transparent. Add seasonings, salt and pepper. Use half of recipe from the dough for yeast bread (use rest for rolls), roll dough to fit a 12-inch round pan (or use a cookie sheet and make it rectangular.) Dough should be thin. Oil the pan, place dough on pan, make a good high ridge on the edge. Place meat mixture on dough. Add tomato sauce. Sprinkle grated cheese on top. Bake 20 to 25 minutes at 375 degrees. Crust should be golden brown.

YEAST ROLLS OR DOUGH FOR PIZZA

1 package yeast	*1 tablespoon sugar*
¼ cup warm water	*1 teaspoon salt*
1 cup milk	*3 cups flour*
1½ tablespoons shortening	*Extra shortening and flour*

Soften the yeast in warm water. Scald milk, add shortening, salt and sugar. Cool to lukewarm. Combine yeast with milk in a large bowl. Add enough flour to make a stiff dough, mix thoroughly and turn out on a floured board.

Knead 5 to 10 minutes ... keep the dough soft. Place the dough in a greased bowl, brush the top with shortening, cover with waxed paper and towel. Allow to rise in a warm place to double in size. Punch down with fist. Fold over so smooth side is on top. Cover and let rise again. Turn out on board. Divide in half, cover with bowl and allow to rest 10 minutes. Roll out half for pizza, half for rolls. Shape rolls, place in greased pan and let rise. Bake at 400 degrees. Follow pizza recipe for finishing pizza.

Mrs. C. L. Leigh

When most people taste tongue, or a tongue casserole, they like it and come back for more, often not knowing exactly what it is. Claire Siskin Binder (Mrs. Samuel) says that every time she makes a lentil and smoked tongue casserole for an informal buffet supper, it is very popular with both young and old, and almost everyone has a second helping.

LENTIL AND SMOKED TONGUE

Boil a large smoked beef tongue until tender. When the tongue is done, and cool enough to handle, plunge it into cold water. Peel off the skin and trim off the fatty and hard portions and the roots. Cut the whole tongue into squares about ¾ inch in size.

Soak 2½ cups lentils overnight in cold water. Drain, cover with cold water, and bring slowly to a boil. Turn down the heat and simmer, uncovered, about ½ hour and drain.

Melt 4 tablespoons margarine or butter in a skillet and add 2 or 3 finely minced cloves of garlic, 2 cups chopped green and red sweet pepper, and 2 cups chopped onion. Saute 5 minutes, stirring often.

In a stewing pan, heat a 10-ounce can tomato puree, 1 cup water, 1 teaspoon salt, 1 teaspoon freshly ground black pepper, 2 tablespoons sugar and 2 tablespoons chili powder.

In a large casserole, put a layer of lentils, a layer of tongue, and then a layer of onions and peppers. Continue with this until the casserole is full, finishing with onion and pepper. Add the tomato mixture. Cover and bake 2 hours in a 350 oven. When finished, the consistency should be moist but not soupy. Add water cautiously if needed. Do everything but the 2-hour baking the day before.

This is good for a picnic supper or any kind of buffet. Add a tossed green salad, relishes and bread.

Mrs. Samuel Binder

My friend Jane Williams and her husband Sumner run a camp in North Carolina. There are always outdoor things to do like horseback riding or hiking on the trails, or canoeing trips. At the same time, Jane does a tremendous amount of entertaining ... the easy informal kind. One of her best menus is Beef Stroganoff, a green salad, French bread, and some French pastries or apple pie from a good bakery nearby. This is her simple way with Beef Stroganoff.

JANE'S BEEF STROGANOFF

2 pounds round steak	*2 cans mushrooms*
1 stick butter	*1½ teaspoons salt*
4 or 5 onions, chopped	*½ teaspoon Accent*
2 tablespoons tomato paste	*Pepper to taste*
2 cups sour cream	

Cut the beef in long thin strips. Melt half the butter in a skillet and cook the beef 'til brown. Salt, pepper, and add any other seasoning you can think of. Remove the beef. Add the remaining butter and saute the onions in the skillet. Now add the tomato paste and the beef and add water to cover (or some canned chicken stock if you have it.)

Cover the heavy pan you have it in and simmer gently for an hour or two or until you finish riding or taking the children swimming. Thirty minutes before serving, add the mushrooms and sour cream. Cook slowly. Too-high heat will make the sour cream curdle. Taste. You might add paprika and parsley. Serve on noodles (about 2 packages for this recipe.) This will serve 10 to 12.

One variation of this recipe is the possibility of serving the sour cream out of a separate bowl on the buffet. A dollop of white fluffy sour cream on the dark meat stew is very attractive.

Mrs. Sumner Williams
Cedar Mountain, North Carolina
Camp High Rocks

About 10 years ago at Christmas one of our favorite Chattanooga families did an unusual thing. They are a large family by the time they get all the uncles, aunts, and cousins together, and they all gathered in the biggest living room among them on Christmas Eve. Everyone fully expected the turkey and all the trimmings, but what they hadn't expected was a short ceremony that took place first.

The host stood up first and began giving a history of the family from the time that they came to this country. He had hunted up all sorts of anecdotes and incidents that go along with the string of misfortunes that the grandparents and great-grandparents endured.

Their first furniture factory down by the Tennessee River was destroyed by fire, and it was only by hard work that they were able to rebuild it. Then, as if that weren't enough to try them, the rebuilt factory was washed away in the terrible flood of 1867.

All those years and the following ones of building the factory again were named by the family "the beef heart years." In the face of hard times and calamity, they survived by eating the cheapest meats to be had ... the heart, the kidneys, the liver, of beef. These are known to be more nutritious and less popular in America than anywhere else in the world. After describing the "beef heart years" in detail, the head of the house reminded the family how good the Lord had been to them, and how they had been prospered and blessed.

And so that they might not forget the hard times the family had come through, and so they might feel especially thankful, he then signaled that it was time to bring in the first course. There on a platter was a stuffed beef heart, and he carved a slice for everyone, young and old. Then after all had tasted beef heart, they all went into the dining room, for the traditional turkey feast.

There is hardly a family in Chattanooga that didn't have a hard time getting started, or that hasn't had some sort of business reverses or misfortunes along the way if you look back far enough.

It is a good way to keep your sense of values to always look back and remember, and to remind children, who cannot even remember the depression, that times may not always be good, but with courage and faith and a stout heart you can live through all sorts of things.

This is a recipe for Stuffed Beef Heart.

STUFFED BEEF HEART

1 beef heart	4 slices bacon
2 cups stock	1½ cups bread stuffing

Prepare a beef heart by washing well and removing all the tubes. Tie it with a string. Place it on a rack in an ovenproof dish. Place in the bottom of the dish either the beef or chicken stock, and place on top of the heart the bacon. Cover the dish and bake at 325 degrees until tender, about 3 hours. Remove the heart to a plate and cool slightly.

Make a bread dressing or whatever kind you would like (a rice and onion would be good) and stuff the heart. Sprinkle with paprika and return briefly to a 400 degree oven to reheat. The drippings may be thickened with flour for gravy. An alternate is to baste frequently with barbecue sauce as it bakes and use a rice stuffing.

A beef fondue party is popular in Chattanooga because it is easy to prepare, fun to do, and different. When Jimmy and Kay Campbell planned a dinner of Fondue Bourguignonne, they approached it with their usual enthusiasm and flair, had a test dinner one night the week before to see what sauces they liked best, and planned the dinner for the pretty old pine table in their family room.

They live in a house which they completely remodeled until now it looks like a Virginia farmhouse, with a long porch, brick walks, and white Williamsburg fences, and inside, a big country kitchen, and a family room full of early American antiques, brass, copper, and red and green prints.

For the meal, they used their copper chafing dish to hold the hot oil, which Kay had heated on the stove first. Each guest was supplied with a long fork to fry his own chunks of steak in oil and the assorted sauces were passed along with plenty of French bread. The Campbells liked the tomato and the mustard sauces best.

FONDUE BOURGUIGNONNE

1½ to 2 pounds beef fillet cut   *Vegetable oil or peanut oil*
in cubes (about ¾-inch)   *Assorted dipping sauces*

Arrange the meat on a platter. Meanwhile heat the oil either in a chafing dish or fondue pot or electric skillet. The oil should be at least 2 inches deep or more. You can put half a potato, peeled, in to prevent splattering. Heat the oil to 400 degrees, but do not let it smoke.

Using long-handled forks or skewers, let each person cook his own meat until done to individual taste. Remove to plate and dip into the following sauces.

A Beef Fondue party is easy to plan and fun to eat since everyone cooks their own dinner. Jimmy and Kay Campbell invited "L. J." and Bob Huffaker to a chafing dish steak and sauce dinner in their family room.

BEARNAISE SAUCE

1 teaspoon chervil
1 teaspoon tarragon
2 shallots, finely chopped

4 or 5 peppercorns, crushed
¼ cup tarragon vinegar
¼ cup white wine

45

Bring to a boil and continue to cook until reduced by one-third. Strain and cool. Combine 3 egg yolks and 1 tablespoon water in top of a double foiler and slowly beat in the strained vinegar-wine mixture. Stir over low heat with a wire whisk until light and fluffy. Soften ½ pound butter and divide into 3 portions. Add the portions of the butter one at a time, stirring until the mixture is thick and smooth after each addition. Season with salt and a little cayenne, and sprinkle a little chervil and thyme into the sauce. Add 1 teaspoon meat extract and serve.

MUSTARD SAUCE

2 cups cream
1 tablespoon cornstarch
½ cup sugar
1 teaspoon salt

2 egg yolks
2 tablespoons dry mustard
1 cup vinegar

Dissolve cornstarch in a little of the cream. Place rest of cream in top of double boiler and bring to the boiling point. Add dissolved cornstarch and continue stirring over hot water. Add beaten egg yolks to which mustard has been added. Cook and stir until thick. Add vinegar and cook one more minute, still stirring. Serve hot or cold.

TOMATO SAUCE

3 or 4 medium to large
   tomatoes
2 tablespoons butter
½ cup tomato paste
1 tablespoon brown sugar

1 bay leaf
1 teaspoon tarragon
¼ teaspoon salt
½ teaspoon onion salt
1 teaspoon tarragon vinegar

Peel, chop, and remove seeds from tomatoes. Melt butter in skillet and add all ingredients. Simmer for about 10 minutes. Remove bay leaf and continue cooking until very thick. Strain and serve.

MAYONNAISE AND SOUR CREAM SAUCE

1 cup sour cream
½ cup mayonnaise

Onion salt to taste
Dill weed to taste

Mix together and serve.

EASY TOMATO SAUCE

½ cup mayonnaise
½ cup chili sauce

Onion salt or grated onion
Lemon juice to taste

Mix together and serve.

Mr. and Mrs. James Campbell

Tender, sweet, rich, and satisfying, ham is always the first choice for Christmas, Easter and all state occasions. I think in our part of the country we are born loving the taste of ham. It signifies the best, the most bountiful thing we can think of when it comes to company or feasting.

Hams attend the biggest weddings, the biggest funerals, buffets, open houses and holiday family dinners. At no time is the prestige of ham greater than during Christmas.

Everyone loves it. We like it for dinner and sliced later for snacks and sandwiches. When our babies have been anywhere from 6 months up, we have occasionally given them a piece of ham to chew (or to gum). Of course, it has to be too big a piece for them to swallow, but I have known it to satisfy and sooth a fussy baby for the longest time while he waits his turn. It's the sweet mellow flavor they love.

I think the most important thing about cooking a good processed ham from the supermarket is to cook it slowly long enough for it to be really done. You don't want it to fall off the bone and be hard to cut, but you do want the meat to be very done. You want a sweet spicy glaze to set off the flavor. And I think it is best to put on the glaze for the last hour of cooking. For Christmas we put the ham on a big platter and garnish the base with sprigs of holly. Then it is ready for the big day.

SOUTHERN BAKED HAM

First get a good tenderized ham from your butcher. Put it in a roaster, and preheat the oven to 325 degrees. We allow 35 to 40 minutes to the pound for our hams, but we like them very well done. Roast uncovered. An hour before you think it will be done, take out and cut off the skin with a knife. Now score the fat and stick in whole cloves at the intersections.

Mix up a glaze using a box of brown sugar, about 1 tablespoon of mustard, and enough sherry or orange juice concentrate to moisten it to a paste. Smooth this over the fat side of the ham, and return to the oven for the final hour. You will know when the ham is done by its wonderful smell, and also by feeling the hock bone. If it is slightly loose and wiggles, it is done.

When Southern men sit down to a dinner of real country ham, they have a feeling of tradition and a sense of well-being that perhaps no other menu can give them, even steak. Country ham, that tangy, smoky, just sweet enough, just salty flavor that happens when a pig's thigh is expertly treated to salt, sugar and spices, and then slowly smoked is a delicacy of which there is no finer.

47

Just as a combination of happenings and responses go to build character in a person, a good ham is built by what is allowed to happen to it. This is why a proper country ham deserves joy and respect.

In families all over the South, hams were cured and smoked according to traditional recipes, and then left waiting for the grandest occasion and the best company. When you ate country ham, you knew you were sharing an important time, and a special sort of festive feeling always accompanies ham. At Christmas it is a must.

The market is now flooded with country hams, from Virginia, Tennessee, and Georgia. Some are good and some are not. Country ham is different from the usual hams you buy in a supermarket. They take longer to smoke and hang. They lose moisture and weight, making them more solid and drier ... this is ham somewhat condensed, or essence of ham. The taste is stronger and to us, more delicious. It costs more. Even the fat on the ham is less moist, and when cooked the proper way, the fat is as sweet and delicious as the ham.

I once had a talk about ham with Chef John Barnes, formerly of the Read House. In the first place, he understands ham and knows how to fry it so that it isn't hard and tough, but a real joy. He also knows how to boil the whole ham and finish it with a glaze so that most people think it is baked. It slices paper thin, with just the right texture. Here is what he taught me.

COUNTRY HAM SLICES

This method works for all ham slices, both country ham and the processed ham that all stores carry. I asked if he soaked the slices first. No, the secret is in slow frying and in paying attention to the rim of fat around the side of the ham. If you put a slice of ham in a pan and fry quickly, the fat will never take on the flavor and color of the ham.

You need to heat a heavy skillet until quite hot with a little coating of grease in it. Then put the slices in and turn down low. You need the initial shock of the hot skillet, but the secret in slow frying is that the fat will gradually take on the flavor and color of the meat. The fat should be golden amber and the ham should gradually get golden brown, too.

When cooked this way, the fat is unbelievably sweet and tasty, and eaten along with biscuit and grits, a pleasure not to be missed. I wouldn't have believed that this simple tip could make so much difference, but it does. Frying both sides of the ham this way, it takes 20 or 25 minutes.

Now for the gravy. Remove the ham and add a little water along with butter. Deglaze the pan so that the gravy takes on color. You can add a little coffee. Be sure to serve with hot biscuits and grits.

John Barnes

BOILED WHOLE COUNTRY HAM

There has been lots of talk about skipping the boiling of country ham, but it needs it. First soak overnight in water to cover. This can be done in the kitchen sink. The next morning wash and scrub the ham well. A big lard can is what people usually boil hams in. Put the ham in and then fill nearly full with water. (One expert adds ½ cup vinegar and ½ cup molasses to cut the saltiness....a good idea.) Let the water just simmer, not boil, until the ham begins to get done. You can tell because the hock bone gets slightly loose.

This takes about 25 minutes a pound. Take it out and remove skin, score the fat and put cloves in the squares. Now make up a mixture of a box of brown sugar, 1 tablespoon mustard and enough sherry to moisten it. Spread this glaze over the ham. Put in a roaster and finish in a 350 oven for about an hour.

Cool and slice the next day, as it slices better when cold. Do make the slices thin and pretty.

John Barnes

There is a new way of cooking Virginia country hams that comes from Richmond, where people who are on to the new method say they will never go back to the old way of boiling.

SOUTHAMPTON HAM

Soak ham overnight. Wash ham and put in roaster. Add 6 or 7 cups cold water. Put top on roaster tight with all vents closed. Preheat oven to 500 degrees. Put ham in oven and cook ham 15 minutes at 500.

Cut off heat for 3 hours. Then turn heat on again at 500 degrees for 15 minutes. Turn off heat. Let ham remain in oven for 3 hours or overnight. It will be done.

Do not open oven during the six hours the ham is cooking. Some Virginia cooks have added their own footnotes. One has found that individual differences in ovens should be allowed for. She cooks her ham at 500 for 20 to 25 minutes instead of 15. Some cook the ham at night with a schedule like this: Soak the ham during the day for 8 hours. Put it in the oven at 7 or 8 at night. Then by 11, you can turn the oven off and go to bed. When you wake up, the ham is done.

The Hunter Art Gallery was given to the Chattanooga Art Association by the Benwood Foundation. It now has a contemporary addition.

In 1899 two young Chattanooga lawyers made a most fortunate investment. Ben F. Thomas and J. B. Whiteside signed a contract with Asa Candler of Atlanta granting them the exclusive right to bottle a new soft drink, Coca Cola, in almost the entire continental United States. A few months later John T. Lupton joined them so that the original total investment of the three was $5,000.

They got responsible individuals to open bottling plants, supplied the syrup, and helped promote sales. Thomas took the northeast, Whiteside the southeast, and Lupton the southwest. The success of their venture is history, and their descendendants and the descendants of friends who invested with them are many of Chattanooga's leading citizens today.

On the death of George Hunter, nephew and heir to Ben Thomas, a foundation was set up called Benwood Foundation, which has granted sums to such worthy causes as hospitals, schools, and various Chattanooga charities. It has been an influence in the cultural, medical and charitable needs of our city. George Hunter's home, formerly the Faxon house on Bluff View, overlooking the Tennessee River, was given to the Chattanooga Art Association for a permanent art gallery and is now the scene of many civic gatherings.

It has often been said that the national drink of the South, at least in Chattanooga and Atlanta, is not water or even wine....it is Coca-Cola. Imaginative cooks include it in punch, salad, and even in baking ham.

HAM IN COCA-COLA

Ham boiled in Coca-Cola has an unusual taste, and may be served with no additional seasoning. Put a medium-sized cured ham into a deep vessel and pour in enough Coca-Cola to half cover the ham. Set on a low flame, cover and boil until ham is tender. (It can be baked in the oven, basted with Coca-Cola.) Test by sticking the long tines of a fork into the meat. Or watch until the bone at the shank end is loose. As the liquid boils out, add more Coca-Cola. When tender, take out and skin. Slice either hot or cold. This ham may be sprinkled with bread crumbs, brown sugar, or any desired glaze, but the meat will already have a sweet flavor.

Martha Bachman McCoy (Mrs. Thomas) lives on Walden's Ridge (now known as Signal Mountain) and enjoys the same sort of rural life, the getting away from town that her father, Senator and Judge Nathan Bachman, did. Her grandfather was Dr. Jonathan Bachman, who for 60 years was the beloved pastor of the First Presbyterian Church, coming here soon after the Civil War from Blountsville, where he grew up.

Any conversation with Martha is apt to be both witty and interesting, for she is not only very elegant looking, but excellent company. I told her that in this Chattanooga cookbook I had said that the Scotch-Irish had left their influence in our region by the independence, the conservatism, the rugged individualists, but then I took it out, because I am not sure we comprise this much of the population. "You're exactly right," she said. "No one but the Scotch-Irish who were used to rugged hills and mountains would have settled in East Tennessee. East Tennesseans are different from Georgia people, we are not like Nashville or Memphis, we are just ourselves." She says she sees it in the mountain people, the town people, in herself, and even in me! We laughed because it is true!

East Tennesseans have a reputation for being shrewd traders, having solid-rock convictions politically and religiously, and demanding the right to do things their own way. Martha has the reputation for serving as delicious a country ham as you will ever eat. She buys two pigs every year, fattens them and when frost comes, butchers them and cures her own hams. I won't go into this, but I will pass along her recipe for cooking country ham.

MARTHA McCOY'S HAM

Soak a 10 to 12-pound ham in water overnight. The next day scrape it clean and put in a large roasting pan which will fit over two burners on top of the stove. Pour over the ham 1 can of Blackstrap molasses, and tea to half cover the ham. Cover the roaster and simmer over medium low heat for 3 hours, turning the ham over once midway. Take off the stove and strip off the skin. Cool in the tea and molasses mixture.

When cool, mix some mustard in with chili sauce. Dice and score the ham with cloves and pour over the sauce. Put in a 400-degree oven for about ½ hour, and then turn down the heat to 300 and roast until the shank bone is loose.

This next suggestion she got from Mrs. Hardwick Caldwell, who says that in Virginia they think a ham is better if it stands after cooking for two or three days before carving. Just keep in a cool place covered, but don't refrigerate. Martha also told me of a new method of carving ham. If you stand it on its small side, you can slice from the front to the back horizontally.

Mrs. Thomas McCoy

Every year on Christmas Eve the H. Clay Evans Johnsons used to have an open house. To this party they invited whole families—hundreds of babies, children, teen-agers, the college crowd, parents and grandparents. Betty Meade decorated the Georgian colonial house, Weswoods, very traditionally. One year she had a life-size manger scene in the stable just as you entered the drive. Another year she had hundreds of miniature lights outside to match the stars.

Some years it actually snowed on Christmas Eve, other years it was almost warm, others just bitter cold, but the hospitality was always the same. Clay had a Christmas red tie and welcomed everyone; Betty Meade saw that the trays in the dining room were full and that each child took home a huge cellophane wrapped Christmas cookie; there were excited little girls everywhere in red and green velveteen; there were children home from college; there were old friends and newcomers to meet.

There was almost always something that stands out in your memory each year . . ..Betsy's little boy, Wayne Farmer, Jr., upstairs in his crib, sleeping soundly in spite of all the admiring peeks; another year Alec Wells just home a few hours before from Parris Island, dashing in his Marine dress blues and soon to leave for Vietnam.

The dining room at Weswoods had eggnog at one end of the table and punch at the other, with trays and trays of cheese biscuits with pecans on top, boiled shrimp on ice with chili sauce dip, sausage rolls, Christmas cookies in many shapes sprinkled with sugar, a cheese board with assorted cheeses and crackers, a ring mold of a sort of ham mousse or pate that you spread on crackers, salted pecans, and anything else Betty Meade might think up. She gave me the recipe for the molded ham, and the punch appears later in the book. Betty Meade and Clay now have a condominium, but their friends will always remember Weswoods.

WESWOODS HAM MOLD

*Soak 1 tablespoon gelatin
in ¼ cup cold water.
Dissolve it in 1½ cups boiling
canned chicken stock.
Chill the jelly. When it is
nearly set, combine it with:*

*3 cups cooked ground ham
¼ cup chopped celery
1 tablespoon grated onion
½ cup mayonnaise
¼ cup India relish*

Season to taste with Worcestershire sauce, lemon pepper, Tabasco and salt. Moisten a ring mold with a little cold water and decorate sides and bottom with stuffed olives (sliced) and sliced hard-cooked eggs.

Chill until firm. This makes 10 servings when used as a salad, but goes much further when used as a spread for water crackers, saltines, beaten biscuits, and so on. We triple the recipe and it fills one large ring mold and one small one. May be frozen ahead.

Mrs. H. Clay Evans Johnson

53

When Dr. Robert Benson came to the University of Chattanooga (now U.T.C.) he brought from North Carolina with him his delightful wife, Helen, and their six handsome children. They are not only additions to the university campus, but to all the various schools the children attend, the church choir, the Tennis Club, and various city affairs. When they come to Wednesday night church suppers, Helen usually brings her oatmeal cake, her brownies, or a hearty casserole like Escalloped Ham and Potatoes:

ESCALLOPED HAM AND POTATOES

1 thin center slice smoked ham	1 cup milk
(¾ pound)	3 cups sliced pared potatoes
2¼ teaspoon flour	1 cup sliced scraped carrots
1 can cream of mushroom soup,	¼ cup minced onions
undiluted	Salt and pepper

Heat oven to 375. In skillet, brown ham lightly on both sides; cut in serving size pieces. Sift flour into fat in skillet. Combine milk with soup. In a 2-quart casserole, arrange layers of ham, potatoes, carrot and onion, until all are used. Sprinkle vegetables lightly with salt and pepper. Pour on soup mixture. Bake covered, 60 minutes, uncovered 15 minutes, or until potatoes are done. Serves about 4. The Bensons double this for Wednesday nights.

Mrs. Robert Benson

PORK CHOPS GRILLED OVER CHARCOAL

Arrange pork chops on a platter about 2 or 3 hours before cooking. Salt, pepper and sprinkle lightly with soy sauce. Now sprinkle with a little vinegar or lemon juice and a little salad oil. This is a marinade and will help keep the chops juicy.

When grilling them, cook over a slow charcoal fire, turning often. Don't let them catch fire and keep a soft drink bottle of water on hand in case this should happen. Pork should be well done, and as soon as you think the pork chops are, test with a knife to see. Potatoes, either baked or in a potato salad, are good with this.

PORK CHOPS WITH MUSHROOMS

This is even easier. Salt and pepper your pork chops and brown in a heavy skillet. Remove and add 1 onion that has been chopped. Saute until soft. Add 1 can of the new clear golden mushroom soup. Return the chops to the skillet and cover tightly. Either simmer slowly or bake in a slow oven for 45 minutes or an hour.

There are all sorts of barbecue sauces. If you have one your family likes, then stick to it. We were still looking for the right one ... not too thick, not too heavy with tomato, not too sweet, not too hot. Then we found this one. It is rather thin, mellow, and tangy. You make up a whole quart at a time, and it keeps indefinitely in the refrigerator just waiting for your whim, whether it be chicken, spare ribs, pork roast or pork chops.

When we have had spare ribs, even the babies would smack and suck the sweet meat off the bones in the most honest and uncultured way. One of the boys used to help me mix up this "witches' brew," as he called it, and was very proud when it went over so well.

This sauce calls for a half-pound of butter and an almost equal amount of vinegar, and acts in almost the same way that a marinade does on meat. It actually tenderizes it as well as flavors it with all the tomato, garlic, onion juice, Tabasco and syrup.

At a food conference years ago James Beard began his meat sauce with a cup of butter and a cup of wine, adding whatever flavoring he wanted in the form of tomatoes, tarragon, and so on. This may be the same principle. If we have any red or white wine on hand, we sometimes substitute a cup of wine for a cup of vinegar. The children complain less about white wine, because it leaves no flavor.

REVISED BARBECUE SAUCE

½ *pound butter*
½ *cup vinegar*
1 *cup white wine (or vinegar)*
2 *cups catsup*
1 *teaspoon Tabasco*
1 *small bottle Worcestershire sauce*

2 *tablespoons brown sugar or syrup*
1 *tablespoon grated onion*
2 *cloves garlic, chopped fine*
Dash black pepper
2 *teaspoons salt*

Bring all ingredients to a boil. Taste. You may want to add more Tabasco, more salt, or more sugar. This makes over a quart, so refrigerate what is not used and save for next time.

The best cook that I know, the one whose instincts about how done bread should be, how to season vegetables perfectly, is Annie Lee Lewis. Annie helps us do all the doing that it takes to raise a big family, and since we do almost everything together, I think of her as my best friend.

She is ingenious at thinking up simple solutions to problems. She figured recently that the apple pies we were making from fresh apples wouldn't boil up and spill over the crust if we just kept the oven temperature lower at first. She figured out how to make a tiny coffee table for the doll house by using a cocoa can top painted black. One day she came with a white nurse's apron that she had made in a size 3 the night before so Ellen could be a nurse and carry trays to Susan when she had her tonsils out.

Annie's barbecued spareribs, fried chicken, roast beef, smothered steak, hash, pork chops, apple pies, biscuits, hoecakes, fried okra, and on and on are without peer. She has a light hand and anything that she would like, I would like, too. Her kind, loving ways make her the most popular member of the household, and although she has taught me much, she is still a better cook than I am.

One day I took down the way she does her spareribs, and this is about it.

ANNIE'S BARBECUED SPARE RIBS

Wash the spareribs well. Salt and put in a roasting pan to bake. These should bake in a 350 degree oven for 1 hour.

Make the following sauce. Mix together ½ cup vinegar, ½ cup water, 1 teaspoon mustard, ¼ teaspoon pepper, one-third tomato catsup, one-third cup Heinz 57 sauce and the juice of ½ lemon. Taste and correct seasoning to suit yourself. Pour over the spareribs and let them bake another hour. Keep them turned in the sauce.

Mrs. Annie Lewis

Perhaps Chattanooga's most colorful hog killing and sausage making project was the one that went on regularly every year in the back yard at Jo Conn Guild's house on Lookout Mountain. On Christmas Eve hundreds of Chattanoogans were sent generous packages of link sausage for their Christmas breakfast that had been personally made and supervised by Mr. Guild.

Virginia Guild Colmore (Mrs. Rupert) says that they usually made the sausage about December 15, his birthday. It had to be after frost, and with many consultations with the weather bureau, he sent to his farm in Columbia, Tennessee, for a truck load of hogs. They were killed and dressed at the packing house here and all preparations made for the big day of sausage making.

It was usually so cold everyone nearly froze, and every pair of hands possible was pressed into service at the long tables set up in the yard. Virginia was always there as was Rupert, who took a day off from the bank. They got their sons, Rupe, Jo and John, off from school to work, and sometimes their friends wanted to come, too. George H. Pettway nearly always came. All the servants of the family came and men from the farm. Sometimes friends pitched in. The day began at 5 a.m. with plenty of hot coffee, and they began cutting the fresh pork into small chunks.

"The big deal was to be through by 3," Virginia says, "and although we were cold most of the time and bone tired, there was lots of laughing and joking, coffee, Cokes and good food to eat. After the meat was cut up, it went to a big electric grinder under the shed and was ground into brand-new aluminum wash tubs from the hardware."

She says that then her father began the weighing, checked from one person to the other, saying, "Put more fat in that," or "That needs more lean meat." He and Mr. H. G. Young had a yearly fuss over the spices and seasoning. Then the sausage was stuffed into hog casings, which make the large fat kind of link sausage.

Although they stopped the sausage making several years ago when Mr. Guild's health began to fail, Virginia says she saw some of the sausage sticks they used to hang the sausage from in the smoke house recently. They look like broom sticks. The hams and bacon sides were put down in salt to cure and were later smoked.

Sausage making on the cold day in December brings back memories for many Chattanoogans who used to drop in to watch or to work. It also brings to mind the hearty breakfasts of sausage, grits, eggs, bacon, apples and biscuits and strong coffee. There are a few simple tricks to cooking link sausage which Virginia passed on.

COUNTRY LINK SAUSAGE

Start the sausage in a cold skillet with a small amount of water over medium heat. Cover the skillet and cook gently. If cooked too fast, they will burst, yet they are fat and must cook through. Properly cooked, they must steam gently about 20 to 25 minutes. Take off the top toward the last and let them brown, rolling them over so that they brown gently. Serve with grits and biscuits.

Mrs. Rupert Colmore, Jr.

Kay Gray (Mrs. John D.) has an unusual way of roasting a leg of lamb with a mint sauce. This is a wonderful company entree.

MINTED ROAST LAMB PROVENCAL

First get a 6-pound leg of lamb. 3 or 4 hours before cooking, chop up some mint leaves, sprinkle with sugar and add some vinegar. Let his stand in the refrigerator for the sauce later.

Slit little holes in the roast and insert pieces of garlic, using about 2½ cloves garlic. Sprinkle the top of the lamb with flour, salt, pepper, Accent, and rosemary leaves. Put in a roaster and pour over it 1 cup dry white wine and 1 cup water. Cover and roast at 500 degrees for ½ hour. Baste with the juices and turn oven down to 350 degrees, cook for 2 more hours, basting every half hour with the juices and also with a little lemon juice.

Skim off the grease. At the end of the 3-hour cooking remove lamb to a platter. In a separate saucepan, make a flour and water paste with 3 tablespoons flour and a little cold water. Take half the juices from the roasting pan and add to it. Now add the vinegar mint mixture that has been steeping in the refrigerator. Taste for the correct seasoning.

With the roaster drippings, make plain gravy using the other half of the liquid. The lamb can be served with both plain roaster gravy and the mint sauce.

Mrs. John D. Gray

One of my Mississippi mother-in-law's company dinners was one featuring leg of lamb roasted with a unique sort of seasoned vegetable coating spread over the top. This combination of carrots, onions, butter, mustard, parsley, and so on seasons the lamb as it bakes.

ROAST LEG OF LAMB

First wash the leg of lamb. Pat dry and rub with lemon juice. Make little pockets in the fat and insert a few cloves of garlic. Now mix up the following mixture: 2 teaspoons salt, ½ teaspoon black pepper, 1 teaspoon paprika, ¼ cup minced parsley, ½ bay leaf, crushed, ½ cup minced carrot, 2 tablespoons minced onion, ¼ teaspoon thyme, ¼ cup soft butter and 2 tablespoons flour and 2 teaspoons mustard. This will be quite a mixture, but you can see that it will be good.

Spread this over the meat and put the lamb in a roaster. Let brown in a hot oven about 425 degrees for 20 minutes. Then cut down the heat to 325 and let roast slowly until done. Don't let the pan dry out, but add a little water as it needs it. Roast about 35 to 40 minutes for each pound of meat.

A different way of fixing lamb for company is to have a leg cut into steaks. This is the idea of Susan Elder Martin (Mrs. John) and the steaks are one of her favorite company dinners. Susan, Jack and their family now live on Elder Mountain, where she grew up in an area now being developed as one of Chattanooga's newest suburbs. When her grandfather, George Elder, bought a large part of Racoon Mountain, they had to ride up on a horse. Now there is a lovely road leading almost to the freeway.

LAMB STEAKS

Buy a leg of lamb and have your butcher cut off steaks an inch thick. Pepper steaks well and place in a buttered baking pan. Cover each steak with a slice of sweet purple onion. Pour a couple of table-spoons of heavy cream over each onion, then sprinkle liberally with Parmesan cheese. Bake for 40 minutes in a 325-degree oven.

Mrs. John Martin

FAIRYLAND CLUB LAMB CHOPS

4 French cut lamb chops
2 tablespoons chopped
  mushrooms

4 ounces fresh chicken livers
2 tablespoons chopped onion
Salt and pepper to taste

Split lamb chops to make a pocket. Saute mushrooms, onion, and chicken livers. Remove from heat, let cook. Chop mixture into a paste and stuff lamb chops. Place in hot saute pan and sear both sides. Remove and place in oven. Bake for 15 minutes. Serve hot with chutney or mint jelly.

Fairyland Club

Some of Chattanooga's most elaborate and many-coursed dinners are the wedding feasts held after the Greek Orthodox weddings. After the marriage of Chrissy Gulas and George Bailey, the wedding party and guests joined hands around a circle for the age-old wedding dance.

The most elaborate weddings in Chattanooga are quite possibly those in the Greek Orthodox Church. The long and lovely service is full of ancient tradition and symbolism, ending in the ceremonial walk around the table, a sort of joyous dance, and a final blessing.

The receptions that follow are usually seated dinners of many courses, and the celebrating lasts far into the night and the early hours of the morning. There is dancing and music.

First there is usually a chicken soup with egg and lemon sauce, then follow several entrees such as roast lamb, macaroni and a ground beef sauce, meat stuffed in grape leaves, chicken smothered in tomato sauce with spices such as cinnamon, garlic and oregano; a rice pilaf; vegetables such as okra or green beans; a Greek salad of lettuce, tomatoes and green onions with a vinegar and olive oil dressing and Feta cheese and black olives over it. The desserts are light and delicate pastries such as Baklava, strudel leaves with almonds, butter and an almond syrup, an almond pecan cake or a Greek rice pudding.

Helen Ellis Pinckney (Mrs. John), who has told me the most about Greek weddings, says that her father, Gus Ellis, and his brother migrated to this country in the early 1900s because of the poor conditions in Greece. He came to see America and worked his way across the country washing dishes in one restaurant after another! He finally settled here and for years had the Ellis Restaurant. Our Chattanoogans of Greek ancestry have certainly contributed to the culinary history of Chattanooga. The recipe for roast lamb is from Mrs. Eva Ellis.

MRS. ELLIS' ROAST LAMB

Rinse a leg of lamb and wipe dry with a towel. Make incisions in the lamb 1½ inches deep and put in them a combination of garlic powder, salt, pepper and oregano. On a 6 to 8-pound leg, make 4 incisions on the top and 3 on the bottom of the leg.

Rub the whole leg with salt, pepper, oregano and paprika. Wrap it in heavy foil and roast about 2½ hours. The first hour, bake at 400 degrees, then turn down to 350 and open the foil and continue roasting. Turn the leg once in a while.

You can tell how done the lamb is by inserting a sharp fork. If the juice runs out pink, it is rare; if the juice is clear, the lamb is well done.

Mrs. Eva Ellis

CHAPTER IV

Poultry and Game

Just south of Chattanooga in North Georgia the broiler industry has grown until nearby Gainesville is one of the chicken centers for the entire country. With modern, scientific methods, a baby chick can be ready for market in ten weeks, raised in the hundreds of broiler houses you see on any drive down into Georgia. Bred to be more tender, plumper, and with more white meat than ever before, chicken is the cheapest meat we can buy, and a long-time favorite in our region.

The real specialty of the town is fried chicken the way fine Negro cooks do it. This takes a light hand, and I have included it in another chapter on their special type of southern cooking not in the books. Gaining in popularity is oven-fried chicken.

It would be safe to say that there are more good chicken recipes in Chattanooga than for any other kind of meat. Chicken adapts to any situation, and in whatever guise, a new sauce or fancy casserole, chicken is an old and dear friend.

When we were little and used to spend the night with our grandmother, we would always ask ahead of time if we could have chicken and dumplings. I'm sure we must have had other things, too, but the chicken and dumplings dinner was the one I liked best.

We would eat the soft, juicy, chickeny dumplings and gravy, and the chicken that was so tender it almost fell off the bones. We remember how good they tasted, how good they smelled, and how stuffed we always were after several helpings.

Chicken and dumplings is a wonderful family sort of dish. A simple type of biscuit dough, rolled thin and cut in strips, is dropped in the simmering chicken juice.

As we get older, we think back on some of the culinary memories that have been stored in the back of our minds for so many years. I can actually remember the fragrant aroma and the delicate taste of the chicken my grandmother fixed for us, although I probably didn't say anything about it at the time. It really should give us resolve and purpose to serve our families often with the foods they like best. They just might remember 20 years from now.

CHICKEN AND DUMPLINGS

3 pounds of chicken (a small hen or fryer) cut in pieces	1 egg
2 cups flour (about)	¼ teaspoon baking powder
½ cup cold chicken broth	1 teaspoon salt
	¼ teaspoon (or a pinch) of sage

Put the chicken in a large saucepan or kettle and cover with water. Put in enough salt to taste, a rib of celery and a small onion, and boil slowly, covered until the chicken is done. This will take about two hours. A fryer cooks faster than a hen. When tender enough, you will know by sticking with a fork.

About a half hour before done, remove ½ cup broth to cool. Make your dumplings by sifting the dry ingredients and stirring in the egg and cold broth. If the dough is too sticky to roll, add a little more flour. Roll out on a board thin, about ⅛ inch thick, and cut into strips 1 inch wide and 3 inches long.

Remove chicken and the celery and onion from the broth. Have it rapidly boiling and drop in the rolled dumplings. Turn down the heat to a simmering boil and cook the dumplings about 30 minutes until done.

Add the chicken until it is hot and serve together on a platter, the chicken, dumplings, and a generous amount of the gravy-like broth.

Everyone loves smothered chicken with rice. This is a favorite standby with families. They sometimes like it better than fried chicken, gourmet chicken or fancy chicken. When Susan was a baby, she would eat all of hers, then climb on her father's lap and finish his. Ellen did the same thing. After dinner there are only plates with skinny, lonesome-looking bones.

This is plain chicken and butter, cooked covered in an oven until the meat almost falls off the bones. Then the juice is thickened to make the gravy, and this is served on the rice. The meat is moist and buttery; the skin and even the gristle are delicious. This is supposed to be the dish you take to sick neighbors, but it tastes even better to healthy people.

Smothered chicken is a simple dish, yet some recipes seem to do strange things to it. They don't tell you to use enough butter; nor do they tell you to cook slowly until the meat comes away from the bones. They forget to say that you can use a whole fryer cut in fourths, a smaller one cut in half, or a cut-up fryer the usual way. They don't insist on a heavy iron skillet. I learned from a cook we had once, Mattie Sinkfield, and this is how she did it.

MATTIE'S SMOTHERED CHICKEN

First you need a heavy iron skillet or Dutch oven with a cover. Wash the chicken well, not just rinsing it, but giving it a bath in a sink full of water. Dry the chicken, and season with salt, pepper and paprika. Put about ½ stick butter and a little oil so it won't burn in the skillet. Add the chicken. Brown it.

Mattie always browned it longer than I would have. She almost burned it. She said it had to get real brown to give a hearty taste to the gravy. When all the chicken was very brown, she took it out of the pan and poured out any excess grease. She put the chicken back in, shook in a lot more paprika to give the broth a hearty color, and added ½ cup water.

I didn't think this was enough liquid, but she said the chicken would add more juice as it cooked. Then she covered the pot or skillet tightly, and put it in a 300-degree oven for 1½ or 2 hours. It must cook until it is tender enough to cut with a fork.

When done, remove the chicken, and you will see why you took such pains to brown it well and add the paprika. The broth is already very rich looking. Take a tablespoon of flour and mix in a little cold water. Add to the hot gravy and stir so there won't be any lumps. Taste to check the seasoning. Serve with rice.

Mrs. Mattie Sinkfield

One of the prettiest parts of town at the turn of the century was Vine and Oak Streets as they extended out from the campus of the University of Chattanooga. The homes were large and stately, tall trees lined the streets, the street car ran regularly out Oak Street to provide transportation.

As times have changed and people have moved farther out into the suburbs, the stately houses have become fraternity houses and clubs. The former Walter Temple home, with its classic Federal lines and its double stairway inside, has now become the Kosmos Woman's Club. They have delicious luncheons after their meetings in such lovely surroundings that they should be the envy of every club in town.

Every year in December the Kosmos plan a Holly Day luncheon and benefit bazaar that is open to the public. They serve from two to three hundred and benefit the auxiliary and psychiatric unit at Erlanger Hospital as well as the juvenile detention home. Their cook, Mrs. Elizabeth Collier, is quite famous for her food, and one year her menu was Escalloped Chicken and Stuffing with Mushroom Sauce, Fresh Cranberry Mincemeat Squares and coffee.

The only change that Elizabeth Collier makes in the following escalloped chicken is that she makes her own old-fashioned cornbread dressing instead of buying the packaged. This is the recipe the luncheon committee gave to me.

KOSMOS ESCALLOPED CHICKEN AND STUFFING

1 package 8-ounce herb
  seasoned stuffing
3 cups cubed chicken
½ cup butter or margarine
½ cup flour

¼ teaspoon salt
Dash pepper
4 cups chicken broth
6 slightly beaten eggs

Prepare stuffing according to package directions or make your own cornbread dressing. Spread in a 13 by 9 by 2 inch baking dish. In a large saucepan melt the butter, blend in flour and seasonings. Add cool broth; cook and stir until mixture thickens. Stir small amount of hot mixture into the eggs; return to hot mixture and pour over chicken. Bake in a slow oven 325 degrees for 40 to 45 minutes or until knife inserted halfway to center comes out clean. Let stand 5 minutes to set. Serve with mushroom sauce.

Sauce: Mix 1 can condensed mushroom soup, ¼ cup hot milk, 1 cup sour cream, and ¼ cup chopped pimento. Heat and stir until hot.

65

In all of Chattanooga there was no more gracious a mother-daughter combination than the late Mrs. T. Allen Lupton and her daughter, Maddin, Mrs. David McCallie. I cannot think of a single kind of party that these two ladies haven't given at one time or another with the warm hospitality that is their trademark.

In my own experience I can remember buffet suppers for the young people at Christmastime, houseparties in Summertown with fried chicken and fresh corn on the cob, and when we were all getting married, clever engagement parties and luncheons to meet new brides. When the babies of the family have been christened, they have had Sunday dinners after church for the families and friends, and these happy occasions always included from thirty to forty.

In spite of the big parties they found themselves in charge of, they both preferred small dinner parties with good food and conversation. At one they had, they featured rolled breast of chicken, with ham and cheese rolled up in a chicken breast and baked. This was so good I fixed it for the children one night, who loved it. A favorite salad they used was tomato and caviar salad, which was really pretty enough for a luncheon, although they used it as a first course. (It is in the chapter on salads.)

MADDIN'S ROLLED CHICKEN BREAST

Preheat the oven to 300 or 350　　*6 slices Swiss cheese*
6 individual breasts of chicken　　*2 cups seasoned bread stuffing*
6 slices baked ham

Debone the chicken breasts. Start on the fat side and slice against the bones, easing and loosening until they come away from the meat. Roll the chicken, then wrap the cheese around it, then the ham around the whole thing. Secure with toothpicks. Do this for each breast. Roll the stuffing into fine bread crumbs. This can be done early in the day. Beat 2 eggs until light. Dip each piece into the egg batter, then in the crumbs. Melt a stick of butter in a shallow baking dish. Lay each piece in the butter, and bake for 45 minutes. During the baking, turn once and baste. Use a low rack in the oven so they won't get too brown.

Mrs. David McCallie

Making the rounds of the young marrieds here is one called Party Chicken. They like it because they can hurry home from their jobs and bake this casserole, which they have assembled the night before. Mar-

The late Mrs. Allen Lupton and her daughter, Mrs. David McCallie, hostessed every imaginable kind of party . . .. luncheons for Colonial Dames and Junior League Conferences, dinner parties, children's birthday parties, and wedding festivities. In this picture Mrs. Lupton was arranging a place card for a formal dinner, while Maddin was looking to see that everything is in place.

tha Elder (Mrs. George) is noted for the fabulous sets for plays that she taught the children at Lookout Mountain School to make when she taught art there. She likes this Party Chicken.

PARTY CHICKEN

8 chicken breasts, skinned
   and boned
8 slices bacon
1 can undiluted mushroom soup

1 cup sour cream
1 package chipped beef
   (4 ounces)

Wrap a piece of bacon around each chicken breast. Using a flat casserole dish about 8 by 12 inches, sprinkle with the chipped beef. Place the chicken breasts on the chipped beef. Mix soup and sour cream and pour over all. Refrigerate. When ready, bake at 275 for 3 hours uncovered. Serves 8.

Mrs. George Elder II

The best curried chicken we have ever made, we got from Mary Anne Lucker, who lived in Thailand for many years while her husband worked there for the United Nations. In Thailand you don't go to the trouble of cutting up little cubes of chicken. You just cut up the chicken as for frying, which makes it much easier. This is curry not just with curry powder, but with curry, Tabasco, soy sauce, and coconut. Even the children love this curry, and we had a very successful dinner party once with this curry and mandarin orange molded salad.

THAI CURRY

Contrary to what people think, curry is a dish, not a spice. The paste or powder that gives curry its distinctive flavor is a combination of spices. In Thailand the cook compounds her own curry with a mortar and pestle immediately before putting it in the stew. The difference in Thai curry, compared to other eastern curries is coconut milk and hot chili powder. Curries are prepared with chicken, shrimp, and sometimes fish. The following recipe can be used with all three.

Cut up enough frying chickens, allowing at least one piece per person. Cut the breasts in half so they will be the same size as the other pieces. Soak 1 package of coconut in 2 cups of boiling water (use real coconut milk if you can get it.) Lightly flour, salt and pepper the chicken parts and fry in a moderate amount of oil until slightly brown.

Put the chicken into a large or heavy kettle or Dutch oven. Pour any remaining fat out of the frying pan, add water, scrape all the good brown in the bottom, and pour over the chicken. Add a can of chicken broth and the coconut water drained from the coconut. The chicken should be swimming in liquid. Add a generous amount of soy sauce. After cooking briskly for a few minutes, turn the heat to low and cook for at least 2 hours or longer. Keep tightly covered.

Now add to taste the following: Enough chili powder seasoning, Tabasco, and pepper to be distinctly recognizable. Thais keep adding pepper, hotter and hotter the more festive the occasion. (At weddings, Thais weep over the curry, not over the bride and groom!) Add ample soy sauce, a few drops of Worcestershire, not too much, a big pinch of garlic chips, a few black peppercorns, and salt. One whole bay leaf, thyme, a few whole cloves, parsley, celery flakes, lemon or lime juice, a dash of wine or sherry if you have any on hand.

Add the curry powder now. Try a tablespoon at first. The Luckers add three. Once you have added all these pinches, you can start over again and add more of each of what you like. Taste as you go. In the meantime peel and quarter a potato or two and a few small white onions and add to the pot. These and all the seasonings may be added any time during the slow cooking so they can penetrate the meat. Do not let it dry out. There must be lots of sauce.

Taste for seasoning. If coconut, curry powder, and red pepper are distinguishable, it will be real Thai curry. The chicken should be very tender, almost falling off the bone.

White rice, cooked in your usual manner, should be served in a big bowl.

CONDIMENTS

The garnishes or condiments come next. Each must be put in a separate little bowl, and each amply ladled over one's pile of rice and curry. This is what gives curry the distinction of being three, five, or ten boy curry, since in the old days a different boy served each item. To most, having curry means to have chutney alongside, but this is Anglo Indian and unknown in Thai. A good choice would be: Sliced bananas, roasted peanuts, small fried onion rings, dried salt fish or shrimp, chopped, hard boiled eggs, chopped, toasted coconut, sliced cucumbers. And happy Thai eating!

Mrs. Harry Lucker

69

One way to fix chicken in an oven casserole is to dip chicken pieces in a seasoned sour cream mixture, roll in herb stuffing, and bake. For a company luncheon, you can use breasts only.

SOUR CREAM OVEN CRISP CHICKEN

1 pint sour cream	*1 teaspoon salt*
4 tablespoons lemon juice	*Dash pepper*
4 teaspooons Worcestershire	*3 pounds chicken breasts,*
sauce	*legs and thighs*
2 teaspoons paprika	*1 package herb*
1 teaspoon garlic sauce	*seasoned stuffing*
2 teaspoons celery salt	*Melted butter*

Mix together sour cream, lemon juice, Worcestershire sauce, paprika, garlic salt, celery salt, salt and pepper. Dip chicken pieces in this mixture. Roll in stuffing. Arrange chicken in shallow greased baking dish. Brush with melted butter and place in a 350 oven for one hour, or until chicken is tender and a crusty brown.

How do you explain the Chattanooga legend of "Dot and Peg?" For years and years Dot (Mrs. James R. Hedges) and Peg (Mrs. Peg Lamb), sisters, have been leaders in the cultural affairs of Chattanooga. They once began a toy business of paper dolls which children could sew for, later branching out into all sorts of other toys. When they went to the toy fair in New York, they made some sort of history and came home with more orders than they had ever hoped for.

Dot and Peg Industries later branched out into satin and lace bedroom scuffs which sold all over the country. When they retired, they took up ceramics, making copies of a Rennaisance Italian nativity scene which they had seen at the Metropolitan Museum. These were sold to benefit the Church of the Good Shepherd, and one is displayed at the Hunter Art Gallery every year.

Dot's French chateau type home has been the scene of many delightful parties, she has been a leading force in getting the Hunter Art Gallery established, the public places of Lookout Mountain beautified, the Community Aid project of providing work to help the people on the back of the mountain started. Dot and Peg collect friends the way they collect beautiful things, and they have been a delightful inspiration to women all over Chattanooga. After being with them I feel that I can do almost anything.

Dot Hedges has given me two chicken recipes. One is Chicken and Orange, a very easy company dish that can be put together at almost the last minute. The other is Chicken Veronique, which she has made in large quantities for the women's meeting at the Church of the Good Shepherd. This recipe will serve 12 and can be enlarged or reduced.

CHICKEN AND ORANGE

6 chicken breasts
1½ cups orange juice
½ cup chutney
½ cup raisins
½ cup slivered almonds
½ teaspoon cinnamon
1 tablespoon curry powder

1 banana, sliced lengthwise
* and then crosswise*
1 can mandarin oranges
* with juice*
Salt and pepper to taste
Nutmeg

Rub chicken breasts with garlic butter. Bake at 475 degrees for 15 minutes with the breast side up, then turn to 350. Make the sauce by combining all the rest of the ingredients, including the juice of the mandarin oranges but not the bananas and oranges. Bake for an hour, basting frequently with the sauce. At the last add the mandarin oranges and the bananas and put back into the oven until heated through.

When Mac Brock (Mrs. Richard) made this, she had some sauce left over. She served it over leg of lamb and says it was as good with the lamb as with the chicken.

Mrs. James R. Hedges

CHICKEN VERONIQUE

Put 3 cut-up fryers in a roasting pan (about 2½ pounds each) with 2 cups sherry, 2 cups water, salt, pepper, a pinch of thyme, basil, a pinch of curry powder, and 3 tablespoons chopped parsley. Cover and roast. for 1½ hours at 300 degrees.

Meantime, take 1 package of onion soup mix and 1 pint sour cream and let it mellow together. When you remove the chicken from the oven 1½ hours later, strain off the liquid and boil it down on top of the stove until you have 1½ cups. Add 1 can mushroom soup very gradually so that it doesn't lump. Add the sour cream mixture.

Now take a box of wild rice and plain rice mixed, cooking as directed. Butter the bottom of a pyrex casserole and put the rice in the bottom. Tear the chicken in chunks off the bones (not diced or cubed) but in nice pieces. Arrange the chicken on the top. Pour the sauce over it and sprinkle with paprika and chopped parsley so that it will look pretty. This should serve about 12.

Mrs. James R. Hedges

71

A good choice for a Saturday night buffet supper is a casserole of chicken and artichoke hearts.

CHICKEN ARTICHOKE CASSEROLE

3 pound fryer,
  cut in pieces
½ teaspoon paprika
¼ teaspoon pepper
6 tablespoons butter
¼ pound mushrooms,
  cut in large pieces

1 can artichoke hearts,
  (12 or 15 ounce can)
1½ teaspoons salt
2 tablespoons flour
¾ cup chicken consomme
3 tablespoons sherry

Season the chicken pieces with salt, pepper and paprika. Brown them in 4 tablespoons butter and place in large casserole dish. Saute mushrooms in remaining 2 tablespoons butter. Sprinkle flour over the mushrooms and add consomme and sherry. Arrange artichokes between chicken pieces, and pour the mushroom sherry sauce in. Cover the casserole and bake at 375 degrees for 40 minutes. This can be made in the morning or even the day before serving.

Mrs. Rupert Colmore III

One of the best new chicken recipes for oven frying chicken is this one that coats the chicken with butter and Parmesan cheese. This is especially good for church suppers or for frying chicken for large groups.

OVEN FRIED CHICKEN WITH PARMESAN CHEESE

2½ to 3 pound chicken,
  cut up for frying
½ stick butter, melted

½ teaspoon salt
Grated Parmesan cheese

Season the chicken with salt and white pepper. Dip it in melted butter and roll it in grated Parmesan cheese. Arrange chicken in a single layer in a shallow baking pan. Bake in a moderate oven (325 degrees) for 1 hour or until tender.

Mrs. G. Rozendale

The Chattanooga Jewish Community Center is now in its beautiful new complex of buildings out in Brainerd near Eastgate. Not only do they have a modern auditorium and dining room, but swimming pool, tennis courts, and a program for every age from the campers in the summertime on up.

I was invited out for a demonstration on gas grill cookery put on for the ladies by Liz Hodes (Mrs. Alvin), who was a home economist with the Chattanooga Gas Company. Liz prepared a delicious outdoor 4th of July supper featuring barbequed chicken, grilled corn, grilled tomatoes, French bread sliced and spread with a mixture of butter and poultry seasoning, and watermelon. She also suggested that while broiling chicken, it is a good idea to prepare more than you need. The additional chicken can be foil wrapped and frozen, then reheated for another night's dinner with no work at all. She made this chicken look very easy and it was delicious.

LIZ HODES' BARBECUED CHICKEN

Soaking Sauce:
1 pint vinegar
1 tablespoon salt
1 tablespoon mustard
3 tablespoons catsup
6 tablespoons lemon juice
Black pepper to taste

Browning Sauce:
4 tablespoons sugar
1 tablespoon salt
6 tablespoons butter,
  or margarine
2 tablespoons mustard
2 teaspoons Worcestershire
1 2 teaspoon black pepper

Soak chicken overnight in soaking sauce, piercing chicken with a fork so that the sauce can penetrate. Place chicken on gas grill and baste with soaking sauce for the first half of the cooking time. Baste chicken with the browning sauce for the last half of the cooking time. Warm any remaining browning sauce and serve along with the chicken.

Tip: Place bony or rib cage side of the chicken down next to the heat first when grilling. Bones act as an insulator and keep chicken from browning too fast. This is enough sauce for two whole chickens. The entire cooking time should be about 45 minutes or an hour. When it is done, the thigh will feel tender when poked with a fork. This is the last part of a chicken to get done.

Mrs. Alvin Hodes

73

It is a great advantage to have individual packets of a specialty in the freezer just waiting to pop in the oven and bake. This is the old principle of pompano in a parchment bag that was madefamous in New Orleans. This version of chicken breasts in individual foil packets came from the late Hilda Spence, the church editor of The News-Free Press for 33 years.

EASY SUNDAY CHICKEN

4 chicken breasts
1 can mushrooms
 (4 or 5 ounce size)

1 small bottle pearl onions
$^1/_4$ cup cooking sherry

Season the chicken with salt and pepper, roll in flour, and then saute until golden brown with real butter. When nicely brown, put each breast on a square of heavy foil. Divide the mushrooms and onions so that they are equally divided for each chicken breast. Save the liquid from the mushrooms.

Put about 1 tablespoon flour into the pan the chicken has browned in, stir and add the mushroom liquid and cooking sherry. Let this sauce come to a boil, and spoon some over each chicken breast.

It would be all right to shake on paprika, add a little chopped parsley or chives or anything else you think up yourself.

Fold the individual serving and put in a shallow baking dish or cookie sheet with a little water in the bottom. (They can be put in the freezer if you are preparing them ahead) The water will keep the foil from sticking to the pan. Bake for 2 hours at 325 degrees.

Mrs. Hilda Spence

At a Food Editors' conference, Sara Spano gave me a Chicken Country Captain recipe with the following story. Mrs. W. L. Bullard of Columbus, Georgia, was going to entertain Franklin Roosevelt. She wanted a very special menu to serve her distinguished guest, so she searched her cookbooks and came up with this now world-famous version of Country Captain.

Soon it became the specialty at "The Big Eddy," a private club in Columbus, where many of the world's great were entertained, including Generals John Pershing, George Patton, Dwight Eisenhower, Omar Bradley and George Marshall.

In World War II, while enroute to Europe with Fort Benning's Second Armored Division, General Patton wired the following message to Mrs. Bullard's daughter, "If you can't give me a party and have Country Captain, meet me at the train with a whole bucket of it."

COUNTRY CAPTAIN

4 pounds chicken breasts,
   split and skinned
Flour, salt, pepper
Shortening
2 onions, finely chopped
2 green peppers, chopped
1 clove garlic, minced
1 tablespoon curry powder
   (more or less to taste)
1½ teaspoons salt

½ teaspoon white pepper
2 cans tomatoes
   (20 ounces each)
½ teaspoon each, thyme
   and chopped parsley
¼ cup currants
¼ pound toasted and
   blanched almonds
Cooked long grain rice

Dredge chicken in flour, salt, pepper. In a large skillet, brown chicken in shortening; remove to ovenproof casserole and keep hot. Meantime add onions, green peppers, and garlic to remaining shortening in skillet; cook and stir until vegetables are tender. Add curry powder, 1½ teaspoons salt, the white pepper, tomatoes, chopped parsley, and thyme. Bring to a boil; pour over chicken.

Baked covered, at 350 degrees for about 45 minutes, or until chicken is tender.

Remove chicken to large heated platter, and around it, pile the cooked rice. Add currants to sauce mixture, and pour over rice. Sprinkle with almonds; garnish with additional parsley; you have food for the gods.

Mrs. Sara Spano
The Ledger-Enquirer
Columbus, Georgia

One year when the women of the Presbytery met at the First Church here, Mrs. Gordon Smith was in charge of luncheons for the two days. Her food was such a hit that for weeks she was sending out recipes to visitors who wanted to know what was in the tomato aspic, how many ginger snaps to put in the ginger pear crumble, and how to make chicken divan.

Mrs. Smith always adds a dash of her own enthusiasm and fun to everything she does.

CHICKEN OR TURKEY DIVAN

Place two packages frozen broccoli which have been cooked (not too done) on the bottom of a large glass casserole. Cover with sliced turkey or chicken breasts which have been boned. Cover this with the following cheese sauce:

1 can cream of mushroom soup	¼ pound grated sharp cheese
1 can cream of chicken soup	½ teaspoon dry mustard
1 can 4-ounce mushrooms drained	½ teaspoon poultry seasoning

Sprinkle about ¼ pound grated cheese over this. Cover with buttered crumbs. She uses half Pepperidge Farm crumbs and half Devonshire crumbs. Place in a hot oven for about 15 or 20 minutes or until heated thoroughly. Serve piping hot.

Mrs. Gordon Smith

One summer we took the children to Williamsburg, and after touring the historic buildings all morning, we had lunch in the garden at Chowning's Tavern. The tables and benches were painted a hearty turkey red and placed under high wide arbors of grapevines. The waiters were in costume, the napkins were heavy crisp checked linen, the sandwiches were from homemade bread, and the Brunswick stew was the best we ever tasted.

CHOWNING'S TAVERN BRUNSWICK STEW

1 hen, 5 or 6 pounds	4 medium potatoes, diced
1 gallon water	4 cups corn
2 large onions, sliced	2 teaspoons salt
2 cups okra	½ teaspoon pepper
4 cups tomatoes	1 tablespoon sugar
2 cups lima beans	

Cut chicken in 8 pieces and simmer for 2¼ hours in water. Remove chicken. Add lima beans, tomatoes, onions, potatoes and okra to the broth. Simmer until beans are tender, about an hour. Add hot water if necessary and stir to prevent scorching. Add corn and chicken, boned and diced, and seasonings. Makes 8 to 10 servings.

A couple of years ago we ran in our column a recipe for Herb Baked Chicken. I misplaced it, but Rowena Frierson (Mrs. Burton) began having it for her family and even gave the recipe to her daughters-in-law. It has gotten to be such a specialty with them that now we call it Rowena's chicken.

ROWENA'S HERB BAKED CHICKEN

1 broiler, (3 pounds), cut up	*¼ teaspoon pepper*
¼ cup lemon juice	*¼ teaspoon rubbed sage*
¼ cup chopped parsley	*¼ teaspoon thyme leaves*
1 clove garlic, crushed	*½ cup flour*
(optional)	*2 teaspoons salt*
1 teaspoon salt	*¼ teaspoon pepper*
½ teaspoon grated lemon peel	*¼ cup shortening*

Place the cut-up chicken in a large bowl. Combine lemon juice, parsley, and garlic, salt, lemon peel and seasonings. Pour this marinade on the chicken, cover, and marinate several hours or overnight in the refrigerator, turning occasionally. Drain but reserve the marinade.

Shake the drained chicken in a paper bag containing flour, salt, and pepper. In a large skillet, brown the chicken in shortening. Remove chicken and place in shallow baking dish. Pour over the reserved marinade. Bake uncovered in a 375-degree oven 45 minutes or until the chicken is tender. The Frierson boys love this on hot steamed rice.

Mrs. Burton Frierson

After the Tennessee River flood waters had receded from the banks in 1896, a group of transplanted New Englanders appeared on the grounds of an amusement park at the end of the Riverview trolley line, north of Hill City. Each picked up a wooden stick attached to an odd-shaped metal head and started swinging at a small round ball. It was golf.

The Chattanooga Golf and Country Club was organized that fall and among the charter members were Chamblisses, Ewings, Voights, Reads, Montagues, among many other names prominent then. In 1902 the first Southern Tournament was played, with a business meeting in town, and the trip out in the trolley or by horse and carriage. The ladies came later for tea and dancing, with ices in the shape of golf balls served on paper tees.

The first club house was copied from a Swiss chalet. The green four-wheel trolley which ran from own to Riverview could hold 40 passengers, carrying golfers to their club; later wives and children, with baskets of food joined the men for dinner. It came across the Walnut Street Bridge, turned right on Frazier Avenue, left at Tremont, and then went on out Riverview Road. They say that the huge fireplace that provided so much warmth and cheer caused the doom of the club house, which caught fire and burned one January in 1914. Number 6 raced from Cameron Hill, but the once-beautiful chalet went up in smoke.

The new clubhouse was built in 1915, and in the years since, it has been the scene of Chattanooga golf, swimming, tennis, and many spectacular social functions. It occupies a lovely bend of the river, and to look out over the river from any porch or terrace, is pleasant whatever the season. The gracious sweeping landscape of the green fairways is always beautiful.

The most current remodeling has been completed recently, including a completely new kitchen. One of the specialties is a slice of ham and one of turkey on a piece of toast, topped with green asparagus, and covered over with a cheese sauce, served piping hot and known appropriately enough as "The Country Club Special."

Cheshire Holmes also told me about a popular new dessert they have been serving....fresh peaches served in iced champagne glasses with a little champagne poured over them. For young people's parties they substitute ginger ale. This is their recipe for the special, very popular at luncheons.

COUNTRY CLUB SPECIAL

First put a thin slice of ham per person in a baking pan. On top of each slice of ham, put a slice of turkey breast. Top with three asparagus spears per serving. Pour over each serving the following sauce:

Make a thick cream sauce using 6 tablespoons butter, 6 tablespoons flour, and 2 cups chicken stock. Season to taste with salt and pepper. Top each serving with a spoon of this sauce, and then sprinkle generously with grated sharp cheddar cheese. Shake paprika on top of this, and run in a 350 oven for about 15 minutes. Serve each Country Club Special on toast, garnished with parsley and a spiced peach.

Chattanooga Golf and Country Club

This is the easiest Mexican sort of chicken tamale pie that we could find. Instead of the tortillas, you could use corn chips.

78

KING RANCH CASSEROLE

1 package frozen soft tortillas,
   cut in bite size pieces
1 large chicken, boiled,
   boned and cut up
¹₂ pound grated cheddar cheese
1 large onion, chopped
1 large green pepper, chopped

1½ teaspoons chili powder
Salt and garlic to taste
1 can cream of chicken
   soup, undiluted
1 can cream of mushroom
   soup, undiluted
1 small can tomatoes, drained

Layer the tortillas and chicken alternately in the casserole. Combine half the cheese with all the other ingredients; pour over the casserole. Sprinkle with remaining cheese. Bake at 375 for 30 minutes. Serve 8 to 10.

One of the easiest chicken dishes is a casserole of browned chicken topped with mushrooms, vegetables, and whatever the late Peg Randolph thought to add to it. Peg and her family were noted for their artistic flair and their good food.

PEG RANDOLPH'S CHICKEN CASSEROLE

Brown chicken in a skillet and season. Place this in a casserole. Add sliced carrots, mushrooms, celery, onions (that have been sauteed), maybe a little garlic. Add bay leaf, a pinch of marjoram and thyme, a package of frozen limas (or left-over lima beans). Top this with a glass of sherry and a little water to cook the vegetables. Cover the casserole and bake at 350 for about an hour. Take the top off at the last so that it browns.

Mrs. Ferguson Randolph

More and more the covered-dish supper is becoming one of the most convenient ways for people to get together and have dinner. It works for large church dinners, for gourmet clubs when the menu is planned way ahead, for neighborhood gatherings, and for buffet suppers in honor of special guests.

For a dinner in honor of the special guests here for a Junior League Garden Club Symposium, the entertainment committee planned a dinner of Chicken Tetrazzini, molded ginger ale salad with grapefruit to provide a tart taste, green peas with mushrooms and artichoke hearts, croissants, and souffle cups of Biscuit Tortoni that were passed along with coffee. All these things were easy for different cooks to bring, and easy to assemble and serve at the Rex Conley's house.

CHICKEN TETRAZZINI

1 large hen	*Make a cream sauce*
1 pound noodles	*of the following:*
2 tablespoons butter	*3 tablespoons butter*
1 large onion, finely chopped	*2 tablespoons flour*
1 large green pepper, chopped	*2 cups chicken stock*
2 cans mushrooms	*1 cup heavy cream*
1 can (4 ounce) pimentos, chopped	*2 tablespoons sherry*
	¹₄ cup Parmesan cheese
	Salt and pepper to taste

First boil the chicken in a large kettle of water seasoned to taste. Cool the chicken in the broth, when tender, then pull from the bones and cut up. Make cream sauce with butter, flour and stock, adding the cream and sherry and cheese at the very last.

Cook the noodles or spaghetti in the chicken stock, adding water if necessary. Saute the onion, pepper, mushrooms, pimento in 2 table-spoons butter. Add this mixture and the chicken and the sauce to the casserole. This will fill a large 3-quart casserole and another small one besides. Top the casserole with ¼ cup Parmesan cheese. This will serve about 20 people. Bake in a 350 oven for 30 minutes or until heated through and bubbling.

Mrs. Rex Conley

Sometimes the young marrieds are the very best ones to get recipes from. One day at the Needlework Shop, where she was teaching crewel lessons, Molly Johnson Nelson (Mrs. Douglas) had a good casserole to pass along when the subject of how to fix chicken for dinner came up.

MOLLY'S CHICKEN CASSEROLE

Wash and pat dry 1 frying chicken cut in pieces. Put the pieces in a buttered casserole. Now make a sauce of 1 can cream of mushroom soup, 1 cup sour cream and ½ cup sherry. Salt and pepper the chicken first and then pour over the sauce. Bake uncovered in a 350 oven for 1 hour. A nice brown crust will form over the top of the chicken. You could brown your chicken in a skillet first, but Molly says the brown crust of the sauce on the chicken makes it taste very good.

Mrs. Douglas Nelson

A familiar Chattanooga landmark is the Hotel Patten. The land itself was first owned by Cincinnati interests who in the 1880s thought Chattanooga would be the coal and iron center of the South. This later developed in Birmingham. The Stone Fort Land Company built the hotel and it was leased to the late J. B. Pound. Ever since its opening in 1908, it has been the scene of many important functions. Chicken Cacciatore was a specialty of the Lamplighter Restaurant at the Patten.

HOTEL PATTEN CHICKEN CACCIATORE

Wash and cut up 1 large fryer, using the neck and back to make chicken stock. Saute the chicken in a small amount of shortening. Put in a baking dish. Add 1 clove garlic, chopped fine, ¼ cup chopped onion, ½ cup tomato paste, and ½ cup dry sherry. Salt and pepper to taste. Add 1 bay leaf and just a pinch of thyme. Finally add ½ cup chopped mushrooms and 2 cups chicken stock. Cover the baking pan and let the chicken simmer in a slow oven until very tender, almost falling off the bones. Serve with either rice or spaghetti.

Chef Robert F. Garrison
Hotel Patten

Whenever we have hen at our house, we have it sliced with dressing, with rice and plenty of good chicken gravy the first night. Sometimes we make more dressing than we will need so we can have a second meal two or three nights later of chicken and dressing casserole. Even a small amount of leftover chicken can be stretched to feed several people this way, and they like it even better than the first time sliced.

CHICKEN AND DRESSING CASSEROLE

Arrange leftover cornbread dressing in a flat casserole. Make gravy with about 2 cups chicken stock. 4 tablespoons butter and 4 tablespoons flour. Go over the hen and slice or chop the chicken meat. Arrange the pieces of meat over the casserole of dressing. Taste the chicken gravy to correct the seasoning and pour over the casserole. Bake at 375 until hot and bubbling.

Mrs. Garrison Siskin has an unusual dressing for chicken or turkey. It is especially easy because instead of making the usual cornbread or breaking lightbread, you just use a box of cornflakes.

DRESSING FOR TURKEY OR CHICKEN

1 large box cornflakes   *2 small onions, grated*
¼ cup chopped celery   *½ teaspoon salt*
3 cups chicken or turkey broth   *Dash of pepper*

Thoroughly moisten cornflakes with the broth. Mash well. Add celery, onion, salt and pepper. Use to stuff fowl. This is also delicious baked in a greased pan for 20 to 25 minutes at 325. Mrs. Siskin got this from Mrs. S.D. Mitchell.

Mrs. Garrison Siskin

My friend, Elizabeth Sparks, Food Editor of the Winston-Salem Journal and Sentinel, has written a book about North Carolina cooking, "North Carolina and Old Salem Cookery," that includes many recipes almost exactly as we do them in Chattanooga. One of them is baked hen. Baked hen is a weekend specialty all over the South, good for dinner the first time around, for slicing or for chicken salad. Readers call to ask how to bake a hen, and the best way is to boil it first. This is Elizabeth's Tarheel recipe and just the way we do it.

BAKED HEN

The modern way of roasting a chicken is to put the prepared bird (stuffed or unstuffed) in an open pan and roast it until done at 325 degrees. That way sometimes you have tender meat, sometimes you don't.

Using the old-fashioned method, you need never worry about tenderness. This is the way to do it. Place the prepared bird in a pot and cover with cold water. Add salt and seasoning as desired. Bring to a boil and simmer (not boil) until there are indications of tenderness. Remove from broth, drain, and place in roasting pan. Stuff with sage rich dressing using some of the dressing to cover the bottom of the pan. Brush chicken with melted butter.

Bake in a slow oven, 325 degrees, for an hour or until chicken is browned and dressing is done. Skim off fat and boil down broth and thicken with flour paste to make a gravy. Diced cooked giblets and chopped cooked eggs are often added to the gravy.

CORNBREAD DRESSING

8 cups cornbread crumbs
   mixed with biscuit or
   light bread crumbs
1 onion, chopped
½ teaspoon pepper

1 to 2 teaspoons salt
Sage to taste (optional)
¾ cup melted butter
Hot water or broth to moisten

Turn in greased pan and bake.

Elizabeth Sparks
Winston-Salem, N.C.
Journal and Sentinel

South of Chattanooga is the town of Rome, Georgia. Years ago one Rome lady, Miss Martha Berry, had the vision of a school where promising mountain boys and girls could get not just a fine education but could be trained as leaders. Too many of them were dropping out of school after a few grades, settling into the routine of low-paying jobs or marginal farming, never having had the chance to develop their potential.

She began in the smallest way but soon came to national attention as she tried to enlist help from American leaders in every field. Once when the late Henry Ford came down to look over her school and see her boys and girls, she put Miss Inez Henry, then a young student, in charge of roasting the turkey that they would serve him for dinner.

Inez was impressed with the awful importance of whether the turkey was the tenderest ever tasted by Mr. Ford, and when Harnett Kane wrote about it in his biography of Martha Berry, "Miracle in the Mountains," I could just see the small hands of a little girl as she opened the oven every five minutes to spoon the drippings back over the bird. It must have been very tender, because Berry School was one of Henry Ford's interests the rest of his life.

The campus today is very beautiful and Berry Academy and Berry College have been an important influence in our area, with students not only from the mountain areas but from all over the South. I never roast a turkey that I don't think about their simple recipe.

MARTHA BERRY'S TURKEY

Season a turkey well with salt, pepper and butter and truss and put in roasting pan. Roast in a slow oven until done, basting constantly.

Bill Brock grew up in Chattanooga and his family spends their
vacations here. Bill, his wife Muffett, and their children Bill IV, Oscar,
Laura and John had this picture taken just after the relays at a July 4
family picnic.

84

Representing Tennessee in the Congress, then the Senate, then with the National Republican Party is Bill Brock. Bill feels that if you believe strongly in good government, you should get involved and work for it. He was quite young when elected Congressman in 1962, and got hundreds of Chattanoogans involved in politics who had never knocked on doors or worked in wards or precincts before.

At home Bill is a family man and likes to cook an inspired dinner for his children or for company. Muffet says that when Bill makes a salad dressing it is better, or when he is hungry for clam spaghetti and makes it, it is very special.

For Thanksgiving, the Brocks have the usual turkey with an oyster dressing separately in a casserole, a cranberry salad mold, candied sweet potatoes, peas and mushrooms, giblet gravy, hot biscuits and pumpkin pie. The following turkey with oyster dressing is the way that Muffet and Mrs. Elizabeth Armstrong and Mrs. Marty Sterling, who take turns helping the Brocks, usually do it every year. The clam spaghetti will be later in the book.

THE BROCKS' TURKEY WITH OYSTER DRESSING

Prepare your turkey and roast in a low oven. Meanwhile make the following stuffing.

2 onions	4 cups cooked cornbread
1 cup diced celery	Salt, pepper and sage to taste
2 cups oysters	Turkey broth
4 slices white bread, torn up	

Crumble the cornbread, and tear up the white bread in a bowl. Add the chopped onions and celery. Moisten with the oyster liquor and enough turkey broth to make a moist dressing. Season with salt, pepper and sage. Add the oysters last and put in a buttered casserole dish. Bake at 350 until slightly browned. Serve with turkey.

Mrs. William E. Brock III

Every year at Thanksgiving and at Christmas the Mountain City Club takes orders from its members for turkeys, which their kitchen will roast to perfection and have ready to be taken home or to be given as gifts. Unelle Johnson, who headed the kitchen before his retirement, roasts his slowly, the old-fashioned way, basting frequently, stuffing the big birds with either plain cornbread dressing or oyster dressing. This is the way he does it:

MOUNTAIN CITY CLUB TURKEY

Get a 10-to-12-pound hen turkey. Clean it and dry it well, inside and out, and then season it with salt, pepper and Accent.

To make the dressing, chop 1 cup minced celery, 2 tablespoons minced onion, and 2 strips bacon, crumbled. Saute the celery and the onion in bacon drippings. Mix 1 cup self-rising corn meal, 1 egg, and ½ cup water and bake in the same pan as the drippings. Bake at 400 until done. Crumble all up together. Moisten with stock and fill the inside of the cavity of the turkey. The cavity is then sewn up with skewers and cord.

Bake in a 350 oven in an open roaster. Start with 1 cup of water in the bottom of the roaster, and the turkey will soon make its own juices. Baste constantly for about 3 hours or until done. When the legs pull away from the breast and when the thigh is done, the whole turkey will be ready. The secret is frequent basting.

Serve with giblet gravy or a light gravy, with a helping of dressing on the side.

If you want to have oyster dressing, make it the same way, except add oysters which you drain and steam, then dry and cut out the hard core of each one. Mix the oysters with the dressing and stuff just as with the plain corn bread dressing.

Unelle Johnson
Mountain City Club

As a family, the Oehmigs are a sporting family. They hunt dove, game, duck, and one year the Von Oehmigs went to Scotland to hunt grouse. Margaret and Von are both good cooks when it comes to game. She prefers the oven method with frequent basting and he prefers char-coaling. They almost always have enough duck or dove in the freezer to have a game dinner.

Unelle Johnson, now retired as chef at the Mountain City Club, has presided over many a feast of ham, turkey, and all the trimmings for the prominent men's club in the center of town. The old clubhouse pictured here, was torn down when the new Williamsburg type building was built.

MARGARET OEHMIG'S DUCK

Defrost duck or game by letting stand at room temperature until thawed. If the duck has been frozen very long, sometimes they take the skin, which might be dry and tough, off. Stuff each duck with a few sliced apples, a few slices of orange, and some celery leaves. Salt and pepper each and cover with a strip or two of bacon. Cook uncovered in a 400-degree oven basting often with red wine and butter. Roast about 20 minutes for rare meat and cook longer for well-done duck.

Mrs. Von Oehmig

At the Signal Mountain Golf and Country Club, there are two or three wild-game dinners every year. These are large banquets of hunters. Chef William Getts says he cooks the game very simply. "Why try to change the flavor of venison so that it tastes like beef? These hunters went to a lot of trouble to shoot deer. I try to cook it as tender as possible with butter and salt, the old-fasioned way, but they want it to taste like venison."

Along with dove, quail, duck, grouse, and venison, he plans a wild-rice casserole with oysters and shrimp, green peas with water chestnuts, home made twisted bread that is freshly baked and pulled apart in chunks, and lots of hot coffee. He gave the following tips on game.

SIGNAL MOUNTAIN COUNTRY CLUB DOVE, GROUSE AND QUAIL

DOVE: Just use the breast. Season with salt and pepper and butter and roast in the oven. Baste and brush often with butter, keeping the oven about 300 degrees for about 45 minutes. Do not cover, just roast slowly and baste often.

GROUSE: Fry grouse like chicken. Coat with flour, salt and pepper, with a dash of ginger in the flour. Fry in deep fat at about 375 degrees.

QUAIL: Use whole quail, split down the back. Roast these in the oven just like the dove. If you want a gravy, thicken the butter and drippings.

Chef William Getts
Signal Mountain Golf
and Country Club

Kinch likes his dove simple . . .broiled with bacon . . . served with Virginia Ham, creamed hominy and spoonbread. This is the way we fixed them for the farewell dinner the night before he had to go back to Vietnam in 1968.

DOVES WRAPPED IN BACON

Wash the cleaned doves and salt and pepper them. Let set for about 30 minutes to thoroughly thaw and to let the seasoning soak in. In a skillet, brown in butter and remove. Some people flatten them, but we didn't. Cover each browned dove with a piece of bacon to fit around.

Arrange the dove in a heavy Dutch oven or casserole and put in a 350-degree oven for about 40 minutes covered. Toward the end, take the top off so the bacon can crisp a little. Squirt with lemon juice and sprinkle with chopped parsley. With the brown bits in the skillet, make gravy with some water and a little flour. Pour this over the dove and arrange on a platter.

The John L. Hutchesons live at Happy Valley Farm in Rossville a short drive from where the Peerless Woolen Mills for years were operated by the Hutcheson family. The dairy business at Happy Valley Farm was just a side line that John L. developed from a very small beginning. He grew up on Missionary Ridge at his folks' handsome home, which they later gave as a manse for the First Presbyterian Church.

They kept a cow, as everyone did, and John L. and his brother Lewis had a route on the ridge which they made every day selling milk. After he was married, he wanted to keep a cow, too, so he went to Middle Tennessee to buy a Jersey one day, bought instead 28 heifers and when he came home, he had to buy a farm to put them on.

He bought the former Leake farm on Dry Valley Road and named it Happy Valley Farm. At first, in addition to running the mills, he loaded up his station wagon every afternoon with 5-gallon cans of milk which he sold and delivered to his relative on Lookout Mountain!

The rest is history, and the fine herd he built up as well as a business that has Happy Valley Milk in every grocery store in town is history. The primary interest at the Hutchesons has always been textiles, but the barbecues at Happy Valley Farm and the horse shows, the cattle sales, the family entertainment, have always interested Chattanoogans.

All the Hutcheson family loves hunting and the week after Christmas every year, all the clan who are able gather at their place in Geiger, Alabama, for a week of hunting, fishing and good eating. Last year there were 38 of them, including a whole generation under 12. They hunt dove, duck and deer and fish in various lakes if it is warm enough.

The children ride horses, have a pony cart and a buggy and just play. The eating is simple, southern and delicious. Edward Little, who cooks for the Hutchesons at Happy Valley, comes along to help Caroline Meeks, who lives at Geiger.

They have big breakfasts of country ham, sausage, grits, eggs, biscuits; they have fried chicken; they have all sorts of game fixed in the simple southern way that makes the meat tender and delicious. This is their method of cooking venison.

GEIGER VENISON

Use a rack of venison that weighs from 5 to 7 pounds. Peel and chop 3 carrots, 3 large potatoes, 2 large onions, and 4 ribs of celery. Put these in a large kettle with 3 cups vinegar, about 2 quarts water, and salt and pepper. Cook for about 1½ to 2 hours.

Put the rack of raw venison in a roaster and pour over the vegetable marinade. Cover and refrigerate overnight. The next afternoon when you want to cook the venison, take out the roaster, put a cover on it, and put in a 375 oven for about 2 hours. It will brown itself.

Slice the venison and serve with wild rice, broccoli and Hollandaise sauce, cooked carrot balls and hot biscuits.

Edward Little

Happy Valley Farm is a beautiful combination of green fields, dairy cows, fine horses, white fences and barns, and various members of the Hutcheson family who love life on a farm.

The easiest way we ever heard of to cook duck is to season it well, wrap it in foil and bake in the oven. This is the way Mrs. Edwin B. Anderson of Nashville does it. She says they gave all their duck away until they discovered this recipe. Now it is one of their favorite dishes.

WILD DUCK IN FOIL

Wild duck	*1 pat butter*
1 onion	*¼ cup red wine*
½ teaspoon thyme	*Salt and pepper*

Rub inside of duck with salt and pepper, and put an onion inside. Lay on large sheet of heavy-duty foil and pour wine over it. Sprinkle thyme on duck, and place butter on it. Wrap closely. Cook at 325 for 3½ hours.

Mrs. Edwin B. Anderson
Nashville, Tennessee

Betty Patten has always been considered quite remarkable by her friends, and has an artistic sense, an eye for the unusual, and everything neat and in order. She is a creative cook, and as long as she is going to cook, she likes to think up an imaginative menu. This is the way she roasts duck with an accompanying wild rice casserole.

BETTY'S ROAST DUCK

Wash duck thoroughly in cold water. Remove oil glands in neck where skin joins the body. Remove rear section beginning at the last back joint. Place 1 onion, 1 piece celery, 1 strip bacon and ½ green pepper inside duck. Salt duck inside and out. Place ½ strip bacon across breast.

Place duck in baking pan and pour 1 tablespoon olive oil (or salad oil) over duck. Place uncovered in 300-degree oven and brown 1 hour. Then cover pan with tight cover and cook at same temperature for 2 more hours or until tender. Do not baste or raise cover. For the fourth hour, leave pan covered, baste duck frequently with following sauce. When ducks are glazed, serve with the following sauce:

Sauce: Prepare for each duck cooked:

2½ ounces tomato catsup
1½ ounces Worcestershire sauce
1 teaspoon Louisiana hot sauce
10 drops Tabasco sauce

2½ ounces sherry wine
1 teaspoon olive oil
1 piece crushed garlic

WILD RICE CASSEROLE TO GO WITH DUCK

1 pound mild sausage
1 pound sliced mushrooms
¼ cup flour
2½ cups condensed chicken broth
1 cup chopped onions
2 cups uncooked wild rice

½ cup coffee cream
1 teaspoon Accent
1 teaspoon salt
⅛ teaspoon pepper (ground)
Pinch oregano, thyme, marjoram

Saute sausage and drain well. In a little of the fat, saute onions and mushrooms until slightly yellow, add sausage and simmer. Wash and cook rice, 15 to 30 minutes. Make white sauce of cream, flour, chicken broth. Sift flour in cream in top of double boiler and then add chicken broth. Don't allow to get too thick. Add seasoning. Mix above together. Bake 30 minutes in 350 oven in roasting pan. This also freezes well.

Mrs. E. W. Patten

CHAPTER V

Seafood

Fishing is a great sport on Chickamauga Lake, in the Tennessee River, and in our various lakes, ponds and streams. Our seafood from the coast has to be shipped in.

From the earliest days, seafood was shipped in by train, and oysters at Christmas were traditional. Summerfield Johnston remembers his mother, "Miss Bess" Johnston (Mrs. James F.), one of Chattanooga's most famous cooks, ordering oysters in the shell and keeping them in her basement in the winter, feeding them occasionally with a little cornmeal.

In this way she could have fresh oysters on the half shell or oyster stew when she wanted them. As a hostess she is still a legend. (In her diary she wrote that her first company meal was when she was nine. She accompanied her father and his friends in a buggy up the rough corduroy road to Walden's Ridge, and cooked supper for them!)

Shrimp, crabmeat and lobster have long been favorites for entertaining and because they are not native to our region, they are considered a little special. When Chattanoogans head for the ocean, they usually go either to North or South Carolina, Georgia, Florida or the Gulf coast.

A good day's journey in any southerly direction will get you to your favorite beach. This means fresh seafood, and all the good cooks bring back numerous recipes. As we try them here at home, before many years we think of them as Chattanooga recipes. The quality of frozen seafood that we can buy here now is very delicious, and almost any seafood recipe can be made.

In the '20s, Garnet Carter, founder of Rock City (where early Chattanoogans used to go on picnics), Paul Carter, O.B. Andrews, and others began to develop Lookout Mountain as a year-round residential section.

They were also interested in getting the mountain families to join in and have a club which was called Fairyland Club. The long English-type building of mountain stone, following the contours of the brow, is as good a place as any to enjoy the magnificent view of the valley and the rides and mountains beyond. On a clear day you can see seven states while having a delicious lunch on the new-enclosed porch.

The Thursday night buffets and the Sunday night buffets are the gourmet type with perhaps the best prime ribs in town, and an assorted selection of country ham, seafood, chicken, beautiful salads and tiny cinnamon rolls along with plain rolls and corn muffins.

Fairyland has been the scene of many wedding receptions, luncheons, dinners, every conceivable form of party and conjures up pleasant memories of Chattanooga happenings as well as being a fine place to just go and have dinner.

FAIRYLAND CRABMEAT WITH ARTICHOKE HEARTS

2 pounds Alaskan King crab	¼ cup olive oil
3 green onions and	1 can artichoke hearts
stems, chopped	1 teaspoon Accent
¾ cup mushrooms	6 tablespoons cornstarch
½ cup white wine	Salt and pepper to taste
3 cups chicken consomme	3 tablespoons pimentos diced

Saute the crabmeat, chopped green onions, mushrooms, pimentos and artichoke hearts in olive oil for 5 minutes. Add salt, pepper, and Accent and let stand. Mix consomme, white wine and cornstarch, bring to a boil, and let simmer 5 minutes. Place crabmeat mixture in casserole. Pour sauce over mixture and serve hot.

Fairyland Club

A good seafood Newburg is one that Nancy Thomas made for a Pilot Club dinner. Served in a chafing dish it can be served on rice, fried noodles, or in pastry shells.

SEAFOOD NEWBURG

2 cans frozen cream	1 pound cooked shrimp
of shrimp soup	½ cup or more sherry
2 packages 6-ounce frozen	1 teaspoon or more bitters
King crab meat	Salt to taste
1 can lobster (5½ ounces)	

Heat soup in top of double boiler. Add crab meat, one package at a time, stirring until melted. Add lobster and shrimp. Add cream to thin to desired consistency. Add sherry and bitters; salt to taste. Serve over rice or in patty shells.

Mrs. Nancy Thomas

Crabmeat is a favorite luncheon dish and there are many ways to fix it. Mrs. Rex Conley has a delicious casserole of crabmeat that adapts itself to either a garden club luncheon or as an extra dish for a larger buffet dinner. This is the way Louise does it.

LOUISE'S GARDEN CLUB CRABMEAT

5 slices day-old bread	½ teaspoon dry minced onion
2½ cups grated cheddar cheese	¼ teaspoon dry mustard
1 can crabmeat (7½ ounces)	¼ teaspoon Lawry's
3 eggs	seasoning salt
1¼ cups half and half	¼ teaspoon paprika
Pinch of brown sugar	½ teaspoon Worcestershire
Pinch of black pepper	

Trim crusts from bread and spread with butter. Cut into 1-inch squares. Place half in the bottom of a buttered casserole. Drain the crabmeat. Spread half over the bread cubes. Spread half the cheese over the crabmeat. Repeat another layer. Beat the eggs lightly with the seasonings and stir into the cream. Pour over the casserole, and place in the refrigerator covered overnight or at least 6 hours. Bake at 300 degrees uncovered for 1½ hours. Serve immediately.

Mrs. Rex Conley

Anne Crimmins Awad (Mrs. George) is a popular soft-spoken brunette who efficiently gets done whatever she is supposed to do for the Junior League, Community Concerts, Symphony or her church. She also fixes an especially good deviled crab. She got this recipe from Betty Cummings (Mrs. Judge), whose family used to vacation in Carter's Quarters, Georgia.

DEVILED CRAB

1 pound or 2 cans 8-ounce	½ cup India relish
crab meat	½ large onion, chopped
2 hard boiled eggs, sliced	½ green pepper, chopped
2 tablespoons Worcestershire	2 tablespoons bacon dripping
½ cup mayonnaise	Salt and pepper to taste

Saute onion and pepper in bacon grease. Mix ingredients and fill individual ramekins or shells or a baking dish. Cover with cracker crumbs and bake in a quick (425) oven for 20 minutes. Serves 4 to 6. This can be made the day before serving and stored in the refrigerator before heating.

Mrs. George Awad

When Chattanooga goes to the beach, it is usually to South Carolina, Georgia or Florida. When we found a spot in South Carolina that suited us, we kept going back year after year, until now, as we rent our cottage each year, we feel a belonging. We all look forward to the tail end of summer when we cross the busy Highway 17 that connects New York and Miami, and drive across the marshy salt creek to the small island called Pawley's. This unique strip of sand restores the spirit, gives rest to the weary, and provides all the excitement and fun of beach living for young and old.

There are the long beach walks, the salt air in your hair, the relaxing of just doing nothing. The main attraction for me is the delicious food fixed by an amazing South Carolina lady, Mrs. R. H. Dingle. Mrs. Dingle runs Tip Top Inn, and each family is assigned a special table. At breakfast, lunch or dinner, you go to your table and await a feast.

Our older boys pass their plates for more roast beef, homemade bread, curried chicken, creole shrimp, fresh green beans, fresh butterbeans, and when it comes to the crab cakes, we have to send back to the kitchen. Ellen and Susan eat as much as grown ups and I embarrass myself with third helpings. This hearty delicious food has a way of easing the lines in the faces of older people, and giving a healthy look to the little ones. The teenagers who surf and fish all day and dance all night even look rested and healthy.

The menus include both a meat and a seafood for dinner, and homemade bread so fresh and tender you could make a meal off of it alone. I even jot down the menus so I can inspire myself some winter day when I can't think of a thing to have for dinner.

I never leave without several new recipes from Mrs. Dingle, who insists that it is just simple food. This is true, but the old fashioned crocheted place mats, the relish and jelly, the individual salt cellars, the magnificent simplicity and style of the food make it our favorite kind of eating.

Her creole shrimp is in a casserole and the crabmeat souffle is light and delicate.

CRABMEAT SOUFFLE

1 pound crabmeat	4 eggs
2 cups milk	½ teaspoon nutmeg
½ cup heavy cream	1 tablespoon sherry
1 cup cracker crumbs	Salt and pepper to taste

Beat the eggs with a beater. Stir in the milk and cream. Add the crabmeat and the cracker crumbs and the seasoning. Put in a well greased casserole and bake at 350 for about 45 minutes. This will rise nicely and not give the trouble with falling the way that one based on cream sauce will.

Mrs. R. H. Dingle

CREOLE SHRIMP CASSEROLE

1 pound shrimp	1 can tomatoes, (303 can)
2 bell peppers, chopped	½ teaspoon salt
2 onions, chopped	½ teaspoon pepper
1 cup bread crumbs	1 tablespoon Worcestershire
2 tablespoons bacon drippings	Dash Tabasco

Cook onion and pepper in bacon drippings until soft. Add all other ingredients. Bake in a baking dish about 20 or 30 minutes in a 350 oven. The bread crumbs and baking it in a casserole give this creole shrimp the effect of being a scalloped shrimp. It is delicious and would be very different to carry to a church supper or to a convalescing friend.

Mrs. R. H. Dingle

Eating at Perdita's in Charleston is a treat. Their recipe for Crab-meat Remick is a specialty.

PERDITA'S BAKED CRABMEAT REMICK

1 pound or more crabmeat	1 teaspoon tarragon vinegar
6 slices bacon, cooked	1 teaspoon dry mustard
and crumbled	½ teaspoon celery salt
1½ cups mayonnaise or	Few drops red pepper
salad dressing	Seasoning
½ cup chili sauce	

Place crabmeat in 6 scallop shells or individual baking dishes; sprinkle with bacon. Place shells in a large shallow pan for easy handling. Heat in moderate oven (350) for 5 minutes while fixing the topping. Blend remaining ingredients in small bowl; spoon over hot crab mixture.

Broil 4 to 5 inches from the heat for 1 minute or just until hot.

Perdita's Restaurant

One night in Savannah, Georgia, we discovered a new shrimp dish, broiled marinated shrimp. They are boiled and peeled shrimp, marinated in classic oil and vinegar dressing until tender, then run under the broiler. This is so simple, I wonder I didn't think of it myself.

SAVANNAH SHRIMP, MARINATED AND BROILED

Get medium or small shrimp because they are more tender. Boil, peel, and clean them. Put in a platter or bowl and pour over them Kraft Italian salad dressing (as it comes in the bottle.) Let them marinate several hours. When ready to serve, remove from bowl and put on a pan. Run under the broiler until golden and pretty.

We also got a good recipe for crabmeat patties. The reason I think it is good is that this is about the way we have been making patties by ear for years. The bread crumbs and eggs seem to form a better base than the thick white sauce that some recipes call for.

CRABMEAT PATTIES

Mix these ingredients:
1 pound crabmeat
2 cups soft bread crumbs
2 eggs

Blend:
1 teaspoon dry mustard

1 teaspoon Worcestershire sauce
2 tablespoons lemon juice
1 tablespoon vinegar
½ teaspoon pepper and
½ teaspoon salt
¼ teaspoon Tabasco
4 tablespoons melted butter

Blend all seasonings. Add to crab mixture. Divide into 8 patties. Roll in flour. Beat 1 egg and thin with a little milk. Dip patties in egg-and-milk mixture and then in cracker meal. Chill about 1 hour before cooking. Drop each patty in hot fat (350 degrees) and brown.

Years ago puff pastry was found only in the best restaurants, and none that we know of in Chattanooga. Now, thanks to frozen patty shells from any supermarket, you can have the finest company dinner with either creamed chicken, lobster Newburg or sherried creamed crab in individual pastry cases. This is a good idea for luncheons or garden club meetings.

SHERRIED CRAB VOL-AU-VENT

¼ cup minced onion
3 tablespoons butter
  or margarine
3 tablespoons flour
1 can frozen condensed
  cream of shrimp soup

½ cup milk
1 can (7 ounces crabmeat,
  (shrimp or lobster
  can be substituted)
2 tablespoons sherry
1 package frozen patty shells

Prepare 6 frozen patty shells according to package instructions.

Meanwhile saute onion in butter until soft, but not brown. Add flour and cook, stirring constantly one minute. Add soup, thawed according to label instructions. Slowly stir in milk and continue to beat and stir until mixture is smooth. (It may have a lightly curdled appearance before it is completely blended.) Add flaked crabmeat and sherry. Taste for seasoning.

Generously fill patty shells. Garnish with tomato wedge and parsley.

Along with the new custom of several couples getting together and each one bringing something for the party, there is new interest in some hearty and different dishes. Marie Crimmins (Mrs. John) brought a hot crab dip to the party her garden club has once a year, and everyone wanted the recipe. Here it is.

HOT CRAB DIP

1½ pounds sharp cheddar cheese
3 packages frozen crab meat

1½ cups mayonnaise
Dash Tabasco

Melt the cheese in a double boiler. Add the thawed and drained crabmeat, which you have picked over. Then add the mayonnaise and Tabasco. Taste to see if you want to add any other seasoning. Serve in a chafing dish with assorted crackers near by.

Mrs. John Crimmins, Jr.

Emeline Ferguson (Mrs. Don) is one of the creative cooks who either looks in the refrigerator and decides to use the vichyssoise from the night before as a sauce for the fish, or tastes a wonderful dish when on a trip and comes home and makes it.

She has an informality, is fairly sure things will turn out all right, and with her common sense, her Hedges flair, and a capability beneath her calm that you might never guess, she has been president of the Junior League, chairman of countless projects, and hostess at some delightful dinners at her French country house.

Her daughters Susan and Lisa have been working alongside their mother ever since they were old enough to sit on the counter, and Susan can cook almost anything her mother can. If all the fourth and fifth generation Chattanoogans are as smart, our city will continue to dine well for years to come.

When Emeline went to Virginia recently, she tasted a flounder and crabmeat dish and came home and copied it.

FLOUNDER AU CRABMEAT

Get about 6 pounds of flounder for 10 people and have it fileted. Take 1 pound crabmeat and saute gently in butter with salt, pepper and 2 teaspoons McCormick fine herbs.

Take the long filets of flounder and line the bottom of a buttered casserole. Put the black skin side on the bottom. Sprinkle the crabmeat over the flounder and put in the refrigerator until cooking time.

Mix 1 can vichyssoise with ½ can chicken stock. Put ½ cup chopped green onions (tops as well as scallions) and ½ cup chopped parsley in the blender, and add the liquid vichyssoise and stock gradually. Season this to taste. Make a roux of 4 tablespoons butter and 4 tablespoons flour and gradually add the blender mixture. Let simmer a few minutes until thickened, stirring all the time. Pour this over the fish. Sprinkle with bread crumbs, Parmesan cheese, dot with butter and slivered almonds and sprinkle with paprika.

Bake in a 350 oven for 30 minutes until bubbly and slightly brown on top. Serve with a salad and French bread.

Mrs. Don Ferguson

The quickest shrimp dish for a family is Shrimp Creole. You can use either a small amount of shrimp or a lot, depending on how much you have. You can use large expensive shrimp or small river shrimp that come frozen and already cooked in a plastic bag. Basically it is a tomato, onion, and celery sauce with shrimp in it, served over rice. The sauce can be made early in the day or half hour before dinner. For company sometimes I add about ½ cup dry white wine as it simmers.

SHRIMP CREOLE

2 tablespoons butter or	Dash cayenne pepper
bacon drippings	1 bay leaf
½ cup finely chopped onion	Pinch sugar
½ cup finely chopped celery	1 can tomatoes or tomato sauce
½ cup finely chopped	2 cups water
green pepper	1 pound shrimp
1 teaspoon salt	Chopped parsley

In a heavy saucepan or an electric skillet, melt the butter and add the onions, celery and green pepper. Saute until golden. Add all the rest ingredients except shrimp and simmer about 30 minutes. This can be thickened at the last with 2 tablespoons of flour in a little cold water. Add the shrimp which have been boiled first. Taste for seasoning. Serve over hot rice.

Almost every family loves a shrimp supper, either fried shrimp or boiled. This is probably because we don't have it nearly enough. Peeling and cleaning shrimp, dipping it in flour, then in egg and milk, then in meal and then frying, takes some doing. Any cook who goes through all the emotions of cooking can remember an experience of cleaning so many shrimp and getting so tired of it that she promised herself that it wouldn't happen again soon!

But ask the rest of the family what their reaction is. They will tell you that they never got enough in their lives. If you take them out to dinner they look longingly at the shrimp cocktail and wonder if it is too extravagant.

Anything this popular ought to get served, so here are two ways to serve shrimp to large families. A dinner of fried shrimp is the biggest hit, but in South Carolina we discovered how easy it is to boil several pounds of shrimp and just serve as is. If you have time, you chill the shrimp but if you don't you just serve them hot.

Each person gets a big plate and a little saucer to make his own dip in. The dips vary. The older people mix chili sauce, horseradish and lemon juice in their saucers. The little ones mix catsup and mayonnaise. Everyone peels his own shrimp, and if he is fussy, removes the little black line. Families who have lived on the coast all their lives just ignore the little black vein. With this we have some potato salad, green peas, and plenty of buttered French bread. We all eat until we are stuffed.

BOILED SHRIMP TO EAT IN SHELLS

In a kettle of boiling water add salt, a rib of celery and the juice of ½ lemon. When the water is boiling, put in the raw shrimp and let cook about 10 minutes. The worst thing you can do is to overcook shrimp, which makes them tough. As soon as they are pinky white they are done.

An alternate method is steaming, which really makes very tender shrimp. Put about 1½ inches of water in a kettle, season with salt, celery and lemon juice, and bring to a boil. When it boils, put in shrimp and cover. They will steam this way. About 15 minutes is long enough, or check to see if the flesh is firm and pink. Let cool in the broth.

Serve hot or cold. Bring a big bowl of boiled shrimp to the table and serve a generous heap to each person. Have on the table mayonnaise, catsup, chili sauce, horseradish and wedges of lemon so that everyone can mix his own dip.

Fried shrimp, however, is the real delicacy. Actually it is not too expensive if you buy the medium shrimp, because a pound will serve about four. If you can, plan to shell and clean the green shrimp, then coat them for frying early in the afternoon. Plan plenty of time for frying, because you can only do eight or ten at a time.

Overcrowding lowers the temperature of the fat too much and makes them soggy and takes too long. They should brown in 375-degree fat as quickly as possible, and when golden, remove and drain. A pound fried makes a heaping platter, and two pounds looks like enough to feed an army. I can think of many easier things to have for dinner, but nothing that fills the hearts and mouths of those present with such genuine delight.

The recipe is the restaurant method of frying and never fails. I have tried the batter method, but the batter drips off and ends up giving my oil a burned taste. This method calls for shaking the shrimp first in a bag of seasoned flour, then dipping in an egg-and-milk combination, finally drying this in finely crushed cracker meal. This browns beautifully.

FRIED SHRIMP

2 pounds raw green shrimp,	Pepper
shelled and deveined	½ cup milk
1 cup flour	1 egg
2 teaspoons salt	Lots of cracker meal

Mix flour, salt and pepper in a paper bag. Mix milk and egg in a small mixing bowl. Pour cracker meal in another bowl. First shake shrimp in the bag of flour, a few at a time. Then dip each in the egg and milk mixture. Finally roll in the cracker meal. (One variation is to spice the egg wash with Tabasco or mustard if you like a highly spiced shrimp.)

Now heat oil or shortening in a skillet or fryer to 375 degrees. It should be at least two inches deep to cover the shrimp. Fry a few shrimp at a time until golden, then remove and drain on towel. Keep in warm place until all are fried. This will take from half hour to 45 minutes.

I must warn you that they will be so pretty and attractive that you will have a problem with people coming in the kitchen and reaching for first one and then another while they talk. I forgot to say that if you split them down the back almost to the tail, and then leave the tail on, you will have butterfly shrimp which cook faster and look bigger.

TARTAR SAUCE TO GO WITH FRIED SHRIMP

1 cup mayonnaise	1 tablespoon chopped parsley
3 tablespoons chopped pickle	1 teaspoon chopped onion

Mix all these together. Add a dash of mustard if you like, and some Tabasco.

Shrimp salad is the perfect summer Sunday lunch specialty.

SHRIMP SALAD

The best shrimp salad is the simplest. Boil and clean the amount of shrimp you will need. To every two cups of shrimp, chop one cup of celery and a very little green pepper. Combine with homemade mayonnaise, the juice of ½ lemon, a little onion juice, and a dash of Tabasco. I have used Accent, some Beau Monde seasoning salt and cayenne pepper, but season it to your taste.

This is a simple uncluttered shrimp salad that shows off the shrimp, but it is much better when garnished with different things around the side. Put the salad on a bed of crisp lettuce. It can be put in a tomato or avocado half. Around the sides put halves of hard-boiled egg, sliced cucumbers, artichokes, olives, radishes or pickles. Either cheese straws or hot homemade rolls are extra good with shrimp salad.

Shrimp also makes lavish casseroles for entertaining. These two have made many Chattanooga luncheons.

CHEESE SHRIMP CASSEROLE

2½ cups cooked shrimp
½ pound cheddar cheese
7 slices bread
3 well beaten eggs

½ teaspoon salt
½ teaspoon paprika
¼ teaspoon dry mustard
2½ cups milk

Remove crusts from bread. Cut in cubes. Grate the cheese. Alternate layers of bread, shrimp, and cheese in a greased 2-quart casserole. Combine eggs, seasoning, and milk. Pour over the casserole. Let stand a few hours or overnight in the refrigerator. Before baking fluff up with a fork. Bake at 325 degrees for 1 hour. Serve with cold asparagus or a green salad.

Mrs. Frank Cater

CHOKED SHRIMP

2 pounds shrimp
3 cups cream sauce:
  6 tablespoons butter
  6 tablespoons flour
  2½ cups milk

1 pound sharp cheese, grated
1 cup sherry, heated
2 large cans artichokes, drained

Shell, clean and boil shrimp for 5 to 7 minutes. Make cream sauce and season to taste; add cheese and stir until melted. Add heated sherry, artichokes and shrimp. Put in a casserole. Grate extra cheese on top, or top with cracker crumbs. Bake at 350 for 20 to 25 minutes.

Mrs. Herbert Suplee

Mildred Montague (Mrs. William L.) lived in Mobile for three years during World War II while Bill was stationed there. When she came back home, she still remembered the wonderful fresh shrimp they could get on the coast and shrimp remoulade was one of the favorite recipes.

In the years since she has been associated with every good cause in Chattanooga from filling almost every job on the board of the Junior League, raising funds for the Cancer Society, helping get the Little Theater building built down on the beautiful river site and being active at the First Presbyterian Church. Mildred and her family, for several generations back, have been very much a part of Chattanooga.

SHRIMP REMOULADE

12 tablespoons olive oil	2 celery hearts, chopped
6 tablespoons vinegar	Parsley
4 tablespoons creole mustard	Salt
(or more)	Pepper
2 tablespoons paprika	Horseradish to taste

Marinate shrimp and shredded lettuce in this sauce for a first course. The shrimp may be drained and served on toothpicks for hors d'oeuvres.

Mrs. William Montague

This shrimp and cheese dip is from The Columns, a tearoom in Lynchburg, Virginia. This was their specialty for Coke parties or teas for Randolph-Macon College students.

THE COLUMNS SHRIMP DIP

1 package 8-ounce cream cheese	Juice of 1 lemon
½ cup chili sauce	½ to 1 cup chopped shrimp
1 small onion,	Salt and cayenne pepper
very finely chopped	to taste

Leave the cheese at room temperature to soften and then cream it. Add the other ingredients. Use as a dip for potato chips or as a sandwich spread. This was featured on a tole tray in Virginia along with chicken salad sandwiches, brownies, cucumber sandwiches and cheese straws at Coke parties.

Oysters have been a winter specialty ever since the first ice house in Chattanooga was built in 1875. Three years later when President Hayes visited Chattanooga, he was treated to a cuisine of Victorian

106

elegance which included oysters which were iced down in the big new bathtub in the upstairs of Judge D. M. Key's home on 4th Street. Since it was frozen every winter anyway, no one could take a bath and "Miss Sarah Key" Patten remembered it being perfect for oysters.

Simple creamed oysters were often served in patty shells and this is still a luncheon or wedding brunch specialty at Fairyland Club.

CREAMED OYSTERS

2 cups milk

4 tablespoons butter

4 tablespoons flour

1½ pints oysters

2 egg yolks

1 tablespoon lemon juice

1 can mushrooms

Make a cream sauce and add the egg yolks just before serving. Simmer oysters in their juice 5 minutes, drain and add to the sauce along with the drained mushrooms. Serve in patty shells or on toast.

One week on the food page we featured one of Chattanooga's earliest cookbooks, called "Selected Receipts," published in the early 1900's. The quaint advertisements (to order groceries from Dewee's you phoned 7) and the recipes called back an age of pressed chicken, chicken croquettes, homemade soups as a first course, hot rolls, elaborate cakes, and desserts such as Spanish cream and Charlotte Russe.

One of the recipes we featured was the minced oysters of the late Mrs. Henry Trotter. Her son Henry called to say that for years they have been wishing they had her recipe, because no one's scalloped oysters were quite as good as hers. Another coincidence was that it appeared on her birthday. Such is life.

MINCED OYSTERS

One quart oysters, 1 pint bread crumbs, 1 small onion, 2 hard boiled eggs, yolks of 2 raw eggs, 2 tablespoons butter, salt and pepper to taste and a dash of cayenne. Drain oysters well and chop very fine. Roll fine the bread crumbs and mix with the oysters, onion (chopped fine,) melted butter, and a spoonful of cream, salt, pepper, nutmeg, and yolks of 2 raw eggs. Mix thoroughly and put on stove to cook, stirring well until oysters are done. After taking from the fire, chop 2 hard boiled eggs and stir in. Fill shells, sprinkle bread crumbs on top, and put in stove until baked a light brown, which just takes a few minutes.

The late Mrs. Henry Trotter

107

The late Dr. Cecil Newell was a Southern gentleman gourmet from Louisiana who liked to make Sunday brunches for his friends. When he died in 1977 he was considered one of the last of a breed, the fine old fashioned family surgeon. Here he and his wife Gretchen posed in their kitchen making soup.

The Newell family has doctored Chattanooga ever since the Newell cousins, Dr. Dunbar and Dr. Ed came to Chattanooga about the turn of the century from Newellton, Louisiana. Dr. Cecil Newell's father came to join his brother in Chattanooga, with Cecil and his cousin, Dr. Ed, Jr., later making the second generation of Newell doctors. Cecil kept his family's reputation for delicious Louisiana food until the day he died in 1977.

If necessary, he would grow Bibb lettuce himself in a cold frame to have it, or spend a Sunday making a fabulous vegetable soup or homemade bread. Like all southern gentlemen, he preferred fresh vegetables rather than canned or frozen, hot homemade bread, beautifully prepared food. At Christmas they ordered fresh oysters from Louisiana and made special Chicken Oyster Gumbo.

CHICKEN OYSTER GUMBO

¾ cup okra	1 stalk celery
1 chicken (2 pounds)	1 pint oysters and liquor
2 medium size onions	Salt and pepper
2 tablespoons butter	1 or 2 teaspoons gumbo file
½ clove garlic	Rice
Dash Tabasco	

Cut okra. Soak in milk and fry. Cut up chicken and cook in 2 quarts water for 2 hours, adding salt, pepper, and Tabasco. Cut up celery and cook the last hour. Slice onions and brown in butter. Add fried okra to the soup. Cook rice separately. Add oysters to soup and cook 5 to 10 minutes. When ready to serve, season with gumbo file and serve immediately with rice.

Dr. and Mrs. Cecil Newell

Louise Newell is originally from Baltimore, and met and married Ed when he was studying medicine at Johns Hopkins. Like all Marylanders she loves fresh crab, and when she can get it, she makes a delicious Maryland Crabmeat Imperial.

MARYLAND CRAB IMPERIAL

1 pound fresh lump crabmeat	3 tablespoons mayonnaise
½ teaspoon salt	2 dashes Worcestershire sauce
⅛ teaspoon cayenne	1 tablespoon chopped parsley

Mix with fork carefully to avoid breaking the lumps. Put in individual shells. Top with pat of butter, sprinkle with paprika. Bake in preheated oven 375 degrees for 15 minutes. Makes 4 large Imperials.

A good salad to serve with this is grapefruit and avocado salad topped with a cream cheese ball and a tablespoon of chutney, dressed with a classic oil and vinegar dressing.

Mrs. Edward T. Newell, Jr.

Mrs. Levi Patton is Chattanooga's most distinguished harpist. She was invited to New York to give a concert for the Kennedy Foundation one year, and the night Ed Sullivan was named Man of the Year, she was one of three artists chosen to play for him. When she worked toward her master's degree in home economics at Columbia University, she also studied music in New York. A creative cook, she gave me the following recipe for oyster loaf as a luncheon or supper specialty.

OYSTER LOAF

Cut off the top from a small crusted loaf of bread and hollow out the center. Brush the inside of both top and bottom with butter, and heat through to toast slightly. Dip medium size oysters in slightly beaten eggs, and then in bread crumbs. Fry in hot fat until brown. Fill loaf with oysters and pour melted butter over all. Put top back on loaf and slice in two.

Decide on the amount of oysters according to the number of servings you need. One small loaf serves two.

Mrs. Levi Patton

The first Christmas my husband wanted fried oysters for Christmas breakfast, it was hard to believe. When on Christmas Eve he garnished the top of every picture with Mississippi holly, it was fine. And when he wanted to deck the mantel with nothing but pine, holly, and red candles, I agreed. But the Mississippi custom of oysters I fought at first.

Isn't it interesting that when we marry a husband, we get not only a whole new set of family, but a whole new set of Christmas traditions. If your husband is not sentimental, or if he is very modern and believes in making his own traditions, then you probably won't notice it much. But if the head of your house is a traditionalist, and remembers family customs in the strongest way at Christmas time, then you have found that you now do all sorts of things differently from the exact way your family did when you were growing up.

In the days before fast transportation, fresh oysters from the coast were a luxury saved up for Christmas in Mississippi. When a whole barrel of oysters came up from New Orleans, they had oyster cocktail

110

on Christmas Eve, fried oysters for Christmas breakfast, with stews and scalloped oysters fitted in during the next two or three days.

It was new to me, but we carried on the tradition, along with a few from my side of the family. And this is a strange confession . . . we have been doing things "his" way for so long, that I now consider these ways a part of me too. In fact between the two of us, we do so many of the exact same things every year, that at least the children will have a wide variety of what they want to keep for themselves and what they want to throw away!

We wouldn't think of having Christmas breakfast now without oysters. Even people who think they hate oysters like them crisp and fried along with a tomato catsup sauce. They are wonderful with scrambled eggs, bacon, fruit bread, grits, fresh orange juice, hot black coffee and all the excited happiness that has been ours on Christmas mornings for over 20 years.

FRIED OYSTERS

1 pint raw oysters	½ cup milk
1 cup flour	1 egg
2 teaspoons salt	Lots of cracker meal
¼ teaspoon pepper	

Mix flour, salt and pepper in a paper bag. Mix milk and egg in a small mixing bowl. Put cracker meal or crumbs in another bowl. First shake two or three oysters at a time in the bag of flour, then dip each one in the egg and milk mixture. Finally roll in the cracker meal. Prepare all oysters this way for frying.

If you have just fried bacon, use the same skillet for the oysters. They are better, though, if you start fresh with an electric skillet and about ½ inch of shortening or oil. Heat to about 375 degrees. Fry a few at a time until golden on both sides. Don't overcrowd or they won't be crisp.

A favorite of Miss Bess Johnston (Mrs. James F.) was escalloped oysters. She was such a noted cook that Chattanoogans still talk about her dinners. She had good cooks, but she always came in the kitchen and tasted to see that everything was good. After her death, with the same cooks and the same recipes and the same kitchen, the food was never quite the same. Her daughter-in-law, Mrs. Summerfield Johnston, was also a noted hostess and used the following escalloped oyster recipe. She passed it along to her sisters and nieces and today it is still a specialty in the Tom Moore, Jr., home where Sarah fixed it recently for her children's friends.

ESCALLOPED OYSTERS

1 quart oysters	1 cup white bread crumbs
¾ to 1 cup oyster liquor	2 cups cracker crumbs
½ cup cream	½ cup (1 stick) melted butter

Mix bread and cracker crumbs with melted butter. Put a thin layer of the crumbs in the bottom of a baking dish. Cover with oysters. Season with salt, pepper, and a little parsley. Add ½ the cream and oyster liquor. Repeat and cover top with remaining crumbs. Chopped celery may be added. Be careful never to use more than 2 layers of oysters. Bake in a 400-degree oven for ½ hour.

Used by the Summerfield Johnston family

In the early 1900's Mr. J. T. Lupton bought some property in Sapphire, North Carolina, near Highlands. It had one big lake for bass fishing and he built a house as well as several smaller guest houses, servants' house and so on. A second lake for trout was built in the '30s. Sapphire has become a beloved retreat for three generations of assorted Lupton kin, and in succeeding years several new houses have gone up.

In 1959 his grandson, Jack Lupton, decided to remodel the servants' quarters and laundry, add a big porch and use it as a vacation house for his family. Alice and Jack say that a weekend or a week in these North Carolina mountains is the most pleasant vacation in the world. The air is different, the trees are greener, life is simpler.

There is no planned entertainment ... the children play in the garden, fish, cook, make orange cakes and churn homemade ice cream. Alice says she suddenly feels like picking apples in the orchard and making a pie and does.

Jack has experimented with cooking almost every kind of meat over charcoal. He does steak, chicken, trout and even calf's liver. He likes to use olive oil, butter, lemon juice and spiced Parisienne seasoning.

One favorite is fish chowder. Alice says that as with any soup, this is an informal recipe. It depends on whether there was any fish left from the meal before, what is in the refrigerator and so on. I am passing on her fish chowder.

112

SAPPHIRE FISH CHOWDER

Use any fish, but bass is best. First boil the cleaned fish in salted water until tender. In another pan chop some celery and onions and add water to boil until they are done. Season this to taste with salt, pepper, Beaumonde seasoning, a pinch of rosemary. Cut up some potatoes and boil along with celery and onions.

This will be the basis of your chowder. When the fish is tender in the other pot, remove and cut in bite size chunks. Add about a pint of half and half (milk and cream), or the proportion that you like and heat. Taste again and see what it needs. You will need to add a square of butter and some chopped parsley.

Serve the chowder with cornbread or crackers.

Mrs. John T. Lupton II

Fried fish has been a standard way of cooking fish for years, but it is not the only way. A cook we had years ago baked fish so tastily that it was a specialty. Butter she used plentifully, along with lemon juice and paprika, cracker crumbs and seasoning, and the moist tender fish was so sweet that it flaked tenderly under its golden top. She lined the baking dish with foil, so she had practically no cleaning.

Her secret wasn't the temperature of the oven, because she used only two speeds, 250 and 450, slow and fast. Yet when the fish came out in a few minutes, it was done and tender. I now think she just seasoned it well with salt, pepper, lemon juice, and lots of butter.

Once I saw her grating a little onion juice on the fish, and a dash of nutmeg, of all things. But she assured me that this was just an impulse, and sometimes she did and sometimes she didn't.

Whenever she reached for the spice cans, she loved to sprinkle a dash of this and a dash of that, and she was a good cook and could get by with it. She was sure that paprika on top put everyone in a good mood, and any food that was white or pale, always got the treatment.

You can use almost any fish, fresh or frozen . . . trout, flounder, sole, bass, red snapper. If you get the frozen filets, remember the trick of thawing them in salty water to which you have added ice and a little vinegar. This seems to plump them.

113

BAKED FISH

2 *pounds flounder*   *Salt and pepper*
  or other fish   *Paprika*
¼ *cup butter, melted*   *1 cup cracker crumbs*
¼ *cup lemon juice*

Place fish in foil lined baking pan. Salt and pepper the fish and pour over the lemon juice and butter. Top with cracker crumbs and paprika. Bake in a hot oven (425) for 15 or 20 minutes until fish flakes easily when tested with a fork. Now turn on broiler and finish off the fish with a golden brown look on top — about 2 or 3 minutes.

One of the most memorable trips of my life was when I was about fifteen and took a four-day Girls' Preparatory School tour to New Orleans. I wish that there were some way to keep all the excitement and enthusiasm of the first time you do things. You may remember the first time that you ate an oyster, or stayed in a hotel, or took a trip apart from your own family, and remember the adventure that life was.

There are many advantages to being older and more mature, a little sadder and a little wiser, and a little more sensible, too. Checking into a hotel, ordering a meal, and planning a day in a strange city are all simple things and have nothing to do with the uncertain, fluttery and excited state that my friends and I found ourselves in the day the bus left the old school on Palmetto Street years ago.

One sunny spring day in New Orleans two days later, Miss Tommy Duffy and Miss Eula Jarnagin, the head-mistresses, took us to the Court of the Two Sisters. We sat at tables in the courtyard to have one of the specialties, Pompano en Papillote. This was filets of pompano with a mushroom and shrimp sauce served in individual packets of parchment in which they had been baked. Maybe it was because I am from such a large family that these individual packets made such an impression. Maybe it was because this was my first bold venture into the world, or maybe it was my age. I remember it as the best thing I ever ate.

POMPANO OR FLOUNDER EN PAPILLOTE

Wipe 6 filets of pompano, flounder or trout and put them in a baking dish with 3 tablespoons olive oil. Sprinkle with 1 large onion finely chopped; 2 teaspoons chopped parsley, and salt and freshly ground pepper to taste. Brown lightly in a moderate 350 oven, turning the filets once. Handle carefully to avoid breaking. Add ½ cup dry white wine, cover the dish tightly, and bake 10 minutes longer in a slower oven.

114

Cut hearts of parchment large enough to cover the fish, and butter well. Lay a filet on each paper. Into pan in which the pompano was baked, put 1 stick butter, 1½ cups finely chopped mushrooms, ½ cup chopped cooking shrimp, ¼ teaspoon anchovy paste, ¼ teaspoon powdered mace, juice of 1 large lemon, and 3 well beaten egg yolks. Stir well and simmer slowly until the sauce is thick. Pour some of the sauce in each paper, put another paper on top and crimp and fold around the edges to seal. Heat a few minutes in a moderate oven until the fish is thoroughly heated and the paper puffed up.

The most outstanding sister team I know when it comes to entertaining, is the combination of Floweree Whitaker (Mrs. Spires) and Janet Mills (Mrs. William, Jr.). Janet now lives in Trenton, New Jersey, but when she comes home for a visit, she and Floweree usually manage to squeeze in a party in honor of somebody. Usually it is for one of the many Patten cousins who is getting married, or a visitor who is distinguished.

If you pop in the kitchen for a visit the day before the party, it is a scene of calm confusion. They are always cutting up chicken, poaching a salmon, decorating a mold or cutting sandwich bread with a dainty daisy cutter. Out of an average size kitchen, the two can turn out a banquet that the finest chef in France would have a hard time duplicating. One buffet dinner featured a Virginia ham at one end of the table, a chicken mousse at the other, with a huge poached salmon glazed and resting on a bed of green cucumber aspic. All these are beautifully decorated with sprays of flowers made out of fresh vegetables. They had hot buttered artichokes in blue cheese, some green vegetables, and for dessert, lemon tarts. Another year they turned the downstairs playroom into a banquet hall, had tables with pink cloths, dahlias and candle light and seated 50.

They are most famous for their congealed mousses which they decorate with lilies of the valley (hard boiled egg whites cut with the tube off an eyebrow pencil and arranged on a parsley stem) and carrots cut like daisies. The decorations are to be copied only by the creative cooks, but the chilled salmon mousse can be copied by anyone.

115

SALMON MOUSSE ON CUCUMBER ASPIC

Cucumber aspic: Dissolve 1 package lemon flavored gelatin in 1 cup boiling water. Cool. Peel and grate 3 small cucumbers. Press through a sieve until you have ½ cup juice. Add 3 tablespoons lemon juice to the gelatin. Tint green with vegetable coloring. Congeal and dice for the mousse bed.

Salmon Mousse: Place a 2 quart fish mold on a bed of cracked ice and add a thin layer of chilled but still liquid aspic. (Use the basic aspic recipe on the envelope of unflavored gelatin.) Swirl it around to coat the bottom and sides of the mold. Chill until set.

Outline the fins, tail and mouth with thin strips of pimento dipped in aspic and line the scales down the back with tiny thin crescents of hard cooked egg white dipped in aspic. Use a round slice of truffle or an olive for the eye.

Sprinkle chilled but still liquid aspic over each piece of garnish to set into place and chill until firm.

Mash 4 cups canned salmon flakes and force through a fine sieve. Season salmon with lemon juice, salt, and cayenne pepper. Soften 2 envelopes gelatin in 1 cup cold water; then dissolve it over hot water. Add dissolved gelatin to salmon and mix thoroughly. Fold in 6 tablespoons mayonnaise and 6 tablespoons whipped cream. Chill slightly. Using pastry bag fitted with a large tube, add mousse to the mold, keeping it away from the sides. Chill until set.

Pour chilled but still liquid aspic to cover mousse and chill until firm. When ready to serve, quickly dip mold in hot water three times. Wipe base dry and invert on large glass or silver platter coated with thin layer of aspic. Garnish with water lilies.

For each water lily, take a hard boiled egg and peel while warm. Remove yolk. With a knife, form petals, trimming thickness from inside with fingernail scissors. Put two together for full blossoms. Fill center with sieved egg yolk. Level bottom to stand straight.

Mrs. Spires Whitaker
and Mrs. William Mills

One of the simplest and best salmon loaves in town is Miss Gertrude Oehmig's. She makes this by adding some crackers, eggs, onion, butter and a little cream of celery soup to the canned salmon. This is easy and good.

MISS GERTRUDE'S SALMON LOAF

1 can salmon (303 size)
1 cup cracker crumbs
½ can cream of celery soup
  (undiluted from can)

2 eggs
1 tablespoon grated onion
1 tablespoon butter

Mince the salmon with a fork and add eggs and other ingredients. Make in a loaf and put in a greased pan to bake. They use a pyrex loaf pan. Bake for 30 minutes at 350 degrees. The rest of the can of celery soup can be diluted slightly to make a sauce.

Miss Gertrude Oehmig

Billy McGinness has a tuna casserole using bean sprouts and chow mein noodles that really does taste almost like chicken if you use the tuna packed in water.

TUNA OR CHICKEN CASSEROLE

2 cans chunk style tuna
  or 2 cups chicken
2 cans mushroom soup
  (undiluted)
2 tablespoons chopped
  green pepper

½ cup minced onions
1 cup water or chicken stock
½ pound cashew nuts
1 can drained bean sprouts
1 can chow mein noodles
2 cups chopped celery

Mix chicken, celery, onions, green pepper, mushroom soup, chicken stock, ½ of the noodles and the cashew nuts. Place in buttered casserole dish and put remaining noodles on top. Bake at 375 degrees until light brown.

Mrs. Joe McGinness

Spaghetti made with clams is one of Bill Brock's specialties.

CLAM SPAGHETTI

3 or 4 tablespoons olive oil
2 cloves garlic
2 onions
2 large cans whole tomatoes
1 cup red wine

2 cans minced clams
1 teaspoon salt
Pepper to taste
¼ teaspoon sugar
¼ teaspoon oregano

Heat oil in a large heavy skillet. Crush garlic, slice onions, and put in the skillet. Saute until the onions are transparent. Add tomatoes with juice. Bring to a rapid boil briefly. Then reduce heat and add wine. Simmer 1 hour more. Add clams. Add salt and freshly ground pepper, sugar and oregano. Continue to simmer while the spaghetti cooks.

Use 1 large package long Italian spaghetti. Boil in large kettle of salted water only until tender. Drain, put in colander, and rinse with hot water. Drain. Put spaghetti in large bowl. Pour the clam sauce over it, sprinkle with Parmesan cheese and enjoy yourself.

Bill Brock

CHAPTER VI

Side Dishes

Sewanee is a unique place on the Cumberland plateau about half way between Nashville and Chattanooga. This is the domain of the University of the South. As you drive down the peaceful tree-shaded streets, look over at the students walking to and from class in the handsome Gothic stone buildings, or waiting outside All Saints' Chapel, you know that this is not like any other place in the world.

Actually started at a meeting of the Southern bishops of the Episcopal Church on Lookout Mountain in 1857, it was founded to train the youth of the South. Academically it was patterned after the colleges at Oxford in England, and consists of an undergraduate college, a seminary, and a military academy.

There has been a spirit about Sewanee through the years. Once a boy gets the love of Sewanee in his bones, it never leaves him. It is a sweet spot away from the world where values are true and certain. For the rest of his life he will come back at every opportunity, and when he can't, he will talk about it!

It is still secluded from the world, and although students first could get there only by train, the new highway that has been cut through the mountains makes the drive to Chattanooga in about an hour. However, it is still trouble to go to town. Nearby Monteagle was for many years one of the famous resorts in our area, attracting families who came for the entire summer from the lowlands of Alabama, Mississippi, Louisiana and South Carolina to escape the heat and malaria. When the Inn burned a few years ago, styles had already changed and people were going to the sea in the summer.

The spirit of Sewanee has remained comparatively unchanged in the hectic modern world. The same old families who have either taught or been connected with Sewanee for generations are still represented, as well as the new families who have been attracted there. There is the small town closeness, but to an average Chattanoogan, the social pace is unbelievable.

In the old days the famous hostesses set aside one day of the week to be "at home." One day between the hours of 4 and 6 everyone would gather at the Myerses, for instance. On another day it would be somewhere else. They still have all sorts of clubs — literary clubs, bridge clubs and so on. They still entertain at home.

It is an academic atmosphere where things intellectual and spiritual are stressed, and conversation is fascinating. You get the feeling that how much money a man has in the bank may be interesting in Sewanee, but it is not the full measure of the man ... a man is what his mind and soul is. And Sewaneeans for generations have delighted in entertaining each other and enjoying each other with some of the most outstanding southern specialties.

Sewanee is the Elliots, the Kirby-Smiths, the Brattons and Gasses, the Myers, the McCradys, the Woods, the Colmores, the Guerrys and on and on. It is long summer days on the front porches of the big old houses. It is dances and fraternity houses for the students on big weekends. It is hiking and exploring caves. It is long conversation after a dinner by candlelight.

One of Chattanooga's most beloved hostesses, we lent to Sewanee for many years. Mrs. Alexander Guerry first entertained as a faculty wife at Baylor School, then at the University of Chattanooga when Dr. Guerry was president there, and when he was named vice-chancellor at Sewanee, she took her famous hospitality there.

Charlotte Patten Guerry could entertain over a hundred at dinner without being ruffled. She had enough English china in the Indian Tree pattern, silver, glasses and so on to operate a fabulous inn. She gave parties for the students, luncheons for her friends, teas and coffees for visiting dignitaries. Once she had a dinner for Lord Halifax when he visited there. Later she entertained the Archbishop of Canterbury.

Mrs. Guerry always had the sort of conscience that promptly planned a gracious gathering of people whom a house guest might enjoy. She chose her list from her old friends, the friends of her children, nieces and nephews, friends in her church, newcomers. After Dr. Guerry's death, she moved back to Lookout Mountain. For years she entertained every club or group that she was interested in with the same warmth and graciousness that made her legendary.

One of her favorite dishes has been copied by people both in Sewanee and in Chattanooga . . . her baked apricots. She had many buffet dinners such as ham or turkey, maybe a corn pudding, baked apricots, a pretty green vegetable, a salad, plenty of hot rolls passed during the meal, hot coffee, and sometimes an angel food cake with strawberries and whipped cream. The menus would always vary, but guests were disappointed if they didn't have the apricots.

The heart of Sewanee is All Saints Chapel on the campus of the University of the South. Built of mountain stone, the bell tower is an impressive one.

MRS. GUERRY'S BAKED APRICOTS

Butter the bottom of a baking dish. You will need two large cans of apricot halves. Drain the fruit, reserving the liquid for later if necessary. Place the apricot halves in a baking dish and dot each half with butter. Sprinkle with brown sugar and a little cinnamon. Top this with a layer of crumbled Ritz crackers.

Repeat this whole process again so that you have two layers of apricots. Top the whole casserole with plenty of Ritz crumbs and butter. You probably won't need to add any juice, but add a small amount if you need to. The casserole should be moist and delicious but not runny. Bake for half hour or 45 minutes in a 375 oven.

The late Mrs. Alexander Guerry

Creamed mushrooms was one of the specialties of Mrs. C. R. Thomas. She served this as a side dish for either a luncheon or dinner.

CREAMED MUSHROOMS

1 stick butter	4 slices bread, toasted
3 tablespoons flour	and buttered
1 pint half and half	1 large package mushrooms
½ teaspoon salt	Salt and pepper to taste
½ cup whipping cream	

Melt the butter and stir in the flour and salt. Gradually add the half and half to make a cream sauce. Toast and butter the bread and cut in small pieces. Wash the mushrooms, break up and boil in a small amount of water until tender. Cook down low until the water has boiled down. Add the mushrooms and the sauce and taste to season with salt and pepper.

In a baking dish put a layer of toast, then a layer of mushroom sauce; repeat so that there are two layers. Add the whipping cream over the top.

Toast 2 slices bread and cut in triangles. Arrange around the sides of the casserole and sprinkle with paprika in the middle. Bake 30 minutes in a 350 oven or until bubbling good.

The late Mrs. Charles Robert Thomas

Another favorite way to fix fresh mushrooms is in a casserole with cream and bread cubes. The first time I had this was at a luncheon with a combination molded cranberry salad and turkey mousse. It is especially good during the holidays.

LUCILLE'S MUSHROOM CASSEROLE

Wash mushrooms and cut off stems. Cut cubes of bread with scissors. Use approximately the following proportions.

1 cup thick cream
1 quart mushrooms,
  washed and sliced
1 tablespoon grated onion
1 cup chopped parsley
Salt and pepper

3 cups bread cubes
1 tablespoon Worcestershire
Dash Tabasco
½ teaspoon oregano
½ stick melted butter

Brush baking dish with butter. Mix all ingredients together. Put in baking dish. Then pour enough cream over the whole thing to moisten. Cover with top and bake at 300 degrees for an hour. Take off top, sprinkle with paprika and let brown.

Mrs. Lucille Hickman

A baked casserole of rice or of corn, such as corn pudding, is traditional for a company meal. It quietly bakes in the oven while you are busy about something else, and when served with something like broiled or barbecued chicken, a green vegetable, a tomato salad, and rolls, it adds a different texture that you need. Corn pudding has many varieties, but this is a good easy one. The rice and almonds baked in consomme is a favorite of Floweree Whitaker, who doubles the recipe and brings a long casserole to Wednesday night church suppers.

ALMOND RICE BAKED IN CONSOMME

1 cup unwashed rice
1 small package almonds,
  blanched

¾ stick butter
2 cans beef consomme
2 very scant cans water

Brown rice and almonds in the butter in a skillet. Place in ungreased casserole. Cover with consomme and water. Bake covered tightly with foil for ½ hour. Stir. Bake uncovered for 45 minutes in a 350 oven.

Mrs. Spires Whitaker

This is Mrs. John O. Fowlers' recipe given me by her daughter, Mary Gaither.

MRS. FOWLER'S CORN PUDDING

2 cups grated corn	4 egg yolks beaten with
1 tablespoon flour	3 cups milk
¼ cup sugar	4 egg whites beaten

Mix together the corn, flour, sugar and the egg-milk mixture. Add salt and white pepper. Fold into egg whites beaten, but not too stiff. Bake for 10 minutes at 400 degrees to get it hot, turn down to 350 for about 15 minutes, then turn down again to 300 and bake until done, about ½ hour or until a knife inserted comes out clean.

This takes about 1 hour, and the secret is to stir about twice as it cooks to keep the egg whites from rising to the top. Mary uses frozen cream-style corn in the winter when you can't get fresh corn, but remember that it is already sweetened.

Mrs. John Gaither

There are several ways to get up Lookout Mountain. Not until recently did I know why two main roads were built. A small summer colony had come to the mountain before 1840 and later Colonel James Whiteside, who owned most of the Tennessee part of the mountain and who built a large hotel, built a turnpike.

This was the only road for 36 years until Chattanooga suffered the yellow fever epidemic and people fled to the mountain as the only escape. (The yellow fever mosquito could not live in high altitude.) Such an exhorbitant toll tax was charged that a group of citizens banded together to build a new turnpike. The next year opened up the Johnson turnpike, built on the other side of the mountain. This was later incorporated into the Ochs Highway.

The steepest incline in the world was built in 1896 from the point of Lookout Mountain, and the incline cable cars carry tourists, school children commuting to town, as well as mountain residents during ice and snow.

As you drive up the Ochs Highway and then out the extension toward Rock City, you are also heading to the Lookout Mountain Golf Club. The golf course is a beautiful site on a point of land that looks out on majestic scenery. The new modern clubhouse with walls of glass to enjoy the view, is a favorite meeting place for parties of members, as well as groups such as clubs, wedding rehearsal dinners, luncheons, dinners, and dances.

Mrs. Medora Berry in the kitchen has put her own special stamp on the delicious food. She makes tiny yeast rolls about 1 inch in diameter, seasons meats and vegetables beautifully, and gives the distinctive touch that you usually find only in a home. After one recent luncheon someone said, "I feel just as if I've been to a party at someone's house. Even the sherried Bing cherry salad is tender with not too much gelatin in it."

Medora is famous for her hors d'oeuvres. She makes pastry the usual way except flavors it with onion juice. Then she rolls into small balls and shapes into a shell with her finger. Baked, these are filled with crabmeat or lobster.

SAUSAGE RING

Her sausage ring she makes by making a simple biscuit dough and rolling it out. She spreads with sausage which must get to room temperature, rolls it up like a jelly roll, and puts it in the refrigerator. When chilled, it is sliced ½-inch thick and the little rings are baked at 450 degrees until done.

A favorite is her rich corn pudding, which she gave me a more exact recipe for.

MEDORA'S CORN PUDDING

6 ears corn,
* grated and scraped*
2 cups milk
4 eggs, separated
2 tablespoons flour

2 tablespoons sugar
Salt and pepper to taste
1 stick melted butter
Small amount chopped
* pimento for garnish*

Heat the milk. Beat the egg whites until stiff. In a bowl put the flour and sugar. Beat in the egg yolks. Add some salt and pepper. Pour in slowly the milk and butter, and finally the corn. At the last fold in the egg whites, pour into a casserole that has been greased with part of the butter. Just before running the casserole in the oven, top with the chopped pimento. Bake at 350 degrees for 45 minutes.

Mrs. Medora Berry

The only early mansion in the Chattanooga area is the Vann House near Dalton, Georgia. The Federal-type house was built in 1804 by James Vann, chief of the Cherokee Nation. His father had been a successful Scotch trader who had married the daughter of the Cherokee chief, and since the title passed through the mother, according to Cherokee custom, James Vann became chief.

He had numerous trading posts, 800 acres of cultivated land, 42 cabins, 6 barns, mills, blacksmith shop, orchards, and over a hundred Negro slaves. His greatest contribution to his tribe was his trip to North Carolina to get the Moravians to establish a mission school at Spring Place, which they did.

The missionaries kept detailed diaries in German of their work and of the Vanns, which can be read today in Winston Salem. Some Moravian missionary craftsmen were involved in the building of the fine house. When James Vann was murdered, his son Joseph Vann acquired the house and much of the property and was even a better businessman than his father. He was known as "Rich Joe Vann."

Ambitious white men had for years been hunting an excuse to seize the Vann properties, and in 1834 the Vanns were turned out of their house. They went to their Tennessee farm near Cleveland for a year or two, but the Treaty of Echota made it clear that they would have to go to Oklahoma. The family traveled to Weber Falls, Oklahoma, before the Trail of Tears when the general exodus of the Cherokees took place, and there they built a duplicate of the Georgia Vann house. It was destroyed by Federal forces during the Civil War.

The house at Spring Place deteriorated for 150 years until Mrs. B. J. Bandy of Dalton led a restoration and money-raising program by the Whitfield-Murray County Historical Society. She hunted original furniture and appropriate antiques, interested Scalamandre, Inc. in giving the material for elaborate period draperies, and supervised the restoration. When it was dedicated in 1958, 8,000 guests were on hand including Georgia leaders, Cherokee representatives and 42 descendants of the Vann family including Will Rogers Jr., a great-great-grandson of James Vann. Mrs. Bandy was made an Ambassador of the Cherokee Nation.

The house is now owned and maintained by the state of Georgia, and represents the high degree of civilization of the Cherokees in this area. It can take its place among the finest restorations in America for beauty, elegance, authenticity, and interest, and is the only mansion in America built by an American Indian.

The grain that the American Indian introduced to the world is corn, now a beloved staple in every American household. It is very probable that with both Indian and Scotch backgrounds, the Vanns took the corn and added eggs, milk and butter from their plantation and had corn pudding.

Their dining room is restored to its former elegance, with a walnut banquet table copied from one owned by John Ross, white china bordered in green to match fragments found near the house, fine woodwork painted in the original greens and golds and Federal draperies by Scalamandre.

The Vann House near Dalton dates from 1804 and is the only mansion type house in America built by an American Indian. With its Federal style, its elaborately carved cantilevered stairway, and the latest in elegant furnishings, it was the showplace of the Cherokee nation.

The following pudding is a recipe given me by the late Dicksie Bradley Bandy (Mrs. B.J.)

INDIAN CORN PUDDING

2 cups corn, fresh or canned	1 teaspoon salt
2 eggs	2 tablespoons melted butter
1 cup moist bread crumbs	Pepper to taste
1 cup sweet milk	

Beat the eggs and the milk, adding the bread crumbs. Add the corn and butter, salt and pepper. Pour into a buttered baking dish and bake in a 350 oven for about 30 minutes.

The late Dicksie Bradley Bandy (Mrs. B.J.)
Official Ambassador of the Cherokee Nation
Dalton, Georgia

Mary and Cliff Duke have always been noted for their delicious food. When Cliff retired, he found that he had more time to experiment in the kitchen and he now makes everything from beaten biscuits, and crullers, to hearty casseroles that he brings to church on Wednesday nights. His baked beans are a favorite.

DUKE BAKED BEANS

1 jar (18 ounce) Brick oven baked beans	½ cup tomato catsup
1 medium sized onion, thinly sliced	3 tablespoons brown sugar
	½ teaspoon dry mustard
	Dash red pepper

Mix all ingredients except bacon and onion. Place in casserole or baking dish. The mixture should be soupy. Cover mixture with onion slices, then with bacon. Bake at 300 uncovered for 1 hour. Cut off heat and leave another hour.

Clifford Duke

Another casserole of the Duke's is a rice casserole.

MARY'S RICE CASSEROLE

½ stick butter	1 package dried onion soup mix
1 cup rice	3 ounce can mushrooms
2 scant cups water	

Brown the rice in melted butter over low heat until golden brown. Add water and soup mix. Next add the mushrooms to the casserole. Mary says that she prefers ½ pound fresh mushrooms sauteed in butter when she can get them. Stir in the rice. Cover and bake at 325 for 50 to 60 minutes.

Mrs. Clifford Duke

Our most popular casserole, especially in the summer, is baked beans. This is one we got from the Carter Padens, who always take some along when they pack up their camper and head for a fishing weekend. It is different because it has onion and bell pepper in it.

THE PADEN'S BAKED BEANS

Drain a large can of pork and beans. Add 4 tablespoons catsup, 2 tablespoons molasses, 2 tablespoons brown sugar, 2 tablespoons bacon grease, 2 tablespoons chopped onion, and 2 tablespoons green pepper. I like to saute the onion and pepper in the grease and then add to the beans. Bake at 375 degrees for 30 minutes.

Mrs. Carter Paden Jr.

A side dish of warm spicy pears is a specialty of Mrs. Gordon Smith. It is especially good served along with baked ham.

GINGER PEAR CRUMBLE

1½ cups ginger snap crumbs　　*1 can pears (2½ size) drained*
½ cup brown sugar　　*1 tablespoon lemon juice*
¼ teaspoon salt
¼ cup butter or
　margarine, melted

Put the ginger snaps through the food chopper to make crumbs, or roll them out. Mix together the crumbs, the brown sugar, salt and butter. Place half of this mixture in the bottom of a buttered baking dish. Place pears, cut side up, on crumbs. Sprinkle with lemon juice and remaining crumbs. Bake in moderate oven at 350 for 35 to 30 minutes. Serve warm. This can be either a side dish with ham or a leg of lamb, or a dessert topped with ice cream or whipped cream.

Mrs. Gordon Smith

Popular with almost any kind of dinner or as a hot accompaniment to a cold salad luncheon is curried fruit served hot. This is the recipe of Mrs. John Kain Jr., who served it years ago at a luncheon featuring chicken.

CURRIED FRUIT

¾ stick butter

2 teaspoons curry powder

1 cup light brown sugar

1 can peach halves, drained

1 can pear halves, drained

1 can pineapple chunks, drained

1 small can cherries, drained

Drain all fruit and arrange in the bottom of a casserole. Mix the butter, sugar, and curry powder and add to the fruit. Bake in a moderate oven at 350 for half hour. Serve either in a casserole or from a compote.

Mrs. John Kain Jr.

Mrs. G. M. Smartt began a tradition in her family of always serving an apricot souffle with the meat dish. It was cooked over hot water on top of the stove and finished in the oven, but never taken off the hot water until serving time. In this way it never fell. Her children and grandchildren still serve apricot souffle on the sideboard at a buffet dinner, or passed and served with a seated roast beef dinner. This recipe comes to me by way of her granddaughter, Betty Meade Smartt Johnson.

The family recipe is a simple one. For each person, allow 1 egg white, 1 tablespoon sugar, and 1 heaping tablespoon apricot pulp. The following amount would serve 4.

APRICOT SOUFFLE

½ cup apricot pulp

4 egg whites

4 tablespoons sugar

Soak 1 package dried apricots in cold water several hours. Then cook and run through a sieve or strainer. Beat the egg whites stiff, then add sugar and beat again. Fold in apricots and put in buttered baking dish. Cook in pan of hot water on top of stove for ½ hour. Put in oven to brown, leaving in pan of hot water. Leave in pan of water until ready to serve, or it will fall.

Mrs. H. Clay Evans Johnson

In the late summer and early fall, everyone is hungry for baked apples. This is the way Mrs. George Fillauer bakes them.

BAKED APPLES

8 Rome Beauty apples
2 tablespoons cinnamon darts
½ cup water

½ cup sugar, (more if
   apples aren't sweet)
2 tablespoons butter

Core the apples, being sure to get all the core and any part that might be stringy and hard to eat. Peel the outside of the apple, leaving a small peel around the middle to hold the shape and keep it from cooking to pieces. Divide the butter and put a dab in the center of each apple. Arrange them in a baking dish and sprinkle with the cinnamon darts and the sugar, getting a little sugar into each hole as well as on top. Pour water around them. Bake in a 450 oven for 20 minutes; then turn down the heat to 350 and finish baking 20 minutes.

Mrs. George Fillauer

What finer breakfast than sausage and eggs, fried apples and lots of black coffee!

FRIED APPLES

Apples (2 medium apples equal
   one serving) cored,
   quartered and sliced,
   but not peeled

2 tablespoons bacon fat
   or butter
½ cup sugar

Melt fat in a skillet over low heat. Add the apples. Cover the skillet and cook gently for 5 minutes or until the apples are very juicy. Turn the apples over and sprinkle with ¼ cup sugar. Cover and lower heat. Cook about 2 minutes more, or until sugar is absorbed, and apples are a delicate brown on the bottom. Sprinkle ¼ cup sugar on apples and remove from pan.

Macaroni and cheese is the sturdy favorite for family dinners that we all remember, yet it is hard to find a recipe. People just presume that everyone knows how. Ann Allen (Mrs. Arthur) has an easy way and sometimes brings a casserole to Wednesday night suppers at church.

MACARONI AND CHEESE

Cook macaroni in salted boiling water until tender. Ann usually cooks it about noon, rinses it in fresh cold water and lets it stand in the cold water until later in the afternoon. Then she drains it in a colander. Grease a casserole with bacon drippings. Cover the bottom with half the macaroni. Sprinkle with a generous layer of mild cheddar cheese, then sprinkle with flour. Repeat with another layer of macaroni, season with salt, and top with cheese. Fill to the top of the casserole with milk. Put in 350-degree oven and let cook about an hour. If it gets too dry, add more milk and cook longer.

Mrs. Arthur Allen

One summer day on Signal Mountain our artist friend Gordon Wetmore took the girls and me to the most unusual place for lunch ... Brown Brothers' Grocery Store on Taft Highway. He explained that he first got to know Mrs. Brown when he stopped in to buy pork chop sandwiches. She cooks on a stove behind the butcher counter, and there are about eight places at a bar down the side. For any more people than this, they turn peck baskets upside down and sit them at another counter. Ellen and Susan sat on baskets. We had a dinner of barbecue, fresh summer vegetables and cornbread. It was delicious.

Mrs. W.L. Brown was born on Signal in the days when mining was going strong. While you wait for your order, you can do your grocery shopping, pick up some tennis shoes for the children, or look at riding boots. This is an old fashioned country store and a charming place. Mrs. Brown gave me an unusual recipe for Macaroni Casserole using cream of mushroom soup. She serves it as a side dish with a meal such as pork chops, green beans, coleslaw, cornbread and apple cobbler. It is an extra and delicious.

MACARONI CASSEROLE

1 box 7-ounce elbow macaroni   2 medium onions, diced
1 teaspoon salt   4 cups boiling water
1 can cream of mushroom soup

Add the salt, macaroni and onions to the boiling water and cook 10 minutes. Don't drain. Add the soup and 1 can of water and bring to a boil again. Pour into a casserole. Cover generously with grated cheese and add paprika over the top. Preheat the oven to 375. Cover the macaroni with foil and put in the oven for 5 minutes, until the cheese is bubbly.

Mrs. W.L. Brown
Brown Brothers' Grocery

As much as people like macaroni and cheese, sometimes it is nice to do about the same thing with noodles. Mrs. Eris Satterwhite told me about her noodle and cheese casserole the day we did a feature on the catered dinners at New Emmanuel Baptist Church.

NOODLES AND CHEESE CASSEROLE

Boil the noodles in a large amount of salted boiling water. Boil about 7 minutes or until tender. Drain. Rinse in a colander. Put half the noodles in a buttered long flat casserole. Spread with dabs of butter and grated cheese. Add the rest of the noodles and sprinkle with cheese and dabs of butter.

For a large casserole beat 3 eggs together and add 2 cups milk. Season with about ½ teaspoon salt and a little pepper. Pour over the casserole and top with more cheddar cheese, grated. Run in an oven to cook at 350 degrees for 20 to 25 minutes.

Mrs. Eris Satterwhite

When we were young marrieds and used to go to more trouble to make fancy recipes, I used to make potato croquettes. These were a delicious way to add a crisp touch to a meal, and you could make them hours ahead. We used to have them to go with chicken and mushrooms in wine. First you creamed potatoes and added eggs and butter plus seasoning.

This is the standard Duchess potato mixture that the French make up ahead and refrigerate. When reheated, it will always be light and good. Make out small balls and put a cooked shrimp in the middle. Roll in flour, then in egg wash, then in cracker meal. The little croquettes are fried until light and crisp.

POTATO CROQUETTES

First make duchess potatoes. Peel two pounds of potatoes, cut, and boil in salted water until tender. Drain and dry by shaking the pan over the eye on the stove until all the moisture disappears. Put the potatoes in a mixer and beat until smooth. Add 2 or 3 tablespoons of butter, 1 teaspoon of salt, pepper and onion juice to taste, 2 eggs and 2 egg yolks. Beat until light and fluffy.

Chill the potato mixture and shape into croquettes. You can bury 1 shrimp in each if you want to be fancy, or if you have any shrimp leftover. Or you can make plain croquettes. Coat the croquettes with flour, then dip in a mixture of egg beaten with a little milk. Finally roll in cracker meal. Chill. At the last minute fry in deep fat at 375 until golden brown.

CHAPTER VII

Vegetables and Pickles

In May, 1906, one of the most unusual housewarmings of the Chattanooga area took place. Mr. and Mrs. Z. C. Patten had completed a handsome country home on the old Crutchfield place in Chattanooga Valley. Ashland Farm, a brick colonial home with Corinthian columns on the porch, a winding stairway inside, and two brick cottages on the back, reminds you of a gracious Virginia plantation. Three miles from the end of the St. Elmo street-car line, the round trip from town would take four hours in a buggy, and you had to ford the creek at Blowing Springs.

In solving the problem of how to get 300 guests out and back, the Pattens thought of the T.A.G. Railroad which ran a local passenger train from Chattanooga to Gadsden every day. They chartered the train for the night of the party, the guests were invited, and it was a long remembered event. Their son Cartter thinks they served chicken salad, ham in beaten biscuits (Miss Sarah called them cracker biscuit), some cake and an ice, punch and champagne.

Christmas at Ashland was a Key family gathering, with Miss Sarah's mother, Mrs. D. M. Key, her brother, Commodore Albert Key, and her sisters, Miss Margaret and Miss Kate and their respective families and children. The traditional menu was Olives and Celery Hearts, Roast Turkey with Oyster Stuffing, Rice and Giblet Gravy, Sweet Potatoes with Marshmallows, Asparagus, Cranberry Sauce, Hot Rolls, Ambrosia and Fruit Cake.

Ashland has been the scene of many lovely parties ... informal tennis gatherings, formal teas in the winter, morning coffees in the spring, young people's parties while Cartter and Elizabeth Patten's children were growing up, luncheons for the Colonial Dames, and dinners for the Preservation of Tennessee Antiquities groups for which Elizabeth works.

Hundreds and hundreds of Chattanoogans love Ashland Farm as one of the still beautiful homes here, as the scene of daffodils in the spring, as a symbol of the gracious living that took place in less hurried years.

Elizabeth Patten (Mrs. Cartter) has given me this recipe for the Christmas sweet potatoes at Ashland.

ASHLAND FARM SWEET POTATOES

Peel, boil, and rice 4 medium sweet potatoes. Add 1 tablespoon butter, ½ cup sugar, dash of all spice, nutmeg and cinnamon, pinch of salt, some milk and some sherry (about ½ cup of liquid). Beat until creamy and light and add ¼ cup raisins and ¼ cup broken nuts. Put into casserole and top with marshmallows. At serving time, put in moderate oven to let marshmallows puff and brown.

Mrs. Cartter Patten

When the Pilot Club had a covered dish supper using recipes from the Pilot Club cookbooks, the tables were laden down with delicious food. Elizabeth Myers brought a very different broccoli casserole that tasted like a good chicken dressing with broccoli.

BROCCOLI CASSEROLE

2 packages frozen chopped
  broccoli
1 package 8-ounce
  Pepperidge stuffing

1 can cream of mushroom soup
¼ pound butter or margarine

Cook broccoli in 1 cup water until tender. Add butter to cooked broccoli. Add remaining ingredients. Pour in 10 by 12 inch casserole. Bake for 40 minutes at 350 degrees. Top should be crusty.

Miss Elizabeth Myers

Every year as spring comes and develops and goes, and then summer begins, always I am wondering when the first homegrown tomatoes will arrive. Tomatoes are available all year long now, but the vine-ripened ones are so delicious that they are almost a different kind of vegetable from their storage sisters. In Chattanooga, it is some time in June.

A vine-ripened tomato is a little sweeter, and at the same time more acid. With one bite of freshly sliced tomato, generously sprinkled with salt, a real tomato lover can experience a zing or a zip or a taste sensation that goes clear to the back of the throat. This delightful experience of summer tomatoes seems to grow on you as the years go by.

I remember one dear person in his eighties who loved tomatoes. He would take a generous helping of fresh sliced tomatoes as they were passed the first time, and toward the end of the meal, he would oblige the cook by finishing as many as were left. He would rather have them than ice cream. I would almost rather myself.

I have known people who loved to eat them in the garden where they grew. This is the same principle as that believed by the French chef at a restaurant in France who had a hen trained to lay an egg into his hand everytime he wanted to make an omelet. The fresher the better! In tomatoes the eating is best as soon as possible after the tomato takes its last breath.

Tomatoes are like potatoes. You can have them every day and still never tire of them. Fresh, sliced and salted is the simplest. Long ago we decided to have a large brunch, and having too many babies and too little confidence, we called the late Fannie Warren, a wonderful Negro cateress here, to see if she would help us. I wish I had watched her more closely.

She sliced tomatoes with a heavy hand. She even featured them. She had scrambled dozens of eggs and packed them gently into a large buttered mixing bowl. When unmolded on a big platter, they were a beautiful round golden heap which she then surrounded with fresh sliced tomatoes. There was another bowl of hominy, another of poached apple rings and sliced ham. We had biscuits and small cinnamon rolls, some sort of juice and coffee. Everyone asked how she did the tomatoes. She said that she had just grated a little onion and used salt and chopped parsley. I have done this since, and it works.

Tomatoes can be stuffed with a hundred different stuffings, whatever you have left over in the refrigerator. Two of the easiest are rice stuffed tomatoes and corn stuffed tomatoes. A friend from California once sent us a tomato and zucchini casserole that we have made so much it is a real favorite. These are all good ways to have tomatoes. Don't forget that a cold platter of sliced tomatoes, green peppers, and onions topped with French dressing is hard to beat, too.

BAKED TOMATOES STUFFED WITH RICE

6 firm tomatoes
2 onions, chopped
3 ribs celery, chopped

¼ cup cheddar cheese diced
1 cup cooked rice

Hollow out tomatoes and let drain. Chop onion, celery, and pepper fine and fry in butter until tender. Add tomato pulp and simmer. Add rice and cook until amost dry. Add cheese. Stuff into tomatoes and bake in muffin pans for 20 minutes.

CORN STUFFED TOMATOES

2 cups cooked corn
½ teaspoon salt and a
   dash of pepper
2 tablespoons butter

1 teaspoon grated onion
6 tomato cases
Buttered bread crumbs

Cut large hollows in the unpeeled tomatoes. It makes sturdier cases to use the stem end as the bottom. Invert them to drain for a few minutes. Salt the inside, mix the corn, butter, onion, and salt and pepper, and fill the cases. Top with the bread crumbs. Place in greased muffin pans and bake 15 or 20 minutes in a 350 oven.

ZUCCHINI CASSEROLE

2 zucchini
2 tomatoes
4 spring onions

Salt, pepper, butter to taste
Cheddar cheese, grated

Boil the zucchini in water until barely tender. Butter a small casserole. Slice a zucchini in the dish, then slice a tomato, salt and pepper. Sprinkle with chopped onion, grated cheese, dots of butter. Do this again to make two layers. Bake for 30 to 40 minutes in a 350 oven.

Sometimes I go out in the herb garden and pick a little fresh basil to sprinkle on the tomatoes. I also use about ½ cup chopped parsley in this casserole to make it pretty sometimes.

There are many ways to fix stuffed squash. Edward Little, who cooks for the John L. Hutchesons, gave this recipe for his specialty to Judy Hutcheson soon after she married Ted. Teddy kept saying, "Judy, your squash is good, but it doesn't taste quite like Edward's. Ask him what he does." This is what he told her.

EDWARD'S STUFFED SQUASH

This recipe makes 6 stuffed squash, but begin with 8 yellow crookneck squash in order to have enough stuffing. Cut off the ends of the squash and wash well. Place in a large pot, covering the squash with water. Let them boil until medium soft. Drain.

Cut off the top of each squash and carefully spoon the inside pulp into another saucepan. Add to the pulp 2 slices of soft bread which have been crumbled very fine. Also add 2 tablespoons butter, ¼ of a large onion, grated, salt and pepper to taste, and 1 egg. Stir and cook until stiff enough to put back into the squash shells. Carefully stuff 6 shells.

On a piece of waxed paper pour ¾ to 1 cup of corn flake crumbs. Melt ½ stick butter and pour over the crumbs, mixing thoroughly. Sprinkle over the stuffed squash and bake at 300 degrees until the crumbs are brown.

Edward Little

Cleveland is about 30 miles north of Chattanooga and is famous for its stove factories, textile mills, Lee College and most recently, Cleveland State Community College. Several years ago Bowaters put in a huge paper plant a few miles away in Charleston, and it is now the largest industry in the Cleveland area. Former Chattanoogan Margaret Wheland Cate (Mrs. James, Jr.), keeps us posted on Cleveland news as well as new recipes that she has tried from her own vegetable garden. We highly recommend her easy way of fixing yellow summer squash.

MARGARET CATE'S SQUASH

Slice small yellow summer squash fairly thin. Put a layer in a buttered casserole. Salt and pepper it. Chop half an onion and sprinkle over the squash. Repeat another layer of squash, onion, and seasoning. Dot with butter. Cover with foil and bake at 400 degrees for 30 to 45 minutes. Uncover and pour in enough milk or cream to see, but not all the way to the top. Grate cheddar cheese on top and put back into a 400 degree oven uncovered for 10 to 15 minutes.

Mrs. James Cate, Jr.
Cleveland, Tennessee

My sister Betsy is the most organized cook in the family. She plans ahead, her kitchen is always neat, and even on the day of a luncheon or dinner, the kitchen is calm and everything has been done in advance ... the croissants already baked, frozen, and ready to heat, maybe a fresh fruit salad with the fruit already cut and the dressing made, and in the oven a hot hearty casserole timed to come out at the exact right time. Betsy's food is always delicious, quite imaginative, but she never gives the impression of spending any more time in the kitchen than necessary. This is quite a trick. People especially like her green bean casserole.

BETSY'S GREEN BEAN CASSEROLE

1 can sliced mushrooms
1 medium onion, sliced
½ cup butter
¼ cup flour
2 cups milk
1 cup light cream
1 teaspoon salt
½ teaspoon pepper
1 teaspoon Accent
¾ pound sharp cheddar
 cheese, grated

⅛ teaspoon hot pepper sauce
2 teaspoons soy sauce
3 packages frozen French
 green beans
1 can (5-ounce) water chestnuts,
 drained and sliced
½ to ¾ cup sliced
 blanched almonds

Saute the mushrooms and onions in butter. Add the flour and cook until smooth. Transfer to double boiler. Add milk and cream. Stir over boiling water until thickened. Add the cheese, hot pepper sauce, soy sauce, salt, pepper, and Accent. Stir until cheese is melted. Cook green beans in salted water until tender. Drain. Mix with mushrooms, sauce, and water chestnuts. Pour into casserole and sprinkle with almonds. bake for 20 minutes at 375 degrees. If made ahead and casserole is cold, allow 40 minutes to heat thoroughly.

Mrs. Lee Anderson

Anne Caldwell McKenzie's great-grandfather, J. L. Caldwell, started a business in Chattanooga making stoves. The first ones used coal and wood, giving way to gas and electric models. Anne's grandfather, Hardwick Caldwell, gave her one of tne new glass topped Modern Maid ranges for her first kitchen so she could act as one of the home testers, which she was delighted to do. The position of the eyes is marked on the special glass top, and to clean the stove, you just wipe it off.

This is the new generation. They cook on glass topped stoves and when they make Hollandaise they use the blender. Anne has a delicious way of fixing an asparagus casserole with a sour cream sauce.

ASPARAGUS WITH SOUR CREAM

2 cans green asparagus or
 2 packages frozen asparagus
1 cup sour cream

¼ cup mayonnaise
2 tablespoons lemon juice
Buttered bread crumbs

Combine sour cream, mayonnaise, and lemon juice. Heat and pour over asparagus. Brown some bread crumbs with butter and spread over the top. Run under the broiler until bubbly. Almonds are also good on top.

Mrs. William McKenzie

Asparagus and broccoli are much dressier with Hollandaise sauce. If you make this once, any other recipe will seem complicated.

BLENDER HOLLANDAISE SAUCE

1 stick butter	½ teaspoon salt
3 egg yolks	Dash cayenne pepper
2 tablespoons lemon juice	or Tabasco

Melt butter to just bubbling. Don't brown. Place all other ingredients into blender. Cover; turn blender on and off once. Turn to high speed and quickly pour in hot butter in a steady stream. Turn off. Sauce will be emulsified with not a trace of curdling. This sauce should be served at room temperature or warm. You can reheat by letting it stand in warm water.

It is a classic truth that so often the hard times of our people have taught us more than the prosperous ones. There is much talk about how to plan economical meals, and we wonder how really poor people get along. Yet after the Civil War, the South was about as poor as you can get. Cash to buy things was rare.

The war was over in April, a good planting month as any farmer knows. All our people had left was the land and the ability to work. You remember that when Moses was called by God and was feeling very scared and hesitant to be a party to such an undertaking, God asked him, "What is in thy hand?" We are always supposed to look around and see what is on hand and ask a blessing on it. In the South it was land. Quick crops of greens were planted . . . mustard and turnip greens. Then corn was planted and some of it was taken to the mills on the rivers and streams to be turned into meal. Chickens were easy to raise because of our climate and they could live on scraps. This provided eggs and meat.

One other principle our people lived by was dried beans and peas. Dried field peas or shinny peas were most common, I think, although you have to go to the curb market to get them today. There is nothing more delicious than field peas cooked with a ham hock or streaked meat. Dried beans and ham hocks or streaked meat have made many a nourishing meal for poor families as well as not so poor families in the hundred years since.

DRIED BEANS OR PEAS

The night before, put dried beans into a large bowl, and cover with water to about 1 inch above the beans. The next day get out a heavy pot or pan. Put a cured ham hock in it and let cook for about an hour. Ham hocks are the lower part of the leg of a pig which have been cured and smoked just like the ham. It is very sweet, being so close to the bone. Now add the beans, a small whole onion, and a little salt. Cook this slowly for 2 or 3 hours. Taste to see if you need to add more salt and pepper. The beans should be very tender but not mushy.

In every New Orleans home they have red beans with rice about once every week or two. It is a simple Creole specialty that has been a beloved family standby through the years. Jessie Beckman got this when she lived in Louisiana many years ago.

NEW ORLEANS RED BEANS

1 pound dried red beans	½ green bell pepper, chopped
1 ham bone or 3 strips	½ clove garlic, minced
bacon, finely cut	3 stalks celery, finely chopped
1 small onion, chopped	Parsley to taste, finely cut
3 shallots, chopped,	Salt and pepper to taste
including some green tops	

Wash red beans in colander and soak overnight in cold water to cover. Add ham bone, chopped onion, and at least 2 more cups of water to the beans, and cook slowly, covered, until the beans are soft. Add remaining ingredients and cook slowly until thick and creamy. Watch the liquid. Add more water if needed, but do not let stick on bottom. Serve over cooked rice with dab of butter or garnish with creamy French dressing and chopped onion. This may be cooked in pressure cooker. This would be a typical New Orleans menu: Ham or pork sausage, red beans and rice, tossed green salad, hot buttered French bread.

Mrs. J. H. Beckman

To have a package of corn in the freezer, or homemade applesauce, is like money in the bank. This is the easy way Mrs. Harold Cooper always has both on hand.

141

HOW TO PREPARE CORN FOR FREEZING

Clean, cut off the cob, and scrape just as if you were going to fry corn. Put on the stove in a saucepan with a small amount of water. Heat just until it is hot through. Put in a pan of cold water to cool quickly, and package in cartons to freeze.

To serve, put in a pan, add butter, salt, and a little sugar. Put over low heat until thawed. Even in the middle of the winter this will taste like fresh corn.

HOW TO FREEZE APPLESAUCE

Core apples and quarter them, leaving on the peel. Cook until tender in a small amount of water. Drain off water, and run through a ricer or sieve while hot. Add sugar to taste while the apples are hot enough to melt the sugar. Freeze in cartons.

One night I had baked a potato for each person to go along with the roast beef dinner. I reached into the oven after about an hour, and with a pot holder picked up each one, giving it a squeeze to open up the top of the skin and let out the steam. One potato actually exploded, sending little spurts of hot airy baked potato on the floor and in the oven. One of the children said, "Don't let that be mine," the way 10-year-old children sometimes do before dinner.

"Don't worry," I said, "this is probably the most elegantly baked potato we have managed in 20 years ...... the heat, the time and the size of the potato were all right. I plan to eat every bit of it myself." And I did.

There is something very distinctive about a potato that has baked in an oven until just the right amount of moisture is baked out. It is just right to soak up the butter and the sour cream. The other potatoes must have been good, too. As Ellen was scooping out the last bit and eating some of the peeling, she said, "Do you know what I like best? I like the wrapper." Modern day children know that everything comes in its own individual wrapper.

There is another way to bake potatoes and that is wrapped in foil. These are good, too, but the texture is entirely different. These are steamed potatoes, with no way for the moisture to escape, so they are not as light and airy as proper baked potatoes. In our family Roy likes these best because they have soft tender skin, and he eats them two at a time. Take your choice.

142

SIMPLE BAKED POTATOES

Wash medium sized baking potatoes and oil the skin with a little salad oil or bacon drippings. You don't have to oil the skins, but it makes them more tender. Preheat the oven to 400 degrees. Allow about an hour for the potatoes to get done. You can tell when they are done by feeling with your finger. They should feel soft. Either slit the top skin with a knife for the steam to escape, or squeeze the potato until the top skin breaks. The inside should be light. Salt, pepper and butter. Or mix sour cream with chopped chive and serve as a dressing.

Corinne Silas (Mrs. J.D.) has a good recipe for escalloped potatoes which she serves in a big casserole along with steak at summer dinners on the terrace. They are topped with onions, cheese, and mushrooms, which make them not only pretty but good.

CORINNE'S ESCALLOPED POTATOES

Boil potatoes half done in their jackets. Peel and slice about ¼ inch thick. Put in layers in a baking dish. Sprinkle with salt, pepper, paprika, and dot with butter, mushrooms, onion rings, chopped green pepper, and grated sharp cheese. Build up each layer in this manner. Pour over the whole casserole 1½ cups coffee cream. Bake in a 300 degree oven for about 45 minutes to 1 hour.

Mrs. J.D. Silas

Middle Tennessee is famous for its gracious recipes and imaginative eating, and Chattanoogans who grew up in Nashville have brought us many ideas. Their recipes are usually simple, and use butter, eggs and cream for their richness. Nashville is famous for chess pie, beaten biscuits, country ham, spoon bread and light rolls, chicken croquetts, rich homemade ice cream. Their ladies are known for the flair with which they serve food. Corinne Spears (Mrs. W.D.) still has the Nashville touch, and this recipe for creamed spinach is one of hers.

CREAMED SPINACH

Bring 1 cup water to a boil in a saucepan and add 2 boxes frozen spinach and about 1½ teaspoons salt. Cook for 6 to 8 minutes. The spinach should then be drained, chilled, and chopped very fine, as fine as it is possible to get it.

Make a cream sauce of 2½ tablespoons butter, 2½ tablespoons flour, 2½ tablespoons chopped onion, and 1 cup cream. Cook the onion in the butter for a few minutes, then blend in the flour. Let this cook over hot water in a double boiler for 10 minutes, and add 1 cup of cream. Season with nutmeg, chopped parsley, Worcestershire sauce, Tabasco, lemon juice and sherry, paprika, thyme. Now mix the spinach and cream sauce thoroughly. Be sure and taste to see that the seasoning is right. Put in a casserole dish and sprinkle the top with cracker crumbs. Heat in a hot oven for 20 minutes.

Another idea is to buy frozen spinach souffle, let it get to room temperature and use it to stuff squash shells that have been parboiled and scooped out. When baked in the squash, the souffle rises in a very dramatic puff.

Mrs. W.D. Spears

Mamie Fowler (Mrs. Calvin) is another native Nashvillian who has brought us both taste and charm. We are always copying the nice things from Middle Tennessee, because they were sipping tea at Traveller's Rest and the Hermitage when Chattanooga was still Indian country. Mamie plans lunches and dinners that have a hospitable southern flair. One recent buffet supper for an out-of-town guest was country ham, squash souffle, creamed lima beans with cheese, a large pretty platter of fresh fruit with a special dressing, watermelon pickle and blackberry jelly, tiny hot homemade rolls, and for dessert, chess tarts. Sometimes when she is in Nashville, she buys a dozen or two chess tarts to keep in her freezer. This is her recipe for Creamed Lima Beans.

CREAMED LIMA BEANS

1 box frozen limas	*1 chopped pimento*
1 cup medium cream sauce	*Season to taste*
1 cup grated cheddar cheese	

Cook the limas according to directions, until tender. Melt the cheese in the cream sauce, add chopped pimento, the lima beans, and taste to correct the seasoning. This can be served in a silver vegetable dish or as a casserole.

Mrs. Calvin Fowler

Chattanooga was settled to Georgia Avenue when the Civil War came along, and like all growing towns, it kept pushing out, as young families moved out to the suburbs. My own grandmother moved way out nearly to the foot of Missionary Ridge in the early 1900s when it was country. My mother and father moved farther out in Brainerd in the 30s and I can remember when it was country. Now Brainerd has moved out with one subdivision after another, shopping centers. The airport built in 1929 was partly responsible and the new airport completed recently is accessible by freeway to all parts of the city.

The most famous landmark in Brainerd is hardly remembered. In 1815 some New England Presbyterians and Congregationalists decided to do something to help the Cherokee Indians. Missionaries were not allowed to locate west of Missionary Ridge.

They sent a missionary to establish the David Brainerd Mission and work with the Indians. He taught them how to read, the principles of Christianity, how to sew, churn, farm. When Andrew Jackson once visited the mission and the Indian children sang hymns for him, it is written that tears came to his eyes. All that remains of the mission today is the cemetery out near Eastgate Center, and the name by which the whole area is still called.

Adjoining Brainerd on the other side of the Ridge is East Ridge, a separate township. This is a thriving community with its own business section, and Highway 41 to Atlanta is lined with attractive businesses and eating places. One is the Tick Tock Restaurant owned by Knox McCardell.

He is one of our best known chefs and gave me the following recipe which he considers a specialty. "Gourmet" magazine wrote recently requesting his Chef's Special Spinach, which they had heard about. It is creamed spinach with mushrooms, tomatoes, onions and cheese — fit for any hungry gourmet.

McCARDELL'S SPECIAL SPINACH

3 cups chopped spinach (frozen)
3 tablespoons finely diced onion
3 ounces diced mushrooms
2 fresh tomatoes,
  peeled and diced
2 tablespoons butter
1 cup rich cream sauce

2 raw eggs, beaten
  only until blended
1½ ounces Parmesan cheese
Salt and Tabasco sauce to taste
Small clove garlic, chopped fine
(optional

Method: Cook the best quality frozen chopped spinach in boiling salted water. Please do not overcook. Drain well. In a heavy saute pan, melt butter, cook onions and mushrooms. Don't brown. Add tomatoes just to warm through. Add spinach and blend lightly with onion, mushrooms and tomatoes. If you use the garlic, it should be sauteed with the onions. Add cream sauce. Blend lightly. Add beaten eggs and cook over low heat, stirring to keep from sticking until the eggs are cooked. Add cheese, salt, Tabasco sauce. Blend and serve.

For something special, stuff a fresh tomato and bake. Or add a jigger of Anisette and use as a base for oysters or shrimp Rockefeller.

Knox M. McCardell
Tick Tock Restaurant

We seem to be a people who delight in extremes. After a few days of feasting on the Christmas bounty of ham, turkey, fruitcake, cookies and candy, we turn the pendulum all the way back and greet in the New Year with black-eyed peas and turnip greens. This is as if to say we love to live high, but down underneath we are southerners, born and bred, and our book calls for down to earth eating. After much rich eating, we crave the things we were born to.

People who have been brought up in other parts of the world will never understand our love for turnip greens and peas. I read that Thomas Jefferson, after he had lived in France and discovered the joys of French cuisine, returned to Monticello with many new recipes. But he always remained faithful to the traditional foods of Virginia ... chicken, ham, greens and cornbread.

There are about four of us here who enjoy three or four helpings of turnip greens with a little vinegar. These are the tops of the turnips that in other areas are thrown away. Here they are known as salad or just greens. We cook them until they are limp, and they comfort our souls.

ANNIE'S TURNIP GREENS

Wash a piece of salt pork or a piece of leftover ham. If it is salt pork, cut thin slices down to the rind, but not clear through. Place in a heavy kettle with enough water to cover the meat, about 1 or 2 inches. Cover, bring to a boil, and cook about 45 minutes until the meat is tender. Add 2 pounds of washed greens from which any tough stems have been removed. Bring to a boil and then lower the heat. Cook covered until tender, about 45 more minutes. Chop the greens, season with salt and pepper and serve hot. Pass a cruet of vinegar with the greens.

Mrs. Annie Lewis

Margaret and Herbert Kaiser used this recipe from the Thursday food column with great success one year, and when they lost it, we all hunted until the exact recipe turned up again.

PICKLED OKRA

4 pounds small tender okra
¾ cup plain salt
8 cups pure vinegar
1 cup water

10 pods red or green
  hot pepper
10 cloves garlic

146

Wash okra. Be sure pods are small, leaving short stem on pod. Pack in hot clean jars. Place 1 pepper pod and 1 clove garlic in each jar. Heat vinegar, water, and salt to boiling. If desired, other seasoning such as mustard seed or celery may be added to vinegar mixture. Pour hot vinegar over okra and seal. Let stand 8 weeks before using. Makes 10 pints.

The Herbert Kaisers

Mrs. J.R. Sheorn makes an artichoke pickle that reminds you of the gracious meals in South Carolina and Virginia when a relish tray of several kinds of homemade pickles, preserves and jellies accompanied every meal. Betty says it is a two day operation...one day to clean the artichokes and another to make the pickle...but these are so special they are worth every minute it takes. They are especially good served with fried chicken, rice and lady peas.

BETTY SHEORN'S ARTICHOKE PICKLE

2 pounds onions, chopped
2 pounds cauliflower,
  broken in small pieces
2 bunches celery
2 green peppers
4 to 6 pounds artichokes,
  scrubbed, scraped, and cut
  in bite size pieces.
  Cover with cold water,
  add ½ cup salt and soak

overnight. Drain well.
6 tablespoons Coleman's
  dry mustard
1 tablespoon tumeric
3 tablespoons celery seed
3 tablespoons mustard seed
5 cups sugar
1 cup flour
2 quarts cider vinegar

Mix sugar and flour. Add spices and enough vinegar to make a paste. Bring rest of vinegar to a boil and slowly add paste mixture. Stir until it boils. Add vegetables, stir often and let come to a boil. Boil 5 minutes. Put in hot sterilized jars and seal.

Mrs. J.R. Sheorn

Julian Lytle is one of the good men cooks around, mainly because he knows exactly how good things should taste. He knows where to get the best corn meal for hoecakes and muffins, makes a real specialty of Sunday breakfasts with smoked mackerel along with scrambled eggs and muffins. The recipe for his pickles is probably his most requested recipe, because everyone who tastes them wants to know how.

MR. LYTLE'S PICKLES

Begin with 1 gallon of large sour cucumber pickles. Drain them and cut off the rough ends. Slice the pickles about ¼ inch thick. Fill a

147

large pan with ice and some water and place the pickles in the ice water to crisp for about an hour. Drain off the water.

Mix a 5 pound bag of sugar with 4 boxes of pickling spices and set aside. Using a 2 gallon crock, put half of the sliced crisp pickles in the bottom of the crock and cover with half of the sugar and spices. Add the rest of the pickles and top with the rest of the sugar. Now slice 2 buttons of garlic and add to the pickles along with 1 cup white vinegar, 3 teaspoons pure olive oil. Top with a piece of cheesecloth over which you put a saucer or lid to cover the crock. Stir every morning for three days, using a spoon that will reach down to the bottom.

The pint jars that you are going to fill do not have to be sterilized, but just clean. First pour off all the liquid in a pitcher. Pack the pickles in the jars by hand, as many as the jars will hold. Fill the jars nearly full with the liquid, and then cap the jars.

Asked if the spices could be kept separate in a bag or cheesecloth, Mr. Lytle said yes, but that the spices are good to eat along with the pickles, and he likes them all together.

Julian Lytle

When you go in Shapiro's, whether it is to get some cheese, some fancy groceries, or just a corned beef sandwich, it is very hard to resist the temptation to buy two or three of Barney Brody's special dill pickles. They are seasoned with dill and garlic, are soft rather than crisp, and when you hold one in a piece of parchment paper and bite into it, it seems to be exactly what you had been wanting.

Barney makes these pickles himself and since he never uses a recipe it is rather hard to get it down on paper. He says the following recipe is about right.

BARNEY'S FERMENTED DILL PICKLES

20 pounds cucumbers
(about ½ bushel)
Black pepper
Red pepper, whole or crushed
Coriander
All spice

Mustard seed
2 bunches dill, or dill seed
if you can't get dill
Garlic
1 cup salt (not iodized)
2 gallons water

Cover cucumbers with cold water. Wash thoroughly and drain. Place some of the spices and a layer of dill in a 5 gallon crock or stone jar. Fill with cucumbers to within 3 or 4 inches of the top of the crock. Mix salt and water and pour over the cucumbers. Place a layer of dill and more of all the spices on top.

Cover with something heavy that won't corrode, like a glass plate. Barney's mother used a board and a brick. Use a weight on top to keep the cucumbers under the brine. Cover loosely with a clean cloth. Keep the pickles at room temperature. They will be ready in 24 to 48 hours, depending on the temperature. Taste when ready, then refrigerate.

Barney has no way of measuring exactly how much of the different spices he uses, but says you can experiment. Just be sure you use enough dill and garlic with the others. He uses Kosher salt, but says any salt will do as long as it is not iodized.

Barney Brody

An easy way to make crisp bread and butter pickles is to start with store bought dill pickles. This recipe is from Mrs. William A. Martin, Jr. and she made some for the Valamont Club Fair.

BREAD AND BUTTER PICKLES

1 gallon dill pickles　　　　　*Bud of garlic*
5 pounds sugar

Drain pickles and slice. Put the sliced pickles back in the jar with the garlic bud. Add 1 pound sugar each day for 5 days. Seal and keep in the refrigerator.

Mrs. William A. Martin, Jr.

Down the west side of Lookout Mountain is Lookout Valley...Wauhatchie, Rising Fawn, New England, Trenton. This beautiful valley is very much a part of Chattanooga because, although Dade County is in Georgia, for over a hundred years, the only way to get over the mountain was to come all the way up to Chattanooga and go around (or go around the southern end of the mountain at Valley Head).

There is now a road across the mountain connecting Trenton with LaFayette with as breath-taking scenery as anything on the Blue Ridge Parkway up in Virginia.

To understand how Chattanooga developed, you almost have to understand how, many valleys all come to a head at the river in Chattanooga. The mountains here are among the oldest in the world. They were once under water, consist of limestone in the lower parts and sandstone on the upper parts, and hardened some 300,000,000 years ago, which makes the Alps young by comparison. If you spread out the middle three fingers of your hand, that is how the mountains, Lookout, Sand and Raccoon have divided up our land, with Missionary Ridge on the other side.

Lookout Valley once had an important city all laid out on paper by northern capital in New England. The city was to take advantage of the rich iron deposits in the mountain, and railroads were built, tunnels into the mountain, a fine hotel, a bank, an office, a depot, building lots for town houses. New England, Georgia, could have become a fine city except for chance. Things didn't work out, the New Englanders went home, and eventually the fine buildings were torn down. Birmingham developed as the iron capital farther south.

Dade County means the Cases, Hales, Morrisons, Tatums, Brocks, Coles, Bates, Carrolls, and Jacoways, and many others. The Civil War is still fresh in the minds of the old families. I have heard that Trenton men looked down from their Confederate unit on Lookout Mountain and saw Yankee tents camping in their meadows.

The cooking in this part of the country is typical of small Georgia towns...home-baked cakes and pies are a matter of pride; the fried chicken, ham, fresh vegetables, plenty of butter, eggs, and cream are Southern stand-bys; and every good cook puts up jellies, preserves and pickles as generations before them have done. Mrs. W.H. Brock of Trenton used to say that homemade pickles are better, which they are.

PICKLED PEACHES

1 gallon freestone peaches	*1 teaspoon whole cloves*
8 cups sugar	*2 cups water*
2 sticks cinnamon	*3 cups vinegar*
1 tablespoon all spice	

Peel peaches and put in water to keep from turning. Tie spices in bag and put in pot with sugar, vinegar, water. Bring to a boil, then put in the peaches and cook until tender. Seal while hot in pint jars.

The late Mrs. W.H. Brock

CHAPTER VIII

Southern Cooking

The best cooking in the world is not French or Italian, or even fancy New York cuisine. The finest cooking in the world is done here in the South by our family cooks.

This is the sort of cooking that you can't find out about in cookbooks, or even by asking our fine Negro cooks. They presume that you know everything they do about turning heat up and turning it down, about seasoning vegetables with streaked meat, about making a rather moist biscuit dough so the biscuits will be light. Through the years the most practical things about cooking that I have learned have been the things copied from the various cooks who have helped our family.

Anyone can season and flour chicken, drop it in hot fat at 375 degrees and in fifteen minutes have fried chicken that tastes as if it came out of a good restaurant. This is not at all like Belle's or Annie's fried chicken. Theirs is crisp on the outside, but inside it is light and juicy and tender. It makes me remember all the good chicken we grew up on for birthday dinners, the first time I came home from college, all the important occasions.

I have tried their method of frying on fried potatoes and hoecakes as well as on chicken. First, you don't use deep fat. For chicken, just an inch or two of hot fat. For potatoes, a little more. Let the fat get hot, but never smoking. (This means it is too hot and bitter.) Into the hot fat, put the chicken or potatoes, and leave it hot until they begin to brown or get crisp around the outside. Then you turn the heat down to medium low and put on a loose cover.

This is sort of poky frying. I've noticed it has to make some noise, spewing, crackling, comfortable little noises. If there are no sounds at all, the heat is too low, and they will get greasy. From time to time, you put in a slotted spoon and stir around and keep checking. Chicken takes about 20 minutes uncrowded, and potatoes about 30 minutes. Turn up the heat again at the last and take cover off to make sure the chicken or potatoes are crisp. Then drain on towel. You can tell if you were good by what the inside is like. It should be light and delicate.

One night we planned to have seven for dinner, and it turned out we were having ten. I looked at the hash and knew I had better do something to make hoecakes, and had only 15 minutes to make about 30. I salted some cornmeal, moistened it with boiling water, and put about an inch of grease (too much) in the big iron skillet. I cooked them as fast as they would cook, and they got nice and brown. After dinner, Roy, who had eaten four, said, "You ought to figure out what you did on those hoecakes. They were good, but they were kind of heavy in the middle."

I didn't even fuss at him, because he was right. I should have used about ½ inch grease, started them hot, turned the heat down so that they would fry poky and light, and then turned them up again to get crisp and get out. You really learn more by your failures than your successes.

This art of changing temperatures when you fry things is fascinating. I don't know why Napoleon's chef didn't experiment more when he found that the fried potatoes returned to very hot fat would puff.

Just as interesting are our fresh vegetables in the South. Americans from other parts of the country are wild about our fried chicken, but they can't understand our enthusiasm for what they call "limp, overcooked vegetables." Those of us who have been brought up on beans cooked with streaked meat, fried corn, fried okra, turnip greens, and rice know that this is the way they taste best. It requires great self-dicipline to stop with just one serving, so you crave second helpings. (This type food is now called "soul food" in other parts of the country, and it is!)

Of all the recipes people call me to ask about, they ask most about green beans and fried corn. The awful thing is that although our cooks have been cooking corn like this for years, you can't find the recipe in any cookbooks. Think of the new generation of brides who won't know anything about the grand tradition of hospitality and cookery that we've had in Chattanooga. It will be a generation "that knew not Joseph" who'll faintly remember how good things used to taste and not know how to make them that way.

An expert when it comes to vegetables is my mother's cook, Mrs. Belle Pettyjohn. Belle's fried corn is not really so much fried as it is creamy. She cooks it with very little fat, scrapes the corn off the cob to get the milk, and finishes cooking it in a slow oven along with butter to make it good. She is the one who taught me to cook green beans with the distinctive flavor of ham hock or streaked meat, well flavored but not greasy. My squash casserole is still not quite as light as hers, but she says maybe I'm not baking it slow enough. It is still the best recipe we know.

We have had several wonderful friends to cook for us. Now Annie Lewis helps me to do all the doing it takes to raise six children. The day the family says my chicken is as good as Annie's or my squash is as good as Belle's, then I will know that I am a good cook! I am grateful to them all.

ANNIE'S SOUTHERN FRIED CHICKEN

In a bowl, put 1 cup of milk. Wash chicken good by putting in the sink in salted water. Dry off. Dip in milk and then in salt, pepper and flour. (People vary. Some use eggs in the milk; Annie uses just milk. Both are good.)

Heat an iron skillet or electric skillet very hot and melt shortening in it ... enough to make about 1 inch deep. When the shortening is hot, but not smoking, put in the chicken. Don't crowd it, about 4 or 5 pieces at a time. When it begins to get brown, turn down to about medium heat. Cover and let cook slow and gently. Turn every once and a while. At last take off cover and turn heat up so that it will be crisp. It will take 20 to 30 minutes.

Heat a heavy skillet with 3 tablespoons shortening or bacon drippings in it. Have the skillet hot when you add the okra. Leave on hot for about three minutes. Keep stirring and turn down to medium low. Let it fry in a very slow way. About every five minutes stir it and see that it isn't sticking. It will take 20 or 30 minutes in all. At the last, turn up the heat. It will be crunchy, but tender.

ANNIE'S FRIED FISH

Salt and pepper the filets of fish and dip in cornmeal. In a heavy hot skillet, melt the grease. It should be deep enough to cover the fish. Cook at high heat the whole time, but be careful that it doesn't get hot enough to smoke. In about 5 minutes it is done and is golden brown. The worst thing to do is to overcook it until it is tough. When we have fish, Kinch and Susan ask for slaw.

SLAW

Cut cabbage very fine. Add a little grated celery, bell pepper, and carrots. Make a dressing of the following: 1 tablespoon vinegar, 3 tablespoons mayonnaise, 1 teaspoon sugar, and 1½ teaspoons salt.

Mrs. Annie Lewis

153

Mother's Sunday dinners are almost an institution. I can remember when we were in our teens and complained about our long Sunday dinners. It seemed so tedious to have roast beef, green beans, and potatoes Sunday after Sunday. We even tried to enlighten Mother and told her how smart and modern it was getting to be to have sandwiches after church, or maybe a sort of brunch.

Then we all got married, my three sisters and my brother. And when we came back home, we all felt overcome with the same sort of warmth and hospitable abundance. Life is so relative.

The advice we gave when we were living at home was not the same thing we felt at all when we were buying our own groceries and doing our own cooking. The two pound roasts we were buying didn't taste nearly as good as Mother's ten pound ones, and no matter how many recipes for green beans I read, none of them tasted like the ones Belle fixed.

Belle and Elmer Pettyjohn are, I suppose, the best friends our family has ever had. Belle has cooked and helped Mother since before I was born, and her husband Elmer knows all about how to make houses and yards run smoothly, either with or without several grandchildren at his heels.

First, on a Sunday dinner, Mother usually has a huge platter of either roast beef, ham or fried chicken. Then she has about three vegetables...beans, squash and corn, for instance. Then some potatoes or rice, sliced tomatoes and bell peppers, biscuits and cornbread, ice cream and cake. You may think this is ridiculous, but there is very little left after we all have second or third helpings. I can remember as a child at the children's table, I wondered what grown ups talked about for such a long time. Now that I am grown-up I wonder why the children finish so fast and want to go in the pool before we have even finished our coffee.

The recipes for the roast beef and the ham are elsewhere in the book. Here are Belle's wonderful fried corn and her squash.

BELLE'S CORN

Take 6 to 8 ears of corn. Cut the kernels off the cob, but not too deep. Then scrape the juice into it. Put about 2 tablespoons of bacon grease into an iron skillet, heat until hot, and pour the corn in. Salt it. Now cook on top of the stove for a few minutes. Put in ½ stick butter and mix until it is melted. Set in 350 degree oven for about an hour until the corn juice is absorbed. Add 1 teaspoon sugar at the last and put back a few minutes longer.

Mrs. Elmer Pettyjohn

154

This is the old sideboard in my mother's dining room at the farm, laden down with fried chicken, ham, sweet potato casserole, corn and green beans, green salad, cantaloupe, cornsticks and rolls. Mr. and Mrs. Elmer Pettyjohn and my mother have engineered many memorable meals like this for family gatherings.

155

BELLE'S SQUASH CASSEROLE

Take 8 or 10 squash. Parboil in salted water until tender. Finely chop 1 onion and 1 bell pepper and saute in a little butter. Drain the squash and mash well. Add 6 crackers crumbled. Now beat ½ cup sweet milk and 2 eggs together and add to the squash. Now add ½ cup grated cheddar cheese, ½ stick butter, 1 teaspoon sugar, the onion and bell pepper to the squash. Taste to see if it needs salt or pepper. Put it all in a buttered casserole and top with cracker crumbs. Bake for 1 hour at 300 or 325 degrees. A low oven makes this a lighter and more delicate affair.

Mrs. Elmer Pettyjohn

BELLE'S ROLLS

¼ cup shortening	2 eggs, well beaten
4 tablespoons sugar	1 package dry yeast,
1 tablespoon salt	dissolved in 3 or 4
2 cups boiling water	tablespoons warm water
7 cups flour, about	

Put the shortening, sugar and salt in a bowl. Pour over the boiling water. Let this cool a little. Then add the flour to make a dough. Add gradually and don't add quite all of it until you see how much you are going to need to make a dough. Add the eggs and then the yeast mixture. This completes the dough. Keep it in the bowl and don't knead it. Cover with waxed paper and then with a newspaper on top. Put a heavy plate on top of this. This keeps all the humidity inside while the dough rises.

Set in a draft free place to rise, about an hour. When the dough has doubled in bulk, mash it down and turn out on a floured surface. Knead a little and work it. Roll out and with a round cutter cut the rolls. Have some melted butter on hand and brush each roll with it, fold over in half, and place on greased baking pan. Let the pan of rolls rise for 45 minutes to an hour, and bake at 350 for 20 minutes or until golden brown.

Belle's rolls are distinctive because they are as light as a feather. Some of this is just know how. Belle says that if you will practice a lot they will be good.

These rolls can be frozen. She either freezes the dough itself or she doesn't bake them quite long enough and freezes them, so they will be just right when the thawed roll is put in the oven for a final few minutes of baking. She has also heated completely baked and frozen rolls by wrapping in foil and heating in a very slow oven.

Mrs. Elmer Pettyjohn

METHOD FOR COOKING SOUTHERN GREEN BEANS, FIELD PEAS, OR LIMAS

For you who have never heard of buying streaked meat and ham hocks to season vegetables, just ask your meat man. He will show you that streaked meat looks a little like unsliced bacon. When you get home, cut off a piece about two inches long, and slice almost through, but not quite, in several places. Put in a hot, heavy, iron pan to brown, then pour in some hot water and a teaspoon of salt.

First wash, string, snap, and wash the green beans. Put into the water and cook slowly until tender. Sometimes for a change, buy a cured ham hock and do the same way. It has such sweet tender ham on it, that it not only seasons the vegetables, but is a prize for the lucky person who asks for it along with the beans.

Field peas are cooked exactly the same way. Some cooks don't brown the streaked meat first, but just cook for a half hour alone in the water to get the flavor out. When the field peas cook down, they take on a rich brownish color, and the juice, or liquor, in the pot is especially delicious. Sometimes I add an onion and a few peppercorns when cooking field peas, and one afternoon recently, when the peas were done at about four, I tasted a few to see that the seasoning was just right. Then without planning it at all, I served myself a little dish of these wonderful fresh peas, and alone and happy, had a sort of teaparty.

Cook fresh limas the same way, and also cabbage.

CLEO'S STUFFED SQUASH

Cleo Smartt, Belle's cousin, helped us for several years. Her stuffed squash was very special.

Take about 6 or 8 small yellow summer squash. Parboil in salted water to cover. In the meantime fry 2 or 3 slices of bacon until crisp. Drain on towel. Saute about 2 tablespoons of chopped onion until soft. When the squash are tender, cut in half, lengthwise. With a spoon, scoop out centers. In a small bowl mash the scooped-out squash and add onion and crumbled bacon. Season to taste with a little celery salt, pepper, and pinch of brown sugar. Refill the squash cases. Top with buttered cracker crumbs and sprinkle with chopped parsley. Bake at 350 for about 20 minutes. These are pretty to serve at a company dinner.

Mrs. Cleo Smartt

CLEO'S BURNED AND BROILED CHICKEN

Cleo had the strangest and most wonderful way to broil chicken breasts. They were so tender that they almost fell off the bone, but with such a brown hearty flavor, that you thought you had never eaten such chicken. The secret was that she nearly burned the things up in much too hot an oven. When in Williamsburg at the Inn there, I saw a fine Virginia chef do the same thing. He put a whole roaster of chicken into a 425 or 450 oven to bake. They were great.

You can do this with breasts of chicken or halves. First wash the chicken. Then salt, pepper, and paprika it. Cleo also sprinkled lemon juice over it. She put the chicken in a roaster, meat side up, and bravely thrust it in the oven which she had turned up as high as it would go. (When I do it, I stop at 450.) Every once in a while, she added a little water to the pan, ¼ cup at a time, and basted it. This chicken roasted uncovered for 35 or 45 minutes. Then she took it out, basted it good, put some foil over it, and put it in a 300 oven for half hour.

She made gravy with the drippings in the bottom of the pan and this is the best chicken you ever ate.

Mrs. Cleo Smartt

SOUTHERN FRIED POTATOES

Peel and slice the potatoes. If you have time, soak in ice water. This is supposed to make them crisper. Heat in a heavy iron saucepan or skillet vegetable shortening about 1½ to 2 inches deep. When it is hot enough, a slice of potato put in it will bubble and sizzle. Put all the potatoes in so that they are rather crowded. Let cook at high speed until the potatoes begin to get crisp and slightly brown. Stir occasionally.

Now turn down the heat to medium or medium low speed and let cook gently and slowly for about 10 to 15 minutes, stirring a time or two, and turning the potatoes over so that they fry evenly. About five minutes before serving, turn the heat up to high again. Let the potatoes get very crisp and brown.

I do not know why, but potatoes fixed this way are soft in the middle and crisp on the outside. They are much better than the method of frying a few at a time uncovered at steady 375 degree heat. Drain the potatoes on paper towels. Salt, pepper, and serve hot.

One year I found out that nearly every Negro church in Chattanooga raises money by selling plate dinners cooked in the church kitchen. Most of these rallies or Women's Day projects are held on the weekends. I visited the New Emmanuel Baptist Church one day when they

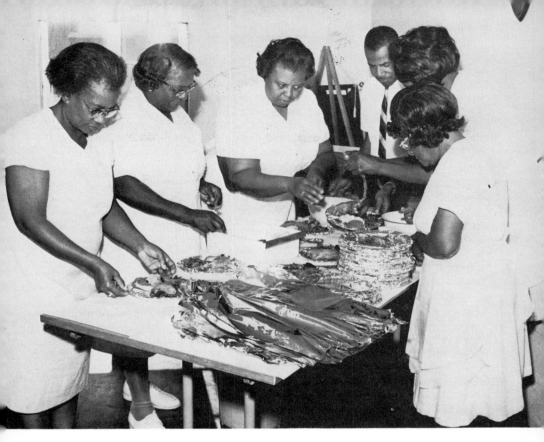

Many churches in Chattanooga make money for their churches by catering plate dinners. New Emmanuel Baptist Church is noted for their fried chicken dinners. Assembling plates are Mrs. Lucille Jackson, Mrs. Belle Pettyjohn, Mrs. Eris Satterwhite, Moses Satterwhite, Mrs. Mattie Patten, and Mrs. Minnie Hambright.

were frying chicken for about a hundred dinners. These are delivered either to offices, factories, or interested groups. And when you have a group of noted cooks who know how everything should taste and how to serve nicely, the dinner is apt to be an experience in the finest Southern cooking.

First was the fried chicken, fried until it is crisp on the outside and moist and tender inside, the way that no electric fryer can achieve. Then they had green beans, pickled beets, new potatoes, a cheese noodle casserole, a tomato and lettuce salad, fresh cornbread and hot homemade rolls just from the oven, and for dessert, a choice of sweet potato pie, apple pie and pound cake.

159

The dinners were served on individual divided plates covered over with foil. The cornbread and rolls were in an individual bag and the dessert was in an individual bag. The plate went down an assembly line, was filled and covered over with foil, then everything went neatly into a sack with a napkin and a fork.

I asked Mrs. Arwin Thomas how she fried the chicken, and Mrs. Eris Satterwhite gave me the recipe for the sweet potato pie.

SWEET POTATO PIE

Pastry for a 10-inch pie
3 cups sweet potatoes
1 stick butter
3 cups sugar
1 teaspoon vanilla

1 pinch nutmeg
½ can evaporated milk
(13-ounce size)
4 eggs, beaten

Boil the potatoes in the jackets until done. Peel and mash. Add the butter, sugar, vanilla and nutmeg. Combine the beaten eggs and milk and mix with the potatoes until blended. Pour into the pastry shell. Bake at 350 degrees for 1 hour or until done. This is a custard pie, so you insert a knife or a toothpick. If it comes out clean, it is done.

Mrs. Eris Satterwhite

NEW EMMANUEL FRIED CHICKEN

Wash the chicken and dry it. Cut into parts, either in quarters or in pieces. Season with salt and pepper. In a sack put some flour that has some paprika mixed in with it. The paprika will help it brown nicely.

In an iron skillet or pot, heat oil or shortening until it is hot but not smoking. Have the fat deep enough to cover chicken. Putting the pieces of chicken in will lower the temperature. When it rises again and you can hear the chicken start frying, turn it down to medium and let it fry. Keep turning the pieces all the time. Use a sharp fork.

You will know when to take the chicken out by looking to see that it is well browned, and also by sticking the fork through it. When the fork slides in easily, you know that the chicken is tender.

When you poke the chicken and it is hard, you have cooked it too long. You want it crisp on the outside and tender and moist on the inside. When done, remove and drain.

This is the way Arwin Thomas fries chicken. She says everyone does it slightly differently, but this is her way.

In the early days, Chattanooga was a meat and potatoes town. It still is in some ways, and a steak dinner is a fine way of celebrating. This view is from the west side of the city looking toward the Blue Cross Building.

"Reflection Riding" is a garden spot at the foot of Lookout Mountain noted for its pleasant three mile drive and collection of trees and wild flowers native to this region. Octavia Chambliss Spring spreads a picnic near the pond.

The Christmas Open House at Weswoods, home of the Clay John-sons, was one of the most festive and beautiful anywhere. Betsy John-son Farmer (Mrs. Wayne) has been helping with the Christmas Eve party for years, and now her excited children share in the good compa-ny and good food.

The Walnut Street Bridge was dedicated in colorful ceremonies in February, 1891, and is still used, along with the Market Street Bridge, the newer Olgiati Bridge, and the recent bridge across Chickamauga Dam. It is Chattanooga's highest bridge, the first to ice up in cold weather, and the most picturesque as seen from the Tennessee River bank.

Don and Emeline Ferguson can gather around their table just their own family or they can have Thanksgiving dinner for the whole Hedges clan of about 75, depending on the occasion. Their children Sue and Lisa help, and Mack and Jim can if they have to.

Ashland Farm in Chattanooga has been the scene of many a delightful party for Chattanoogans. Mrs. Cartter Patten is not only a gracious hostess, but has been involved in saving our historic sites, planning attractive landscaping, and being a good citizen and friend to Chattanooga.

Mrs. Calvin Fowler served a buffet supper on the terrace for her family the night this picture was taken. Mrs. Dick Fowler is on the left, Frank is having a chunk of watermelon, young Chappell and Calvin are in line, then Mrs. Frank Fowler, Mrs. Calvin Fowler, Dick and Margaret.

Chattanooga is a city of churches, and downtown is dotted with steeples. Some play chimes during the week; others ring bells from the bell tower to call people to worship on Sunday. This classic steeple belongs to the First Christian Church on McCallie Avenue.

The Hobby Law family enjoys inviting friends to their house on Chickamauga Lake in the summertime. Martha sets the picnic table with a gay cloth, flowers from the yard, and informal accessories.

This is a picture of my father, Roy McDonald, with the newest excitement in our family newspaper business....his fifth press, a new Goss Mark II. It is a far cry from his first press of the ancient flat-bed type that seemed very exciting to us forty years ago when he first got into the newspaper business.

This is a picture of a landmark that must be in this book in color because it is so much a part of the life of my family and friends...McDonald Farm. The house at McDonald Farm has undergone about three re-modellings since my grandfather helped build the standard farmhouse for that time...four rooms downstairs and four rooms up, with a hall down the middle, nearly a hundred years ago. The trees planted then are now huge and have sheltered many a picnic and family gathering for his 21 grandchildren and their children.

The best place to get vegetables and fruit, fresh from the farm, is the Farmers' Market on 11th Street. There are dozens of stands and tempting produce.

The late Colonel Creed Bates, the beloved former principal of Chattanooga High School, was a favorite resident of Summertown on Walden's Ridge. He lived in a wonderful log house, grew every variety of apple, and made cider every year which he delivered to his friends in town.

This hot apple pie was made by Annie Lee Lewis out of apples from our yard. The mountains around Chattanooga for some reason grow excellent apples.

This is the Exum family, whose steady appetites and love of good dinners has inspired most of the cooking we do, although the children have grown up since the memorable dinner for our international guests. Sitting on the steps in front of our house are clockwise, Jonathan on the left, Susan, Roy, his wife Anne, Kinch, Jr., Franklin, and Ellen. I am in the middle.

The Grand Canyon of the Tennessee as viewed from Elder Mountain.

CHAPTER IX

Salads and Dressings

What kind of salads does Chattanooga eat? Just about every kind you can think of. We make old fashioned potato salad and chicken salad, the newest molded salads, and the tossed green salad in recent years has gained a host of admirers. For some reason children do not care for some of the molded aspics and molded vegetable salads, but they love the raw vegetables in the tossed green salad. Since this is easy and complements every meat, this is getting to be standard fare.

There are all sorts of salads and some are meals in themselves. Our hotels and restaurants feature chef's salads which contain strips of ham, chicken, cheese, vegetables and greens, a complete and delightful meal. One Sunday after church I made everyone an individual chef salad in our largest soup bowl and served a blue cheese dressing as well as a French one. It was a great success.

One Wednesday night at a church supper, I watched to see what salads the women would bring, and which ones would be the most popular with the 350 people going down the line. There was slaw, green salad, molded strawberry salad, tomato aspic, peach halves filled with cottage cheese, and many many more. The tossed green salad and the potato salad were gone first, but they were all eaten by the time I went back to get my salad bowl, which shows that variety tastes good to everyone.

The first lady of food with thousands of Chattanoogans is certainly Miss Gertrude Oehmig. For many years she has set a standard for southern hospitality and for food, elegant but simple, that we all find ourselves wishing we could duplicate everyday for our own families.

In 1924 she and her sister, Miss Bessie Oehmig opened the Coffee. Shop on Georgia Avenue. For 23 years these ladies gave luncheons, catered for weddings, and made themselves famous. There was always chopped parsley on the butter balls, dainty bread trays with homemade clover leaf rolls (both white and whole wheat), homemade ice cream churned on the back porch with such rich cream that it stuck to the roof of your mouth in a most pleasant way. They made chicken salad to go in tomatoes that has never been surpassed. (Miss Gertrude cut the white meat in chunks and minced the dark meat so that it appeared to be all white.) For dinner at night you could go and have a filet mignon with fresh mushrooms from Bert Wills' mushroom farm, two vegetables, rolls, coffee and ice cream for $1.25, which was considered very expensive.

The Oehmigs lived on East Fifth Street right across from the Loveman house (now Dr. Cecil Newell's clinic) and the Dunbar Newells lived next door. It was a fascinating neighborhood of old Chattanooga.

When the Coffee Shop closed, Miss Gertrude became head of all the food for Girls Preparatory School, and when she retired, Chattanoogans followed her to Loveman's Tearoom where she served chicken salad, tomato aspic, her famous caramel cake, homemade rolls, and all sorts of specialties that readers called me regularly to get the recipes for. Her most famous salads were her chicken salad and her frozen fruit salad. Her many other recipes are scattered through this book, a very delicious part of this Chattanooga collection.

MISS GERTRUDE'S CHICKEN SALAD

Clean well and salt a medium sized hen (about 4 pounds). Boil gently until tender. Then cool in the broth. Pull the meat from the bones and cut up. Cut the white meat in larger chunks and the dark meat in smaller pieces. Add 1 cup chopped celery to every 2 cups of chopped chicken. Add juice of 1 lemon and enough homemade mayonnaise to make a moist salad. Season to taste with salt, white pepper, and a dash of cayenne pepper.

MISS GERTRUDE'S FROZEN FRUIT SALAD

This specialty has been a real favorite with our readers, and when hot weather comes and people start wanting a salad they can make ahead for the weekend or a summer luncheon, someone always calls to ask the recipe for this frozen fruit salad again. It contains miniature marshmallows along with the fruit, and is delicious.

1 large can fruit cocktail, drained (2½ can)
1 cup homemade mayonnaise
1 cup cream, whipped
½ package miniature marshmallows

2 bananas, sliced
1 small can Royal Anne cherries, drained
1 small jar maraschino cherries, drained

Drain all fruit and mix together in large bowl. Add the mayonnaise and whipped cream and fold in. Miss Gertrude Oehmig puts in a bread pan and freezes so that it is easily sliced. You may freeze it in whatever you like.

Miss Gertrude Oehmig

An unusual luncheon dish is the chicken salad made by Helen Siskin Pregulman (Mrs. Mervin) using cucumber balls, green pepper and pink grapefruit along with the chicken, and served with a curry dressing.

CURRIED CHICKEN SALAD

Combine 2 cups cooked white meat of chicken, cut into tiny cubes, ½ cup skinned, thinly shredded green pepper, 12 small cucumber balls, and the sections of 1 pink grapefruit. Add ½ cup French dressing and toss well. Chill thoroughly.

Press out the excess dressing gently but thoroughly, and toss the mixture again with ½ cup mayonnaise mixed with 1 teaspoon curry powder and 1 tablespoon each grated onion, parsley, and chives. Line a salad bowl generously with crisp water cress and spoon the salad over it. Decorate with mayonnaise and dust with paprika. chopped parsley, cinnamon and curry powder. Sprinkle with 2 tablespoons drained capers and serve.

Mrs. Mervin Pregulman

A refreshing and simple molded fruit salad is grapefruit aspic. This version calls for almonds along with it, but we think pecans are good, too.

OLD CHARLESTON GRAPEFRUIT ASPIC

2 grapefruit	1 cup grapefruit juice
2 ounces almonds or	¾ cup boiling water
pecans, chopped	1 tablespoon lemon juice
1 package lemon gelatin	1 tablespoon sugar

Peel grapefruit with a sharp knife, cut out and dice segments; drain, reserving juice. Add chopped almonds or pecans to the fruit. When cool, refrigerate until slightly thickened, then fold in the grapefruit and nut mixture. Pour in mold and refrigerate.

Some molded salads are wonderful hits at ladies' luncheons and for some reason don't go over at all with the children. Apricot salad is one of these. I like it and tell the children that probably they will, too, when they grow up and get some sense. This salad compliments a luncheon of ham or chicken.

APRICOT SALAD

1 package lemon gelatin
1 can apricot halves
1 package cream cheese
  (3 ounce)

¾ cup nutmeats
Juice of 1 lemon
Juice of 1 orange

Use 1 cup of hot apricot juice in dissolving the gelatin. Use 1 cup of the lemon juice, orange juice, and remaining apricot juice in addition. Put the apricots through a sieve and add to the gelatin. When the mixture begins to thicken, add the nuts. Drop a ball of cream cheese in each of the individual molds and then add the gelatin. Chill until firm.

Baird McClure unmolds a ring of orange salad on a big silver platter, surrounding it with all sorts of fresh fruit and wedges of melon, and serving it with a cream cheese and ginger dressing. This compliments a shrimp curry luncheon or a cold sliced country ham and biscuits buffet. This pretty salad is almost a trademark at her parties.

BAIRD'S MOLDED ORANGE SALAD

1 package lemon gelatin
1 can orange juice
  concentrate (6 ounces)
1¼ cup boiling water
1 tablespoon lemon juice

1 small can mandarin
  oranges, drained
  or 4 canned pear halves
½ cup white grapes

Dissolve the gelatin in the boiling water. Add the thawed concentrate. Cool until thick and arrange a small ring mold with the fruit and gelatin. Increase the recipe for large molds.

PINEAPPLE AND GINGER DRESSING

1 package cream cheese
  (3 ounces)
½ can crushed pineapple,
  drained (small can)

¼ cup candied ginger,
  chopped fine

Soften cream cheese and add pineapple and ginger to the right consistency.

Miss Baird McClure

164

A tart tangy molded grapefruit salad to compliment chicken Tetrazzini was the one Mrs. Don Ferguson brought to a garden club supper.

EMELINE'S MOLDED GINGERALE SALAD

4 envelopes plain gelatin
2 cups pineapple juice
¾ cup sugar
Pinch of Salt

1 quart gingerale
Pinch of ginger
1 cup lemon juice

Dissolve the gelatin in the pineapple juice. In a large saucepan, put the gingerale, sugar, pinch of salt. Heat, then add the gelatin mixture to dissolve. Add a pinch of ginger and the lemon juice. When cool, add:

1 cup chopped celery
1 cup chopped apples
1 large can crushed pineapple
3 cans strained grapefruit
    sections

3 cans white grapes, strained
Chopped Almonds or pecans

Pour all this into the largest ring mold you have. This serves a large group of about 20. This is also easy to decorate if you have time. The gelatin is clear so that strawberries, pineapple, or other arranged fruit will show through. It can also be garnished on the outside with other fruit. Unmold on a bed of lettuce with some mayonnaise or cream cheese dressing to go with it.

Mrs. Don Ferguson

An especially good version of the molded Bing cherry salad is one that the late Winnie Holmes made. It calls for pineapple, nuts, and for a tingly zip of a bottle of Coca-Cola.

BING CHERRY SALAD

1 can pitted Bing cherries
1 large package cherry gelatin
    (or 2 small packages)
1 envelope plain gelatin
    (optional)

1 large can crushed pineapple
1 cup nuts
1 bottle 6-ounce Coca Cola,
    unchilled
2 cups water

Drain cherries, mix juice with water and bring to a boil. Dissolve gelatin in a little cold water, empty cherry gelatin into it, pour juice and water mixture over and dissolve gelatin. Add cherries and let cool. Add pineapple, nuts and Coke. Chill until set.

Winnie says the plain gelatin was not included in the original recipe, but she adds when she is planning to carry a congealed salad out. It keeps it set better until serving time.

The late Miss Winnie Holmes

The interesting thing about strawberry salad is the unusual dressing. No one can every guess how it is made, but it is delicious and makes the salad distinctive. It is also a little different to use frozen strawberries in a molded salad.

SURPRISE STRAWBERRY SALAD

1 package strawberry gelatin	*1 small can crushed pineapple*
1 package cherry gelatin	*2 packages frozen strawberries*
2 cups hot water	*Juice of ½ lemon*

Dissolve gelatin in the hot water and allow to chill until partially set. Meanwhile thaw the strawberries. Stir the strawberries and the pineapple in the gelatin, add the lemon juice. (You can also add a can of drained mandarin oranges to this.) Chill until firm.

SURPRISE DRESSING

Cut up 10 marshmallows in ½ pint sour cream. Stir and allow to stand for several hours until dissolved. This takes a few hours or even overnight if possible. Some marshmallows dissolve easier for some reason...the soft spongy ones.

Mrs. Willard Steele, Jr.

Jellis Moncure (Mrs. Richard) has the gracious imaginative ways that Virginia seems to bestow on its daughters. From our days together at Randolph-Macon Womens College, and then later when she and Dick moved to Lookout Mountain, Jellis has always planned a luncheon, furnished a room, decorated a doll house or groomed her yard, with a very distinctive and tasteful touch. She makes spoonbread, keeps the brass on her lovely old furniture polished, and is ever on the lookout for new recipes. For a recent meeting of the Investment Club at her house, she served chop suey salad and homemade ginger ice cream.

CHOP SUEY SALAD

Dice the following:
Green Pepper
Cabbage
Green onion
 (tops and bottoms)
Celery
Water chestnuts

Black pitted olives
Swiss cheese
Bean sprouts
 (freshen under cold water)
Chicken, cubed
Broken Romaine lettuce

Toss the above with diced chopped bacon and the following dressing. Dressing: 1 cup mayonnaise, ¼ cup oil, ¼ cup soy sauce, ¼ cup lemon juice, 1 teaspoon Worcestershire sauce, salt and pepper.

Mrs. Richard Moncure

During the depression, one of Franklin Roosevelt's plans for developing the South was to create water power by harnessing the waters of the Tennessee River valley, thus attracting industry, lowering electric rates and so on. Norris Dam was built in the Knoxville area and Chickamauga Dam was built at Chattanooga.

When the waters began to back up and the lake began to form, the scenery that had always been here became rather breathtaking with vast areas of water as a base. Hills dropped sharply to the water's edge, coves and harbors took shape as if they had been planned, visitors compared our scenery to Switzerland.

The TVA has been very important to our region economically, but the lake has opened up a whole new way of life to our people. Before, our family had a boat, which we kept between the bridges on the river and took cruises down to Hales Bar Dam, and Sunday excursions. Now all the activity has moved above Chickamauga Dam on both sides of the lake. Gold Point Marina, the TVA boat dock, the Rod and Gun Club, the yacht club, all became places to meet for a day on the lake.

We later had a cruiser that even careful teen-agers could manage, and we learned to read the buoys, follow the maps, look and see how deep the water should be and how to keep in the channel.

There is something about a few hours in the sun and on the water that relaxes people. We enjoyed the lake in the summer sun, in the fall as the autumn colors appeared on the shore and the September sun

167

Chickamauga Dam, a part of the TVA system, spans the Tennessee River 4 miles up stream from Chattanooga. Dedicated in 1939 by President Franklin Roosevelt, it has provided power for the industry of the area, and recreation and boating for thousands of people.

shone with a different angle on the water. Sometimes at night we lay on the top of the boat and looked at the stars.

Always someone was going to the galley for something else to eat. Most of the time Mother cooked ahead and brought food . . . fried chicken, potato salad, sliced ham, buns, potato chips, cake. We also ate deviled ham on crackers, cheese on crackers, peanut butter sandwiches . . . you get less and less particular when you are hungry.

I think the food is probably more elaborate in the thousands of homes that now line the sides of the lake than on the boats where it is more practical to take along a picnic. We have lugged many a thermos of iced tea and lemonade, basket after basket of food, and enjoyed many a fine day on the lake.

Every weekend in the summer, thousands of Chattanoogans seek out the lake and build traditions of picnics, water skiing, boating, swimming for their families to remember years from now. There is no real recipe for potato salad. You just make it. But this one is about right.

POTATO SALAD

3 cups mayonnaise
2 hard cooked eggs
  chopped
2 tablespoons vinegar
Salt, pepper, Tabasco
  to taste
Dash of mustard

10 large white potatoes
2 cups finely diced celery
½ cup finely diced onion
¼ cup finely diced
  green peppers
½ cup finely diced sweet pickle

Boil potatoes. Let them cool in their skins. When cool, remove skins and cut up potatoes in small bite-sized pieces. Mix all other ingredients together and add potatoes. Mix all together and taste. Correct seasoning.

When Martha and Hobby Law ask friends to have dinner with them at their place on Ware's Branch, there is bound to be an afternoon of boating on Chickamauga Lake, water skiing, and sunning. Martha has an unusual menu for hungry lake people that features German sausage grilled over charcoal. (She gets these at the Rathskeller), German potato salad, a big platter of sliced tomatoes, artichoke hearts, imported Swiss cheese, sliced dill pickles, homemade mayonnaise and horseradish mustard. She has a bowl of chilled marinated bean salad, plenty of rye bread, and small pecan and lemon tarts. This is her way with bean salad.

MARINATED BEAN SALAD

½ cup vinegar
¼ cup (or less) sugar
1 teaspoon garlic vinegar
¼ cup oil
   (olive oil if you like it)
2 teaspoons soy sauce
Celery salt to taste
1 can (1 lb.) Blue Lake
   cut green beans
1 can (1 lb.) kidney beans,
   drained

1 medium onion,
   sliced in thin slices
   (purple onions best)
1 can (5 oz.) water chestnuts
1 small can tiny lima beans,
   drained
1 carrot, cut up
2 ribs celery, cut up
Dash Tabasco
Lemon pepper
Dry mustard

Marinate all these ingredients for several hours or overnight. Martha uses a large jar which can be screwed tight and that can be turned from time to time so the marinade can get through all the beans. Sometimes she includes the following when available: wax beans, fresh mushrooms marinated in French dressing, raw cauliflower, green pepper, corn, olives.

Mrs. Halbert Law

For a Pilot Club buffet supper, Lillian Cathcart brought a German Potato Salad that was so good, people went back for second helpings. She used new potatoes, onions, celery and parsley, with a vinegar and mayonnaise dressing.

GERMAN POTATO SALAD

6 pounds small new potatoes
1 cup sweet onions
   (either red or yellow)
   sliced thin
2 cups celery sliced thin
1 cup parsley, snipped fine

3 cups mayonnasie
1 tablespoon sucaryl,
   or 2 tablespoons sugar
Salt, pepper and MSG
4 tablespoons vinegar

Boil the potatoes with the jackets on until tender. Chill thoroughly, then slice very thin. Mix the mayonnaise with the vinegar and the sugar. This is assembled in layers to avoid breaking the potatoes. First arrange a layer of potatoes in a large bowl, sprinkle with salt and pepper and a little MSG, the onions, celery, parsley, and mayonnaise mixture. Make another layer of potatoes and do the same. Repeat until all ingredients are used. Mix carefully so that the slices do not break unnecessarily.

Miss Lillian Cathcart

One of the greatest salads ever invented is certainly the tossed green salad. As we think over the salads that we have most often, by far the best is the combination of salad greens and fresh vegetables with a vinegar and oil dressing. No other salad so well complements meat or contrasts so nicely with cooked vegetables. In all parts of America, this is getting to be "the" salad. Yet with minor changes in the combinations of ingredients, we never seem to tire of a green salad, day in, day out.

It was while we were at Stanford the first year we were married that we found out about the salad customs of one delightful California family. We had dinner with our next door neighbors, Shirley and Leonard Ely, and Leonard tosses a salad at the table, using a little salt cellar, a grinder of fresh peppercorns, and cruets of vinegar and oil—a simple combination of lettuce, tomatoes, onion slices and avocado.

I had never eaten anything so delicious. We had seconds. And before the week was out I had gotten my new husband to buy me a wooden salad bowl, red wine vinegar, a pepper grinder, and was experimenting with do-it-yourself classic salad dressing.

This was a family tradition with the Elys. Leonard's grandfather was Chancellor Ray Lyman Wilbur of Stanford, and at any dinner when he was present, he was considered the finest salad maker. The bowl of broken lettuce, sliced onions, tomato wedges, and other raw vegetables in season was always brought to him for the authoritative finishing with oil and vinegar.

Just as he had watched his grandfather for years, Leonard would pour about ½ teaspoon salt in a wooden salad spoon. This he covered with black pepper, ground fresh from the mill. Then he finished filling this same spoon with red wine vinegar. (The salt and pepper will dissolve in the vinegar but not the oil.) He poured this over the salad. Now he filled the same spoon with salad oil and poured over the salad, doing it three times.

If this were a very large salad, he repeated the whole procedure, just remembering to use three spoons of oil to every one of vinegar. He tossed the salad all together, then picked up a piece of lettuce to taste. If it didn't suit him, he usually added more salt.

It can be made with plain salad oil and cider vinegar. We think it is best using red wine vinegar and salad oil. Gourmets seem to prefer olive oil, but plain families who haven't gotten to be gourmets yet seem to like plain oil. Sometimes I have been out of vinegar and substituted lemon juice, and think it is extra good for a change. This classic mixture is equally at home with salads using fruit. The only way I have tampered with it down through the years is by adding a little monosodium glutamate and sometimes a little celery salt.

When we were at the Four Seasons in New York, the head waiter dramatically tossed a salad for us over a salad cart pushed up to our table. He used exactly the same method except he added a pinch of powdered mustard with the salt and pepper in the spoon. I asked him why, and he explained that the Bibb lettuce was young and tender and needed a little tang of something. He used white wine vinegar and olive oil.

The salad ingredients can be arranged in the bowl an hour or two ahead of time. The tomatoes, onions, and avocado are cut and sliced in the bottom of the wooden bowl. Any other wet or heavy ingredients are put in the bottom. The lettuce is broken with the hands (never cut) into small pieces and put on top.

When thinking about your ingredients, choose three or four things and don't cut them all alike. When everything is chopped alike, it isn't pretty. Too many ingredients in a salad are confusing. Our favorite is lettuce plus tomato wedges, sliced spring onions, bell pepper, and avocado. For an extra zip in the flavor of the salad when the lettuce is not so good, for instance, use crumbled bacon or sliced olives or anchovies. You wouldn't use them all at once, but any of these lend flavor and energy to the whole thing.

Sometimes when we think ahead, we fry croutons. First cut the edges from white bread and then cut in cubes. In the electric skillet, melt about 2 tablespoons butter and 2 tablespoons salad oil. Set the dial so that the croutons fry slowly in this mixture until they are very crisp . . . about 10 or 15 minutes. Add at the very last minute.

Through the years we have had this tossed green salad several times a week, and have passed on the method to all the friends and relatives who like it, too. Any of the children can toss it. There are so many of us that we toss it at the last minute in the kitchen and bring the bowl to the table ready to serve.

We have made this salad at buffet suppers for 25, making up the ingredients ahead of time in the vegetable drawers of the refrigerator. Recently we made enough for a dinner party for 80 and served it in a huge clear plastic bowl that looked like crystal. After measuring the salad spoons several times, just wash your hands and use them to toss the salad.

One reader says she made enough for 200 people at church by this recipe and never had so many compliments. I have tried to make it in large quantities in a jar, but for some reason, it is never as good as on a salad.

THE CHANCELLOR'S SALAD DRESSING

½ to ¾ teaspoon of salt,
* measured with the eye*
Black pepper to cover

1 salad spoon of vinegar
3 salad spoons of oil

Put the salt into the salad spoon (or any large spoon). Cover it with pepper. Then pour this same spoon full with vinegar. Since the seasoning will dissolve in vinegar but not in oil, take a fork and stir the seasoning in the spoon. I usually shake in some monosodium glutamate here. Now pour it out on the bowl of salad ingredients. Fill the same spoon with oil and spill over the salad. Repeat with oil twice more. Now toss the salad with the fork and spoon and taste. It may need more salt and pepper. To vary it you can add celery salt, dill, parsley, Tabasco, and so on, but you can really not improve on the simple formula which seems to bring out the best flavor in each of your salad ingredients.

The late Dr. Ray Lyman Wilbur
Stanford University

Perhaps the most dramatic molded salad to serve around the holidays is this combination of molded chicken or turkey with a cranberry mixture on top. Lucille Hickman makes this in a large ring mold.

CHICKEN CRANBERRY MOLD

Molded Chicken or Turkey layer:
3 cups chopped chicken
2 cups finely chopped celery
2 cups mayonnaise
* (homemade)*

1 cup chicken broth
2 tablespoons gelatin
¼ cup cold water

Soak the gelatin in cold water. Add to mayonnaise and broth. Add chicken and celery and season to taste with salt and pepper.

1 cup ground
* fresh cranberries*
½ cup sugar
1 package orange gelatin
1 package raspberry gelatin

1 cup hot water
½ cup pineapple juice
1 cup crushed pineapple
1 cup chopped celery
½ cup broken nuts

Combine cranberries and sugar. Dissolve gelatin in hot water. Add juice. Chill til slightly thick. Add cranberries, pineapple, walnuts and celery. Pour into 2-quart ring mold and chill until firm. Then put chicken mixture on top.

Mrs. Lucille Hickman

An easy way to make molded cranberry salad is in the blender. This is very creamy looking when it is all molded, and very pretty.

BLENDER CRANBERRY MOLD

2 envelopes unflavored gelatin
½ cup cold water
½ cup boiling water
1¼ cups sugar

½ orange,
   cut in pieces and seeded
3 cups cranberries

Sprinkle gelatin over cold water in blender container; allow to stand while assembling other ingredients. Add boiling water; cover and process at high speed until orange is finely chopped. Stop blender and add cranberries. Cover and process until cranberries are finely chopped. Turn into 4-cup mold or individual molds. Chill until firm.

Right across from the site of the old Union Station on Ninth Street is the Read House. This was built on the site of the old Crutchfield House which had been one of the early hotels. The Read House with its beautiful panelled lobby and elegant Green Room has been the scene of many dinners and parties, or just a lunch or dinner in town with a friend. Its fine food is a tradition.

READ HOUSE CRANBERRY SALAD

1 package strawberry gelatin
1 tablespoon gelatin
   unflavored
1 cup hot water
1 tablespoon lemon juice

2 cans whole cranberries
¼ cup pecans
½ cup celery, chopped
½ orange,
   chopped or ground

Heat the cranberry sauce. Dissolve the strawberry gelatin in the hot water and add to the sauce. Soften the plain gelatin in the lemon juice and a tiny bit of water. When soft add to the sauce. Add the other ingredients. Mold in individual molds. Serve with homemade mayonnaise.

John Barnes

One day we went up to Sewanee and had lunch with our friend, Marie Woods (Mrs. Cecil). In her pretty dining room looking out over the distant view of the valley below, we had a summer salad that I have used many times since.

174

On a piece of Holland rusk was a slice of ham, a slice of white meat of chicken, a tomato, a hard-boiled egg stuffed with egg yolk and anchovy paste, and over all a Russian dressing topped with caviar. You really don't need another thing, but she had fresh asparagus to complement it, rolls, coffee in her green Rockingham cups, and meringue filled with peaches for dessert. Here is how you build the salad.

SEWANEE CHICKEN AND HAM SALAD

For each person, arrange on a plate crisp lettuce. On it place a round of Holland rusk with a slice of ham and a slice of chicken or turkey. Peel a small tomato or use half a large one, slicing a little off the top and bottom to make it level so it will stay on the chicken. Have hard-boiled eggs ready. When mixing the yolks to stuff, mix with a little mayonnaise, mustard, and anchovy paste. This depends on your guests and whether you think they would like anchovy paste. Turn the stuffed egg half upside down on top of the tomato.

Now make a Russian dressing. Use 1 cup of mayonnaise, ½ cup chili sauce, the juice of half a lemon, Worcestershire sauce and celery salt to taste. Pour some dressing over each salad. Then top with some red caviar.

Now garnish the base of the salad with some parsley, olives, artichoke hearts, or whatever you like to use.

Mrs. Cecil Woods, Jr.

MRS. LUPTON'S TOMATO AND CAVIAR SALAD

For each serving, trim a slice of bread into a circle. Either toast it or saute it, which keeps it crisp longer. Spread this with mayonnaise, and top with half a peeled ripe tomato seasoned with Lawry's seasoned salt. On top of the tomato, spread a generous dollop of cream cheese dressing. This is made from softened cream cheese mixed with a little mayonnaise, onion juice, and whatever you feel inspired to get off your spice rack and shake into it. The dressing should be soft but rather thick. Top each salad with a final garnish of red caviar. Serve on a bed of lettuce. This is especially pretty when served on a pink tablecloth and china with a pink or red color scheme.

Mrs. Allen Lupton

Signal Mountain was used during the Civil War as a point from which signals were sent by Federal soldiers observing shipments up and down the Tennessee River. It was one of Chattanooga's greatest promoters who began its development in the 1880's.

Charles E. James planned to use the Chattanooga Western Railroad to bring coal and iron from Walden's Ridge to the furnaces in town. He also planned a community on the spur of the Ridge called Signal Point City. The project was unfinished, but 30 years later Mr. James did get a street car line built up Signal Mountain, and it began to develop. He would be amazed at his own vision today, because about 10,000 people now live on the mountain top. It is both flatter and larger than Lookout, and one of the fast-growing suburbs.

Several years ago Mrs. Claude Givens of the Signal Mountain Garden Club had the idea of planting dogwoods, which are natural to the mountains, along the streets, in the yards, and wherever anyone would plant them. In April when the dogwoods bloom, Signal Mountain has a festival; homes and gardens are open; and the whole city comes up to enjoy the lacy white grandeur that masses of dogwoods in bloom make. There are special teas and sometimes luncheons. If Signal Mountain people are going to plan a party in the spring, they usually do it to coincide with the dogwoods.

Mrs. Gordon Smith, whose garden is sometimes on tour, makes a dill tomato aspic that would be good with any sort of chicken dish.

TOMATO DILL ASPIC WITH ARTICHOKE HEARTS

Soften 3 envelopes unflavored gelatin in ½ cup tomato juice. Meanwhile, heat together 5 cups plus 2 tablespoons tomato juice, ½ cup lemon juice, 1 tablespoon grated onion, 1 clove crushed garlic, ½ teaspoon dried dill and 2 teaspoons salt, a pinch basil, a pinch oregano, and 1 bay leaf, crushed. (You can adjust these herbs to suit yourself.) Simmer all together for 10 minutes, stirring occasionally. Season to taste. Remove from heat and strain hot tomato juice through cheese cloth.

Add softened gelatin to the hot juice and stir until dissolved. Cool. Drain 1 can artichoke hearts and slice the hearts in half. In the bottom of 2-quart ring mold, arrange a design of the hearts. To seal in the design carefully, add enough of the tomato mixture to measure about ¼ inch deep in the bottom of the mold and chill until the gelatin is thickened but not firm. Add remaining artichoke hearts and tomato juice mixture and chill until firm. Unmold and garnish with crisp greens. Serve with caviar mayonnaise.

CAVIAR MAYONNAISE

Mix well together 1 cup each of mayonnaise and sour cream, 1 tablespoon lemon juice (add a little more if you like a tart dressing), and 2 teaspoons prepared mustard. Fold in the contents of a 1-ounce jar of black caviar.

Mrs. Gordon Smith

The easiest tomato aspic is made with V-8 juice. This needs only some Tabasco and some lemon juice along with gelatin, to make a tart tomato mold to serve with tuna fish, crabmeat, or just plain with home-made mayonnaise.

V-8 TOMATO ASPIC

2 cups V-8 juice	1 teaspoon lemon juice
⅛ teaspoon Tabasco	1 envelope unflavored gelatin

Save ½ cup of the vegetable juice to dissolve the gelatin in. Heat the remaining juice and add the Tabasco and lemon. Add the gelatin and stir well. Taste to see that the seasoning is correct. Pour into individual molds. This makes 5 or 6 individual molds.

This frozen salad is one that Mac Brock (Mrs. Richard) brought back from Arizona to Chattanooga.

MAC'S FROZEN SALAD

1 cup crushed pineapple	1 cup chopped celery
1 cup chopped cabbage	1 cup mayonnaise
1 cup whipped cream	1 teaspoon lemon juice

Freeze the above mixture and serve on top of a thick slice of tomato with the fruit dressing below.

FRUIT DRESSING

1 cup oil	1 teaspoon dry mustard
¼ cup vinegar	1 teaspoon paprika
1 teaspoon salt	1 teaspoon grated onion
1 teaspoon celery salt	½ cup sugar

Add 1 teaspoon oil to combined dry ingredients and beat in mixer slowly for a minute. Add vinegar and oil alternately until used up.

Mrs. Richard Brock

When the Federal army began to press down on Chattanooga midway through the Civil War in 1863, the Confederates were afraid their supply line to Atlanta would be cut off. They pulled out of Chattanooga without a battle.

The Union army followed and they bumped into each other in the woods at Chickamauga. This was a small rural community. There was the Lee and Gordon Mill on the creek, and a Mrs. Thedford had a house nearby. When the fighting began, it lasted two days and was the bloodiest in the history of all warfare, with 35,000 killed and wounded in 48 hours. The Confederates won and the Union army retreated into Chattanooga.

The Confederates got on the ridges and mountains to besiege them, and General Grant was sent in to command the Union forces. He got reinforcements and first fought the soldiers in the mountains with the Battle Above the Clouds. The Confederates were pushed off Lookout, and Grant then concentrated on Missionary Ridge. When this fell, Sherman marched through southward from the end of the Ridge and began his march to Atlanta and down through Georgia to the sea.

General D. H. Hill said that day, "Chattanooga sealed the fate of the Confederacy."

The best way to understand what happened here during the Civil War is to visit Confederama. My brother-in-law, Lee Anderson, has been interested in the history of this war since he was a young boy and hunting Minie balls in Chickamauga Park and on Missionary Ridge.

Several years ago he planned a miniature layout of the Chattanooga area, showing Chickamauga Creek, the Tennessee River, the various mountains, the ridge. He and Pendell Meyers ordered miniature soldiers in gray and in blue, set up a series of lights to indicate where the action took place, and wrote a narrative. This is the way Confederama became a tourist attraction to emphasize the historical aspect of Chattanooga.

This 30 minute narration and re-enactment of the battle with tiny guns that smoke as they are shot, made me understand for the first time our Civil War history and also the geography of this region. It is located at the foot of Lookout Mountain and is seen by thousands of tourists and school groups each year.

Today Chickamauga is the pleasant town just to the south of Chickamauga Park. You can drive through the park any day and see all the markers, the monuments to the brave men on both sides, the museum, the well-kept green planting with big pines, maples, oaks. There are many cannon so heavy and awkward that you wonder how they were carried across mountains and ridges.

There is a peace about this place. One day I took the children for a picnic there, and we unpacked our lunch beneath the big trees. I told them about the battle and it was said that the creek had run red for days afterward.

As we packed up to leave, Susan's friend, Anne Glascock, said, "Hand me that last paper cup to put in the sack. It wouldn't be right to leave trash in a holy place." We all felt the same way. Chickamauga Park is a beautiful place that has seen enough suffering and fighting to command respect and honor.

Chickamauga, Georgia, just south of the park is a thriving community. Just across the state line, you get the feeling immediately that you are in Georgia. The people are immediately soft spoken, they have the graceful way of sounding "r's" at the end of words the way Atlanta people do. They entertain often in their homes and churches, have fried chicken, roast beef, fresh vegetables, pie, cakes, homemade ice cream in the bountiful Georgia way that has always made Chickamauga a favorite place for Chattanoogans to visit. This is the land of the Bowens, Jewells, Callaways, McMillans, Andrews and others.

Vera Jewell (Mrs. Ashley) got a recipe for chicken mousse years ago from the Frances Virginia Tearoom in Atlanta. This was a lovely old-fashioned tearoom on Peachtree near Five Points, and people used to go there when they went to Atlanta to shop.

CHICKEN MOUSSE

2 tablespoons plain gelatin

1 cup chicken stock

1½ pound chicken, cooked
  and minced

1 cup chopped blanched almonds

2 cups finely chopped celery

2 cups green peas

5 tablespoons sweet pickle relish

4 hard boiled eggs, chopped

1 cup mayonnaise

1 teaspoon salt

1½ teaspoons white pepper

Dash red pepper

Juice of 2 lemons

1 cup whipping cream,
  whipped

Heat the chicken stock. Dissolve the gelatin in it. Combine the chicken, almonds, celery, peas, relish, eggs, mayonnaise, and salt and peppers. Add gelatin and lemon juice. Fold in the whipped cream and spoon into molds. Chill until firm. Yields 12 servings.

Mrs. Ashley Jewell

The party giver in our family is my aunt, Kitty McDonald. She manages to bring together this group and that, usually at her house on the lake in the summertime, and with a magic blend of good food, lots of things to do, comfortable chairs and hammocks, and a well-chosen guest list, everyone has a wonderful time.

She usually has a Sunday crowd of 20 to 30 and plans either fried chicken or ham, vegetables from the garden and a couple of salads. Kitty knows all the shortcuts and when to use them. She makes gallons and gallons of lemonade, but confided that it was Wyler's lemonade mix, served in tall clear glass pitchers with thin slices of real fresh lemons floating in it. She says people drink more this way when they can see the lemon slices than when it is served in crocks.

Two salad recipes follow, but I can't guarantee that you or I could use them and give a Kitty party. Kitty's conscience and mind are stirred with the impulse to invite some people up when other people would dismiss such a wild thought as too much trouble. She and Estella Bolder, her chief helpmate, have presided over many a gathering with success.

KITTY'S KIDNEY BEAN SALAD

2 (1-pound) cans kidney beans	8 scallions chopped fine
1 cup diced peeled cucumber	½ teaspoon salt
1 cup diced celery	⅛ teaspoon pepper
½ cup minced green pepper	¼ cup mayonnaise

Drain the beans. Add the cucumber, celery, green pepper, and scallions. Season with the salt and pepper. Add just enough mayonnaise to make it a good juicy consistency. Blend well and adjust seasoning. Kitty adds a teaspoon or two of sweet pickle juice. This is better made about a day ahead.

KITTY'S COLE SLAW

1 small head cabbage, grated fine	Dressing:
1 scallion, minced fine	½ cup mayonnaise
1 carrot, grated	¼ teaspoon salt to taste
½ green pepper, minced fine	1 teaspoon sugar
1 rib celery, minced fine	2 tablespoons cream
	1 teaspoon vinegar

Taste, and if not sweet enough for teenagers, add a teaspoon or two of sweet pickle juice.

Miss Kitty McDonald

Apricot Cheese Delight was a specialty brought by Margaret Hobday to a Pilot Club supper. It is a congealed fruit salad frosted with its whipped cream dressing.

APRICOT CHEESE DELIGHT

1 large can apricots
1 large can crushed pineapple
2 packages orange gelatin

2 cups hot water
1 cup miniature marshmallows

Drain fruits, reserving juices. Chop apricots. Chill fruits. Dissolve gelatin in hot water; add 1 cup of reserved juices. Chill until mixture begins to jell. Fold in fruits and marshmallows. Pour into large pan. Chill until firm.

TOPPING

½ cup sugar
3 tablespoons flour
1 egg, slightly beaten
1 cup apricot and pineapple juice

2 tablespoons butter
1 cup whipped cream
¾ cup grated cheese

Combine sugar, flour and egg. Add juices. Cook until thick, stirring constantly. Remove from heat, add butter. Cool and fold in whipped cream. Spread over congealed salad; sprinkle cheese over top. Serves 24.

Miss Margaret Hobday

A simple molded cucumber salad is a great boon to have in the refrigerator when you are trying to think of something different to have for lunch. This one is made with sour cream.

MOLDED CUCUMBER SALAD

1 package lime gelatin
¾ cup hot water
¼ cup lemon juice
1 teaspoon onion juice

1 cup sour cream,
   whipped smooth
1 cup chopped cucumber

Dissolve gelatin in hot water and add lemon and onion juices. Chill until thick. Fold in cucumber and sour cream. Taste for seasoning... you may want to add Worcestershire sauce or Tabasco. Pour in individual molds and chill until firm. Garnish with tomato wedges and ripe olives on lettuce.

When it comes to mayonnaise, we probably have all bought jars at the store numerous times, but we know that the only great mayonnaise is the kind you make yourself. Several years ago Frenchie Hagan (Mrs. William III) taught me how to make the most amazing mayonnaise I have heard of before or since.

It takes about two minutes, it always turns out well. She puts up with no such nonsense as adding the oil drop by drop...she pours in a whole glob at a time, and when it is blended, she adds another helping. In no time she has a beautiful heap of yellow mayonnaise flavored with lemon juice and cayenne pepper.

This method is easy. You beat a whole egg until it is light, add seasoning, add blobs of oil until thick and then add the juice of a lemon. This has never failed for anyone. When Susan was three, she was sitting on the kitchen counter as usual when I needed to make mayonnaise. "Please let me do it this time," she begged.

"Well, I'd better break the egg for you," I said.

"No, I can do that, too," she insisted. So while I did the dishes, she broke an egg in a cup (and fished out two or three pieces of shell), then put the egg in a mixing bowl. I added a teaspoon of salt, some cayenne pepper, and a little white pepper. She turned the mixer on, of course, and let it beat a minute or two until it was light.

She added the oil, a little at a time usually, and once a lot at a time. When it really did begin to thicken, she was beside herself with the same sort of giggling that used to break out when she sewed a stitch with a needle. Discovering how to make things work is a great thing for your confidence.

After all the oil was in, I squeezed the juice of a lemon and would have added it if she hadn't been determined to do it herself. We both tasted it and we needed a little more salt, but the texture was fine. From that day on Susan has been our mayonnaise maker, for picnics, for parties, or just when she is in the mood. For some curious reason, her emulsion is better than mine, the texture is nicer, not stiff, but with just the right body. If a 3-year-old can make this mayonnaise, anyone can!

FRENCHIE'S 2 MINUTE MAYONNAISE

1 whole egg	*Juice of 1 lemon*
Salt, cayenne pepper,	*Salad oil (about 1 to 1½ cups)*
white pepper, paprika	

Put 1 whole egg into the small bowl of an electric mixer. Put the seasonings in on top of it. Start with about ½ teaspoon salt, and a good dash of white pepper and red cayenne pepper. I use Tabasco if I don't have cayenne pepper. Follow with a dash of paprika.

Now turn the mixer on high speed and beat the seasoning into the egg. Add the first spurt of oil, and you don't have to be especially careful. Beat until it is absorbed. Then add another spurt. Continue this until the mayonnaise gets thick. It may take more oil...I have used 2 cups sometimes. When it is nice and thick, get out a lemon and add the juice of it.

The main thing is to taste it. You want it to be thick enough to hold its shape, and to taste salty enough with a nice lemon tang to cut the taste of oil.

Mrs. William Hagan III

One of the favorite salads at the Winborn Willinghams is one that they call Addie May's salad. It is lettuce pulled apart in chunks with a Roquefort dressing, and sometimes Mary brings this to Wednesday night church suppers.

The Willinghams live in a big sprawling house in Summertown, winterized so they can live up there all year round. Mary loves company, and the house is almost always full of either children's friends, their friends, foreign visitors, or visiting missionaries. They are a hospitable family who with their various family connections of Sharps, Poindexters, Strangs, and Powells typify the spirit of Summertown.

ADDIE MAE'S SALAD

1 teaspoon dry mustard	1 tablespoon sugar
Paprika	1 tablespoon lemon juice
1 teaspoon salt	1 tablespoon olive oil

Beat all this smooth with a wire whisk. Add 2 tablespoons olive oil, and 2 tablespoons lemon juice and beat with a wire whisk. Add 3 more tablespoons oil and 2 tablespoons vinegar and add slowly. Continue to beat until thick. Add 2 buds garlic, cut in half, 2 hard-boiled eggs, chopped, and 1 large package Roquefort cheese, mashed. Mix all these ingredients in the dressing.

Pull lettuce apart in chunks, not leaf by leaf. Use different kinds of lettuce when you can get it. Pour the dressing over the lettuce and crumble bacon on it.

Addie May Lillard

TOWN AND COUNTRY BLUE CHEESE DRESSING

4 ounces Blue Cheese
1 tablespoon bell pepper,
  chopped very fine

1 tablespoon chopped onion
½ cup tarragon vinegar
3 cups mayonnaise

Mash the cheese and add mayonnaise. Add onion and pepper, and vinegar and blend in a mixer. Season to taste with Tabasco.

Town and Country Restaurant

A Roquefort cheese dressing was a specialty at the old Beef and Liberty Restaurant.

ROQUEFORT DRESSING

½ pound Roquefort cheese,
  crumbled
1 tablespoon lemon juice

1 cup mayonnaise
1 cup sour cream

Mix all these ingredients. Refrigerate. This keeps very well.

Some like a cucumber and cream cheese dressing to serve on tomato salads and tomato aspics. This is especially pretty, because the skin is left on the cucumber and grated, making pretty green touches in the creamy dressing. This is Mrs. W.J. Hagan, Jr.'s and is as elegant as it is simple.

CUCUMBER CREAM CHEESE DRESSING

1 package cream cheese
  (8 ounces)
1 cucumber

Lemon juice
Salt and Tabasco

Let the cream cheese get to room temperature. Then beat it very well indeed so it is creamy. Wash the cucumber well, since you are going to use rind and all. Grate the cucumber into the cream cheese. Add salt to taste, as well as Tabasco. Then add lemon juice until you get the right consistency for a dressing. You can add all sorts of seasonings, but this seems best when seasoned very simply with the things mentioned. Serve on any vegetable salad, but this is usually good with tomatoes.

Mrs. W.J. Hagan, Jr.

Kay Gray (Mrs. John D.) is famous for her salads. She uses this version of the famous San Francisco Green Goddess Dressing over Bibb lettuce and avocados.

GREEN GODDESS DRESSING

1 cup mayonnaise
3 tablespoons finely
    chopped anchovies
3 tablespoons chopped chive
    or green onions
1 clove garlic, grated

1 tablespoon lemon juice
3 tablespoons tarragon
    wine vinegar
⅛ cup chopped parsley
Salt and freshly ground pepper
½ cup whipping cream

Mix all ingredients. This may be made in a blender.

Mrs. John D. Gray

One good dressing to pour over a simple fruit salad is poppy seed dressing. This is especially good on avacado and grapefruit in the winter time.

POPPY SEED DRESSING

½ cup sugar
¼ cup honey
1 teaspoon onion
6 tablespoons vinegar
3 tablespoons lemon juice

1 cup salad oil
1 teaspoon dry mustard
1 teaspoon paprika
¼ teaspoon salt
2 teaspoons poppy seed

Mix the dry ingredients. Add honey, onion, vinegar and lemon juice. Pour oil in very slowly, beating constantly and continue to beat for a few minutes. Add the poppy seed last. This is best made in an electric mixer and should be very thick. It keeps well in the refrigerator.

CHAPTER X

Breads

If I were trying to think of one cooking principle that would raise the standard of living more than anything else and actually save you money, I would vote for hot homemade bread. Hot bread has always been a specialty in the South and in Chattanooga. With a little corn-meal or flour, a good cook can quickly make enough tender flaky biscuits, fry delicate but hearty hoecakes, turn out piping hot cornbread muffins or cornsticks, and given just a little more time, can make rolls that melt in your mouth.

These traditional breads have been made here regularly ever since Mrs. Henderson opened the first boarding house on Second Street just up from the river landing. It was also the first house in Chattanooga. (Chattanooga was called Ross' Landing until 1838.) Good hot bread can be found from the lowliest little house to the finest mansion, depending entirely on the cook. It is the best meal stretcher in the world.

Yet times are changing. Southern cooking, just like French cooking, takes time. Chattanooga, just like the rest of the country, has found out that frozen breads, brown and serve breads, sliced French bread from the bakery, and just a package of bakery rolls are both quick and good.

I, who love to bake, sometimes do just as my friends do and buy some bread for dinner. Although I do it when I'm in a hurry, I do know that homemade hot bread adds a quality to a meal that bought bread doesn't. Sometimes I wonder if it is a fact or if it is just in my mind that there is a warm family unity and spirit around the table when I plan a dinner complete with biscuits or hoecakes or cornbread or rolls. I do know that hot bread from the oven adds much pleasure and is worth every bit of effort.

Probably the wisest way is to know how to cook both ways...from scratch and from all the convenience foods developed by the modern world. The following bread recipes I can promise will add much to the meals you serve them with, as well as promoting a warm and happy spirit to the satisfied diners.

186

In the old days everyone had to have their wheat and corn ground at a mill before making bread. Ketner's Mill is the last active mill on the Sequatchie River.

Sequatchie Valley lies between high mountains, Waldens Ridge on the east and the Cumberlands on the west, and on a spring day if you drive over the Ridge and look down into the lovely green valley, you really have to catch your breath, because not even Ireland could be as fresh and green and lovely. The Sequatchie River runs for seventy miles down the valley which is almost 4 miles wide the whole way.

My father's mother grew up in the valley where her family operated a mill on the Sequatchie River. Ketner's Mill is the last mill still in operation on the river, and family reunions there were great events when we were children. It is now run by third-generation Ketners, Paul and Clyde. My father's memories of the mill all concern the two-story brick front, all handmade on the place from a hill of clay in the 1870s. He can remember my grandmother telling how she helped tend the brick kiln fires as a small girl along with her brothers and sisters. The mill wheels were from France, having quite a trip before they reached the valley.

The mill ground corn and wheat, and also carded wool for several years. All the women of the family placed great importance on whole wheat flour and made Graham biscuits, called for a Dr. Graham who was a great nutrition expert of the day.

I remember very little about how the mill worked. My memories all had to do with the wonderful river, about as wide as a very wide creek and quite clear and green. We played by the side of the creek and made mud lollies with our toes in the fresh mud while we waited our turn to go out in a boat that you could paddle. Every summer when the water was low, the dam had to be repaired, and as to how bad the dam was leaking and the best way to fix it were annual conversations.

Now that I am older, I know how hard it is to find good water-ground flour and meal. Whole wheat bread and biscuits have a rich nutty flavor that beg to be drenched with real butter. Our grandmothers knew that good bread really is the staff of life. Sometimes we have Graham biscuits or whole wheat biscuits and think of these days.

WHOLE WHEAT BISCUITS

2 cups whole wheat flour	2 teaspoons baking powder
1 teaspoon salt	½ teaspoon soda
1 teaspoon sugar	¼ cup shortening
1 cup buttermilk	

Sift flour, sugar, salt, baking powder together. Add soda to the buttermilk and stir into a dough. Turn out dough on a floured board and knead for a minute. Roll out the dough to about ½ inch thickness and cut individual biscuits. Bake in baking pan at 450 degrees for about 10 minutes. Butter immediately.

Measuring flour and mixing bread at the last minute is never easy, so we usually keep on hand a mixture of self-rising flour and shortening. This is the most fool-proof ready mix there is, and it makes biscuits, cornbread, plain muffins, pancakes and waffles, depending on what you add to it. Once I made up some for a schoolteacher, who lived alone, with the directions for one biscuit (a tablespoon of mix moistened with just enough milk to form a nice ball of dough for a biscuit).

Just remember that there is exactly enough baking powder, salt and shortening for the flour. Wet it with milk or buttermilk for biscuits. For muffins, add an egg and a little more milk to make a batter. For pancakes do exactly the same thing but make the batter thinner like a pancake batter. For cornbread use an equal amount of cornmeal and mix, with egg and milk to make a nice batter. It's quick, foolproof and you don't have to measure.

EASY READY-MIX

2 pound package self-rising
flour (about 8 cups)

1½ cups shortening

Cut the shortening into the flour. Now you have a mixture of flour, salt, baking powder and shortening. You can make anything that calls for these ingredients. This does not need to be refrigerated. Just keep in canister. It has a more homemade taste than bought biscuit mix. Bread made with this mix is very economical.

HOMEMADE BISCUITS FROM READY-MIX

2 cups mix

½ cup milk, about

Put the mix in a bowl. Pour in milk and stir with a fork (not a spoon) until the batter forms and makes a sort of ball. With practice you can tell how much milk you will need and will not have to measure anything...just dump in the amount of mix you will need and moisten with milk. You can use buttermilk, but if you do, add ½ teaspoon soda.

Buy a pastry cloth at a department store or Sears. Keep it floured and rolled up in a drawer, and use over and over again so you will never have flour messes to clean up. Turn your dough out onto the floured cloth, and knead six or eight times. Roll out biscuits, cut them, put away cloth until next time, and bake biscuits at 450 degrees about 10 minutes. Butter in the kitchen while hot.

CORNBREAD FROM READY-MIX

1 cup ready-mix
½ teaspoon soda
1 to 1½ cups buttermilk

1 cup cornmeal
2 eggs

Beat the eggs and add buttermilk. Now add the ready mix, corn-meal and soda. This is all a matter of the right consistency. It takes a soupy batter to make light cornbread.

Get out either an iron skillet, muffin pans, or cornstick pans and grease very generously indeed with shortening. Heat in oven. When hot, pour in the batter about two-thirds full. Bake in a 425-degree oven for 20 to 30 minutes.

BREAKFAST PANCAKES WITH READY-MIX

1½ cups ready-mix   1 egg
¾ cup milk

In a bowl, mix the egg and milk. Now add enough of the mix to make a good pourable pancake batter. You will know whether your family likes thick or thin pancakes. Drop the pancakes on a hot griddle or electric skillet and bake on either side until golden brown. We always turn the first brown side up and put a square of butter on it while the underneath side is browning. This makes them good and buttery.

Swedish pancakes are different from any other kind. They are soft inside like custard, very tender and delicious, and really better with raspberry or strawberry preserves than with syrup. The only thing is, they must be mixed up the night before to mellow in the refrigerator. The next morning they are ready for making in the electric skillet.

SWEDISH PANCAKES

1 cup flour   ¼ teaspoon salt
2 tablespoons sugar   3 whole eggs,
3 cups milk   beaten well

Mix flour, salt and sugar into the eggs; then add the milk. Stir with a wire whisk. It should be as thin as cream. These must sit in the refrigerator to mellow for 6 to 12 hours. Fry on top of stove at second heat or in an electric skillet. Use small amount of oil to grease the grill.

My mother makes the best cornbread I know. It is as light as a feather, and we put generous squares of real butter in the middle of the steaming bread as soon as it is served. This is the way she makes it:

190

MOTHER'S CORNBREAD

1 cup meal	1 teaspoon salt
1 cup flour	2 eggs
3 teaspoons baking powder	1½ cups buttermilk
¼ teaspoon soda	½ cup shortening

Beat eggs and pour in the buttermilk. Sift the dry ingredients and add them. The batter will be rather thin, and this is right because it takes a thin batter to make light, tender bread. In an iron skillet or square cake pan, heat the ½ cup of shortening. This greases the pan. Pour the shortening into the batter, mix well, and pour into the pan to bake. Bake in a hot 450-degree oven for 20 or 25 minutes.

Mrs. Roy McDonald.

Mrs. W.D. Pettway brought back a new recipe from a visit to Jackson, Tenn. It is a corn light bread. It isn't an anadama bread because it has no yeast in it. It is just cornmeal, flour, a little baking powder and soda, blended with buttermilk and shortening and baked an hour in a loaf pan. You slice it like bread while hot and butter it.

CORN LIGHT BREAD

2 cups white corn meal	1 teaspoon salt
½ cup flour	1 teaspoon baking powder
¾ cup sugar (I used just ¼ cup)	½ teaspoon soda
2 cups buttermilk	2 tablespoons shortening

Sift the dry ingredients. Put the shortening in a loaf pan and set in a 350 oven to melt. Now pour the buttermilk into the meal and flour mixture. At the last add the shortening. I use butter. Make sure that the loaf pan is very well greased, because this tends to stick. The new teflon pans are nice for something like this.

Bake for one hour and turn out on a bread board. Slice in medium thick slices with plenty of butter.

Mrs. W.D. Pettway.

The true Southern specialty that has never received proper recognition is the hoecake. A mixture of meal and water, it used to be shaped into pones and baked on a hoe over a fire on the early days when people worked in the fields.

It is made best by any of our fine Negro cooks who fry the small cakes in a little hot shortening in a heavy iron skillet. These are thicker than pancakes, buttered while hot, and when fried properly, are light as a feather. They are best with soup, hash, stew, fried fish, or fried chicken. Some people make a thin batter and have them for breakfast.

They fit simple family meals and are not considered fine enough for company, which explains why they are relatively unknown except to homefolk. But children who grow up on hoecakes will remember them as the fabulous specialty that they are.

SOUTHERN HOECAKES

Put a pan of water on to boil vigorously. Sift the amount of plain white corn meal that you will need (2 or 3 cups) along with a teaspoon of salt, in a good-sized bowl. When the water boils, begin pouring it into the meal. It takes more water than you think, because the meal absorbs a lot. Stir and keep adding boiling water until you have a mushy batter, not too stiff, not even holding its shape. We use a wire whisk to stir it smooth.

Let the batter stand for a minute or two while you heat fresh shortening in a heavy iron skillet. We start with ½ inch of shortening melted. When the shortening is hot (but never let it smoke), spoon about 4 of 5 hoecakes in the skillet with a kitchen spoon. Let brown on one side with the heat pretty hot. Now turn the cakes over with a pancake turner to brown on the other side. In a minute or two you will need to turn down the heat a little.

If you leave the shortening on at high heat the whole time, the cakes will be brown on the outside and mushy in the middle. After you turn down, fry at a pokey speed until the second side is brown. Now turn the heat up again. This is the principle. When golden on both sides, drain on a paper towel on top of the stove and butter with a pat of butter on top of each while hot. Keep warm while the next ones are frying.

Absolutely the fastest bread when it comes to mixing time, and the most spectacular when it comes to the table is one that is made in a blender. No talent is required...just this recipe for Sky-high Blender Popovers. They have never failed to pop.

SKY-HIGH BLENDER POPOVERS

2 eggs	1 cup sifted all-purpose flour
1 cup milk	¼ teaspoon salt

Preheat oven to 450 degrees. Place eggs and milk in blender. Cover and turn to high speed until frothy. Stop motor. Add flour and salt and blend again until smooth. Pour batter in muffin pans or custard cups that have been very well greased. You don't have to preheat the pans. Bake in a 450-degree oven for 20 minutes. Reduce heat to 350 degrees and bake 10 to 15 minutes longer. This makes 8 to 10 popovers.

Whenever we have a roast or sometimes when we have fried chicken, our favorite bread is spoon bread. This is a Virginia delicacy...just cornmeal, milk, eggs and butter. It rises like a souffle and some recipes call for more eggs than others.

Have you noticed that the richest recipes are the hardest to make? They rise beautifully and fall before you get them to the table. We tried dozens of recipes before we settled on the one we now use. It is quick to put together, not too rich; it rises and falls just the tiniest bit. The children like it so much they scrape the last bit of crust from the casserole it is served in, and there is never a crumb left.

If you have never seen spoon bread served, it is brought to the table in a Pyrex casserole, or we use a white souffle dish, and put alongside the meat and vegetables for the head of the house to serve. He serves it with a tablespoon onto the plate and puts a dab of butter in it. Sometimes the boys want roast beef gravy on theirs. This is a fool-proof recipe. Everyone who tries it has good luck.

VIRGINIA SPOON BREAD

½ cup white cornmeal	2 cups milk
1 tablespoon of butter . . .	3 eggs, separated
no substitute	1 teaspoon salt

Heat milk in saucepan to scalding. Add cornmeal gradually to prevent lumping. Add butter and salt. Stir until butter is melted. Cook over moderate heat, stirring constantly until thickened.

Beat egg yolks until light. Add small amount of the hot mixture to egg yolks. Mix well. Combine both mixtures. Beat egg white stiff and fold into cornmeal mixture. Pour into well-buttered 1-quart baking dish. Bake at 350 or 375 degrees for about 45 or 50 minutes. Serve in dish in which it was baked. Serves 4.

On a trip to Williamsburg we were served hot Sally Lunn. At the King's Arms Tavern, the waiters were all in costume, the lighting was all by candles, we had huge yard-square napkins on our laps and the food was bountiful. Our waiter brought hot, fresh Sally Lunn just turned out of a Turk's head mold and sliced. It was a cross between cake and regular yeast bread...just delicious.

After we got home, I tried the recipe. It is very easy, requires no kneading. The only thing is you have to think about it 2½ hours before dinner. Make this one afternoon when you are going to be home and not in a hurry.

WILLIAMSBURG SALLY LUNN

Put 1 yeast cake in 1 cup warm milk. Cream together 3 tablespoons shortening and 3 tablespoons sugar. Add 2 eggs and mix well. Sift together 3 and one-third cups flour and 1¼ teaspoons salt. Add this alternately with the milk. Beat well.

Cover the bowl with a moist towel and let rise in a warm place about one hour. Turn out on floured board and knead lightly. Put into a well-greased Sally Lunn mold or an angel food 10-inch tube pan. Let stand and rise again until double. Bake in a slow 300-degree oven for an hour.

At a food editors' conference years ago, we got the recipe for cranberry muffins. They were beautiful, light muffins with the red, sweet cranberries in every bite. These are wonderful for luncheons and family dinners, especially with chicken.

CRANBERRY MUFFINS

1 cup fresh cranberries, halved or chopped	1 tablespoon baking powder
	1 teaspoon vanilla
¼ cup sugar	½ teaspoon salt
2 cups flour	1-3 cup margarine
1-3 cup sugar	1 egg, beaten
¾ cup milk	

Combine the cranberries and the ¼-cup sugar. Sift together the flour, one-third sugar, baking powder and salt. Cut in the shortening until the mixture resembles coarse crumbs. Add the combined eggs, milk and vanilla. Stir just until the ingredients are blended. Fold in the cranberry mixture. Fill greased muffin pans two-thirds full. Bake in a hot oven, 400 degrees, for 15 to 20 minutes.

Miss Dorothy Holland, Kraft Kitchens

The extra light biscuits using yeast as well as baking powder took Chattanooga by storm several years ago. This recipe comes from Kathryn V. Wallace.

ANGEL YEAST BISCUITS

1 cup buttermilk	1 teaspoon salt
½ teaspoon soda	1 tablespoon sugar
1 yeast cake	4 tablespoons shortening
1 teaspoon baking powder	2½ cups flour

Sift flour, baking powder, sugar and salt together. Cut shortening into above mixture. Dissolve soda and yeast cake into buttermilk (have buttermilk at room temperature). Stir into flour mixture to make a soft dough. Use more or less flour at end of mixing as needed on dough board. Roll dough thin and cut with small cutter. Stack two together with smaller one on top, brushing between and on top with melted butter. Place on biscuit pan and let rise 1 hour or as needed, depending on temperature of room. Bake in oven 450 degrees.

Miss Kathryn V. Wallace

Every cook has a favorite recipe for hot yeast rolls. Rolls are served at fancy ladies luncheons and garden clubs, for family dinners on Sunday, for out-of-town company and when the children come home from being away at school. Refrigerator rolls are a big advantage because the work can be done ahead and the rolls themselves shaped about an hour before dinner. This is the late Mrs. Richard Fowler's recipe made with mashed potatoes, and one of the best I know:

REFRIGERATOR ROLLS

1 cake or package of yeast,	Flour to make a dough
dissolved in ¼ cup	(4 sifted or more)
warm water	1 cup mashed potatoes
2-3 cup butter	1 cup scalded milk
½ cup sugar	2 eggs, well beaten
1 teaspoon salt	

Melt the butter and add to the scalded milk. Next add the sugar and salt and let cool to lukewarm. Add beaten eggs, potatoes, yeast and flour. You have added almost enough flour when it is hard to stir and you have to turn it out on a board and knead it with your hands. Add flour until the dough will not stick to the board, and knead until it is smooth and elastic. This may be put in a bowl to rise or stored in the refrigerator for future use. If it is to be used at once, let the dough rise in a bowl until double in bulk. Roll out and shape the rolls, place on a baking sheet and let rise again until light. Bake at 400 degrees until nicely brown.

If you have never tried rolls, be sure to try these. I have never tasted a bad yeast roll. They are hot, and even if you make every mistake, work in too much flour so they have a tough crust, let them rise too long, your family will still think they are delicious.

Mrs. Hugh Maclellan

Mary Gaither gave me the recipe for her mother's rolls that have apricot centers.

MRS. FOWLER'S APRICOT ROLLS

2 cups scalded milk	¼ cup lukewarm water
½ cup sugar	1 teaspoon sugar
2 teaspoons salt	2 well beaten eggs
½ stick butter	4 cups flour
2 cakes yeast	

Cool the scalded milk, sugar and salt together until lukewarm. Dissolve the yeast in the lukewarm water with the teaspoon of sugar, let it stand a few minutes and add to the milk. Add 2 well-beaten eggs. Now add the flour and beat well. Add enough more flour to make a dough that will not be necessary to knead. At this stage the dough may be covered with melted butter and put in a tightly covered receptacle in the refrigerator.

When you take it out to make rolls, allow to rise until double in bulk, and then make in rolls.

To make apricot rolls, cut out with a large round cutter (the size of the top of a 1-pound baking powder can . . . about 3 inches). Put a spoon of stewed apricots and a dab of butter in the center. Pinch ends together tightly, brush with melted butter and put upside down in a greased muffin pan to let rise. When light, bake at 400 degrees until slightly brown.

Mrs. John Gaither

Croissants are very flaky yeast rolls. They are kin to puff paste, but contain yeast, and are much easier to make. A little like Danish pastry, they contain no filling and are not sweet. They can be served for lunch or dinner, but for breakfast they are supreme. When we are listening to every detail of some friend's trip abroad, she always comes to the part where she describes the food on the boat going over, the huge strawberries in England, a wonderful little restaurant in Paris and, finally, the delight of sitting in bed and ordering a continental breakfast ... a cup of very strong coffee, a little fruit and a croissant.

After hearing about croissants, so flaky, chewy, warm, light, fresh, perfect, one day we decided to make them and did. They were all that had been described ... just delicious. The second batch we discovered a wonderful thing. They freeze. Bake until done, cool, put in a plastic bag and freeze. When ready to serve, take one, six, or two dozen out of the bag, run them in a hot oven for three or four minutes until hot, and serve. They seem better than the first time out of the oven.

These have gotten to be our favorite roll for company luncheons or dinners, because they can be made ahead and reheated at the last minute. The crescent-shaped rolls served hot with strawberry preserves are the hit of every party they have been a part of.

Someday I am going to Europe, order a continental breakfast, and see how authentic croissants taste. Until then, I hope there is always a supply in the freezer, ready to eat with tea for a guest, for luncheons, or as a nice surprise for Kinch and Franklin, the boys in the family who love them best.

CROISSANTS

Soften 2 envelopes of yeast in ½ cup warm water in a mixing bowl. Add about 1 cup flour and stir. Cover with a damp towel and set in a warm place to rise for about an hour, or until double. This is your sponge.

Sift into another bowl about 3½ cups flour, ½ teaspoon salt and 1 tablespoon sugar. Add gradually 1½ cups milk and stir well. Add the yeast mixture to this, stirring well. Turn out on a board and knead, bounce, spank and mix with a little more flour until it doesn't stick to the board and is elastic. Add flour if you need to. Cover and let it rest for 10 minutes.

Now roll out in a long rectangle about a half inch thick. Arrange 3 sticks very cold butter on the dough (I sometimes use 2 sticks butter and ½ cup lard.) Just cut in squares and cover the dough. Fold one-third of the dough over the center third, and then fold the remaining third on top to make 3 layers. Roll this out and fold into three layers again. This is called a "turn."

Some recipes want you to refrigerate the dough between turns to keep the butter flakes cold, but I have never had time. Remember that each flake of butter makes a flake of pastry. Make one more turn. Wrap the chunk of dough in a moist cloth and put in the refrigerator overnight.

Next day, roll out, fold and turn. Make two more turns. Let it rest. If you have three layers each turn, and they multiply themselves, you should now have dozens of distinct layers of butter. Be ever so gentle about not letting these get blended or kneaded. Now cut the dough with a knife into four squares. You will see all the nice layers of butter I am talking about.

Roll one square out large enough so that you can cut a circle using a 9-inch cake pan as a pattern. Now cut the circle into 8 triangles. Starting with the wide part, roll each triangle toward the point, pulling on the point as you roll. Curve the roll into a crescent and arrange on a baking sheet. Roll out the rest of the croissants the same way. Cover with a towel and let rise in a warm place 30 minutes.

Now for the trick that makes them shine. Make an egg wash of an egg yolk beaten with a little milk, about ½ cup. Brush each roll with this. Bake for 20 minutes at 400 degrees. This will make about 3 dozen rolls.

When an Orthodox Jewish boy is 13, he becomes a "Son of the Commandment," a Bar Mitzvah. The ceremony takes place at the B'nai Zion Synagogue on Vine Street, and some of Chattanooga's finest citizens are men who have lived up to the vows they made when they were 13, had completed several years of study with the rabbi and cantor, and assumed their responsibilities as members of the Jewish community. My Jewish friends have often told me about the receptions following these ceremonies.

A 1969 Bar Mitzvah was Lonnie Jacobs. His mother, Phyllis Jacobs (Mrs. Al), explained that first there was the service in the synagogue. Lonnie was called up to read from the Torah, he made a carefully prepared speech, he pledged and covenanted his duties to God, led the musaf (the chanting) and received a special blessing from the rabbi. He was thus received into the ranks of the elders, and should anything happen to all of them, the young would be trained in the faith of the oldest nation on the face of the earth. This was a very impressive service.

The reception afterward could be either very simple or very elaborate, done by the family and friends or catered. It is primarily a spiritual occasion, and in the very old days consisted of simply a glass of wine and honey cake for everyone. Phyllis says that she would never have gotten everything prepared had it not been for all the friends who helped.

It is a Jewish tradition that a boy at thirteen, becomes a religious adult, assuming his responsibilities in the congregation. After the worship service in the synagogue, Lonnie Jacobs sliced the Challah bread at the reception following his Bar Mitzvah.

199

All the food must be prepared at the synagogue or from a Kosher bakery, which means the one in Atlanta. She and her friends made the lekach (honey cake) at the synagogue kitchen, where another friend baked the challah (Sabbath egg bread.) There were beautiful trays of molded tuna salad in the shape of a fish, molded egg salad, gefelte fish, herring, fresh fruits. There were no meat or dairy dishes. All the trays were garnished with radishes, carrot curls, olives, parsley, until they looked like pictures. She did go to Atlanta and get some of the dainty cookies, sweets, candies and pastries that look and taste so good. There was fresh chilled fruit.

First Lonnie made a blessing and thanked God for the challah bread. Then he sliced it and everyone had some, along with wine, the honey cakes and all the other refreshments. Phyllis says the lekach or honey cake symbolizes sweetness and goodness, because knowledge of the Torah is sweet to the mouth. It is served on the Sabbath because the Sabbath is sweet, and also at Rosh Hashonah, the New Year.

HONEY CAKE
(Lekach)

2 eggs	⅛ teaspoon salt
½ cup sugar	¾ teaspoon baking powder
¼ cup freshly brewed coffee	½ teaspoon baking soda
½ cup honey	1 cup soarsely chopped nuts
1 tablespoon salad oil	(filberts, almonds, walnuts)
1¾ cup sifted flour	2 tablespoons brandy

Beat eggs in a bowl. Add the sugar and beat until light and fluffy. Mix coffee, honey, and salad oil together, and combine this with the eggs. Sift the flour with the baking powder and soda and salt. Add nuts and stir. Gradually add to the egg mixture, stirring constantly. Add brandy and mix.

Preheat the oven to 325. Oil a loaf pan and line carefully with wax paper. Pour the batter in and bake 45 minutes or until cake tester comes out clean. Remove the cake from the oven and allow to cool thoroughly in the pan. Remove carefully. Cut in squares or small pieces.

Mrs. Al Jacobs

On Friday evening in traditional Jewish homes, there is the Sabbath meal. Challah, a Sabbath twist loaf, is the usual bread. First there is the lighting of the candles by the mother, who teaches her daughters how to do it. Then the father asks a blessing on the bread and it is passed around the table so that all can have a piece. The father then takes a sip of wine and passes the glass around the table for each family member to have a sip. And Sabbath dinner begins.

Helen Siskin Pregulman (Mrs. Mervin) says she has just learned how to make egg bread to have Friday nights for their family's Sabbath supper. She says it is much easier than she thought it would be, and that freshly baked, it is ever so good.

CHALLAH
(Sabbath Egg Bread)

2 envelopes dry active yeast

8 teaspoons plus ½ cup sugar

7¾ cups flour

2¼ cups warm water

½ cup plus 1 tablespoon oil

2 tablespoons salt

3 eggs

Place the yeast, 2 teaspoons sugar and 2 tablespoons flour in a tall tumbler. Add ¾ cup warm water and mix well. Set in a warm place, uncovered.

Place 4 cups flour in a big bowl. Add 1½ cups warm water, ½ cup oil, ½ cup sugar, the salt and 2 eggs and mix well. When the yeast mixture reaches the top of the glass, add it to the batter in the bowl. Mix well and gradually add 3 more cups of flour. Knead the mixture right in the bowl until very smooth and elastic. Cover and set in a warm place about 5 hours.

Knock down dough and add about two-thirds cup more flour, kneading well to give a soft but not sticky dough. Oil the top of the dough with remaining oil. Cover and let rise again until double, about 2½ hours. Knead again. Divide dough into halves, each half into three pieces. Roll each piece into a 9-inch roll. Pinch 3 rolls together at one end, and braid into a high twist. Repeat with remaining 3 rolls. Set on a greased baking sheet. Cover, let rise until double, about 1 hour.

Preheat oven to 350. Combine the remaining egg and the remaining 6 teaspoons sugar and brush over top of the loaves. Bake 40 minutes or until done.

Mrs. Mervin Pregulman

Sometimes the yearning comes over you to make some plain homemade bread, to smell it while it is baking, and then to slice a piece while still warm and eat it with butter. Sometimes this feeling hits me on a snowy day in winter, sometimes on a glorious spring day when the birds have been singing since dawn. Making bread works a sort of therapy, and it puts you in such a good humor that you needed to make it as much as you wanted to eat it.

BEST HOMEMADE BREAD

1 package active dry yeast	2 cups milk, scalded
¼ cup water (warm for dry yeast, lukewarm for compressed yeast)	6 cups sifted all-purpose flour
	¼ cup butter
	2 teaspoons sugar
2 teaspoons salt	

Dissolve yeast in water; let stand while you mix milk, sugar, salt and butter in a large bowl. Let stand until lukewarm, then add yeast mixture and 3 cups of flour. Beat until flour has disappeared; then add remaining flour, stirring and mixing constantly. Turn out on floured board. Knead until satiny smooth. Place in greased bowl, turn over once, cover with clean cloth. Let rise in warm place for 90 minutes until doubled.

Now punch the dough down, cover and let rise for 30 minutes. I dampen the cloth. Shape into two loaves in greased bread pans. Cover with a cloth and let rise until double again. Bake at 400 degrees for about 30 minutes.

South Pittsburg, Tennessee, was first settled about the same time as Chattanooga and called Battle Creek. In the booming 1870s an Englishman named James Barron came to this area seeking a location for the iron and coal industry that British capitalists wanted as an investment.

After searching he found the Sequatchie Valley, with coal near Whitwell and an iron supply near Inman. He decided to locate the smelters at Battle Creek. Since they had interested manufacturers from Pittsburgh, Pennsylvania, to move their plants south, they organized the town as South Pittsburg.

They began smelting the iron at South Pittsburg, getting the coal from Whitwell, coking it at Victoria, and getting the raw iron from Inman. This was a $3 million investment in those days, and there came to South Pittsburg many plants. The Perry Stove Company, which became U.S. Stove, and the Lodge Manufacturing Company are still in business today. Leonard Raulston at U.S. Stove is the chief historian of

Sarah Lodge is pictured with a collection of iron skillets, corn pone pans, corn stick pans, popover pans, and fluted muffin pans, some old, some new. Sarah's great grandfather, Joseph Lodge, came from Pennsylvania in 1896, and organized his foundry, the Lodge Manufacturing Co., during the coal and iron boom in Sequatchie Valley. The family company still makes all sorts of cast iron cookware.

203

the area who has filled me in on these details, and his firm makes ranges, heaters, and most recently has renovated the Ben Franklin stove, the most practical instant fireplace ever invented, which is enjoying great popularity all over the country.

South Pittsburg and the Sequatchie Valley area has produced many prominent families of our region......the Raulstons, the Lodges, the Kellermans, Rogers, Allisons, Spears, the Fraziers who supplied two congressmen, the Moores, the Standifers, and many others.

If you should go to Williamsburg and buy a cast iron molded bundt pan to make Sally Lunn in, the tag would tell you that it is manufactured in South Pittsburg, Tennessee, by the Lodge Manufacturing Company. Good cooks all over the world, whether the French, the Dutch or the Creoles in New Orleans, know that cast iron gives an evenness and a distribution of heat to cooking that makes breads and cakes better, give a better crispness to fried chicken, roast a ham or beef cut to great succulency, just plain out-cooks any other kind of utensil.

Cornstick pans, Dutch ovens, popover pans, skillets of all sizes, bundt pans, and even French bread pans are the specialty of this plant, run by the Kellerman and Lodge families. They say that the secret to iron pots and pans is to simply rinse them or to wipe out with cooking oil, and they will never rust. If they should, or to season them, just oil well and place in a slow oven an hour or two. A well-seasoned pan is a joy forever and seldom will anything stick.

I got the French bread recipe used by the Kellerman family for many years and baked in their unique pair of French bread pans, which is two loaves connected in the middle.

These twin bread pans, along with other such wonderful pots as cast iron Dutch ovens, chicken fryers, griddles, cornstick pans, Sally Lunn pans, and square iron skillets for frying bacon, can be ordered by mail from J.D. Walton, Arts and Crafts Center, South Pittsburg, Tennessee, or most of the cast iron pots can be found at Agnew Hardware in Chattanooga.

FRENCH BREAD

Use twin loaf cast iron bread pans. This makes 4 loaves. Dissolve the following ingredients, one at a time, in a deep pan with a tight fitting lid. Stir in ingredients by swirling the pan gently.

3 cups lukewarm water *2 tablespoons salt*
1 package dry yeast *¾ cup powdered milk*
1-3 cup sugar *¼ cup salad oil*

Add 10½ cups plain flour, unsifted. Plunge hands in, with pan at a comfortable level, and knead until dough pulls freely away from the fingers. Knead until dough is firm and smooth. Work at this.

Cover the pan with a tight fitting lid and place in a warm place (85 degrees or so). You can slightly warm your oven, but cut it off before placing dough in oven to rise.

When two or three times its bulk, divide into four parts. Shape and place in generously greased cast iron pans. Allow to rise until at least double in bulk.

Place in 375 degree pre-heated oven and allow space to grow one third in rising. Bake for 40 minutes. If it's golden brown, it is done.

Mrs. Francis Kellerman
South Pittsburg, Tennessee

Mrs. R.S. Dingle, who runs Tip Top Inn at Pawleys Island, South Carolina, serves homemade bread at every meal to her guests. It is much richer than any other bread you have tasted, and when you eat it, barely cool from the oven, it is almost chewy. One of our boys at dessert time once said, "No, I think I'd rather have another piece of Mrs. Dingle's bread with some butter."

When we printed the recipe in the paper, some readers wondered if the shortening was correct. It is. This is a very rich bread that can also be made into rolls.

MRS. DINGLE'S BREAD

6 cups flour	1 package yeast
1 cup shortening	1½ teaspoons salt
1 pint milk	1 tablespoon sugar

Dissolve yeast in a little lukewarm water. Heat milk to scalding and then let cool to room temperature. Sift dry ingredients. Add the cooled milk to the flour mixture along with the shortening and yeast. Mix well. Of course you may need more flour or less flour to get the right dough . . . elastic but not sticky. Knead on a floured board, put in a greased bowl, cover and let rise until double 1½ to 2 hours. Shape into 2 loaves. Let rise until light, about 45 minutes. Bake in a slow 300-degree oven for 1 to 1¼ hours. Rolls may be made from the same recipe.

Moccasin Bend

As the Tennessee River winds its course around the foot of Lookout Mountain, its path makes the outline of a foot, and the resulting peninsula, when viewed from 2,000 feet up at the point of Lookout Mountain, does indeed look like an Indian Moccasin. The familiar Moccasin Bend is for many, the trademark of Chattanooga.

It has always been farm land, which has made it especially pretty when viewed from above. Chattanooga, however, is the manufacturing center of the Southeast, with over 1,500 products made in this area and a metropolitan population of 317,000. Our stoves, nylon, textiles, parts for ships, autos and planes, clothes, machines find their way all over the world. As new factory sites are needed, Chattanooga is excited about progress and at the same time hates to give up historic and scenic sites.

Moccasin Bend several years ago was slated for an industrial park on the river until a group of patriotic ladies crusaded against it. Miss Zella Armstrong, Mrs. Sim Perry Long, Mrs. Cartter Patten, Mrs. Dudley Porter, Mrs. Alice Milton, Mrs. W.H. Wilson and many others including Mrs. Ernestine Lyle and Mrs. Raleigh Crumbliss, interested in preserving the worthwhile antiquities and important places, called everyone they knew, met with the Mayor dozens of times, wrote Washington, made speeches, enlisted the aid of Dr. James Fowle, and never gave up until the city and county governments acquired the land and dedicated it to public use in 1961.

"Miss Sophia" Long was an amazing lady. She was one of the Scholze clan, who have been important to Chattanooga through their large tannery and by their leadership. She loved beauty, flowers, music (her garden in Riverview was designed in the shape of a violin), good food and home-made whole wheat bread. Whether she was choosing a stained-glass window to give to the First Presbyterian Church, or saving Moccasin Bend, or making homemade bread, Miss Sophie imparted her unusual talents, her intelligence, and her own strength of character to the project.

She said some years ago when she was not well, her doctor suggested some old-fashioned whole wheat bread. She made some and her family liked it so much, she baked bread every Tuesday and Friday since. This was her recipe.

MISS SOPHIE'S WHOLE WHEAT BREAD

Scald 1 cup milk and pour into a large stone bowl. Add 2 tablespoons lard, 2 tablespoons butter, 2 tablespoons honey, 2 tablespoons Sand Mountain sorghum, and ¾ tablespoon salt. When dissolved, put in 1 cup water. The bowl should be warm but not hot ... about 80 degrees. Now dissolve 1 package yeast in ¼ cup tepid water and put aside for a minute.

You will need about 2 cups of white flour and about 6 cups whole wheat flour. Put the white flour into a large sifter first, then fill it with the whole wheat. Begin sifting into the liquid in the bowl. When part of it is in, put in the yeast. Stir with a heavy spoon to make a moderately stiff dough, adding the rest of the flour in the sifter. Knead it on a floured board. Toward the last you can finish out with whole wheat and white flour. You want the dough smooth and elastic, but not too stiff.

Use an aluminum roasting pan with a rack in it, and fill the bottom with hot water. Grease the bowl that you mixed the dough in, put the dough in it again, and set the bowl on top of the rack. Cover the bowl with a lid and put a tea towel over all of it. This is your own proofer, since all bakers know that bread should rise in a warm, moist atmosphere for the best bread.

Sour cream coffee cakes are a specialty that Baird McClure bakes
and takes to friends. One afternoon young Charlotte Grant came over
to help.

Set the timer to go off in 1 hour. It actually takes 2 hours for the bread to double, sometimes longer, but it is good to start checking on it from 1 hour on. When the dough has doubled, dump onto a bread board. Cut into three pieces for three loaves. Knead each piece a little, and put into a greased bread pan.

Set the time to go off in 40 minutes. The dough should rise in the pans, covered with a towel for 40 minutes or more, so when the timer rings, turn on your oven to 350 degrees.

When the oven temperature is 350, put the loaves in. They should brown in 8 minutes. Start checking the loaves for doneness in 40 minutes. It takes about 50 minutes usually for the loaves to be done.

When you take them out of the oven, rub with butter, and set on ends on a rack to cool. Put a towel over them while they cool. When ready to store, roll in aluminum foil and keep in the bread box.

The late Mrs. Sim Perry Long

The perfect Sunday morning breakfast is coffee cake. Baird McClure makes up a sour cream version, several at a time, and keeps them in the freezer. She always has some on hand to take to friends who have moved in a new house, been sick, had a death in the family, or to friends who are perfectly healthy and happy and just might enjoy a coffee cake. This recipe is especially moist and spicy.

BAIRD'S SOUR CREAM COFFEE CAKE

2 sticks butter	2½ cups flour
1½ cups sugar	1 teaspoon almond flavoring
3 eggs	1 cup brown sugar
1 cup sour cream	1 tablespoon cinnamon
1 teaspoon soda	½ cup pecans
1 teaspoon baking powder	

Cream butter and sugar and add eggs. Sift dry ingredients, flour, baking powder and soda. Add alternately with sour cream. Grease and flour three 9-inch aluminum coffee cake pans or small loaf pans. Pour out batter among them. Sprinkle with half of the mixture of brown sugar, cinnamon and pecans. Cut into batter with knife. Sprinkle the remaining mixture on the tops. Bake 25 minutes at 350 degrees. This freezes well. When serving, heat in oven just until hot.

Miss Baird McClure

Whoever heard of a coffee cake made with 12 egg yolks. Or one whose rich dough was laced with currants, blackberry jelly, cinnamon, butter and both ground almonds and pecans. This ridiculously rich yeast bread is made regularly next door by my neighbor, Mrs. George Fillauer, and many times when we have just gotten home from a trip or on a special occasion, she will come over with a whole wonderful coffee cake to welcome us. When she makes this specialty for charity bake sales at the church or at the annual carnival for the school, people will pay as high as $10 for the honor of getting anything as elegant as this.

MRS. FILLAUER'S COFFEE CAKE

2 yeast cakes	1 teaspoon vanilla
1 teaspoon sugar	½ cup milk
½ cup milk	5 or 5½ cups flour
1 cup flour	1 cup currants
2 teaspoons grated lemon rind	Blackberry jelly
1½ sticks butter	4 tablespoons cinnamon
1 cup sugar	4 tablespoons sugar
2 teaspoons salt	4 tablespoons butter melted
12 egg yolks	6 tablespoons ground almonds
6 tablespoons ground pecans	

Have the half cup of milk barely warm, and dissolve the yeast in it along with the teaspoon of sugar to feed the yeast. Mix with the cup of flour and set aside in a small buttered bowl.

In a mixer, cream the butter and sugar, lemon rind and salt. Add the egg yolks (the yolks make the dough light, the whites would make it heavy). Make an angel food cake with the whites. Add the vanilla, another ½ cup of milk and the flour to make a shiny satiny dough. The yeast can be added any time. This batter is thoroughly creamed and mixed on the mixer before much of the flour is added.

When the dough gets too heavy for the mixer to beat, when it gets pully and rubbery, put some flour on the counter, dump the dough on it and begin three or four minutes of kneading. You knead until it hardly sticks. Now it is ready to rise. Place in a large crockery bowl coated with melted butter. Cover with foil and tie the foil around the bowl with a string.

Because this is such rich dough, it will take 4 or 5 hours or overnight to double in bulk. When it is doubled, then punch down and divide in two portions. (Mrs. Fillauer lets the dough rise in the laundry room sometimes, so that the steam from the warm dryer will make the atmosphere fight). Roll each portion out, and begin sprinkling each with ½ cup currants, 2 tablespoons cinnamon, 2 tablespoons sugar, 2 tablespoons melted butter, 3 tablespoons pecans, 3 tablespoons ground almonds and daube of blackberry jelly all over it.

Now roll up each as tightly and firmly as you can. Put in a buttered loaf-size pan, butter the top and let rise till double. This makes two large loaves.

Bake at 300 degrees for 30 minutes and at 250 degrees for 15 minutes. Turn out on rack and let cool. Keep in plastic bag in refrigerator. This keeps very well.

Mrs. George Fillauer.

Dr. James Fowle grew up in North Carolina in the Piedmont country, and remembers having rice waffles as a child. He says these are popular all over the Carolinas. "You must mean rice cakes," I said, thinking that we mix leftover rice from the night before with beaten eggs and fry like cakes. He says that the rice waffles he remembers were like a waffle batter but with rice in them and crisp and light as a feather. I hunted and finally found this recipe.

CAROLINA RICE WAFFLES

1¾ cup flour	2 tablespoons sugar
2 teaspoons baking powder	1½ cups milk
1 teaspoon salt	4 tablespoons melted shortening
2 eggs	¾ cup cold cooked rice

Sift the dry ingredients together. Beat the eggs, shortening and milk together. Mix with the rice and other ingredients. Bake in a hot waffle iron.

Years ago there was a popular tea room here called Shop Hounds. Lunches and brunches were the specialty and everyone loved their waffles with chicken hash, their hot chicken and tomato sandwiches baked in shirred egg dishes and their lemon pie. The waffles are very crisp and light and can be made up ahead of time.

SHOP HOUNDS WAFFLES

1 egg	½ cup shortening
½ cup sweet milk	3 teaspoons baking powder
1½ cups water	2 cups flour
1 tablespoon sugar	Thin with ice water

Mix all ingredients and then blend in ice water to the right consistency. This should be a thin batter. We make it in the blender.

The old Shop Hounds Restaurant used to feature a delicious hot chicken sandwich on a bun with tomato, bacon, and a hot cheesy sauce. Mrs. Gloria Lamb Greene doesn't remember the exact recipe, but this recipe is a good guess. She served them in individual white flat casseroles.

SHOP HOUNDS SPECIAL SANDWICH

On a toasted bun or a Holland rusk arrange sliced white meat of chicken and sliced tomato. Top with a slice of bacon already cooked. Put each serving in a small baking dish. Make up the following cream sauce: 3 tablespoons flour, 3 tablespoons butter, 1 cup chicken broth, 1 cup milk. When it is thickened, grate some cheddar cheese in it, grate a small amount of onion, then taste for the correct seasoning. Pour some sauce over each sandwich, and put in a hot oven until it bubbles.

At Christmas time, anyone who has ever made bread or yeast doughs gets a strange yearning to bake some sort of fancy bread. The rich good taste of homemade bread, laced with candied fruit, rasins, and nuts, is more delicious than I can describe. Heated or toasted for breakfast, or served with tea or coffee after a long busy day, home-made bread is a special part of the holiday season.

If you like to bake, or if you can master simple dinner rolls, you can make bread. The kind we make most is not quite as rich as stollen, but just an adaption of a rich sweet dough, the same kind used for cinnamon rolls. At the last add mixed chopped candied fruit and a few raisins and nuts, and shape the loaves either in tin cans or in small tea loaf pans. These, when baked and cooled, are iced with powdered sugar icing and decorated with bits of fruit and nuts.

On the day we bake bread, the whole house is filled with a sweet yeasty aroma, there are batches of bread at all stages, in every available bowl and pan, and everyone who wants a turn at kneading and spanking the dough, gets one.

I have learned everything about making bread the hard way. Kneading the dough was a great mystery to me, and my bread never was light until I noticed the dough mixed in a huge bakery. There is nothing gentle about the machinery that kneads those big batches of dough . . . it is thrown around and beaten with a terrific force.

It is said that Margaret Rudkin of Pepperidge Farm fame, when recruiting workers for her bakery, wanted women who had no preconceived notions about kneading. She wanted them to spank the dough, pound it, turn it, and push it with real vigor. So when handling your dough, work in just enough flour to keep it from sticking, let it rest a few minutes to stiffen, and then start kneading it as roughly as possible. For as long as five minutes, throw it down, hit it, spank it, and pound it. You will develop the bread protein and provide an elastic structure strong enough to hold the gases released by the yeast.

One more thing that makes light yeast bread is the place you put the dough to rise. The temperature is supposed to be warm (86 degrees) and away from drafts. I have tried every place from the hearth by the fire to a closed cupboard next to a bowl of hot water. Recently I came upon the perfect solution. Put a shallow pan of hot water on the bottom shelf of the oven. Then turn the oven on to preheat for about 30 seconds. Turn it off quickly. You will have a proofing box for your dough to rise in undisturbed and out of the way. Just to be safe, stick you hand in to see that it is about 80 and no higher.

Here is the recipe for Christmas bread. It is wonderful for breakfast on Christmas morning.

CHRISTMAS FRUIT BREAD

1 cup lukewarm milk	4½ to 5 cups flour
½ cup sugar	1 cup chopped candied fruit
1 teaspoon salt	¾ cup light raisins
2 cakes yeast	½ cup almonds or pecans
2 eggs	Grated rind of 1 lemon
½ cup butter	1 teaspoon vanilla

Mix together the milk, sugar and salt. Crumble into the mixture the yeast and stir until dissolved. Then stir in the eggs and shortening. Now mix in the sifted flour, first in the mixer, and when it begins to get too thick, by hand. Add the flour gradually, using the amount necessary to be able to handle without sticking too badly. Keep the dough as soft as possible, almost sticky, and the bread will be more tender. Too much flour will make it dry and tough.

Turn the dough out onto a floured board and let rest 10 minutes. Knead in the fruit and remaining ingredients. Continue to knead and pound the dough until soft and elastic......about 5 minutes.

Set into a large greased bowl to rise, covered with a damp cloth. In 1½ to 2 hours it will be double. Now punch it down and turn completely over and let rise again until almost double, about 30 minutes.

After the second rising shape the dough into loaves, filling the pans or cans about 2-3 full. Let rise again until light (about 30 minutes) and bake at 375 degrees for 30 or 40 minutes or until done. This will make 4 small loaves or 2 good sized ones. Turn out immediately on wire rack and while still warm, ice the tops with powdered sugar icing.

One of Chattanooga's outstanding projects is the Siskin Memorial Foundation. In a beautiful modern building there are three floors where some sort of therapy or other is going on daily for handicapped people. It had an unusual beginning. In 1942 two brothers, Garrison and Mose Siskin, were enjoying modest success in the scrap iron business, when Garrison was seriously injured by a heavy iron girder, which fell on his leg, forming a clot. Three surgeons told him it would be necessary to amputate the leg and gave him a 50-50 chance of recovery.

Garrison Siskin says that he prayed all night, and he promised God that if he recovered he would spend the rest of his life helping those less fortunate than he. It was a long and hard convalescence, his first introduction to physical therapy, but he pulled through. The Siskins have a very deep Orthodox faith, and ever since that time both brothers have crusaded to help provide medical attention for the lame, the needy and the unfortunate.

They established the Siskin Memorial Foundation in memory of their parents. This is a rehabilitation center providing facilities that Chattanooga did not have. There is one floor for the training of pre-school mentally handicapped children, another for pre-school physically handicapped children, and a third floor for a hearing and speech center. There are specialists trained in teaching those with cerebral palsy, audiologists to test hearing, and physical therapists. Another building is a cultural, civic, and charitable meeting place with a museum of religious artifacts.

You can't really know what a special place this is unless you go on a tour as we did when our third grade Brownie Scouts gave their cookie money profits to the 365 Club, a fund raising drive for the center. Children are fitted with hearing aids, braces, learning to walk, learning to read, and are brought from home to discover a whole new world they never thought they could enjoy.

Hundreds of families have benefitted from the Siskin Center, including my own . . . a little niece with cerebral palsy and a son with a slight speech defect. Both Mr. Garrison and Mr. Mose have been nominated for the Lasker Award for service to mankind and Chattanooga is justly proud of them.

The feminine side of the Siskin family are noted cooks. Their recipes are throughout the book. The following coffee cake made by Mrs. Mose Siskin is rich with butter and egg yolks but is quite easy to put together. The egg yolks give it a tender moist quality.

MRS. SISKIN'S COFFEE CAKE
(Babka)

2 packages or cakes yeast	1 cup sugar
½ cup warm water	4 cups flour
1 cup milk	6 egg yolks
½ cup butter or margarine	Icing
1 teaspoon salt	

Dissolve yeast in warm water and set aside. Scald the milk and add butter, salt, sugar and 2 cups flour. Beat with mixer until smooth. Add egg yolks, one at a time, beating well after each addition. Add yeast mixture and remaining 2 cups flour and knead until smooth.

Let rise in a warm place until doubled. Turn out onto a floured board and knead until smooth and elastic. Place in a greased fluted pan or mold and let rise to rim of mold. Bake at 350 degrees 35 minutes. Remove from pan and cool. Spread with icing, if desired.

Mrs. Mose Siskin

The most famous orange bread in town is probably Anita Patton's (Mrs. John Evander). This is because she has taken it to friends at Christmas or just as a "thinking of you" present throughout the year. This is best on a cold afternoon in front of a fire to accompany a cup of tea. It is also good for breakfast.

ORANGE BREAD

2 cups orange peel, ground fine in chopper	1 cup water
	1½ cups sugar

Add water to orange and cook until tender. Add sugar and cook until thick. Cool. For the orange part, she uses halves left from squeezing orange juice and puts them pulp, rind and all through the food chopper.

1 egg	1 cup milk
1 cup sugar	3½ cups flour
1 tablespoon (generous)	3 teaspoons baking powder
Melted butter	½ teaspoon salt

Mix the eggs, sugar, butter, milk, and flour mixture. Add the orange syrup to it, and mix well. Grease and flour lightly 3 small loaf pans (about 4 by 8 inches). Divide batter among the pans. Let set 20 minutes. Bake at 350 degrees for about 40 minutes.

Mrs. John Evander Patton

Craven's House, on the side of Lookout Mountain, was the home of an ante-bellum industrialist. It served as Confederate and Union head-quarters. Almost stripped by souvenir hunters after the war, it has been restored as a State Historic Site.

At Craven's House, the home on the side of Lookout Mountain restored by the Association for the Preservation of Tennessee Antiquities, there is a tea every fall. Usually the trees are in their prettiest fall colors and there is a nip in the air. One year they served mulled cider that was warm and delicious, and cranberry nut bread sandwiches. The cranberry nut bread was made from a recipe of Mrs. Cartter Patten's.

CRANBERRY NUT BREAD

2 cups flour
1 cup sugar
1½ teaspoons baking powder
½ teaspoon soda
1 teaspoon salt
Juice and grated rind
  of 1 orange

2 tablespoons melted salad oil
1 egg plus enough water to
  make ¾ cup
2 cups cranberries, cut in half
½ cup chopped nuts

Sift together the dry ingredients. Add the orange juice and rind, oil, egg and water. Stir until the mixture is damp. Fold in ½ cup chopped nuts and 2 cups cranberries. Spoon the batter into a 9 by 5 by 3 inch loaf pan or two smaller tea loaf pans. Be sure to grease the pans first, and when you put the batter in, make the sides and corners higher than the middle. Bake at 350 degrees for 50 to 60 minutes. Store overnight for easier slicing.

Mrs. Cartter Patten

My doctor sister Martha insists that her talent is medicine rather than cooking, and she doesn't really have time to do lots of cooking. One day soon after she got a new blender, whe got hungry for banana bread and went in the kitchen and did it the modern scientific way in the blender. This was fast and easy and the bread was good.

MARTHA'S BLENDER BANANA BREAD

2 eggs
½ cup soft shortening
2 ripe bananas, cut
¾ cup sugar

1¾ cup flour
¾ teaspoon soda
1¼ teaspoons cream of tartar
½ teaspoon salt

Into container of blender put eggs, fat, bananas and sugar. Cover and blend about 20 seconds until smooth. Toss flour, soda, cream of tartar and salt in mixing bowl. Pour contents of container over flour mixture. Mix gently to combine. Pour into greased 8 by 4 inch loaf pan. Bake in moderate oven, 350 about 45 minutes until golden. Cool on rack.

Dr. Martha McDonald

CHAPTER XI

Cakes

When you go to any supermarket, you can easily get the idea that no one makes cakes from scratch anymore. Yet when you go to luncheons and suppers at church, nearly everyone brings their very best homemade cakes. When the News-Free press has office parties, the array of homemade cakes is honestly as beautiful and impressive as any spread in a magazine.

Chattanooga families like homemade cakes......rich pound cakes, light fluffy angel foods, dark moist chocolate cakes, tender layer cakes made with butter, simple old fashioned tea cakes. When I was growing up, I can remember visiting my great-grandmother on Sunday and going back to the dining room where a white tablecloth was spread over the table of leftovers from Sunday dinner. There were always at least two or three cakes to choose from. There would be a caramel layer cake, a sunshine cake, and maybe a pound cake.

Later I can remember my mother making a cake every Saturday morning for the weekend. She usually wouldn't let us cut it until Sunday, and my sister Betsy promised herself that when she grew up and made cakes, whe was going to have a slice right away, while it was still warm. I think she does!

When I got married and was mistress of my own kitchen, I began making a cake on Saturday, too. My pitiful little thin layers of cake made my mother's best recipe were a far cry from the ones I knew she was making 2,000 miles away. I finally learned, and in this chapter I will pass on the tips that helped me.

The most famous cake in Chattanooga just may be Miss Gertrude Oehmig's caramel cake. She made it for years and years at her Coffee Shop, then at G.P.S. and later at Loveman's Tea Room.

When a whole town has grown up loving fine cakes, biting into delicate layers of sweet buttery goodness, exchanging new recipes, getting into the habit of keeping a cake on hand to offer friends or family, then the art of cake making will never die out.

The most famous cake in Chattanooga is undoubtedly Miss Gertrude Oehmig's caramel cake. Having served thousands of these at the Coffee Shop, G.P.S., Lovemans' Tearoom, she cuts one more slice for her niece and namesake, Trudie Stone.

We will take the mixes and adapt them and add our own personality to them. We hope that we will always be known for our good cakes.

There is only one other thing about cakes, and that is, you must be in the mood. One day when Susan was making a cake that none of us had ever tried, I asked why she didn't make a 1-2-3-4 cake or some brownies instead. She said, "When I make the cakes you say, sometimes they don't turn out for me. I like to make a cake because it was my idea and because it sounded good to me." I could understand this, and sure enough, the sour cream cake she made was delicious, as was the spice cake, although she didn't have such good luck on another one, but they were hers. You have to make what inspires you, and then it will give pleasure to other people.

HOW TO MAKE A CAKE

The things I learned the hard way, by trying and failing, boil down to a few simple rules which can turn anyone into an expert. When you have made a few, you can turn out a cake quickly, yet with no risk, because you have followed the rules.

First, all the ingredients must be exact. In soups, salads, and even simple baked goods like biscuits and cornbread, a simple pinch of this, "about a cup" of that can get by. But in cakes the chemical balance of each ingredient is relative, and contributes to the other. All the weights and measures have been planned. So always level off every solid measurement with a knife edge (use those nested measuring cups for solids.) And be as exact as you know how with every ingredient.

The following procedure is the best I know for butter cakes:

1. Cream the shortening. By using half butter and half shortening, you get a better flavor and texture.

2. Add the sugar to the shortening and cream it until light and fluffy. Beat as long as you want at about medium speed on the mixer. I have never heard of this being overdone. The air incorporated here gives the cake volume.

3. While this creaming is going on, sift the flour, measure and resift with baking powder and salt. Set aside.

220

4. Add the whole eggs or egg yolks to the butter mixture and beat vigorously until quite thick, fluffy and pale. Beat thoroughly. Hurrying through the creaming and adding the sugar and eggs too fast without beating enough is about the worst mistake you can make.

5. Add flavoring to the creamed mixture. The shortening and egg yolk absorb and hold the flavor best at this point.

6. Turn down mixer to a very low speed. Add the sifted dry ingredients and liquid alternately. The dry ingredients are added in about 4 additions and the liquid in 3. Start with flour and end with flour. This must be done on the slowest speed and just as quickly and deftly as you know how. Hurry, hurry lightly. If you overbeat at this stage, you lose the air and volume you built up in the first stages.

7. If making a cake using egg whites only, beat them separately until stiff but not dry. If you do this first, you don't have to wash the beaters. Some people also put a little of the sugar that the cake calls for into the egg whites to help hold the air. The egg whites can add a large amount of air so handle lightly and fold in the batter quickly.

Keep these principles in your mind while putting a cake together, and with practice, you can mix a cake in about 15 minutes ... one you can be proud of down to the last crumb.

Possibly the most popular cake all over the South is the 1-2-3-4 cake, a butter cake that can be made in layers or in a tube pan. It is called this because it calls for 1 cup of butter, 2 cups sugar, 3 cups flour and 4 eggs. It never fails and the white version using 8 egg whites instead of 4 eggs is just as elegant as its yellow sister. We ice the yellow cake with either an Orange Butter Cream Icing or an Orange Glaze. White Mountain Icing tops the white.

BEST YELLOW 1-2-3-4 CAKE

1 cup butter	*1 teaspoon salt*
2 cups sugar	*3 teaspoons baking powder*
3 cups cake flour, sifted	*2 teaspoons vanilla*
4 eggs	*Grated rind of 1 lemon and*
1 cup milk	*1 orange (optional.)*

Grease and flour a tube pan. Cream the butter and sugar well. Add one egg at a time and beat until light and fluffy. Sift the flour and dry ingredients three times on a paper towel. Add the flavoring and the grated rind to the batter. Now alternate the flour mixture and the milk, combining into the batter at a very low speed until just blended. Pour into the tube pan and bake at 325 degrees about 1 hour and 15 minutes or until done.

WHITE 1-2-3-4 CAKE

Follow the above recipe except use 8 egg whites instead of 4 eggs. Beat the whites until stiff and set aside while you make the rest of the cake. Fold into the batter the very last thing. Leave out the rind of the lemon and orange and use only the vanilla as flavoring.

This bakes in either 2 or 3 nine inch layers at 325 degrees.

ORANGE BUTTER CREAM ICING

1 stick butter, softened
to room temperature
Juice of ½ orange

Sifted powdered sugar to
the right consistency

Beat the butter and orange juice and add 2 or 3 cups of powdered sugar until it will hold its shape.

QUICK ORANGE GLAZE

½ box powdered sugar, sifted   *Orange juice*

Add the orange juice a little at a time until the glaze is thick but can be stirred smooth. Put on the cake while still warm, about five minutes after you have turned the cake out on a rack. It will dry and have a nice sheen.

The favorite chocolate cake we make is the famous $100 Waldorf Cake. It is a rich cake, but the real secret is the icing that sets it off. This is a chocolate powdered sugar icing with a difference......it is flavored with a combination of vanilla flavoring and lemon juice to cut the too-chocolate taste. This is so delicious that I use a similar version on the top of brownies and the same icing without the nuts to ice anything that needs to have chocolate on top.

$100 WALDORF CHOCOLATE CAKE

4 squares bitter chocolate
½ cup shortening
2 cups sugar
2 eggs
2 teaspoons vanilla

2 cups cake flour
2 teaspoons baking powder
1 teaspoon salt
1½ cups milk
1 cup chopped pecans

Melt over hot water the squares of chocolate; cool. Cream the shortening, gradually add sugar and cream until fluffy. Add eggs and vanilla. Beat well. Now reserve 2 tablespoons of flour in which to dredge the nuts. Sift the remaining flour with the baking powder and salt. Add alternately with milk to the creamed mixture. Beat batter about 1 minute. Now fold in the floured nuts. Bake in 3 layer cake pans that have been greased and floured. Bake in 350 oven about half hour or until the sides of the cake come away from the pan. Cool 10 minutes in pans; turn out on wire rack.

FROSTING

2 squares bitter chocolate	1 tablespoon vanilla
½ cup butter	1 tablespoon lemon juice
1 cup powdered sugar	1 cup powdered sugar
1 egg	1 cup chopped pecans

Melt the chocolate and butter over low heat. Add the powdered sugar and blend well. Now take off the stove and add the egg, lemon juice and vanilla and the rest of the powdered sugar, enough to give the right consistency. Add the nuts and spread on the cake. If this icing is warm when it goes on the cake, it will dry to a nice shine.

The tenderest Devil's Food Cake is the one we got in California from our friend Margaret Gibson. It is dark, moist with buttermilk and brown sugar, and light as a feather. White Mountain Icing is best on this.

MARGARET'S DEVIL'S FOOD CAKE

¾ cup butter	2¼ cup cake flour, sifted
1⅞ cup brown sugar (1 box minus 2 tablespoons)	1½ teaspoons baking soda
	¾ teaspoon baking powder
3 eggs, well beaten	¾ teaspoon salt
¾ cup boiling water	1½ teaspoons vanilla
3 squares bitter chocolate	¾ cup buttermilk

Pour the boiling water over the squares of chocolate and let sit until they melt. Cream the butter and sugar. Add the eggs, one at a time, and sift the dry ingredients three times. Now add to the butter and egg mixture the chocolate and vanilla. Add the flour and buttermilk alternately. Pour the batter into three 8 inch layer pans that have been well greased and floured. Bake at 350 degrees for 25 minutes. Let stand in pans for a few minutes after they are done, as this cake is very tender. Frost with 7 Minute or White Mountain Frosting.

Mrs. Margaret Gibson
San Jose, California

WHITE MOUNTAIN FROSTING

1 cup sugar   2 egg whites
6 tablespoons water   1½ teaspoons vanilla
¼ teaspoon cream of tartar

Boil the sugar, water, and cream of tartar slowly without stirring until a thermometer registers 242 degrees, or the syrup spins a 6 inch thread. While syrup is cooking whip 2 egg whites until stiff. Pour the hot syrup slowly over the egg whites, beating constantly. Add the vanilla and spread between the layers and the top and sides of a layer cake.

Roselle Bender, as the wife of former Mayor A. L. Bender, made a charming first lady of Chattanooga. She is also a noted cook who is famous for chocolate cakes, not only in political circles but also among the press reporters and photographers who have sampled them. She says the chocolate cake part was originally from her sister Juda, the fruit filling from Chunk's mother, and the chocolate glaze on top, her own. She has often taken this cake to the Brainerd United Methodist Church and to the Chi Omegas Mothers' Club at the university.

THE MAYOR'S CHOCOLATE CAKE

¾ cup shortening   2 cups flour
2 cups sugar   3 squares unsweetened chocolate
5 eggs   1 teaspoon vanilla
1 cup buttermilk plus   Pinch of salt
1 teaspoon soda

Cream shortening until fluffy. Sift the sugar and the flour before measuring. Slowly add the sugar. Add salt and vanilla. Add eggs, one at a time, beating well after each. Alternately add flour and milk (let the soda foam in the buttermilk). Lastly, pour in the melted chocolate. Pour into a 10 by 14 by 2 inch pan which has been greased, then lined with waxed paper, and greased again. Bake at 325 degrees about 35 minutes. Turn out on waxed paper on a board and remove paper. Cool. Flip cake over. It can be cut in half and layered with your favorite chocolate or divinity icing, or filled with this fruit filling and iced on top and sides. It can also be left in a sheet, topped with fruit filling and then glazed with chocolate.

FRUIT FILLING FOR CHOCOLATE CAKE

¼ cup stoned chopped dates
¼ cup seeded chopped raisins
¼ cup chopped figs,
  (or more dates)
¾ cup evaporated milk

¼ cup water
1 teaspoon vanilla
¾ cup sugar
½ cup nuts, chopped

Dilute milk with water. Put in a double boiler with sugar. Stir until sugar is dissolved. Add fruit and cook until thick. Cool. Add vanilla and nut meats.

CHOCOLATE ICING

1 package 6-oz. semi-sweet
  chocolate bits
½ cup sour cream
¼ cup butter

1 teaspoon vanilla
¼ teaspoon salt
3 cups confectioner's sugar

Melt chocolate and butter over hot water; remove. Blend in sour cream, vanilla and salt. Gradually beat in sugar to make frosting a spreading consistency.

Mrs. A. L. Bender

City Chaplain of Chattanooga is Dr. James L. Fowle. He is a large man with a big heart and kind twinkling eyes. For nearly 40 years he was pastor of the First Presbyterian Church until his retirement in 1967. He is interested not only in the affairs of his own church, but in almost every good cause in Chattanooga.

During World War II, he and the late Professor Spencer McCallie traveled all over the state raising money for war bonds. He has been a leader in the fund raising campaign for the University of Chattanooga, the Cancer Society, and Tumor Clinic at Erlanger, the Y.M.C.A., new churches as the town has grown into the suburbs, new churches for his Negro friends, and many other needs that he has seen. He is a legend, an inspiration, and a wise comfort. When he squeezes your hand with his big pudgy strong one and says, "God bless you, child," you have a warm feeling that everything is going to be all right.

225

Dr. Fowle's appetite and his appreciation of good things to eat, especially cakes, is also legendary. At the women's meetings it may be that he accepted a slice of every cake just so that no feelings would be hurt, but it is more probable that he really appreciates good cakes. His wife Katherine was a noted cook, and Mary Payne Fowle has given me the following recipe of her mother's.

MRS. FOWLE'S DEVIL'S FOOD CAKE

1 stick butter	1 cup sweet milk
1¼ cups sugar	1 teaspoon soda in milk
2 eggs	2 squares baking chocolate
1¾ cups flour	1 teaspoon vanilla
1 teaspoon salt	

Cream butter and sugar, add eggs, one at a time, beat well. Add flour, milk, chocolate and vanilla. Pour batter in 2 greased and floured cake pans and bake at 350 for about 25 minutes or until done.

CHOCOLATE ICING

4 cups brown sugar	1 teaspoon vanilla
4 squares baking chocolate	1 lump butter
1 small can evaporated milk	

Stir constantly until it begins to boil, and let cook slowly until it reaches the stage where it forms a soft ball. Take off the stove, let stand in cold water until cool, then beat. Put on the cake when creamy and thick.

Miss Mary Payne Fowle

A caramel frosting can be made that never needs to be caramelized. The caramel fudge that Miss Gertrude Oehmig makes turns a soft pale gold as the cream and sugar cook down. This is possibly Chattanooga's favorite dessert.

MISS GERTRUDE'S WHITE LAYER CAKE

¾ cup butter or shortening	2 teaspoons baking powder
2 cups granulated sugar	5 egg whites, beaten stiff
1 cup sweet milk	1 teaspoon vanilla
3 cups sifted cake flour	

Beat the egg whites until stiff. Set aside. In another bowl cream the shortening and add the sugar, creaming until smooth. Sift the baking powder with the flour, and add this flour mixture to the sugar and shortening alternately with the milk. Add the vanilla. At the last, fold in the egg whites. Pour the batter into two 9-inch layer pans that have first been greased and floured. Bake at 350 degrees for 25 or 30 minutes until done.

MISS GERTRUDE'S CARAMEL ICING

3 cups granulated sugar   *½ stick butter (no substitute)*
2 cups heavy cream   *1 tablespoon vanilla*

Stir well and let boil until it forms a soft ball in cold water. (As added insurance that it won't be grainy, I butter the saucepan first and add ¼ cup white corn syrup.) Don't add the vanilla until last. When it reaches the soft ball stage (I have to use a thermometer, Miss Gertrude can look and tell), let cool a little. Then beat until creamy enough to ice cake. Use two layers of white cake.

Miss Gertrude Oehmig

Dr. and Mrs. Ben Haden are attractive additions to Chattanooga, who came when Ben was named to succeed Dr. James Fowle as minister of the First Presbyterian Church. Ben had been a lawyer with the C.I.A. during the Korean War and later a newspaperman; Charlyne had been a fashion model in New York before they married. The story of how they came to the ministry is ä fascinating one. Ben's Christian leadership and Charlyne's thoughtful graciousness, as she has hostessed various church classes and groups at the manse, have endeared them to many Chattanoogans.

Charlyne has a fool-proof caramel icing that she has given many friends. You don't have to worry about fudge that doesn't cook long enough or that cooks too long. After bringing the butter and sugar to a boil, you finish out with powdered sugar. This is one everybody can make.

NEVER FAIL CARAMEL ICING

Bring to a boil 1 stick oleo, ½ cup evaporated milk, and 1½ cups brown sugar. Cool. Then add 1 teaspoon vanilla and 1½ cups powdered sugar. Beat in the mixer, adding powdered sugar until you get the right consistency to spread on cake.

Mrs. Ben Haden

Alice Lawwill makes a 1-2-3-4 cake in three layers and ices it with a caramel frosting she got from Mrs. Robert McCallie. This freezes well, she says.

227

ALICE'S 1-2-3-4 CAKE

1 cup butter
2 cups sugar
3 cups cake flour, sifted
4 eggs, separated
1 cup milk

1 tablespoon baking powder
1 teaspoon vanilla flavoring
1 teaspoon lemon flavoring
1 teaspoon almond flavoring

Beat egg whites stiff. Add 1 cup of the sugar and set aside. Cream butter and sugar; add egg yolks. Add baking powder to cake flour. Add the flour mixture alternately with the milk to the butter mixture. Add flavoring. Fold in whites. Divide into 3 layer pans that have been greased and floured, and bake in preheated 425 oven twenty minutes. This was in the old "Mrs. Dull's Southern Cooking."

CARAMEL ICING

1½ sticks butter
1½ cups dark brown sugar packed
½ teaspoon salt
½ cup milk

1 pound box powdered
   sugar, sifted
2 teaspoons vanilla

Melt the butter, brown sugar and salt. Add the milk. Bring to a boil and then add the powdered sugar and vanilla. Beat well and ice the cake.

Mrs. Stewart Lawwill, Jr.

This applesauce cake can be made in layers, or in a long rectangular cake pan so that you can cut it in squares. I have also made it in a big cookie sheet like brownies so that I could ice it with lemon icing, cut in squares and pass, to be eaten with the hands like brownies.

APPLESAUCE CAKE

1½ cups applesauce
½ cup shortening
2 cups sugar
1 egg
2½ cups flour
¼ teaspoon salt
½ teaspoon cinnamon

½ teaspoon cloves
½ teaspoon all spice
1 cup chopped raisins
½ cup nuts
2 teaspoons soda
½ cup boiling water

Cream shortening and add sugar gradually. Add beaten egg and applesauce. Sift flour before measuring. Use a little of the same flour to sift over fruit and nuts. Sift remaining flour with salt and spices.

Dissolve soda in boiling water. Then add flour mixture alternately with water to the creamed mixture. Add the floured raisins and nuts. Pour into cake tins, in sheet pans, or it can be baked in a tube pan. Grease and flour the pans first.

Bake for 1 hour at 350 for a cake, but if you are baking in a sheet or cookie pan, keep an eye on it, as it will bake faster. When the cake comes away from the sides of the pan, is rather firm when felt with a finger, and leaves no batter when a broom straw is inserted, you know it is done. The oven should be 350.

A glamorous dessert worthy of a European chef is the Black Forest Cake topped with cherries. The eye appeal of this is as spectacular as the flavor.

BLACK FOREST CHOCOLATE-CHERRY FUDGE CAKE, CHANTILLY

1 cup butter	½ cup chopped walnuts
1¾ cups sugar	or pecans
3 large or 4 small eggs	2½ cups of cake flour
1½ teaspoons vanilla flavor	(sift 2 or 3 times)
1 teaspoon red food color	½ cup cocoa
1 cup cold milk	3 teaspoons baking powder

Mix butter and sugar until fluffy. Add eggs, color and nuts. Sift dry ingredients 2 or 3 times; add alternately with milk. Mix for about 3 minutes. Do not over mix. Scrape mixing bowl so that dry ingredients are mixed in well. Pour into 3 8 or 9 inch cake pans. Bake in preheated oven 325 degrees for 25 minutes until done. Test with tooth pick.

FROSTING

2 sticks butter	4 ozs. semi-sweet chocolate,
1½ lbs. powdered sugar	melted
2 egg yolks	

Beat butter and sugar in mixer until fluffy. Add egg yolks and melted chocolate. (Not too hot.)

Ice cake between layers and on sides. Not on top.

TOPPING

1 can No. 2½ dark sweet cherries. Drain juice, place in sauce pan, add ½ cup of sugar. Bring to a boil and thicken with 2 tablespoons corn starch until thick. Remove from heat and let cool.

Add cherries and place topping on top of cake. Garnish with whipping cream, cocktail cherries and toasted almond slivers. This cake is very elegant and delicious.

Chef Gunther Krupp
The Read House

"*I will lift up mine eyes unto the hills   *" *Mrs. G. M. Smartt who was born the day after Sherman marched through Chattanooga, was a beloved citizen of our city. Here she was photographed on her 99th birthday at the home of her son, Polk Smartt, in Chattanooga valley.*

One of Chattanooga's most unforgettable characters was certainly Mrs. G.M. Smartt, matriarch of the large Smartt clan. She was a part of Chattanooga from as far back as anyone can remember. When Chattanooga was occupied by the Union army, her young and pretty mother was sent to relatives in Athens so she wouldn't fall in love with any attractive Yankee soldier here. In Athens she met Henry Knox, a Confederate boy who had been wounded in New Orleans so gravely that he was sent home to die. They fell in love and were married on her 19th birthday.

Emma Sue Knox was born the next year, the day after Sherman swept through Chattanooga on his march to Savannah and the sea, leaving total destruction in his wake. There was nothing to eat, but the day before Sherman came, neighbors concerned about the baby, gathered the few remaining apples on the trees and hid them so the new mother would have the strength to nurse the baby.

She grew up to be proficient at whatever needed to be done. She played the organ at the First Baptist Church for 50 years and sometimes at the Cumberland Presbyterian Church, too. She raised seven outstanding children, who have been leaders in almost every phase of Chattanooga's growth. She was full of life, and even when blind, never gave up making things and doing things for other people......she fringed napkins by feeling them, crocheted bedroom slippers for the whole family, covered coathangers, listened to books for the blind on records.

She had a strength of character that still inspires her family. When her son Matt died in Montana, Dr. Fowle came by and had prayer with her, then at 2 o'clock, the exact time of his funeral thousands of miles west, she gathered the family, had her son Polk read from the Bible, and then she sat at the piano and played all the familiar hymns.. ."Abide With Me," "Rock of Ages," "Fairest Lord Jesus," "The Old Rugged Cross," "Faith of Our Fathers," and on and on. It was she who comforted all the rest of the family.

On her 99th birthday, still alert and bright, "Granny Smartt" received her children, grandchildren, nieces, nephews, friends and neighbors at a birthday party at Isabel and Polk Smartt's house in Chattanooga Valley. It was a memorable party for a memorable lady, and this is the cake they served.

GRANNY SMARTT'S BIRTHDAY CAKE

3 sticks margarine	3 cups plain flour
1 pound powdered sugar	1 teaspoon vanilla
6 eggs	

Cream margarine in large bowl of mixmaster. Add powdered sugar and cream well. Add eggs, one at a time. Then add flour in 3 or 4 portions. Add vanilla. Pour into greased and floured stem pan. Bake at 350 degrees for 30 minutes, then 325 degrees for about 40 minutes. Cool in pan 1 hour. Ice with Italian Meringue Icing.

ITALIAN MERINGUE ICING

1 cup sugar
¼ cup water
¼ teaspoon cream of tartar

4 egg whites
1 teaspoon vanilla

In small saucepan, combine sugar, water, cream of tartar, and stir until sugar is dissolved. Place on heat, cover pan and bring to a boil. Remove cover and boil rapidly until candy thermometer reads 242 degrees. Pour hot syrup in thin stream on stiffly beaten egg whites. Add vanilla.

Given me by Mrs. Polk Smartt

One of the most requested recipes we have ever had is Mrs. List's Sour Cream Cake. This is a pound type cake extra rich with sour cream. It can be made in a tube pan or in two loaf pans. It freezes beautifully, so you can always be ready for company. At Moccasin Bend Hospital, they make up 10 at a time to keep on hand in the freezer for special occasions.

MRS. LIST'S SOUR CREAM CAKE

1 cup butter
3 cups sugar
6 eggs, separated
3 cups flour

1 teaspoon salt
¼ teaspoon soda
2 teaspoons vanilla
1 cup sour cream

Beat egg whites until stiff and add ½ cup of the sugar so they will hold their air. Now cream the butter and the rest of the sugar. Add the egg yolks. Sift the flour, salt, and soda and add alternately with the sour cream. Add the vanilla. Fold in the egg whites last. Turn into a greased and floured tube pan or two loaf pans. Bake in a 325 degree oven for an hour and 15 minutes or until it is done. Turn out on cake rack to cool. This needs no icing because the crust is very crunchy and special.

The late Mrs. W. H. List

The most consistent prize winner at the Hamilton County Tri-State Fair for cakes and cookies is Mrs. Earl Brown. When asked what is the cake she most frequently makes for her own family, she gave me this simple yellow cake using a one bowl method. Making this cake is as easy as a cake mix and much better.

QUICK YELLOW CAKE

¾ cup shortening or margarine   1 ½ teaspoons vanilla
2 cups sugar   3 cups self-rising flour
3 eggs   1 ¼ cups milk

Put all ingredients except eggs in a large mixer bowl. Mix on medium speed for about 2 minutes. Add the eggs, one at a time, until blended. Bake in three 9 inch layer pans that have been greased and floured. Put them in a 375 oven for 30 to 35 minutes or until done. Cool 10 minutes. Then turn out on rack.

QUICK CHOCOLATE ICING

Mix together one-third cup sifted cocoa, 1 box powdered sugar, 1 stick butter, or margarine, 1 teaspoon vanilla, and 4 or 5 tablespoons scalded milk.

Mrs. Earl Brown

MOTHER'S BEST LAYER CAKE

½ cup butter   1 ¾ cup cake flour
½ cup milk   2 teaspoons baking powder
1 cup sugar   Grated rind of 1 orange
7 egg yolks

Cream the butter and sugar. Add the egg yolks, two at a time, sift the dry ingredients together. If you use butter, you won't need salt. Add the flour alternately with the milk and put in the orange rind last. Pour into a 9 by 13 inch pan since this is batter for a small cake. (Two 8 inch pans might do, but she has never tried it.) Bake at 325 degrees for 25 minutes. Cut in half and this makes a nice little rectangle shaped layer cake. It needs a moist icing. She uses chocolate or coconut.

Mrs. Roy McDonald

Mrs. Ira Trivers was one of the co-editors of a cookbook published a few years ago by the Women's Auxiliary of the Chattanooga Jewish Community Center. This is her recipe for pound cake which is baked in the unusual way of putting it in a cold oven and then turning the heat on.

MRS. TRIVERS' POUND CAKE

1 pound butter	*8 tablespoons light cream*
2 ¾ cup sugar	*1 teaspoon vanilla extract*
(reserve 6 tablespoons)	*1 teaspoon lemon extract*
8 eggs, separated	*6 tablespoons*
3½ cups sifted flour	*(reserved) sugar*

Cream together butter and sugar (less 6 tablespoons). Add egg yolks, 2 at a time, beating well after each addition. Add flour, light cream, vanilla and lemon extracts.

Beat egg whites until foamy. Gradually add the 6 tablespoons sugar, continuing to beat until stiff. Fold egg whites into first mixture. Pour into a lightly greased and floured 10 inch tube pan.

Set cake in cold oven. Set thermostat at 350. Turn on heat. Bake for 15 minutes. Reduce heat to 300. Bake until cake tests done, a total of about 1 hour and 10 minutes. Let stand in pan 10 minutes before turning out.

Mrs. Ira Trivers

A couple of summers ago Kitty Stone (Mrs. Harry) told me about a new chocolate cake making the rounds. We printed it and the chocolate pound cake got taken to church suppers, picnics, and to sick or grieving friends. It can be made plain or iced, and the rich solid texture of a pound cake is very attractive made with chocolate.

CHOCOLATE POUND CAKE

1½ cups butter	*4 tablespoons cocoa*
3 cups sugar	*½ teaspoon baking powder*
3 cups flour	*1 tablespoon vanilla*
1 cup milk	*½ teaspoon salt*
5 eggs	

Cream butter and sugar. Add eggs one at a time and beat well. Sift dry ingredients 3 times and add alternately with the milk. Pour into greased and floured tube pan. Bake 80 minutes at 325 degrees.

FROSTING

2 squares unsweetened chocolate
4 tablespoons butter
  or shortening
½ teaspoon salt
1 teaspoon vanilla

1½ cups sugar
½ cup milk
1 teaspoon corn syrup
1 cup chopped nuts

Grate chocolate and combine all ingredients except vanilla and nuts. Bring to a boil and cook two minutes. Remove from heat, cool and beat. Add vanilla and nuts and spread. It will be a thin fudgey glaze.

Mrs. Harry Stone

The late Winnie Holmes was a sweet fine lady who was secretary to the publisher. She had a new way with a German Chocolate Cake mix. She added sour cream, eggs, butter and baked it in a tube pan glazed with a chocolate icing.

WINNIE'S GERMAN CHOCOLATE CAKE

1 package German Chocolate
  Cake Mix
¼ cup water
2 eggs

1 cup sour cream
2 tablespoons softened
  butter or margarine

Combine cake mix, water, eggs, sour cream and butter in a mixing bowl. Blend at low speed just to moisten. Beat 4 minutes at medium speed of mixer, or vigorously with a spoon until creamy.

Pour batter into tube pan or 8 by 12 inch pan, which has been greased and the bottom lined with wax paper. Bake at 350 for 30 to 35 minutes, or until top gently springs back when pressed with finger. Cool in pan 10 minutes, then remove to rack to cool before putting on glaze.

CHOCOLATE GLAZE

2 squares unsweetened chocolate
½ teaspoon salt
1½ cups sugar
1 tablespoon corn syrup

4 tablespoons butter
1 teaspoon vanilla
½ cup milk

Grate chocolate and combine all ingredients except vanilla. Bring to a boil and cook 2 minutes. Remove from heat, cool and beat until it begins to thicken. Add vanilla and spread on cake. This is a thin sort of fudgy glaze.

The late Miss Winnie Holmes

Certainly adding much to the world of culture and arts in Chatta-nooga has been the Wallace Clements family. Doris and Wallace start-ed a small antiques business about 20 years ago, going to New York, buying estates, and bringing them back to Chattanooga. Then they began getting estates from England and Scotland. Their Hixson shop now occupies the space of about three warehouses, is the largest in the South, and they have encouraged thousands of Chattanoogans as well as out-of-town buyers to start their own collecting.

Their own home is tastefully furnished in mostly fine English and American pieces, but whenever I have been in the homey American kitchen, there has always been a homemade cake under the cake cov-er, hot coffee on the stove, and a mellow old pine lazy-Susan table to sit at and enjoy a piece of cake and a visit. The cake makers are Doris, her sister Lois Johnson, or one of the three girls. The Red Velvet Cake with chocolate icing is a favorite.

RED VELVET CAKE

½ cup butter plus 2 tablespoons	2 tablespoons cocoa
	1 teaspoon salt
1½ cups sugar	1 cup buttermilk
2 eggs	plus 2 tablespoons
1 ounce red food coloring	2¼ cups cake flour
1 teaspoon soda	½ teaspoon baking powder
1 tablespoon vinegar (cider)	1 teaspoon vanilla

Cream the butter and the sugar. Add the eggs one at a time. Add the coloring, coconut, and vanilla. Beat well. Add sifted salt, baking powder and flour alternately with the buttermilk. Put the soda in the vinegar. Sprinkle over batter. Fold (don't beat) until well blended. Bake in 3 8-inch layer pans at 350 for 25 minutes.

Frost with a cooked chocolate icing.

Mrs. Charles Wallace Clements

This cake is from one of our local church cookbooks, The Avondale Methodist. They dedicated it to the late Emma Wolfe, who had a repu-tation of knowing who was sick, bereaved, had just moved into a new house or had come home with a new baby. She always appeared at the right moment with sometimes a whole meal, or one of her famous cakes. The fastest one that she could put together and get to the right people was her Bake and Take Cake, rich with spices and oats. To see it at a covered dish supper was to know she was there.

BAKE AND TAKE OATMEAL CAKE

1¼ cup boiling water	½ teaspoon salt
1 cup oats	1 teaspoon soda
½ cup brown sugar	1 teaspoon cinnamon
½ cup butter	1 teaspoon nutmeg
1 cup white sugar	2 eggs
1¼ cups flour	1 teaspoon vanilla

Pour boiling water over the oats and let stand. Cream the butter and sugar well. Add eggs, one at a time. Sift flour with soda and spices. Add flour mixture with oats, add vanilla and bake 25 minutes at 350 degrees. Remove from oven and spread topping over the cake. Return to oven for 15 minutes.

TOPPING

1 stick melted margarine	2 egg yolks,
1 cup nuts	slightly beaten
1 cup brown sugar	1 cup coconut

The late Mrs. Emma Wolfe

At old fashioned Christmas open houses, there was always a dark fruit cake made with jam and a very light cake using nuts and cherries. To have a light cake and a dark cake, a country ham sliced thin, beaten biscuits, small sandwiches of turkey and plenty of eggnog, was to have a gracious open house indeed. This Christmas Cake of John Barnes is a good moist dark one.

CHRISTMAS CAKE

1 cup butter	1 teaspoon allspice
2 cups sugar	¾ cup buttermilk
3 whole eggs	2 ounces brandy
1 cup blackberry jam	(or brandy flavoring)
1 cup chopped walnuts	1½ cups sifted cake flour
1 cup glazed cherries	1½ cups sifted
1 cup chopped raisins	all purpose flour
1 cup mashed potatoes	1 teaspoon soda
1½ cups shredded coconut	A little salt

Cream butter and sugar, add eggs, beating well after each addition. Add jam, walnuts, cherries, raisins, potatoes, coconut and allspice. Stir in buttermilk. Add brandy. Add sifted flour with soda and salt and fold into the batter until smooth.

Bake in two or three layers or in a tube pan in a 250 oven (slow) for about 1½ hours or until done. Use any preferred icing with nuts.

John Barnes

An old fashioned white Christmas cake is this one from the family of Mrs. Arthur Paty.

ELEGANT WHITE FRUIT CAKE

2¼ cups cake flour
1 teaspoon baking powder
½ teaspoon salt
1 cup butter
1 cup sugar
5 eggs
1 tablespoon brandy or
  brandy flavoring

1 teaspoon lemon flavoring
¾ cup blanched almonds,
  chopped
1 cup fresh shredded coconut
½ cup candied lemon peel,
  chopped
½ cup candied cherries

Mix as you would any cake. Turn batter into greased and floured 9 inch tube pan and bake at 325 for about 1¼ hours. Frosting: Cream a 3 ounce package of cream cheese with 4 tablespoons cream. Add ⅛ teaspoon salt and about 2½ cups powdered sugar.

Mrs. Arthur Paty

Mrs. Levi Patton, as our most distinguished harpist, has recorded albums and given concerts here, in New York, and in Japan. Sometimes after a concert, she invited out of town guests to dinner at her home on Missionary Ridge where the dining room looks out over all the lights in the city below. She is a thoughtful hostess who likes to plan a beautiful table and a dinner to fit the occasion. She and Dr. Patton have been cultural and civic leaders in Chattanooga.

BANANA CAKE

1 whole egg, well beaten
2 cups sifted flour
1 teaspoon baking powder
1 teaspoon soda
½ cup shortening
1½ cups sugar

1 cup ripened
  mashed bananas
¾ cup sour milk
  or buttermilk
1 teaspoon vanilla
½ teaspoon salt

Sift flour, add baking powder, soda and salt, and sift together. Cream shortening well, add sugar, beat in the egg and mix. Mix in the

238

Mrs. Levi Patton as Chattanooga's most distinguished harpist, has performed in concerts both in New York and Chattanooga. She and Dr. Patton like to give after concert dinners at their home on Missionary Ridge.

bananas. Add flour alternately with the milk. The vanilla goes in last. Bake in 2 greased 8 inch pans at 375 degrees for about 25 minutes.

Frost with butter cream icing.

Mrs Levi Patton

A very quick dessert can be made with a can of blueberries and a yellow cake mix. Mrs. Cartter Patten used to make this when they summered in Maine, either with fresh or canned blueberries.

BLUEBERRY UPSIDE DOWN CAKE

Butter a 9 inch cake pan and add drained blueberries from a No. 2 can or a quart of fresh blueberries. Sprinkle liberally with sugar and pour over a simple one-egg cake batter. Bake in a quick oven 375 degrees until done. Turn out on a platter while hot and serve with whipped cream lightly sweetened and flavored, or a foaming brandy or rum sauce.

A yellow cake mix is a good substitute, but will be enough for two cakes.

Mrs Cartter Patten

One of the specialties at a recipe fair sponsored by the faculty at Bryan College in Dayton, Tennessee, was Apricot Nectar Cake. It is a delicious pound cake starting with a yellow cake mix. When we ran this in the column it was a readers' favorite.

APRICOT NECTAR CAKE

1 box yellow cake mix
5 eggs
1 cup salad oil
1 cup apricot nectar

1 box lemon gelatin
(regular size)
1 teaspoon lemon extract

Put all ingredients in a large bowl and beat 2 minutes at medium speed. Pour into a pan about 9 by 11 inches. Bake at 350 for 30 to 40 minutes.

GLAZE: Mix 1 cup sifted powdered sugar and the juice of 1 lemon. Pour over hot cake while still in the pan. Keep covered with foil. This cake will keep well, as it is very moist.

Bryan College Recipe Fair

Mrs. Paul Kruesi has always had a flair about serving food elegantly, keeping an eye out for the newest thing in recipes, needlepoint, gardening, house ideas, or menus. She is a creative person with very high standards, and she regularly inspires all her friends When she told me about a strawberry cake that you make by doctoring up a cake mix with strawberry gelatin and frozen strawberries, I knew it would be good if she said it was.

STRAWBERRY CAKE

1 package white cake mix
1 3-ounce package strawberry
 gelatin
½ cup water

½ cup salad oil
3 whole eggs
1 10-ounce package frozen
 strawberries, thawed

Stir gelatin into cake mix. Add the salad oil and water and beat 2 minutes in the mixer. Add eggs and beat 5 minutes more at medium speed. Fold into the batter the drained and defrosted berries, saving the juice. Pour into 2 9-inch greased and floured cake pans. Bake in a 350 oven for 20 to 25 minutes Don't overcook. Take from oven and let stand in pans 10 minutes before cooling on rack.

ICING

Soften two-thirds stick margarine and mix with 1 box sifted powdered sugar, adding the sugar gradually with 4 tablespoons strawberry juice. It may take a little more juice or a little less. When you have the right consistency, frost the cake.

Mrs. Paul Kruesi

An unusual cake to bring to Wednesday night suppers is a Rum Cake which Jean Evans (Mrs. John) got in Durham years ago when Jack was a medical student.

RUM CAKE

½ cup butter
½ cup margarine
2 cups sugar
4 eggs, added one at a time
3 cups sifted cake flour

½ teaspoon baking powder
½ teaspoon salt
1 cup buttermilk
½ teaspoon soda
1 teaspoon vanilla

Cream the butter, margarine and sugar. Add the vanilla. Add eggs, one at a time. Alternate the flour mixture and buttermilk. Bake in a greased and floured tube pan at 325 degrees. Bake 1 hour or 1 hour and 15 minutes until done. Glaze with the following syrup.

SYRUP

1 cup sugar
½ cup water

1½ teaspoons imitation
rum flavoring or rum to taste

Bring the sugar and water to a boil and take off the stove. Cool and add the flavoring. When you take the cake out, let stand 5 minutes in the pan. Turn out on a cake plate and spoon the syrup over the tops and sides of the cake as a glaze.

Mrs. John T. Evans

Interested readers have been time and again the source of many columns and articles, and one day I got a nice note from a reader suggesting her minister's wife as the subject for a future column.

"Josephine Mathis Johnson (Mrs. J. Fred)," she wrote, "is quiet and gracious; it is incredible how much visiting and baking she does among the congregation of the First Cumberland Presbyterian Church. She bakes pies, cakes, fresh bread, and her buffet suppers defy description. I have been the recipient of a number of loaves of fresh bread, cakes, salads, and I doubt that we have a family in our church of 1600 members that hasn't been brought something that she has baked along with a delightful visit."

Mrs. Johnson is an old friend of ours and as much as she would like to keep her doings a secret, I had already heard how she had brought dinner often to one member in a nursing home, how she seemed to know just what to bring to bereaved families, or to people in trouble.

So many people stop cooking when their families grow up. Mrs. Johnson has never stopped as long as someone is on her heart who needs a visit and a gift from her kitchen. She makes ice cream pies with meringue shells and keeps them in the freezer, since they will be good anytime; she takes mainly hams, salads, chicken or cake when there is a funeral in a family. Dr. Johnson is a beloved and outstanding minister whose influence is city wide. The Cumberland Youth Foundation in conjunction with their church has a sports program for thousands of young people all over the city, and their swimming team usually wins the championship.

Mrs. Johnson makes the following Upside Down Apricot Cake to take to a friend or to a church dinner. When she takes it to church, she

242

cuts individual squares and arranges on a tray, topping each serving with whipped cream and a cherry or pecan.

APRICOT UPSIDE DOWN CAKE

½ cup sugar
½ cup butter
1 egg
1 cup molasses
2½ cups sifted flour
2 teaspoons soda

¼ teaspoon cinnamon
½ teaspoon ginger
¼ teaspoon cloves
½ teaspoon salt
1 cup hot water

Cream butter and sugar. Add egg and stir well. Add molasses. Sift flour with soda and spices. Add to butter and sugar mixture. Add hot water last.

Place ¼ cup melted butter and ¾ cup brown sugar in the bottom of a 9 by 15 inch cake pan. Put in 1 can drained apricots and 1 can cooked prunes. Arrange over the sugar and butter alternately. Pour the cake batter over the fruit and bake at 350 degrees for 45 to 60 minutes. Cut into squares and serve each topped with whipped cream.

Mrs. J. Fred Johnson

We have a cousin, who, when she comes for a visit, always brings along a cake or two, some divinity candy she has made, a big box of nuts, and whatever else her gracious mind thinks up. Once she brought us an unusual kind of date nut cake with an orange glaze. Here it is.

COUSIN MILDRED'S ORANGE DATE NUT CAKE

1 cup butter
2 cups sugar
4 eggs
2 tablespoons grated
   orange rind
1 teaspoon vanilla
3½ cups flour

2 teaspoons soda
1 teaspoon salt
1¼ cups buttermilk
½ cup sifted flour
   (for dates and nuts)
1 cup chopped dates
1 cup broken pecans

Cream butter and sugar. Add eggs, one at a time, beating after each. Add orange rind and vanilla. Sift flour, salt, and soda together, and add to first mixture alternately with milk. Mix ½ cup flour with dates and nuts; fold into batter. Pour in greased tube pan. Bake at 325 degrees for 1 hour and 15 minutes.

ORANGE GLAZE

Blend together 1½ cups sugar, 1 cup orange juice, and 2 table-spoons grated orange rind. Cook on stove until sugar melts. Pour over cake while still warm. The cake is better if made a day ahead.

Mrs. E.L. McMurchey
Duncan, Mississippi

Surely one of the miracles in Chattanooga is the Chattanooga Free Press. Begun as a throw sheet to advertise my family's grocery chain, the Home Stores, it began as a regular Sunday paper in the spring of 1936 and went daily that August. The motor for the press that my father bought in Chicago was delayed weeks in the Pittsburg flood, and when it did arrive, erecting the press was one of those day and night affairs.

The first Sunday paper, with beautiful full color front page illus-trations was finally off the press the following Thursday, with my fa-ther and Charlie Bledsoe, the mechanic (who from memory of what the press looked like in Chicago, put it together), working four heart breaking days and nights in a row.

All the stories and adventures as we later became the Chattanooga News-Free Press, then in 1942 joined with the Chattanooga Times as the Chattanooga Publishing Company, then in 1966 became an inde-pendent again, with not only a daily, but with a resumed Sunday paper, would fill another book. For me, his daughter, Roy McDonald, my father, is Chattanooga's most unforgettable character.

No other newspaper has been started from scratch this way in the United States in these times and made it. We are a small East Tennes-see family, and the success of the paper is in some part due to the remarkable spirit of all the people who worked to put it out.

There is a family feeling and loyalty in every department. Almost everyone works hard and at capacity. From the advertising salesmen, the sports writers, the women's staff, and the boys on the city desk to the business side, there is a dedication to the conservative principles the paper stands for and an esprit de corps. With all the laughing, jokes, and friendships, it is amazing that any work gets done, but this group of great people turn out an uncommon amount of talented re-porting of the news.

In 1935 the Free Press was a weekly, and this picture shows the first plant at 1214 Broad Street. The editorial room, the composing room and the press room were one and the same, next to the Home Store warehouse. In early 1936 the paper bought a new press and moved to 815 Chestnut Street, publishing the first Sunday issue on Easter. It began daily publication on Monday, August 31st of that year, and in January, 1940 became the Chattanooga News Free Press after acquiring the News a month before. From small beginnings......

On this family newspaper, my father, Roy McDonald is publisher, my brother Frank McDonald is president, my brother-in-law Lee Anderson is editor, my aunt, Kitty McDonald writes a Sunday feature, I write a food feature and a Sunday feature each week, and there is a grandson in every department. We like to think we represent all the people of Chattanooga and the counties that surround it.

When Time and Newsweek came to report on our operation in 1966 when we became independent again, they printed in detail that my father felt his buying the old Davenport Hoisery Building for what he thought was a fraction of its real worth, was an "answer to prayer." We all consider it by the grace of God, as well as the paper's very existence today.

The recipes of News-Free Press people are sprinkled through this whole book......Eunice Bales' pound cake, Winnie Holmes' cherry salad, Laura DeArmond's cake. Whenever there is a party, every department is represented, from the mechanics at the garage, the people in the composing room, press room, editorial,and so on.

We are a close unit, and I have gotten to know many of the various departments through my four sons who have ever since they were ten or twelve, "helped" on a rather informal basis. They have swept, washed cars, and helped mechanics at the garage, and when the paper moved to the new building, they helped get it ready with a remarkable crew of men.

Carl Tallent, Cecil Craun and Landon (Tang) Floyd taught them how to drive a nail, lay floors, knock down partitions, and put up new ones, helped build the foundation for the press so that it would be exactly level, and then one exciting day they poured the concrete for the press, having to go to Uncle Herman's Shoe Store and buy special rubber boots small enough for Jonathan.

Ronald Owens, who is called Skinny by nearly everyone, is the expert in the press room. His ears can listen to the roll and whirr of a press and tell exactly how it is doing. He was in charge of completely assembling the press from the crates of parts and hundreds of photographs taken as it had been dismantled. It was put up one piece at a time, and when it completed its first run, the boys jubilantly brought home a souvenir copy. They were so dirty with printer's ink that I didn't recognize them.

In the succeeding years the boys have run errands, hunted mats, sold ads, written sports features, kept linage reports, done bookkeeping, run the elevator and the switchboard, along with their cousin

Frank McDonald. Their cousins, Corinne Anderson and Elizabeth McDonald, have been more ladylike in the art department and classified.

The same Chattanooga story has been repeated over and over, with variations, as other Chattanooga families have built their businesses. It might be a store, a carpet factory or a dry cleaners, but it gives a family a purpose.

Through the years one thing I have heard over and over is "You should get Mrs. Floyd's recipe for cake. Tang always has a piece of homemade cake in his lunch." Or "Carl brought a great lunch today. He said his wife used one of your recipes." I finally decided that nothing I could put together and send along with the boys could match Carl's or Preacher's or Tang's lunches.

I am also so conscious as other parents are, that we are very indebted to many people who put up with them and influence them to do as they are supposed to do. We are very lucky that we all love this newspaper, have plenty of work to do, and enjoy the deep friendships with the people who have helped make it what it is.

I finally got Tang to bring me his wife's cake recipe that the boys like.

QUICK POUND CAKE

1 box Duncan Hines lemon
cake mix

2 eggs, unbeaten
1 cup orange juice

Empty the mix in a large mixing bowl. Add the unbeaten eggs and the orange juice. Mix in the mixer until well blended. Grease and flour a tube pan. Pour in the batter and bake at 350 degrees for 25 minutes until well done.

ICING

1½ cups powdered sugar
1 tablespoon soft butter

1 tablespoon cream

Add orange juice until icing is thin enough to spread. Ice the cake while hot.

Mrs. Landon Floyd

E. T. Bales, now retired, was for many years our sports editor. When his wife Eunice brought a cake to News-Free Press gatherings, everyone wanted a sample, because she learned to bake from her mother-in-law, who was one of Chattanooga's noted cake experts.

EUNICE'S POUND CAKE

1 pound butter	8 tablespoons coffee cream
2¾ cup sugar	1 teaspoon vanilla
3½ cups sifted flour	1 teaspoon lemon
8 medium sized eggs	

Separate eggs, whip the whites, adding 6 level tablespoons of the sugar while beating. Place this mixture in the refrigerator until the rest of the cake is mixed.

Cream butter, gradually add the rest of the sugar. Add the egg yolks, about two at a time, beating after each addition. Add flour and cream alternately. Whip until as light as possible. It takes 10 minutes at least by electric mixer. The longer you beat, the lighter and fluffier the cake is. With the mixer at low, whip egg whites in only long enough to mix well. Pour batter into lightly greased tube pan or into 3 small loaf pans. Start oven at 350 for 15 minutes, then turn to 300 degrees and bake 65 minutes more or until done.

Mrs. E. T. Bales

When the Valamont Club had a country supper as a fund raising project, they made a huge assortment of cakes and sweets, made by their members. Two rather unusual cakes were Marshmallow Fudgkins brought by Mrs. Richard Cunningham, and Mrs. Bill McCool's Apricot Brandy Pound Cake.

MARSHMALLOW FUDGKINS

2 squares unsweetened chocolate	1½ cups all purpose flour
	1 teaspoon baking powder
2 sticks margarine (1 cup)	1 cup broken nutmeats
4 eggs	2 teaspoons vanilla flavoring
2 cups sugar	

Melt chocolate and margarine in double boiler. In electric mixer, beat eggs until foamy, add sugar, beat well, then add all other ingredients and the chocolate mixture. Spread in greased 11 by 13 inch pan and bake at 325 degrees about 35 minutes.

Meanwhile prepare topping as follows: in double boiler, melt 1 stick margarine, 2 squares unsweetened chocolate, 1 small can evaporated milk, and 1 cup sugar. Add 1 teaspoon vanilla. Beat in 1 box confectioner's sugar. The mixture will be thin. As soon as the cake is done, cover with a 6 ounce bag of miniature marshmallows. Then pour on he hot icing.

Eleanor says to bake this recipe the day before you want to serve it. The next day cut into 1 inch squares.

Mrs. Richard Cunningham

APRICOT BRANDY POUND CAKE

3 cups sugar	1 teaspoon vanilla
2 sticks margarine	1 teaspoon butter flavoring
6 eggs	3 cups flour
½ teaspoon rum flavoring	¼ teaspoon soda
1 teaspoon orange flavoring	½ teaspoon salt
¼ teaspoon almond flavoring	1 cup sour cream
½ teaspoon lemon flavoring	½ cup apricot brandy

Cream sugar and oleo; add eggs one at a time, then add flavorings. Add dry ingredients alternately with sour cream and brandy. Bake in greased tube pan at 325 degrees for 1 hour and 10 minutes.

Mrs. Bill McCool

Our neighbor Kathy Lyon was one of the smart young marrieds who combined houskeeping with a career as an audiologist at the Siskin Speech and Hearing Center. On her days off, she brought over some old fashioned tea cakes just as her neighbor in High Point, North Carolina used to bring to her.

HIGH POINT CUP CAKES

4 eggs	2 cups sifted plain flour
2 cups sugar	1½ teaspoons baking powder
1 cup milk	1 teaspoon vanilla
1 stick butter	

Cream the butter and sugar. Add eggs and beat well. Mix flour, baking powder and eggs. Add to the batter alternately with milk. Add vanilla. Pour batter into cup cake pan that has been lined with paper liners. Bake in a 375 degree oven for 12 to 15 minutes.

Mrs. Richard Lyon

Whenever there is a birthday among the Free Press staff, there is usually cake and coffee in that department, and from time to time, there are office parties either on the lake or at the paper. Usually there is a long table of cakes and cookies to choose from, and they are all good enough to want the recipes. The following cakes all made a memorable picnic on the lake.

Laura DeArmond is a member of the display advertising department, and a good cook who is always trying new recipes. When the sour cream cake came out several years ago, she experimented by using more eggs to make it lighter. Here it is.

LAURA'S SOUR CREAM CAKE

1 cup butter	1 teaspoon salt
3 cups sugar	2 teaspoons vanilla
8 eggs, separated	1 cup sour cream
3 cups cake flour	

Beat egg whites until stiff, and gradually add ½ cup of the sugar so they will hold their air. Now cream the butter and the rest of the sugar. Add egg yolks. Sift the flour, salt, and add alternately with the sour cream and vanilla mixture. Fold in egg whites. Pour into a greased and floured tube pan. Bake in a 325 oven for 1 hour and 15 minutes. Turn out on cake rack to cool.

Mrs. John DeArmond

My grandfather moved to Knoxville in 1922 to start the White Stores, a chain of grocery stores, and two years later my father returned to Chattanooga to begin the Home Stores here. This pattern of a Knoxville branch of the family as well as a Chattanooga branch has been experienced by several East Tennessee families, and makes for many pleasant memories of family reunions, summer gatherings of cousins, weddings, and always good food.

My uncle, the late Dwight McDonald, headed the White Stores, and he and my aunt Bernice had the family record for beautiful weddings with outdoor receptions in their gardens. Their big back yard on Kingston Pike is actually geared for their children, grandchildren and friends, with tennis courts, swimming pool, and all sorts of activities, but for the weddings, everything was manicured, planted in geraniums and begonias, and the summer wedding day was beautiful four different times.

For a summer party down by the pool Bernice tried a new apple cake recently which she passed on to me.

250

BERNICE'S APPLE CAKE

2 cups sugar
2 cups flour
1⅛ cup corn oil
2 cups chopped apples
1 cup nuts, chopped
2 eggs, well beaten

1 teaspoon soda
1 teaspoon vanilla
1 teaspoon rum
   or black walnut flavoring
½ teaspoon salt

Combine the ingredients in a large bowl and pour into a greased rectangular cake pan. Bake at 350 for about an hour or an hour and ten minutes. Do not open the oven for the first 45 minutes. Serves 12.

Mrs. Dwight McDonald
Knoxville, Tennessee

A Centennial Cake (also called the Robert E. Lee Cake) is a big elegant one. It deserves to get taken to church when it is your time to bring dessert, and there isn't a man in America who wouldn't be flattered to have a birthday cake like this ... three layers of light tender cake with a lemon filling and Seven Minute Frosting topped with coconut.

The spectacular thing about this cake is its height ... it is six to eight inches high. People will gasp and ask if you beat your egg whites separately, and what on earth you did to get such volume. You can either tell them or not. When you look through the ingredients ... 4 cups flour, 2½ cups sugar, and so on ... you will suddenly realize that the reason it rises twice as high as any other cake is that it has twice as much batter! Very impressive.

CENTENNIAL COCONUT CAKE

4 cups sifted cake flour
5 teaspoons baking powder
1½ teaspoons salt
6 egg whites
½ cup sugar
1 cup shortening

2 cups sugar
2 cups milk
2 teaspoons vanilla
   Lemon filling
   Seven Minute Frosting
1 package frozen coconut

With butter, use 1½ cups milk; with vegetable shortening, use 2 cups milk. This cake made with margarine is unsatisfactory.

Measure sifted flour, add baking powder and salt, and sift three times together. Beat egg whites until foamy, add 1 cup sugar gradually, and continue beating until meringue will hold up in stiff peaks.

251

Cream shortening, add 2 cups sugar gradually, and cream together until light and fluffy. Add flour mixture alternately with the milk, a small amount at a time, beating after each addition until smooth. Add vanilla. Then add meringue and beat thoroughly into batter.

Pour batter into 3 round 9 inch layer pans, which have been greased and floured. Bake in moderate oven 375 degrees for 20 to 25 minutes. Cool layers. Spread 2 layers wih lemon filling and cover top of third layer and the sides of the cake with Seven Minute Frosting. While frosting is still soft, sprinkle liberally with coconut.

LEMON FILLING

¾ cup sugar	1 cup water
¼ cup cornstarch	¼ cup lemon juice
¼ teaspoon salt	1 tablespoon butter
2 egg yolks, slightly beaten	1 teaspoon grated lemon rind

Combine salt, sugar, and cornstarch in top of double boiler. Blend together egg yolks, water and lemon juice in small bowl. Add to sugar mixture gradually, blending well. Cook over boiling water, about 5 minutes, or until mixture thickens, stirring constantly. Remove from heat. Add butter and lemon rind. Cool slightly before spreading on cake.

SEVEN MINUTE FROSTING

2 egg whites, unbeaten	¼ cup water
1½ cups sugar	2 teaspoons light corn syrup
Dash of Salt	1 teaspoon vanilla

Combine egg whites, sugar, salt, water and corn syrup in top of double boiler. Beat about 1 minute, or until thoroughly mixed. Then place over boiling water and beat constantly with sturdy egg beater (or at high speed of electric beater) for 7 minutes or until frosting will stand in stiff peaks.

Remove from boiling water. For a very smooth and satiny frosting, pour at once into large bowl for final beating. Then add vanilla and beat 1 minute or until thick enough to spread.

The Fowlers and the Sterchis have been in the furniture business in East Tennessee for generations, and there is probably not a home between here and Knoxville that is not prettier and more comfortable because of their furniture. (Dick Fowler, the most recent Fowler to

open his own business, Richard Fowler Galleries, is the fourth generation in the business.) The feminine side of the family has distinguished
themselves as fine Southern cooks. Chattanooga cooks have enjoyed
Mrs. John O. Fowler's recipes in the food column for years.

Her daughter, Charlotte Fowler Maclellan (Mrs. Hugh), says that
even on Christmas Eve with a big family of children, Mrs. Fowler
would make four or five cakes and take down to serve to the truck
drivers who were working on late deliveries. She loved to cook, and
although she taught her cook, Annie B. Williams, to make her specialties, she was a worker and constantly making these herself. The Date
Nut Bread was always served at the Summertown Labor Day Picnic. It
is very moist but calls for no butter.

MRS. FOWLER'S DATE NUT BREAD

1 package 8-ounce pitted dates	2 teaspoons baking powder
1 cup boiling water	2 cups flour
1 scant teaspoon soda	1 cup pecans
1 cup sugar	½ teaspoon salt
2 eggs (beaten slightly)	

Pour boiling water and soda over cut-up dates. Stir and let stand
until cool. Add sugar, pecans and 2 eggs. Sift flour before measuring.
Sift 2 cups flour with baking powder and salt. Add to wet ingredients
until just well mixed. Bake at 350 for 1 hour until broom straw comes
out clean. Makes 1 loaf pan about 9 by 5 by 2½. Serve sliced with butter.

Mrs. Hugh Maclellan

To make high fluffy angel food cakes is the desire of every cook.
And actually the angel food cake is the easiest and quickest to make.
Years ago I took an angel food cake to our Hamilton County Fair,
and the minute I walked in, I wished I hadn't. One older lady had entered an angel food that was the highest, most beautiful thing I ever
saw. All I could think of in my honest envy was that she must have
doubled the recipe and baked it all in one pan. When I asked her how
many egg whites she used, she assured me it was a dozen, but she
laughed and said she had been baking them all her life.

Now I know that she had just picked up some rules. I knew then that
I wouldn't be happy until I could make as high an angel food cake as
anyone could, so I took pains to learn.

My friend Luci Carter makes tall tender angel foods. One afternoon I took my ingredients over to her kitchen so she could tell me what
I was doing wrong. It turned out that I was trying too hard and was

253

beating my egg whites too stiff. I polished up this point and thought up some procedure rules for myself. That year I went on a real angel food binge, and made them so fast that I always had one to take to friends or just for my own hungry boys.

Now for the rules that make angel food cake making foolproof. First, in sponge cakes, the only leavening is the air that is incorporated into the beaten egg or egg whites. Therefore the main thing is to beat the most air into the egg whites, and then to handle very lightly indeed, so that most of this air will be kept while mixing in the regular ingredients. It is the expansion of air that makes the cake light. If the air is lost in mixing, the cake will be heavy and too compact in texture.

This is the way to mix an angel food. Sift and measure the flour. Be sure to use nested measuring cups and level off the tops exactly with a knife. Mix the flour with the required amount of the sifted sugar and sift several times. Have egg whites at room temperature; sift salt and cream of tartar over them and beat until just stiff, but not dry. I had been overdoing this. Add flavoring and gradually beat in the rest of the sugar, a little at a time. (If you dumped it all in, you would lose some precious air.) Then turn off the mixer and fold in the flour and sugar mixture lightly and carefully until it is all incorporated. Pour into ungreased tube pan and bake according to recipe.

The traditional baking temperature is a slow one, 325 degrees. The newest method is in a hotter oven 375 or 400 degrees. Bake until the cake springs back when lightly pressed with the finger tips, or until you can see no beads of moisture in the cracks on the top of the cake.

Remove from oven, and invert over a soft drink bottle so that the cake doesn't rest on the upper crust. After about two hours when it is completely cool, loosen the sides and work around the tube with a thin bladed knife.

The most ideal time to put together an angel food is just after breakfast. You can be doing the dishes at the same time. The rewards are great, because you can build a great culinary reputation. Lucy says she doesn't know how to make any other cake, but she doesn't have to!

When you make a real angel food cake, see how fast it goes, and taste the flavor and texture that fresh eggs contribute, you'll promise yourself to do it often.

The yellow and white angel food, made by adding some yolks to half the finished batter and then marbling the yellow and white mixtures, is a favorite with the family. So is a chocolate angel food.

LUCI'S ANGEL FOOD CAKE

1¼ cups sifted cake flour
½ cup granulated sugar sifted
1½ cups (about 12) egg whites
¼ teaspoon salt
1¼ teaspoons cream of tartar

1 teaspoon vanilla
¼ teaspoon almond extract
 (optional)
1¼ cups sifted granulated sugar

Measure the sifted flour, add ½ cup sugar, and sift the mixture four times. Combine egg whites, salt, cream of tartar, and flavorings in a large bowl. Beat with beater until moist soft peaks form. Add rest of sugar in 4 additions, beating until blended each time. Sift in flour mixture in four additions, folding in with large spoon each time; turn bowl often. Pour batter into pan. Bake at 375 degrees for 35 to 40 minutes. Invert pan on a bottle; let stand until cool. Then loosen from sides and remove.

Mrs. J.O. Carter

CHOCOLATE ANGEL FOOD

Follow the regular angel food recipe, but leave out the almond flavoring. Substitute ¼ cup cocoa for ¼ cup of the flour and sift well with the flour mixture. The boys like this frosted with whipped cream.

I had always heard that Mrs. Mose Siskin was famous for her cakes, and once I tasted her sponge cake. It was high and light, and the whole confection seemed to weigh only a few ounces. This is the type I can remember at my great-grandmother's. It really melts in your mouth. Mrs. Siskin sometimes bakes several cakes at a time and puts some in the freezer, has one on hand, and gives away others.

MRS. SISKIN'S SPONGE CAKE

9 eggs, separated
½ teaspoon salt
¾ teaspoon cream of tartar
1¼ cups sugar
2 tablespoons lemon juice

1¾ teaspoon grated lemon rind
 (optional)
2½ tablespoons water
1¼ cups sifted cake flour

Beat egg whites and salt until foamy. Add cream of tartar, continue beating until shiny peaks are formed. Gradually add ½ cup sugar, sprinkling 2 tablespoons at a time. Continue beating until stiff meringue is formed. Beat egg yolks until very thick and lemon colored.

Gradually add rest of sugar until well blended. Combine lemon juice and water to egg white mixture. Beat well. Add to egg white mixture. Fold in flour thoroughly but gently.

Pour into ungreased tube pan. Cut through batter with knife to remove air bubbles. Bake in a 350 degree oven for 45 or 50 minutes.

Mrs. Mose Siskin

An uneventful night one summer the phone rang and someone asked Kinch, who was on the board of the Chief John Ross House, how a group of Cherokee Indians who were here from Oklahoma, could get in to see it. They were a delegation from Oklahoma making the trip back east to see their native mountains and their distant cousins, the Cherokees, near Gatlinburg in the Smokies.

Impulsively I said, "I made a gold and white angel food cake this afternoon. Call back and invite them to come up for coffee." The Indians in our country were treated very unfairly. I don't know what solution would have been fair, but I have always wanted to tell a Cherokee face to face that I am sorry. After talking a few minutes, one of us did call back and invite them over.

Chattanooga was the last of the Tennessee towns to be settled by the white man because it was the last citadel of the Cherokee Indians. They had once owned from the Blue Ridge Mountains of Virginia down to Rome, Georgia, and had ceded one vast domain after another. Here they gathered in the one area they loved best.

The Cherokees had actually been a very civilized tribe when they lived on this land. They had a constitution and declared themselves a nation with their capital at New Echota just south of Chattanooga near Dalton. They wore white men's dress, had an alphabet and a newspaper, good schools for their children and prosperous plantations. Chief John Ross, who had a landing on the river of Chattanooga, was part Indian and a leader. The Cherokees fought on the side of Jackson against the warlike Creeks, and at one time saved his life. When he ordered them west on the "Trail of Tears" in the 1830's, they were very bitter.

Some of the Cherokees, knowing they would have to go, began to move West in small parties. General Winfield Scott with 2,000 men came to enforce the removal of the rest in 1838. The Indians, who had been intelligent, civilized and prosperous, were treated with systematic cruelty, dragged from their homes and prodded with bayonets into stockades, which had been built. They were kept for weeks, and when their strength was sapped, they left Ross's Landing in the middle of winter to walk to Oklahoma. 13,000 left and 4,000 died on the way.

The Ross House, one of the oldest homes in the region, was the home of Cherokee Chief John Ross in Rossville, Georgia. The house, dating from about 1790, has been restored.

The missionaries who had worked with the Indian schools at Sale Creek, Hiwassee, Brainerd, and at Spring Place, accompanied the Indians west.

One band of Indians responded to the cruel treatment by the soldiers by fleeing to the inaccessible Smokies and their descendants live in Cherokee, North Carolina, to this day.

That night, about 20 well dressed Indians came up our front steps, came to the dining room for coffee and cake, and then sat in the living room to talk. They told of the hard trip west. One old grandmother wanted to take her large iron pot which she used for washing and cooking. In crossing the mountains, on an arduous winding mountain path, the heavy pot slipped and fell clear to the bottom. The soldiers wouldn't let her go back to get it.

It was a hard trip with many sick and dying. When they got to the land in Oklahoma, it seemed a desolate place indeed when they remembered the green mountains and the rich river soil. For years they wondered what happened to the part of the tribe who refused to leave and instead hid in the inaccessible Smoky Mountains to the north.

Along the banks of the river and the lake today, often arrow heads turn up; there is one section on Lookout Mountain where many have been found.

The Indian way of life lasted many hundred years before the white man came to Chattanooga. It was a memorable night that we have never forgotten — all because we happened to have a fresh cake on hand.

GOLD AND WHITE ANGEL FOOD

Make an angel food cake but leave out the almond flavoring. When you have finished the batter divide it into two parts. In a separate bowl beat 4 egg yolks until lemon colored and add the rind of 1 lemon, grated. Add half the white batter to the yolks and mix gently until blended. Now drop by spoonfuls in the tube pan, alternating white and yellow batter. Cut through the batter with a knife, going around three or four times. Bake as usual. When the cake is cooled, sift powdered sugar over it. This is pretty and the light lemony flavor is very refreshing.

CHAPTER XII

Cookies

In Chattanooga at Christmas time, almost everyone you know bakes some sort of special cookies. There are teas, open houses, Coke parties, and coffees. Some are very elaborate and some are quite simple, but all of them feature some sort of cookie along with coffee, tea, punch or Cokes.

In our town cookies go in waves of popularity. When we taste a good cookie, we get the recipe and make it. Many of the recipes in this chapter are favorites that have made many festive occasions for many different cooks.

It would be hard to say who really made the Fruitcake Cookies first. I got the recipe from my mother, who got it from Mrs. Hilda Spence, who got it from Mrs. John O. Fowler, who must have gotten it from someone else. Of all the recipes that we have published in the column, copies of this have been requested more than any other recipe. The Luscious Squares have also made the rounds in such an area that I am not sure who makes them the most. There are simple cookies and complicated cookies, coolies that can be passed in place of dessert, and plain oatmeal cookies to have in the cookie jar for the children. Cookies are a part of happy homelife, to be shared both in recipe and in the actual finished cookie.

One day when we needed lots of brownies to have for one of the children's parties, I experimented with doubling the standard brownie recipe and baking the batter in our largest cookie pan. This made 48 brownies to a pan, even if they were thinner than usual. Then since they looked thin, I glazed them with the famous $100 Chocolate Icing that has lemon juice in it to cut the too-chocolate taste. Put on while warm, the frosting dried to a shine, with all the rich pecans showing. We liked them so much that we have never made them any other way since, and call them $100 Brownies because of their frosting.

259

$100 BROWNIES

Melt over low heat in a heavy saucepan, 1 stick of real butter and 4 squares bitter chocolate. Let cool. Drop into the cooled mixture 2 cups of granulated sugar and stir until well mixed. Now add 4 eggs, one at a time, and mix well. Finally add 1 cup sifted all purpose flour, ½ teaspoon salt and 1 teaspoon vanilla.

Grease and flour a large cookie pan about 10 by 15 inches. Pour in the brownie batter and bake in a 350 oven for 20 to 25 minutes. You must watch to see that they don't overcook. Since they are thin, you must keep them on the soft and moist side. They are done when they first begin to pull away from the sides of the pan and get a dull look on the top.

$100 BROWNIE FROSTING

Melt over low heat ½ stick butter and 1 square of bitter chocolate. When melted, add about ½ box of powdered sugar. Mix. Take off stove and add 1 egg. Mix well. Add 1½ teaspoons vanilla and 1½ teaspoons of lemon juice. This combination of flavors cuts the too-chocolate taste. Finally add 1 cup chopped pecans. Your consistency should be about right, but if not, add more powdered sugar. Remember that it is warm and will get harder. This acts as a chocolate pecan glaze, and should have a lovely sheen if it is put on while the brownies are warm. This frosting is the secret of the popularity of $100 Brownies.

These fudgecake brownies bake over hot water in the oven, which accounts for the extra moist chewy quality. many people make these brownies now. I got them from Corinne Spears (Mrs. W.D.) and she got the recipe originally from Margaret Killebrew (Mrs. Robert).

FUDGECAKE BROWNIES

2 ounces baking chocolate	1 cup broken pecans
1 stick butter	Pinch salt
3 eggs	¾ cup flour, unsifted
1½ cups sugar	½ teaspoon baking powder
1 teaspoon vanilla	

Melt chocolate and butter in double boiler and let cool. Add other ingredients. Line an 8-inch square pan with waxed paper. Put the batter in and place in a large pan of water. Bake in a 350 oven for 35 to 40 minutes. Let cool in the pan. Turn out, peel off paper, and cut. Sprinkle with powdered sugar. Store in tin box.

Mrs. Robert Killebrew

For years it has been the tradition for the Chapin clan to have Sunday night family dinners with the E. Y. Chapins, Jr. Mrs. Chapin usually has a ham or turkey or a casserole plus a salad. Her specialty as far as her grandchildren are concerned is her Butterscotch Brownies.

BUTTERSCOTCH BROWNIES

1 stick butter
2 cups light brown sugar
2 well beaten eggs
1 cup flour, sifted
2 teaspoons baking powder

½ teaspoon salt
1 teaspoon vanilla
1 cup black walnuts,
    chopped

Cream the butter and the sugar. Add the eggs, one at a time. Sift the dry ingredients and add them plus the vanilla and the nuts. Grease and flour a brownie pan and pour in this batter. Cook at 350 degrees for 25 minutes. The main thing is not to let these overcook, and you will have to watch the first time. They may seem too soft when you take them out, but remember that you want them chewy. Cut into bars while warm.

Mrs. E. Y. Chapin, Jr.

When the Philoptochos Society (Friends of the Poor) of the Greek church has its annual luncheon at the Hunter Art Gallery, they usually have a capacity crowd. Where else can you taste the delicate specialties for which they are noted! Mrs. Gus Vlasis is famous for the delicate crescent cookies rolled in powdered sugar.

SWEET CRESCENT COOKIES
(Kourabiedes)

1 pound unsalted butter (sweet)
2 egg yolks
4 tablespoons confectioner's
    sugar
¼ cup bourbon (optional)

4 to 6 ounces blanched almonds,
    chopped and lightly browned
    in oven (cool before adding)
5 to 6 cups flour
    (or a little more)

Beat butter with electric mixer for 20 to 25 minutes until light and fluffy. Add egg yolks, sugar, bourbon, and mix well; then add toasted almonds. Start adding flour, mixing by hand. Mix well as you blend and add enough flour so the dough will be soft but not sticky.

Shape into crescents or rounds and bake on greased pan at 350 degrees about 15 to 20 minutes, until very lightly browned. Allow to cool, then sprinkle with sifted confectioner's sugar. Makes 40 to 50 cookies. These keep well in an air tight container.

Mrs. Gus Vlasis

Knoxville had been settled by Governor Blount and had a town and college when Tennessee became a state in 1796. From that time on, settlers came farther south into Indian country, and Hamilton County was formed in 1819 with a log court house on the farm of Asahel Rawlings at Dallas.

There were 765 white settlers and some of the families are still represented......the Pattersons, Jones, McDonalds, Eldridges, Coulters, and Hutchesons; the McGills, Lewises, Thatchers, Clifts, Hixsons, and Rawlings. Settlers could settle north of the Tennessee River, but the other side of the river where Chattanooga now is and on to Missionary Ridge belonged to the Cherokee Nation until 1835. The northern end of Hamilton County is older than Chattanooga, which wasn't organized until 1838.

When my grandfather was growing up on the farm north of Sale Creek, he promised himself that if he ever got a chance, he would leave and go in business, which he did. Then just to show that sometimes life plays strange tricks on us, when in 1933 he and his children had a chance to buy back the old farm and the house that had been out of the family for years, they did. This is the way that his city grandchildren grew up with all the fond memories of summers on a farm.

My aunt and uncle lived there, and I will never know how Aunt Clara and Uncle Gene Ketner put up with so many children who begged, when our parents came up on Sunday, to stay "just one more week." To get up early and go out to the barn seemed fun; we played in the loft, stepped on rusty nails and had to be taken to Dayton to the doctor, swam in the new swimming pool which was filled with the coldest well water you ever felt. We rode horses, and a big brown one called Old Frank could carry at least three of us.

We rode horses back to the foot of Walden's Ridge which stretches all the way up the valley (named for John Walden, a "long hunter" of the Daniel Boone era. He was gone all winter and would come back a year later if he hadn't been killed by Indians. Since he was gone such a long time, they called him a "long hunter"). We actually thought we were the first children to discover a place called "Blue Hole" up on the side of the mountain, where there was a lovely pool of water, fish, gnats, laurel and mosquitos.

On Sundays there were big dinners, ball games in the front yard, Aunt Clara's homemade ice cream. One year Uncle Gene built us a tree house down over Sale Creek big enough to sleep about 4 or 6 with a porch that extended way out over the creek in the trees. During the day we would build rafts out of old railroad ties and pole our way down the

My family's farm is in the northern part of Hamilton County, where there are many happy childhood memories for grandchildren and friends.

creek a mile or two to Sale Creek, where we would call the farm and someone would come and get us.

We learned to drive by learning how to drive the tractor in the field. Then when we were nearing sixteen and driving age, each one of us would practice backing, shifting gears, making turns, and so on, by taking a car down to the front meadow. You can develop great skill this way without bothering anyone or anything but an occasional cow. Uncle Gene usually thought enough of them to put them in another pasture.

After my brother and my sisters were grown, my own mother and father did over the old house for the third or fourth time and lived there, providing memories for still another generation of 15 grandchildren. After Mother's Sunday dinners, my father would usually get out the jeep for a Sunday ride through the woods for the children. To go through the woods, over rocks, up an old logging road, down a glen is to know that this valley and these mountains are the loveliest in the world.

On summer afternoons, he would hitch up the pair of team horses to a talley-ho and take 20 or 30, including my grandmother, who was getting quite old, for a more leisurely ride to the West Side. These were wonderful rides.

There is the unique sensation of being pulled in a wagon by a horse, the clippity clop of the hoofs, the sounds of the wheels, the steady jerking sensation of being pulled. There were times I have been scared, and if you haven't experienced the uneasy doubt and the pang in your stomach that happens when the horses haven't been driven in a long time, and when your fearless father is sure that they are completely under control, but they do seem to be going the homeward stretch mighty fast . . . then you haven't lived.

But we got home every time. The only times we didn't get home on schedule were when the jeep broke down. And even these experiences can come in handy. When Kinch was on the DMZ in Vietnam, the Marine jeep broke down with a broken clutch in enemy territory. Kinch says that after they had all tried everything, he remembered that in a jeep the bolt that holds on the mirror is a lot like the bolt they needed on the clutch. He tried it and drove it on in to camp!

After getting home from a jeep ride or a tally-ho trip, whichever grandchild was the baby was asleep and the rest were thirsty. This was Coke time with one of the boys usually getting a handful of Mother's sugar cookies from the canister. The following recipe is the one she makes most often.

A tally-ho is an old-fashioned buggy long enough to hold a large group of people. There is a driver's seat, with long bench-type seats behind. Seat cushions and good springs make this a smooth-riding and beautiful carriage, which is pulled by large and strong team horses. It was a popular conveyance during the horse and buggy days of America.

MOTHER'S SUGAR COOKIES

1 cup sugar	1 teaspoon soda
1 cup shortening or margarine	½ teaspoon nutmeg
1 egg plus 1 egg yolk	1 teaspoon vanilla
3 cups flour	

Mix shortening and sugar; cream well. Add egg, well beaten, and vanilla. Sift soda, nutmeg and flour together and add to mixture. Put in refrigerator for ½ hour. Roll out on pastry canvas, cut and bake in a 325 degree oven. They should be lightly brown in about 10 minutes.

Mrs. Roy McDonald

If you ever serve Apricot Cookie Bars at a coffee, you will have many recipe requests. They are very different and we have made them many times since Gail Brody gave the recipe to me.

APRICOT COOKIE BARS

½ cup soft butter	1 cup sifted flour
½ cup light brown sugar	

Set the oven for 350. In a small bowl at medium speed, cream the butter with the sugar until light and fluffy. At low speed, mix in the flour until blended. Pat the dough evenly into the bottom of a 9 by 9 inch pan. Bake 10 to 20 minutes or until golden brown. Let cool in the pan 20 minutes. While cooling, make the filling.

1¼ cup dried apricots	1 tablespoon grated orange peel
½ cup light brown sugar	1 cup coarsely chopped walnuts
2 tablespoons cornstarch	or hazelnuts
(or 1 tablespoon arrowroot)	2 eggs
¼ cup orange juice	3½ ounces flaked coconut
1 teaspoon grated lemon peel	

In a saucepan over medium heat cook the apricots in enough water to cover. This takes about 30 minutes or you can do it faster in a pressure cooker. Drain. Reserve 2 tablespoons liquid. Cut in quarters.

Combine in saucepan with the reserved liquid, sugar, cornstarch, salt, orange peel, lemon peel, and juice. Bring to a boil and reduce heat. Simmer 2 or 3 minutes, stirring constantly until thickened. Stir in nuts and smooth over cooled crust. In a small bowl, beat 2 eggs until frothy. Stir in the coconut. Spread over apricot mixture and bake 25 minutes at 350 degrees. Cut into 24 bars while still warm. Cool.

Miss Gail Brody

The R. J. Maclellans, long associated with the Provident Insurance Company here, had a wonderful cook, Grace Hill. When Hugh Maclellan was attending Cornell, Grace missed him as much as his folks and used to send regular boxes of cookies which the Maclellans always called "Grace's Rocks." They are a little like Hermits, and still a family favorite.

GRACE'S ROCKS

1½ cups light brown sugar
1 cup butter
3 eggs
1 teaspoon sugar, dissolved in
   3 tablespoons water
1 teaspoon vanilla

2 teaspoons cinnamon
½ teaspoon salt
3 cups flour (more if needed)
½ cup English walnuts
1 pound dates

Cream butter, sugar, and egg yolks. Add soda, flavoring, and one cup flour at a time. Add walnuts and dates in the last cup of flour.

Drop by spoonfuls on a greased cookie sheet and bake at 350 to 375 for 12 to 15 minutes. Keep rocks in a stone jar. They are better when a day old.

Mrs. Hugh Maclellan

A good bar cookie to compliment Brownies or to pass for dessert is Lemon Meringue Squares.

LEMON MERINGUE SQUARES

½ cup shortening
½ cup sifted confectioners sugar
2 tablespoons grated lemon rind
2 eggs, separated

1 cup sifted all purpose flour
½ cup granulated sugar
1 tablespoon lemon juice
½ cup finely chopped nut meats

Cream shortening and confectioners sugar together until light and fluffy. Blend in lemon rind. Beat egg yolks until thick and light. Add to first mixture. Add flour slowly and mix til smooth. Spread and pat this stiff mixture in a thin even layer in a greased 9 by 13 by 2 inch pan. Bake in a 350 degree oven for 10 minutes. Meanwhile beat egg whites until fluffy. Add sugar gradually while beating. Beat until stiff but not dry. Fold in lemon juice a little at a time. Fold in nuts. Spread over baked layer. Return to oven and bake 25 minutes longer. Cool about 3 minutes and cut into 48 squares.

Mrs. William Ragland III and Mrs. Jack Stephenson are sisters who enjoy entertaining together with an annual holiday coffee.

Mrs. William Ragland III and Mrs. Jack Stephenson are a pair of Chattanooga sisters who have gotten quite a reputation for entertaining together with a coffee, which they think up about every other year. Jane and Carol grew up as the Keese sisters here, trade recipes, have many of the same friends. Carol says they learned many things from their own parties.

First they get some close friends to help by checking when things run short in the dining room, and getting refills from the kitchen, showing guests where to take their coats. They have found it best in a party like this to stay close to the door to visit and be where people can find them. Another thing they do is to stagger the guest list, with half the guests invited from 11 until 12:30 and the other half from 12:30 to 2. This keeps the house from being too crowded.

Since the party is held during the lunch hour, they feel they need something more substantial than just cookies, so they add a molded salad. One year they had an orange salad mold, some open-face shrimp sandwiches, and some small hot biscuits filled with country ham, along with an assortment of sweets. Another year they had a strawberry congealed salad with cream cheese balls, date nut balls, cheddar cheese olive balls, sugar cookies, mincemeat dessert, some mints.

CHEESE OLIVE BALLS

¼ pound cheddar cheese, grated *¾ cup flour*
30 medium size olives, pitted *⅛ teaspoon salt*
¼ cup butter *½ teaspoon paprika*

Blend cheese with butter. Add flour, salt and paprika and work to form dough. Shape around olive. Bake on greased cookie sheet at 400 degrees for 12 to 15 minutes.

MINCEMEAT DESSERT

1 package dry mincemeat *1 cup sifted flour*
1 cup boiling water *1½ cups quick cooking oatmeal*
½ cup shortening *½ teaspoon salt*
1 cup brown sugar, packed

Break mincemeat into boiling water. Cook 3 minutes and cool. Cream shortening and sugar and beat until fluffy. Add dry ingredients. Mix well. Spread one-half oatmeal mixture into a 9 inch square shallow pan. Press mixture down firmly. Then spread mincemeat mixture evenly over this, and finally top with other half of oatmeal mixture. Press firmly. Bake in 350 degree oven 30 to 40 minutes. Serve warm with whipped cream and cherry.

These are rich squares to pass for a buffet luncheon dessert. They are very popular for coffees and teas, too. We got these from Helen Austin, who used to make them for the young people at church.

LUSCIOUS SQUARES

1 stick butter	*2 tablespoons sugar*
1 cup flour	

Knead the above ingredients to a dough and pat in a 9 inch greased pan. It will be crumbly. Bake 15 minutes until light brown in a 350 oven. While baking, mix up the next layer.

3 eggs, beaten
1½ cups brown sugar
2 tablespoons flour
1 teaspoon baking powder
1 cup nuts

½ cup coconut (I leave
  this out and add ½ cup more
  pecans, making 1½ cups)
1 teaspoon vanilla

Spread this over the first mixture and bake for 25 minutes. When cool, put on the following icing.

½ box powdered sugar
3 tablespoons melted butter

3 tablespoons cream

Cut in rather small squares, because this is very rich eating.

Mrs. L. B. Austin, Jr.

Having a canister filled with crisp cheese straws on the pantry shelf is a real luxury. Our best recipe is from our Mississippi aunt, Meadie. She puts them through the star opening of a cookie press, bakes them crisp but not brown, and always makes plenty for family gatherings to snack on while we rock on the front gallery and keep an eye on the children fishing on the pond.

MEADIE'S CHEESE STRAWS

1 pound New York sharp
  cheese (black rind)
½ teaspoon red pepper

2 cups flour
1 teaspoon salt
½ cup butter

Let cheese get to room temperature and grate coarsely. Let butter get soft. In a mixer beat the butter and cheese together, season, and gradually add the flour. Sometimes it doesn't take quite 2 cups of flour so check to see if the dough will be too stiff with the full amount. Use a cookie press to push out cheese straws about 2 of 3 inches long. Bake in a 425 oven for about 10 or 12 minutes. Watch them so that they are very pale brown. If they get too brown, they will have a bitter taste. Store in air tight tin.

Mrs. George Montgomery
Yazoo City, Mississippi

It is said that the only thing you own in this world is your reputation and the influence that you have. One of the most influential ladies ever to live in Chattanooga was "Miss Ellen" Poindexter (Mrs. John). With her brains, her charm, and her loving ways, she grew up as one of the beautiful Sharp girls, lived on the corner of Sixth and Georgia where the Provident Building is now, and as a young married, was one of the best golfers at the Country Club. When Billy Sunday came to Chattanooga, she decided to start a Bible class at her house. From that beginning she taught sometimes four and five classes a week, either at church, the Kosmos Club, a Lookout Mountain class, a Summertown class, and others.

For over fifty years she was a leader in any kind of Christian work in Chattanooga, and influenced women of every denomination. She saw needs of the community before anyone else. She was either "Miss Ellen" or "Aunt Nelle" to hundreds of Chattanoogans who loved her because she was loving, wise, tactful, non-controversial, and a practical Christian. Some people, like me, even named their babies for her.

Miss Ellen always said she could not cook, but since she always had a cook, this made no difference. She entertained beautifully always, whether at a large tea, a luncheon for 12 with broiled chicken, an informal summer lunch at Summertown of a salad and creamed eggs, or afternoon tea in fine English cups served on a tray with cheese cookies. The cheese cookies she always served us were cut in rounds and topped with a pecan half.

MISS ELLEN'S CHEESE COOKIES

2 cups flour	1 teaspoon salt
1 stick butter	Dash of nutmeg
½ pound New York cheese	Dash of cayenne pepper
½ pound Wisconsin cheese	

Grate the cheese and let get to room temperature. Let the butter get soft. Cream the butter and the cheese. Add seasoning. Work in flour. Roll out and cut with a small cutter. Press nut on top of each.

Bake in a slow oven. Miss Ellen's cook baked them at 250, but I am always in more of a hurry, and bake at 350. They should be done and crisp, but never brown.

The late Mrs. John S. Poindexter

When the Church of the Good Shepherd has its annual Christmas bazaar, one specialty is the shortening canisters that have been gaily painted and decorated and then filled with Cheese Krispies. Edna Washington, who helps Martha (Mrs. Hobby) Law, not only made many wreaths and pine cone arrangements, but made about 60 dozen of these Cheese Krispies one year, keeping them in top condition in the freezer.

CHEESE KRISPIES

Work together 1 cup grated cheese, 1 stick butter, 1 cup flour, a dash of Tabasco and Worcestershire sauces. When this is well mixed, work in gently 1 cup Rice Krispies. Form in small balls on a cookie sheet and flatten each with your finger. Bake at 300 degrees for 10 minutes or until done.

Mrs. Edna Washington

A little different version of cheese straws are cheese biscuits. These are made by Joan Heywood (Mrs. Barrett) who got the recipe from Mrs. Mary Pack, who has made cheese biscuits for the E. Cecil Phillips family for years. All the various Talleys and Phillips' have loved snacking on these tidbits. And when Barry was in Vietnam, he loved to get them.

CHEESE BISCUITS

2 cups flour	¼ cup salad oil
¼ teaspoon red cayenne pepper	¾ cup cold milk
3 teaspoons baking powder	½ cup grated cheese
1 teaspoon salt	

Sift dry ingredients. Add milk to salad oil; stir into dry ingredients. Mix all together. Place dough on waxed paper; pat out ¼ inch thick. Put cheese on top. Put another sheet of waxed paper on top of cheese. Roll as thin as you can. Cut into finger strips about 2 inches long. Bake at 400 degrees until slightly brown. This will take about 5 minutes, so watch closely to see that the cheese does not burn. Lift with spatula onto rack or waxed paper to cool. It helps, by the way, to grease the pan slightly.

These cheese biscuits have amazing keeping qualities. They will keep for months wrapped up in foil in a tin. They can also be reheated in a slow oven.

Mrs. Barrett Heywood

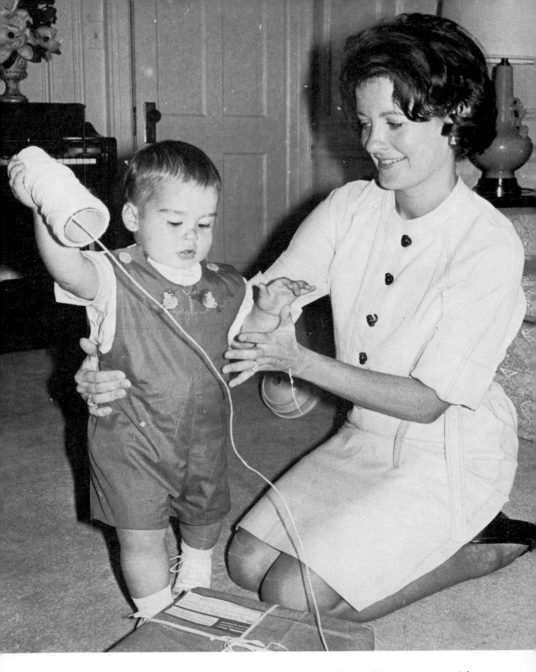

When Dr. Barrett Heywood was doing orthopedic surgery with the Army in Vietnam, his wife Joan and young son Barry mailed boxes of cookies to him regularly.

One year Anne Elizabeth Pettway (Mrs. W.D.) decided to ask a few friends over to see daughter Emmy's wedding presents. With several other things like the wedding on her mind that week, she had very simple refreshments, but I never have forgotten how delicious and how delightful it was. She has a gift of appearing very relaxed and informal, while everything she does from flower arrangements at church to a simple luncheon has a great deal of taste and originality. It was in the winter, so she had Russian tea, fruitcake, and macaroons iced with a hard sauce and topped with a cherry. You will hunt a long time before you find a better cookie than macaroons fixed this way.

MACAROONS ICED WITH HARD SAUCE

First buy as many macaroons as you will need at the bakery. Then make a hard sauce by creaming a stick of butter, adding a box of sifted powdered sugar, a tablespoon or two of cream, and flavoring to taste with bourbon, brandy or rum. When this is the right consistency, ice the macaroons and top each with a maraschino cherry half.

Mrs. W. D. Pettway

When Adolph Ochs went to New York, bought the New York Times, and guided it to great success, his brothers remained here to run The Chattanooga Times. Milton Ochs and his family lived on North Crest Road, and to their children's and grand-children's friends, Colonel Ochs and Miss Fan were favorites. Miss Fan, with warm expressive eyes, witty conversation, pretty clothes (never black,) and always the faint whiff of Bellodgia perfume when she kissed you, charmed Chattanooga for over ninety years.

If you were spending the night with her granddaughter, as I did, she made you feel like a most important guest and was very interested in you. She kept up with everyone she knew, planned little luncheons, and parties, and her social conscience and loving interest endeared her to everyone. Her children and grandchildren all seem to have this gift of friendship, and of doing for other people.

Miss Alice Ochs (Mrs. Van Dyke) is famous for the morning coffees that she has during the summertime visiting season. One of her specialties is Cheese Puffs.

CHEESE PUFFS

½ cup butter	1 cup flour
1 cup sharp cheese	Red pepper

Melt butter. Add cheese and flour and pepper. Roll in balls the size of a marble. Put in plastic bag and keep in refrigerator until firm.

Cook in a 400 degree oven for 20 to 30 minutes. These are supposed to be a little soft inside.

Mrs. Van Dyke Ochs

A reader sent this in as the easiest cookies she had ever mixed. Actually you melt butter in a baking pan, dump in the other ingredients, and bake ... no dishes to wash, and very quick! Melt in a 7 by 11 inch pan, 4 tablespoons butter. Spread over this:

PEARL'S EASY COOKIES

1 cup crushed graham crackers   *1 cup nuts*
1 cup chocolate chips

Pour over all this 1 can of condensed milk. Bake in a 350 oven for 30 to 35 minutes. Cool completely before cutting in squares. Makes 16 to 18 squares.

Mrs. Leon Caldwell

Mrs. Humphrey Heywood makes some Italian shortcake cookies called Biscotti. When her son, Dr. Barry Heywood was serving in Vietnam, he enjoyed getting these.

BISCOTTI

½ cup butter   *1 teaspoon vanilla*
1 cup sugar   *1 egg*
2 cups flour   *Milk...just enough to hold*
Pinch salt   *   dough together*

Cream the butter. Add the sugar and beat until fluffy. Sift flour, salt, baking powder together. Add to butter and sugar and blend. Add the egg and beat, add the vanilla, and then just enough milk to make a nice dough.

Roll out dough to ¼ inch thickness. Cut into pencil size strips about 1½ inches long and twist into "S" shapes. Brush with beaten egg yolk. Sprinkle with sesame seeds. Bake at 350 degrees for 10 to 12 minutes.

Mrs. Humphrey Heywood

Each December the Sisters of Charity of Nazareth give a tea at Memorial Hospital to say thank you to all the Pink Ladies, Gray Ladies and other volunteers who have given their time at the hospital. For the doctors and their wives, there is a buffet supper. These two holiday parties are very memorable for the people who attend them every year. One doctor's wife said, "It's one party I wouldn't miss. The nuns are so excited that they are greeting everyone, the decorations are beautiful and I come home feeling very loved and very important."

Mrs. Donna Murrey is the dietitian who helps get all the homemade cookies for the tea done. She says everyone helps. A tablecloth of satin and lace was handmade by an admiring Chattanoogan to be used for these parties. The decorations are different every year. One year an epergne of frosted fruit was the centerpiece with red candles in the candelabra. Another year they used fresh holly and carnations.

Sister Thomas de Sales, administrator, and the other sisters wear their most formal habits and pour coffee, tea or serve punch. The menu is like a high tea......fancy cookies, pinwheel and open face tea sandwiches, ham in tiny biscuits, cream puffs filled with chicken salad, nuts, mints.

For the doctors' buffet supper, they serve finger food and things that can be passed easily. There are hot rolls for the ham, plenty of shrimp with cocktail sauce, assorted cheese logs with different crackers, dips and chips, fruit cake, cookies, and some tiny meringue shells filled with dabs of raspberries (just frozen raspberries thickened with cornstarch.) There is coffee, fruit punch, and a favorite pink champagne punch. Both parties have a warm personal spirit that no one who has ever been can forget.

Mrs. Murrey gave me the recipe for the date balls they serve at the volunteers' tea.

MEMORIAL TEA DATE BALLS

1 pound dates, chopped	4 cups Rice Krispies
1 pound butter	2 cups chopped nuts
2 cups granulated sugar	4 teaspoons vanilla

Melt butter with sugar and dates. When the sugar dissolves, cook slowly 10 minutes. Stir often. Remove from heat and add other ingredients. Let cool. Roll into small balls. Sprinkle with powdered sugar or roll in grated coconut. This makes 12 dozen balls. Keeps well in an air tight container. This can also be frozen.

Mrs. Donna Murrey
Memorial Hospital

We got this recipe at a Food Editor's Conference in New York and passed it on years ago. Then I lost it. One afternoon I tasted these currant cookies again that had been made by our teenage friend, Margaret Williams. Now we call them Margaret's Currant Cookies.

MARGARET'S CURRANT COOKIES

1 cup butter or margarine	½ teaspoon ground cloves
3 cups rolled oats	½ teaspoon cinnamon
1 cup sugar	½ cup dried currants
¾ cup sifted flour	¼ cup milk
1 teaspoon baking soda	

Soften butter and blend in sugar and oats. Mix the rest of the ingredients. Shape in small balls 1 inch in diameter. Put on a greased baking sheet 3 inches apart. Bake at 350 degrees for 12 to 15 minutes.

These cookies are very thin and crisp, and are really more delicious than a regular oatmeal cookie made with raisins.

Miss Margaret Williams

About the crispiest oatmeal cookies are well named, Oatmeal Crispies. I had printed them and about forgotten them until Mrs. Harris Gregg told me she makes them more than any cookie. Then we started making them again. They call for a whole cup of almonds, which may be the reason they are so good.

OATMEAL CRISPIES

1 cup sugar	1 cup sliced almonds
1 cup brown sugar, packed	1¼ cups sifted flour
1 cup soft butter	1 teaspoon soda
2 eggs	1 teaspoon salt
1 teaspoon vanilla	3 cups quick cooking oats

Cream sugars, butter, eggs and vanilla. Stir in almonds. Sift flour with soda and salt. Add to creamed mixture. Stir in oatmeal. Divide dough in half and shape into two rolls on waxed paper. Chill until firm. Slice thinly and place on lightly greased baking sheet. Bake in 350 oven for 7 to 10 minutes. Makes 5 dozen.

Mrs. Harris Gregg

In the old days the Little Cakes that Mrs. Bernard Loveman used to bring to fancy Riverview Garden Club teas were much admired. Everyone asked for the recipe.

MRS. LOVEMAN'S "LITTLE CAKES"

½ pound butter
1 cup sugar
3½ cups flour

½ lemon...juice and
grated rind

Cream the butter and sugar. Sift the flour before measuring. Mix and roll a small amount of the mixture in hand to a little ball, and make a depression in the center. In this put a nut or a drop of tart jelly. Bake quickly, about 375 degrees, until lightly brown. Roll in powdered sugar.

Given to me by Mrs. Hugh Maclellan

My sister-in-law Mimi has a good recipe for Oatmeal Cookies. Oatmeal cookies are classics. They are fairly easy to put together, bake quickly, and always please whatever children come through the kitchen and reach in the cookie jar.

MIMI'S OATMEAL COOKIES

Cream 1 cup shortening, 1 cup brown sugar and 1 cup white sugar. Add 2 well beaten eggs and 1 teaspoon vanilla and beat well. Sift 1½ cups flour, 1 teaspoon salt, 1 teaspoon soda, and add to mixture. Then add 2½ cups oatmeal and ½ cup nuts.

Drop by teaspoonfuls on greased cookie sheet. Leave space between, since they spread with baking. Bake 10 minutes at 350 until slightly brown.

Mrs. Frank McDonald

When "Lyndhurst," the home built by the J. T. Luptons in Riverview was torn down an era ended. For several decades this beautiful house was presided over by Mrs. J. T. Lupton, who loved to have friends in for luncheons, teas, dinners, or balls. The ballroom had a real pipe organ and hundreds of little ballroom chairs that are now scattered all over Chattanooga. There were debuts, open houses, wedding receptions. (When Kate Rawlings married Jack Poindexter, the wedding reception was there.

On New Year's Day there was always an open house. One of the Lupton nieces remembers seven or eight dozen red roses in the centerpiece on the table, great silver punch bowls of eggnog, and heavy lace tablecloths.

Mrs. Lupton loved to plan parties and menus, and had many recipes for party delicacies. Chocolate Rings were among her favorite cookies, and she contributed the following recipe to the old Presbyterian Cookbook.

CHOCOLATE RINGS

2 cups chopped almonds	3 eggs
1½ cups granulated sugar	1 square bitter chocolate
1 teaspoon vanilla	1 square sweet chocolate

Beat the eggs until light and lemon colored; add almonds and grated chocolate. Let stand two or three hours, then shape into rings about the thickness of a pencil. Bake about 15 minutes in a slow oven at 300 degrees.

The late Mrs. J. T. Lupton
From The Presbyterian Cook Book

When Mrs. Hilda Spence, church editor of the News-Free Press, died, she left behind hundreds of friends who had at one time or another been on the receiving end of her culinary gifts. She loved to cook, and always had the knack of knowing just what each person liked the most. Given an hour or two on the phone, she could organize an office party for several hundred or just a smaller ·group of a hundred with 10 or 15 homemade cakes promised. She used to bring these ice box cookies to the boys on the city desk.

ICE BOX COOKIES

1 cup brown sugar, firmly packed	1 egg
1 cup powdered sugar	6 cups flour
1 pound butter (margarine can be used)	½ pound nuts, chopped
	1 tablespoon vanilla

Cream butter and sugar. Add the egg, then flour, nuts and vanilla. Roll in waxed paper in rolls and chill in ice box. Slice then and bake in moderate 350 oven until barely brown. This recipe she got from Mrs. Harris Gregg.

Mrs. Hilda Spence

At one food conference in New York, we were served a delicious coffee cake at a morning coffee. The only sugar in it is in the frosting, but it is so short with butter, and the top layer does a puff very much like a cream puff, that all the editors raved over it. Try it at your next tea or coffee, or just make it for the family in place of a cookie. This is the kind of thing people can't figure out and want the recipe for.

DANISH PUFFS

1 cup butter or margarine (2 sticks)	3 eggs
2 cups sifted flour	2 cups sifted confectioner's sugar
2 tablespoons cold water	1 tablespoon butter or margarine
1 cup boiling water	4 tablespoons cream
1 teaspoon almond flavoring	1 teaspoon vanilla
	⅛ teaspoon salt

Cut ½ cup butter or margarine into 1 cup of flour until it resembles coarse meal. Add cold water and stir until well blended. Divide dough in half. Press each half into a 3 by 12 inch oblong on an ungreased baking sheet.

Place boiling water and remaining ½ cup butter or margarine into a saucepan. Bring to a boil. Add almond flavoring and remove from heat. Stir in remaining 1 cup of flour. Add eggs one at a time, beating well after each addition. Spread this mixture over the oblongs. Bake in a hot oven 425 degrees about 20 minutes, or until dry and golden brown.

Meanwhile combine confectioners sugar, cream, butter, vanilla and salt. Beat smooth and frost cakes while hot. Cut into slices and serve warm.

When Dr. Lawrence Lassiter was in medical school at Vanderbilt, his wife Teeny taught the first grade in Nashville. The mother of one of her first graders used to bring some delicious sugar cookies to the class for various parties at Christmas and Valentine's. Teeny says maybe the reason they were so good was that they are flavored with both lemon and vanilla. She made sure she got the recipe, and through the years it has become a favorite Lassiter specialty.

TEENY'S SUGAR COOKIES

2 cups sifted flour	1 cup sugar
2 teaspoons baking powder	½ cup butter (1 stick)
⅛ teaspoon salt	½ teaspoon vanilla
1 egg	½ teaspoon lemon flavoring

Let the butter soften so it can be worked by hand. Beat egg in mixer and set aside until the flour, baking powder, and salt are sifted. Add sugar and butter, egg and flavoring and mix well in a large bowl with the hands until the flour is taken up. Place on lightly floured board. Roll ⅛ inch thick. Cut in various shapes and add sugar or Christmas decorations to the tops.

Bake on ungreased baking sheet at 375 degrees for 6 to 8 minutes, or until edges are slightly brown. This makes 3 dozen and they will stay thin and crispy in a cannister.

Mrs. Lawrence Lassiter

When the Christmas season finally arrives, like other families over the land, we get a tree, we deck the mantels with pine and holly from our back yard, and cones that we picked up at Pawley's Island, and I see to it that the baking is done, the Christmas ham ready, and the Chocolate Yule Log made.

Surely one of the little miracles that happens to all of us at Christmas is that we somehow manage to get all the special and extra things done. Almost always a couple of weeks beforehand, I go through a moment of panic. My heart sinks as I wonder when we will do all the baking, make the wreaths, get the packages off, do the things at church that we want to do. Then we remember all the Christmases past. It is amazing how, taken a day at a time, things fall right in place . . . the cookies, the greens, the packages, the church services. On Christmas Eve each year, as in all other years, we will sit down before the fire and feel the peace of Christmas.

Christmas baking is the most exciting baking of all. In a big family of children, the very air is charged with excitement, Christmas carols play from every radio in the house, and someone always seems to be turning the tree lights on and off, calling Santa Claus on the phone, or begging to help make the boxwood and fruit wreath for the front door. The day we bake, the kitchen will be a mess, but the whole house will smell wonderful. If you go out to get the mail and come back in out of the cold, one sniff will say that it is Christmas time. We will fill jars, cans, cookie tins, and even start lining boxes with foil.

Of all the favorites over the years, the best-loved cookie among our readers is the Fruitcake Cookie. One friend says that she was spring cleaning one year and found one lone cookie in a cake tin. She couldn't resist eating it, and it was good! Ours never last that long, but they will if given a chance. The butter cookies, cut out in star shapes are old faithfuls, as are the chewy date nut bars.

If things ever got really desperate, we would choose the fruitcake cookies and the cheese cookies and let that be it. We make as much as we have time to, and this varies with the years. We've learned though,

At Christmas we make a simple tree of apples for the centerpiece, bake cheese cookies, a chocolate log, and various confections and pies, and ask the neighbors in for coffee. For this picture I made some of our Christmas favorites.

that it is better to stop before you get too tired and cross. Better a simple and sweet Christmas than a mother who has overworked. And this is easy to do. All of these baked goods can be made and then frozen, and some year we are going to do this.

The secret of Fruitcake Cookies is that they are full of good fruit and nuts, and that the fruit has mellowed overnight in sherry. There is no taste of wine, but the mellowness and moistness that this fruit has makes it far superior to any other fruitcake cookie.

The boys like the Mexican wedding cakes and the date nut bars. It seems such a few years ago that they were licking the beaters and watching the oven for me. Now all these boys just walk through the kitchen and check the cookie cannisters, assuming the role of appreciative eaters. And the girls make up my companionable staff!

FAMOUS FRUITCAKE COOKIES

½ pound candied cherries   *½ pound chopped citron*
½ pound candied pineapple   *½ pound chopped white raisins*

Soak the above overnight in 1 cup sherry or fruit juice.

½ pound pecans, chopped   *1 cup brown sugar*
½ pound almonds, chopped   *¾ cup melted butter*
3 cups all purpose flour   *1 tablespoon buttermilk*
1 teaspoon powdered cloves   *1 teaspoon soda*
2 teaspoons cinnamon   *1 teaspoon vanilla*
3 eggs

Sift together the flour, which has been sifted before measuring, and the cloves and cinnamon. Beat the eggs and add the brown sugar and melted butter. Next dissolve the soda in the buttermilk and add to the egg mixture. Now add the dry ingredients, the vanilla, the fruit and the nuts.

Drop by ice tea spoonfuls and bake at 325 for 15 minutes until very light brown. Do not overcook. Store in a cookie jar. If you want them really crisp, wrap each individually in a square of waxed paper. This way they will keep for months in a cannister.

MEXICAN WEDDING CAKES

1 cup soft butter   *1 teaspoon vanilla*
1 cup sifted powdered sugar   *2 cups all purpose flour*
1 cup finely chopped pecans

Stir butter until smooth and creamy. Add sugar a little at a time, beating constantly. Add nuts and vanilla. Gradually add flour and mix to a dough. Refrigerate dough until it is firm. Form round balls with a teaspoon of dough, then roll into little logs. Bake at 375 degrees for 12 to 14 minutes or until light golden. When cool, roll in sifted powdered sugar. Makes 3 dozen.

DATE BARS

2 eggs	1 teaspoon vanilla
1 cup flour	1 cup chopped pecans
1 teaspoon baking powder	1 package dates, cut fine
1 cup sugar	

Sift baking powder and flour together. Beat eggs; add sugar, flour, vanilla, dates and nuts. Bake at 375 degrees in a greased and floured pan for about 20 minutes. Cut in finger lengths and roll in powdered sugar.

Simple butter cookies are the best all-around cookie ever invented. Although rich in butter, they are not too sweet, and we like them better than sugar cookies. We have made them in many shapes. Once I made a 4-inch-tall Christmas tree for each child in Kinch's and Roy's classes ......about 50 cookies, iced in green, decorated with colored candy and with each child's name written on them. I did it for Jonathan's class on Valentine's Day with red icing and white names. For Christmas we make stars iced with yellow icing.

BUTTER COOKIES

1 cup butter	3 cups all purpose flour
½ cup sugar	½ teaspoon baking powder
1 egg	½ teaspoon salt
3 teaspoons vanilla	

Mix the soft butter, sugar, and egg together. Stir in the flavoring. Sift together the flour and baking powder and stir into the batter. Chill the dough for 10 or 15 minutes. Roll very thin and cut into shapes. Bake at 425 degrees for 5 to 7 minutes. Ice with simple icing.

Simple Icing: Sift a box of powdered sugar and thin with just enough water to make a rather stiff icing. Allow for 1 teaspoon vanilla flavoring. Add a pinch of salt. If this is put on a very low eye of the stove and warmed, it will dry to a shine when glazing a cookie. (This is also a simple glaze good for warm fruit bread, or a 1-2-3-4 cake that has just come out of the oven.)

Some of the most beautiful cookies and cakes in town are made by a remarkable Chattanooga couple, Margaret and John Matusek. There are butter cookies decorated with Christmas trees, wreaths, and dainty poinsettias that have a very Old World sort of delicacy; cup cakes topped with red Santa Clauses which Margaret quickly molds out of her pastry tube, even down to black boots and white beard; Dobos Tortes, layers of puff paste filled with creme patisseries, and European specialties you would expect to find only in a very large city.

Their story is a fascinating one. Back in 1956 John had been elected food manager of all the food stores in Papa City, Hungary. They had been owned by the government since 1948 when all private businesses and farms were confiscated. He says you cannot imagine how it feels for a government official to come to the door one morning, ask for the keys, and demand that you leave. Margaret's father lost his farm this way. John had been a full baker since he was 16, but was more famous as a professional soccer player, and 17 times represented Hungary in different countries of Europe. His business was food, however. During the famous uprising, John refused to sell to the Russians for three whole days, not milk, not potatoes, not anything. One night friends warned him he would have to leave in the three hours granted for freedom fighters, or the Russians would pick him up and send him to Siberia. He and Margaret left their house, their belongings, everything. First they went to Austria, then West Germany, then to the United States at Camp Kilmer, New Jersey.

They needed a sponsor, so Ed J. Chitko, who lives in Chattanooga Valley, offered to be responsible for them, and they came to Chattanooga. John got a job at Koch's bakery, then Manhattan Bakery, and made many friends.

Their story is the story of America. They arrived in 1957 and by 1958 had saved enough to buy a house. He paid $1,000 down with an 11-year mortgage, yet all he could think of was somehow paying back what he owed. He says that when he wanted a cigarette, he just put the thought out of his mind, because the house was so important. Five years later in 1963 they paid off their mortgage . . . 6 years early. By then they were United States citizens and owned their own home. "It could only happen in America," he says.

Their dream was to have their own bakery, so they started saving for that. The story of how they started the Incline Bakery and Pastry Shop and the people who encouraged them is a thrilling one. As the customers come and go, there is usually the smile and conversation of old friends.

Margaret is lovely looking, charming, cheerful and gracious. She works quickly, whether it is icing a chocolate cake or swirling Santa Claus bodies for the cup cakes. She showed me how to roll up a parch-

Margaret and John Matusek came to Chattanooga as refugees after the 1956 uprising in Hungary. They now have their own home, their own bakery, and many admiring friends. This is the story of America.

ment cone, and with no pastry tube at all, with two snips of the scissors, she formed an opening so that the icing came out to make the tiny leaves for a wreath.

Margaret and John are warm in their praise of America that has given them a chance. "God bless this land and all its people," he says. "The people here who want to appease the Communists should have to go live with them for three months. Then they would know the truth and want to swim the ocean if necessary, to get home."

The Matuseks are probably the most patriotic couple in Chattanooga, and represent the many refugees who have brought their skills and talents to Chattanooga. They give every visitor a warm boost, and incidentally, make not only their dainty cookies and cakes, but the best Cuban bread and pastry cases in town. The following recipe is a Hungarian one for Donkey's Ears.

DONKEY'S EARS

2½ cups flour
½ cup shortening
1 cake yeast

3 tablespoons milk
1 teaspoon vanilla

Put the crumbled yeast in a cup together with lukewarm milk and 1 teaspoon sugar. Leave to rise. Rub the shortening into the flour, add risen yeast and knead into a smooth dough. Roll out to matchstick thinness and cut into squares. Put a spoonful of jam on each square, roll up, and by twisting corners, shape small crescents of it. Bake in medium oven for about 18 or 20 minutes. As soon as ready, roll in sugar.

Sweets with sugared nuts, poppy seed and jams are special to Hungary, and using jams in cookies and sweets makes a very colorful appearance.

Mr. and Mrs. John Matusek
Incline Bakery

Mrs. Arthur Paty makes Orange Coconut Bars as a different sort of cookie for a coffee or tea or just to pass as dessert at informal suppers.

ORANGE COCONUT BARS

½ cup butter
1 cup flour

¼ cup powdered sugar

Cream and bake in a buttered 8 by 12 pan at 325 degrees for 12 to 15 minutes, or until slightly brown.

1 cup coconut

1½ cups brown sugar

1 cup chopped pecans

½ teaspoon vanilla

½ teaspoon salt

2 tablespoons flour

¼ teaspoon baking powder

2 eggs, beaten

Mix and cover crust. Bake at 325 for 20 minutes. Cool and frost.

1½ cups powdered sugar

3 tablespoons orange juice

3 tablespoons butter

Sprinkle with chopped nuts. Cut in small squares.

Mrs. Arthur Paty

Our pediatrician, Dr. Eleanor Stafford, is a North Carolina Tarheel who, when she goes back home for a visit in the late fall, brings back a big cannister of Moravian ginger cookies. Her grandfather was a Moravian minister, and she says in the old days, the frugal Moravians always baked a small batch of cookies after breakfast. While there were still enough coals in the stove to provide a little more heat, the housewife would stir up a small amount of cookie dough, roll it out, and put it in the dying oven. There were always cookies cut out with pewter cookie cutters in the shapes of crescents, stars, trees, and scalloped circles, to offer anyone who might come in. It is a Carolina custom that you must offer company a little something, and if you have ever been company, you know that there is no way to say no to such hospitality.

MORAVIAN COOKIES

¼ cup light molasses

¼ cup soft butter

2 tablespoons granulated sugar

1¼ cups sifted all purpose flour

½ teaspoon salt

½ teaspoon baking soda

¼ teaspoon cinnamon

¼ teaspoon ginger

¼ teaspoon cloves

Blend together light molasses, butter and sugar. Sift together flour, salt, baking soda and spices. Blend dry ingredients into creamed mixture; mix well. Cover with plastic wrap and refrigerate at least 2 hours before rolling. Use a pastry cloth and roll out very thin. Cut in various shapes and place on greased cookie sheet. Bake at 375 degrees for 5 or 6 minutes until only slightly brown. Don't let burn. This makes about 6 dozen very thin cookies.

Dr. Eleanor Stafford

The finger dessert that can be passed after lunch or dinner is getting to be very popular. Bubbles (Mrs. Thornton) Strang makes small meringues topped with a chocolate filling.

ANGEL KISSES

2 egg whites	½ cup sugar
⅛ teaspoon salt	½ teaspoon vanilla
⅛ teaspoon cream of tartar	½ cup chopped pecans

Beat egg whites with salt and cream of tartar until foamy. Add sugar 2 tablespoons at a time, beating well after each addition. Continue until very stiff. Fold in vanilla and nuts.

Put wax paper on cookie sheet. Drop mixture on by teaspoon and bake at 250 degrees for 50 to 55 minutes.

FILLING

1 bar German chocolate	1 teaspoon vanilla
3 tablespoons water	1 cup whipped cream

Stir chocolate in water over low heat until melted. Cool until thick. Add vanilla and whipped cream and fold into chocolate. Put on shells. Makes 16 to 18.

Mrs. Thornton Strang

One year on the Sunday before Christmas, Mrs. George Henshall's mother, Mrs. Sam Taylor of Raleigh, North Carolina, brought me some samples of her Orange Blossom Cup Cakes. These are her specialty, and she dips the small sponge cake muffins in a glaze. For wedding parties she even ties a tiny yellow bow around an orange blossom and tops each cake with a blossom and bow. They are also nice for coffees and teas.

The little cupcakes were delicious and melted in your mouth. She gave me the recipe which I promptly misplaced. Two years later I found the typed recipe stuck in a book about Christmas, and it was like finding a prize. I promptly transferred to to the loose leaf notebook where I keep all my recipes, and consider this very special.

ORANGE BLOSSOMS

Make the orange dip frosting first.

Orange Dip:

*Grated rind and juice
of 2 lemons
Grated rind and juice
of 2 oranges*

*1¼ pounds powdered sugar,
sifted (1¼ boxes)*

Sift the sugar and add the juices and rinds. Cream together until very smooth. It is very important that the sugar be sifted.

Cake Batter:

CAKE BATTER

*3 eggs
1¼ cups sugar
½ cup water
1½ cups plain flour*

*1½ teaspoons baking powder
½ teaspoon salt
1 teaspoon vanilla*

Beat the whole eggs in an electric mixer until creamy, adding the sugar gradually. Add water alternately with the flour, salt, and baking powder, that has been sifted three times after measuring. Then add vanilla. Slightly grease the muffin pans. Bake in a moderate oven at 350 degrees about 12 to 15 minutes. Remove from muffin pans right away and dip in glaze while hot. This is absolutely necessary. Place muffins on waxed paper to dry a little. They remain very moist if kept in metal containers.

To dip cakes, place one or two at a time in a shallow bowl or saucer and cover with the orange dip. After each dip, rake the remaining frosting back in the bowl and start over.

This recipe will make 24 muffins. For luncheons or parties, place a cluster of artificial orange blossoms tied with a small bow of narrow yellow satin on top of each cake.

Mrs. Sam Taylor
Raleigh, North Carolina

CHAPTER XIII

Pies

Pies have been the favorite dessert of Americă ever since the settlers first came to the New World. Pies are easy and quick; they are not as delicate as cake; they make the most of whatever fruit is in season.

Chattanooga has cooks who make pies several times a week. Our men especially like apple pie, cherry pie, pecan pie, just about any kind of pie. These are for family dinners. When we put on airs, we make macaroon pies, cream pies, black bottom pies. The chess pie, loved all over the South, has a place here, too.

When I first began to cook, the two of us could never have eaten a whole pie. This was before the day of the freezer, so I usually took half a pie, still warm, to a neighbor in the apartment. This was when I found out that the best way to get to know your neighbors is to take them something. Every day or two I made another pie and took to another neighbor. If I thought it strange that they didn't bring a plate of food back, I don't remember. They were the first neighbors of my own that I had ever had, and we soon became close friends.

I look back on these learning days with real nostalgia. When we came back home to Chattanooga, I kept doing the same thing. The warm friendships that have developed over exchanging good things to eat are sweet and good to this day. I found out that no one can hate you if you appear at their door with a pecan pie saying you had just been in the mood to bake it. They will decide you are an intriguing, if strange, person, and want to know you better.

First learn how to make tender crust. It is very easy. Then make it often for your family. Make two pies instead of one and put in the freezer. Then experiment with many different kinds of pie. The Pecan and the Sale Creek Strawberry Pie have been the ones that Chattanoo-gans have requested the recipes for most often. The Black Bottom Pie found in a later chapter is the one we make most often for company dinners.

As I write this the apples are so bountiful on the two trees in our back yard that we have been feasting on green apple pie, which you make like any other apple pie except you add ½ cup more sugar. Pies are a definite part in the culinary story of Chattanooga, and beloved in almost every family.

SOME THINGS I HAVE LEARNED
ABOUT MAKING PASTRY

Every time I make a pie, I wonder why I don't do it every two or three days, because it goes so quickly. First you sift 1 cup of flour with 1 teaspoon of salt into a small bowl. Measure 1-3 cup soft shortening into it and use a pastry blender of about 4 wires shaped into a hoop (from the dime store) to press the shortening about the size of corn kernels. These bits of shortening when rolled out will make the flakes of pastry. This is why I like to use shortening rather than oil.

All this takes just a minute. Now comes the part that seems hard to people who have only done it once. Fill ½ cup with cold or ice water although you won't need it all. Add two or three drops at a time, tossing with a fork or using your hand, which works best for me. You want to add enough water to hold the flour together. If you don't add enough, it will be dry and you will go wild having the pastry break off when you try to roll it. If you add too much water, it will be tough and hard to roll out. The best thing to do is not to think about it, and just make it as quickly as possible, using a light fast hand both in mixing and in rolling out. Bearing down with a rolling pin can make it tough, too.

Invest in a pastry canvas and stockinette for your rolling pin. The job is not only easier, but there is no flour mess on your counter to clean up.

The recipe for a two-crust pie is just double . . . 2 cups of flour, 1½ teaspoons salt, 2-3 cup shortening, and enough cold water so that the dough comes away from the sides of the bowl when added gradually.

The first pie I learned to make was a rich pecan pie, and since we usually had a supply of Mississippi pecans on hand, we had it often. It also makes delicious tarts.

SOUTHERN PECAN PIE

4 eggs	*1 cup sugar*
1¼ cups cane syrup	*4 tablespoons butter*
1½ cups broken pecan meats (I	*1 teaspoon vanilla*
now use 1 cup)	*Pinch of salt*

Boil sugar and syrup together two or three minutes. Beat eggs until mixed, pour in slowly the hot syrup, add the butter, vanilla, and the pecan meats, broken rather coarsely. Turn into a raw pie shell and bake in a moderate oven 350 degrees about 45 minutes or until set. This recipe will also make 12 little tarts.

A pecan pie that is a little different is the one baked regularly by Queenie McCallie (Mrs. T. Hooke).

PECAN PIE

3 eggs

1 cup white corn syrup

¼ cup sugar

¼ cup melted butter or oleo

Pinch of salt

1 teaspoon vanilla

1 cup chopped pecans

or ½ cup walnuts

and ½ cup pecans

Combine ingredients and pour into unbaked pie shell. Bake at 350 degrees for about 40 minutes.

Mrs. T. Hooke McCallie

Once Peggy Chambliss planned a picnic for the Junior League Garden Club at Reflection Riding and asked Mary Rozendale (Mrs. G.) to help. Mary can cook for large numbers of people with quite a flair. She insists that she cooks very simply, and she does, but it is always elegant. Down by the log cabin at Reflection Riding, she served everyone individual basket lunches wrapped inside a calico napkin.

There was Fried Chicken, Deviled Eggs, Cucumber and Cream Cheese Sandwiches, Potato Salad, some delicious little Pecan Pastries and a light punch that was so different that everyone drank two or three tall glasses full. I asked how she fried so much crisp chicken. She browned it in hot shortening and then put it in an open roaster in the oven to finish getting tender. This is a good idea for a large group. Her stuffed eggs she seasoned with homemade mayonnaise, salt, pepper, a little mustard,and some melted butter, which she thinks is the secret.

Everyone wanted to know how to make the pecan pastries and the pale pink punch. The punch recipe should be circulated among all people who despise sticky sweet punch made from fruit juice and ginger-ale. Mary thinks the success of it is because it is lightened and dried with soda water along with the ginger-ale. It is in a later chapter.

MARY'S PECAN PASTRIES

1 3-ounce package cream cheese

½ cup butter

1 cup sifted flour

Soften the cream cheese and butter at room temperature. Shape into 2 dozen 1 inch balls. Place in tiny ungreased muffin pans and shape into tarts. Pecan mixture:

1 egg

¾ cup brown sugar

1 tablespoon melted butter

¾ cup coarsely broken pecans

Beat eggs, sugar, and butter together. Add pecans to egg mixture. Fill cups ¾ full. Bake in 325 oven til slightly firm.

293

During the Revolutionary War, British agents supplied the Indians along the Tennessee River with arms to stimulate their warfare against the settlers. In 1779 Colonel Evan Shelby left the Hiwassee Garrison with a group of frontiersmen and cleared the river of Indian villages. On his return, he conducted an auction of the confiscated supplies at the site of a creek known afterward as Sale Creek because of the sale. Later Gideon Blackburn the missionary, established a mission and the first school in Hamilton County at Sale Creek.

The late Mrs. W. H. List of Sale Creek, Tennessee, had a recipe for using fresh strawberries in a pie that was so good we have to print her recipe every year in May when the local strawberries come in. She combined the berries with pastry, like the best shortcake, and then to bring out the best flavor, poured thickened strawberry syrup while hot over the prettiest berries in the pie shell. The syrup formed a glaze. Whipped cream finishes this elegant pie.

SALE CREEK STRAWBERRY PIE

1 baked pastry shell
1 quart strawberries
1 cup sugar
1 cup boiling water

3 tablespoons cornstarch plus
  enough cold water
  to make a paste
1 cup whipping cream,
  whipped

Bring to a boil and strain 1 cup of the smaller berries, the sugar, and the boiling water. Now add the cornstarch mixture. Cook over the fire for a couple of minutes, stirring constantly. Remove from fire and beat. Return to a slow fire and cook slowly until thick. Have ready a baked pie shell. Arrange the rest of the berries, which have been washed and picked over, in the shell. Pour the hot sauce over them. When cool, spread whipped cream that has been sweetened with powdered sugar over the top.

Of all the ways to enjoy strawberries, this is the very best. It is better than shortcake, and a very beloved recipe all over the Chattanooga region.

Mrs. W. H. List
Sale Creek, Tennessee

One day I looked everywhere for the recipe for strawberry cream pie using a package of frozen strawberries and a package of strawberry gelatin. I couldn't find it, so I made up the following recipe. The family loved it, and when I found the recipe later, it said to include 2 beaten egg whites. This recipe will work with or without the whites!

QUICK STRAWBERRY CREAM PIE

1 package frozen strawberries,
 thawed
1 package strawberry gelatin
1 cup boiling water
1 tablespoon lemon juice

1 cup whipping cream,
 whipped
2 egg whites, beaten
 (optional)
Baked pastry shell

Dissolve the gelatin in the boiling water. Add the frozen straw-berries, juice and all, and the lemon juice. Let cool. Fold in the whipped cream, pour in a baked shell and chill. Or fold in the whites, beaten stiff, along with the whipped cream and chill.

At Callaway Gardens in Pine Mountain, Georgia, they make a macaroon pie that is unusually good. Most macaroon pies are very rich anyway with egg whites and pecans, and sometimes are too sweet. This recipe is just sweet enough and my favorite version.

CALLAWAY GARDENS MACAROON PIE

6 egg whites
¾ cup sugar
1 tablespoon baking powder

1½ cups Ritz Cracker crumbs
1¼ cups chopped pecans

Beat the egg whites and sugar together and add baking powder while beating. When mixture becomes stiff enough, fold in pecans and cracker crumbs. Bake in floured greased pie pans at 300 degrees for 45 minutes.

Callaway Gardens

A Macaroon pie made extra chewy with chopped dates is this one.

DATE MACAROON PIE

20 double soda crackers
1¼ teaspoons double
 acting baking powder
4 egg whites,
 room temperature
1¼ cups light brown sugar

1 teaspoon almond extract
½ cup chopped dates
½ cup chopped nuts
1 cup heavy cream,
 whipped (sweeten if desired)

Crush crackers into fine crumbs between waxed paper. There should be about 1 1-3 cups. Stir in baking powder and set aside. Beat egg

After dinner coffee in the living room is the nicest way to end a dinner. Mrs. Hardwick Caldwell pours the coffee in this picture while her daughter-in-law Ellen, Mrs. Phil Whitaker, serves.

whites until stiff but not dry. Gradually beat in sugar. Continue beating until mixture holds soft peaks. Gently fold in almond extract, dates, nuts and crumb mixture. Pour into buttered 9 inch pie plate. Bake in preheated moderate oven (350) for 25 to 30 minutes, or until top is brown and crusty to the touch. Let cool in plate on a rack; pie will sink a bit and be crispy on the outside, and chewy on the inside. When ready to serve, garnish with whipped cream and nuts.

The hickories that grow in our region and furnish us with rich smelling logs for the fireplaces and smoke for fine country hams, also are loaded with nuts in the fall. The nutmeats have a flavor different from other nuts, and are prized for special recipes in old cookbooks. Mrs. Hardwick Caldwell has a Hickory Nut Pie that is much like a pecan pie except that it uses hickory nuts instead of pecans and maple syrup instead of cane syrup.

HICKORY NUT PIE

1 cup maple syrup
2 eggs, beaten
1 cup dark brown sugar
2 tablespoons butter
2 tablespoons flour

Pinch of salt
1½ cups hickory nut meats,
   chopped coarsely
1 unbaked 9-inch pie shell or 8
   small unbaked tart shells

Cream butter and sugar. Add eggs, flour, salt and syrup. Add nuts and mix well. Pour into unbaked pie shell. Bake 5 minutes at 400 degrees. Reduce heat to 375 degrees and bake until mixture sets, about 30 to 40 minutes. Serve plain or topped with whipped cream flavored with vanilla.

Mrs. Hardwick Caldwell

Mrs. Herbert Supplee used to make lime pie for all her daughters' friends, who still remember it and have written for the recipe. Make it, freeze it, and serve it frozen.

FROZEN LIME PIE

½ cup lime juice
2 tablespoons grated rind
6 eggs

1 cup sugar
2 cups heavy cream
Green Coloring

Make two 9-inch pie crusts of graham crackers. Cook lime juice, egg yolks, and sugar in a double boiler until it thickens. Cool. Beat whites of eggs stiff but not dry. Whip cream, fold into egg whites. Add a few drops of green coloring. Fold in yolk mixture. Pour into the crusts. Sprinkle top with more crumbs.

This lemon chiffon pie uses 5 eggs and the meringue stands way up.

LEMON MERINGUE PIE

1 9-inch baked pie shell	*2 tablespoons flour*
1 tablespoon butter	*5 egg yolks, beaten*
1 cup hot water	*Juice and grated rind of 1*
1 cup sugar	*large lemon*

Melt the butter in the hot water in the top of a double boiler. In a bowl, mix the sugar and flour. Add beaten egg yolks, lemon rind and lemon juice. I add a pinch of salt. Add this to the double boiler and cook until thick, stirring constantly. Cool thoroughly, and turn into the pastry shell. Cover with meringue and bake in a 400 degree oven for 12 to 15 minutes until brown.

MERINGUE TOPPING

5 egg whites	*Pinch of salt*
10 tablespoons granulated sugar	

Beat the egg whites with a pinch of salt until they hold a firm peak. Then add the granulated sugar, a tablespoon at a time. Keep adding sugar until all of it is used and you have a marshmallow-like shiny consistency. Some cooks add ¼ teaspoon cream of tartar at the end to insure stiffness. It should be so thick and stiff that it must be packed down and spread smoothly across the top. A too rough top results in an uneven browning. The meringue should stay in the oven for 12 to 15 minutes (at 400). Then it will be thoroughly cooked and will stay high and fluffy. Do not expect a good meringue to result from quick broiler browning.

The town crier of Chattanooga Luther Masingill, whose morning radio show is a daily part of the lives of thousands of Chattanoogans as they have breakfast and drive to school and work. He passes on the phone numbers of people with dogs or kittens to give away; he offers suggestions to the mayor and commissioners; he passes on the word when women have driven off with their purses on the top of their cars and lost them. "If I've told you once, I've told you a thosand times to lock your cars and when you unlock them, don't put your purses or packages on the car." Luther is a familiar voice who plays melodic and good music in a world of strange noise, and is considered a good friend by hundreds of people whom he doesn't know.

When snow hits Chattanooga, which is three or four times a winter, the whole town tunes in. Luther passes on the word which schools will meet and which will be closed. He tells what streets to avoid, how much snow is on the mountains, whee the accidents are, which hills have been salted. We have many good announcers and local programs in Chattanooga, but Luther has been at the mike for so many years that he is an institution and a favorite.

I asked his wife Mary to give me one of his favorite desserts, and she says either lemon pie or devil's food cake with white icing is always popular at the Masingill house. Her lemon meringue pie has an espeically good crust made with sour cream, and the filling is rich with four eggs.

LUTHER'S LEMON PIE

Pie Crust:

1 cup all-purpose flour	¼ cup shortening
½ teaspoon salt	3 tablespoons sour cream

Mix flour and salt, cut in shortening. Add sour cream and mix well. Roll out to 9 inches. Line a 9-inch pie pan, and bake at 425 until slightly brown.

Filling:

¼ cup cornstarch	4 egg yolks, slightly beaten
3 tablespoons flour	½ cup lemon juice
1¾ cup sugar	1 tablespoon grated lemon peel
¼ teaspoon salt	1 tablespoon butter
2 cups water	

In medium saucepan, combine cornstarch, flour, sugar, and salt, mixing well. Gradually add 2 cups of water, stirring until smooth. Over medium heat, bring to a boil, stirring occasionally. Boil 1 minute. Remove from heat. Quickly stir some of the hot mixture into the egg yolks. Return to hot mixture; stir to blend. Return to heat. Stir in lemon juice, lemon peel, and butter.

Pour into baked pie shell. Preheat oven to 400 degrees. Make meringue. Spread over lemon filling, carefully sealing top to edge of the crust and swirling top decoratively. Bake 7 to 9 minutes. Let pie cool completely on wire rack. Makes 8 servings.

Meringue

4 egg whites	½ cup sugar
¼ teaspoon cream of tartar	

Beat the egg whites and cream of tartar together until stiff and gradually add the sugar until well dissolved and quite stiff.

Mrs. Luther Masingill

Chess pie is baked in the oven like a custard pie. When you find a version that calls for a cup of milk or cream, then you have a custard pie but not a a chess pie. The rich combination of butter, eggs, and sugar, when baked has a consistency all its own ... very solid, almost pully, but quite tender. In Middle Tennessee they add a teaspoon of white corn meal to add an extra crunch to the top crust. This is a Nashville recipe that Mrs. J.W. Boyd served me on an interview for a series on our local ministers' wives. Her husband is minister of the Red Bank Church of Christ.

NASHVILLE CHESS PIE

½ cup butter   1 teaspoon vanilla
1½ cups sugar   3 eggs
1 teaspoon corn meal   1 pie shell or individual
1 teaspoon vinegar   pie shells

Cream butter and sugar until light and fluffy. Add cornmeal, vinegar, and vanilla. Beat in eggs, one at a time. Fill either an unbaked pie shell or individual shells. Bake at 375 for about 25 minutes. Be sure to get the pastry crisp.

Mrs. J.W. Boyd

Frances Wilson (Mrs. Shields) is known for her Middle Tennessee specialties, her extraordinary way of preparing food for large numbers of people in the most gracious way. Without really meaning to, for years she got involved in catering for parties as well as for the Brainerd Kiwanis Club. Now this one time officer in the Waves, P.T.A. president, and church worker, is using her masters in education as a reading specialist. Frances' Chess Pie is one of the best. She mixes it by hand and flavors it with lemon.

FRANCES WILSON'S CHESS PIE

½ cup butter at   Grated rind and juice
   room temperature   of 1 lemon
1¼ cups sugar   1 teaspoon vanilla
2 teaspoons cornmeal   Unbaked pastry shells
3 whole eggs

Cream butter; add sugar and meal. Add eggs, one at a time, beat-

300

ing well after each addition. Mixture should be light and fluffy, but do not use an electric mixer as it beats in too much air. Add flavorings and pour into pastry lined tart tins or a 9 inch pie shell. Bake at 325 for about 45 minutes, or until knife in center comes out clean.

Mrs. Shields Wilson

About ten years ago Kathleen Brock Stott (Mrs. Avery) and Elenora Varney (Mrs. Vic) got out a delightful cookbook of their special recipes. Here is Mrs. Stott's version of Bavarian Cheese Pie, which is a specialty at one of our hotels.

BAVARIAN CHEESE PIE

2 envelopes clear gelatin	½ teaspoon salt
½ cup cold water	1 teaspoon vanilla
2 beaten egg yolks	1 teaspoon grated lemon rind
1 cup sugar	2 teaspoons lemon juice
½ cup sweet milk	½ pint whipping cream
1 carton (8-ounce) cottage cheese	2 egg whites

Soften gelatin in cold water. Combine egg yolks, sugar, milk, and salt and cook in double boiler until slightly thickened. Add gelatin. Chill until thick but not set. Add cottage cheese which has been sieved smooth and flavored. Last fold in egg whites which have been sweetened to taste, and cream which has been whipped but not sweetened. Pour into tender cooked pastry shell. Sprinkle buttered graham cracker crumbs on top for a garnish.

Mrs. Avery Stott

When the World Book people here got out a small cookbook to raise money to build Sir Edmund Hilary's school for Sherpa children in Nepal, we ran some of the recipes in our column. For some reason the French Coconut Pie by Gay Wigley struck everyone's fancy, and our readers have been making it ever since. The original recipe made two pies, so I am revising it so that the following amount is for one pie.

FRENCH COCONUT PIE

1 pie crust	1½ tablespoons flour
¼ stick butter	1 cup milk
½ can coconut	1 cup sugar
2 eggs	1 teaspoon vanilla

Melt butter in a pan while making the crust. Coat the bottoms of the pie crust with butter. Mix flour with sugar. Beat the eggs and add the coconut, then the milk and vanilla. Add the liquids to the flour mixture. Pour into the pie shell and bake in a 350 oven for 1 hour.

Miss Gay Wigley

We Chattanoogans are often asked if we have any hillbillies in our Appalachian hills. You can hear the plaintive ballads of country music, whose center is in Nashville, on radios and television wherever you go, and the expert on country music in my own family is my brother Frank.

About twenty years ago when he was at McCallie School, he and some teen age friends got up a guitar and musical group called, of all things, "The Dismembered Tennesseans." They appeared on the radio, in theaters, and at various entertainments. We all assumed that it was a temporary thing. He played the harmonica and guitar. Fletcher Bright played the violin or mandolin, and Ansley Moses played another fiddle or banjo.

They went off to college, then came home and got married, had families. Fletcher is a leading real estate expert, Ansley a banker, and Frank a newspaperman, but whenever they get together for fun, they pick and sing. Strangely enough, for twenty years they have regularly appeared whenever asked for political rallies, wedding rehearsal dinners, anniversary parties, fund raising dinners for the Art Association, dinners for foreign dignitaries, fancy and unfancy occasions. They know many stories and songs and often make them up on the spot. The wit is pure corn, the songs are of love lost and the tragedies of life, the stories have us all laughing until we cry, but sometimes late at night when the mood is right, the plaintive melodies have a haunting beauty. If only they weren't so busy running a newspaper, a bank, and managing property, they might be famous for their country music.

The songs are not all the sad ones about train wrecks, lost love, and dying. Some are about food. There is a song about peas, another about cabbage, a watermelon song, and one about sweet potato pie. This is a favorite not just in the Appalachian mountains, but all over the South.

SWEET POTATO PIE

½ cup mashed sweet potatoes *Pinch salt*
2 egg yolks *Flavor to taste with vanilla*
1 cup sugar *and allspice*
1 cup milk

Pour into pie pan lined with unbaked pastry. Dot generously with butter and bake at 350 for about 30 or 40 minutes until done.

In the fall the children soon begin to ask when we are going to get our apples. Several years ago we got our first box of Red Delicious apples from Virginia as a gift. There were about a hundred apples in the box, which we kept on the back porch. We discovered how wonderful it is to enjoy crisp, cold apples when the boys came in from school, after dinner along with cheese, baked or made into a pie.

All winter long we keep apples,   and have found that the Golden Delicious is probably the most versatile, good to eat and fine for pie making. One year Jonathan requested an apple pie for his October birthday instead of a cake. The secret of making good apple pie is using plenty of butter, we think.

OLD FASHIONED APPLE PIE

Pastry for double crust	*3 tablespoons butter*
8 tart apples (Stayman,	*Dash of nutmeg*
Jonathan, or Golden Delicious)	*⅛ teaspoon salt*
1 cup sugar	*1 teaspoon lemon juice*
1 teaspoon cinnamon	

Roll dough, line pie plate. Fill shell with sliced apples. Mix sugar, spices and lemon juice together. Sprinkle over the apples, which have been peeled and sliced. Dot with butter. Moisten edge of pie crust with water. Fit top crust over apples and seal edge of pie. Cut or prick top of crust to allow steam to escape. Bake in hot oven, 425 degrees, for 50 or 60 minutes.

Chattanooga has a mild climate. The winter is sometimes damp and cold and bitter, but it doesn't last. Our neighbors Jane and Peter Branton built a swimming pool recently, had it heated, and it is actually possible to swim from April when the dogwoods are in bloom until frost in October. One day we were enjoying a swim with the children when I asked "BB" Branton, "Tell me something good that your mother has made lately." He said I should make an Apple Crisp recipe that he first had at his friend, Tom Heys' house, and that he brought the recipe home for Jane to try.

Jane is the comfortable sort of old friend who after school at G.P.S. used to wait on McCallie Avenue with us for the old Brainerd Bus when you could go two ways on McCallie. Then we went to Virginia to Randolph-Macon together, were worshipful students of the same legendary Latin professor, and kept taking Latin many more years than we meant. Sometimes we still say "Carpe diem," and can remember when he used to say, "Young ladies, seize the day, make the most of every opportunity, take hold of life."

We both married Mississippians, bought adjoining property, and settled down to the pattern that Chattanooga has repeated so many times...long pleasant friendships, church together, children. I never have to apologize to Jane when Roy brings a new Labrador Retriever home who looks as if she might have puppies, because Jane's sons do the same thing. This is her Apple Crisp by way of Mrs. Tom Heys.

APPLE CRISP

Put 4 cups sliced and peeled apples in a buttered casserole. Pour over this ¼ cup water and 1 teaspoon cinnamon. Mix together ½ cup flour, ¾ cup sugar, one-third cup softened margarine and spread over the apples. Bake at 350 for 40 minutes. Top with ice cream or whipped cream and serve warm.

Mrs. Peter Royal Branton III

Christmas in Shepherd Hills is a rather special event. They have a community project of lighting candles inside paper bags filled with sand. Set in front of every house, the effect as you drive through at night is lovely, and thousands of cars from all over Chattanooga make the trip to see the various lighting effects that their committee thinks up each year. One year the Shepherd Hills Club had a recipe tea in which each member brought one dish and the recipe. Mrs. Stan McCullough's Cherry Pie was one popular dessert.

CHERRY PIE

Pastry for 2 crust pie:
1 can frozen cherries
¾ cup sugar
3 tablespoons flour

¼ teaspoon almond flavoring
¼ stick butter
* (no substitute)*
6 drops red food color

Let cherries thaw, and add other ingredients. Bake in 9 inch pan lined with pastry. Use scalloped strips for top pastry. Bake at 400 degrees for 15 minutes, reduce heat and bake 30 minutes longer.

Mrs. Stan McCullough

Mrs. Harold Cooper makes a blackberry specialty that is a favorite of friends who come for a weekend with her on the lake. When blackberries are in season, she gets them and simply washes them, puts them in plastic bags, and stores in the freezer. She is always ready to make a cobbler.

BLACKBERRY COBBLER

Get blackberries from the freezer and put in a pan and sprinkle tapioca over it. Put in the berries and dot with butter generously. Top with the following pastry made with an egg as the French do.

Pastry:

2 cups flour	*1½ teaspoons sugar*
½ teaspoon salt	*¾ cup shortening*

Cut the shortening into the flour as for any pastry. Break 1 egg into a measuring cup and pour over it ¼ cup milk. Beat until blended. Pour over the flour a little at a time, stirring all the time until the pastry makes a ball. Chill. Roll out and cut in strips. Criss cross over the pie. Dot with plenty of butter and sprinkle with sugar. Bake at 400 degrees for ½ hour, then turn down to 350 for another ½ hour or until done.

Mrs. Harold Cooper

You can go through 20 cookbooks and still not find a recipe for apricot cobbler. One of the best here was made at the old Tomlinson's Restaurant. Years ago I called Mrs. Bob Tomlinson and asked for her secret. She said that theirs was a very simple version, no fancy spices, but just apricots, sugar, and lots of butter. This last is the secret, if there is any. Never substitute margarine for butter in cooking, because it doesn't perform the same way. Plenty of butter in any fruit pie is the secret to quality. In a cobbler, by the way, the pastry is on the top only, with none on the bottom.

TOMLINSON'S APRICOT COBBLER

1 size 2 can of unpeeled	*2 tablespoons flour*
apricot halves	*½ stick butter*
1 cup water	*Pastry for the top of cobbler*
1 cup sugar	

Mix the sugar, water, and the can of apricots in a shallow baking dish. Sift the flour lightly over it. Dot with butter. Arrange the pastry in strips across the top, with the strips pretty close together. Bake in a 400 degree oven for 30 minutes. Serve either plain or with vanilla ice cream.

Tomlinson's Restaurant

Every town has a farmer's market. Ours used to be the old Market House on Georgia Avenue across from the Key Hotel and next to the Volunteer Building. I can remember going there as a child with either my mother or grandmother and choosing the stall that had the prettiest tomatoes or the first watermelons or pumpkins, depending on the time of year. There were always flowers for sale, whatever was in season...the first jonquils in the spring, bunches of zinnias, marigolds, chrysanthemums later. The people who had the stalls were busy and their children helped by shelling peas or butterbeans, sweeping, arranging the various baskets, or whatever. There was always a great deal of trading, because the local farmers would come by to sell a load of peaches or potatoes or tomatoes to the owners of the stalls.

When the market house was torn down to make Patten Parkway, the market moved to Eleventh Street, where it is known as the Farmer's Market or just the Curb Market. There are the long rows of stalls, the choice vegetables, the fresh produce, the lively trading, the competition between the stalls. The wonderful smells of the vegetables and fruits just in from the farm and the drama of choosing among such a wondrous and colorful variety is still the same.

If you should stop at Granny Bettis' stall on a September day, you chould choose from locally grown pole cat peas, sugar crowder peas, purple hull crowders, both prune plums and damson plums, Hale peaches from Virginia, new green peanuts, corn, squash, cucumbers and okra. She would have all sorts of beans like butter-beans, October beans shelled for you, green beans, new sweet potatoes, green peppers, red peppers, and banana peppers, yellow and red tomatoes, preserving pears, watermelon, cantaloupe, pepper plants and cider.

She still weighs vegetables on scales that hang down from a chain, does her figuring informally on a small white pad, and makes wise observations about the weather and the crops. In mid conversation a truck will come by to ask how much okra she will need tomorrow, and she guesses about two or three baskets since she still has some on hand. She will ask about your husband, your children, "Did the boy in Vietnam get back," and suggest good ways to fix any of the fresh summer vegetables or fruit.

Just to see the variety and bounty of fresh vegetables in season is to inspire great menus. Such fresh butterbeans almost inspire a ham dinner, and when peaches are so pretty, you can't help asking Granny's recipe for cobbler. Chattanoogans who regularly go by the Curb Market, are bound to enjoy a greater variety of fresh vegetables as well as an enjoyable visit to a picturesque scene that doesn't change.

Granny Bettis has a different way of making cobbler by including 3 layers of pastry.

GRANNY BETTIS' PEACH COBBLER

First make a crust of 2 cups self rising flour, ¼ cup shortening cut in, and enough butter milk to make a biscuit type dough. Divide the ball of dough in 3 parts.

Prepare the peaches by peeling and slicing them. Put in a saucepan with a small amount of water and cook it slightly.

In the meantime, grease a rectangular type pan with butter. Roll out one-third of the pastry so that it covers the bottom and sides of the pan and laps over. Put in half the peaches and add butter and sugar. Turn the pastry over the peaches and add another layer of pastry rolled with the second third of the dough. On top of this crust dot with butter, sprinkle with sugar, and put in a 400 degree oven until the pastry is slightly brown. Take out and put the rest of the peaches on top. Add sugar, butter, and then the last layer of pastry. Sprinkle with sugar, flour, and butter and return to oven until the top crust is brown. Cook until very tender and done.

Granny Bettis

Elenora Varney (Mrs. Vic) has made some sort of culinary history in Chattanooga by making Moccasin Bend Hospital famous for its excellent homey food. She serves hundreds of people the kind of wholesome delightful food that might be served in a gracious Middle Tennessee home...fried chicken, roast beef, turkey, well seasoned vegetables, and homemade breads and esserts. Several years ago she was co-author of a cookbook here. This is her chocolate chiffon pie.

ELENORA'S CHOCOLATE CHIFFON PIE

2 eggs
1 cup white corn syrup
2 packages plain gelatin
½ cup cold water
1 teaspoon vanilla

1 pint whipping cream
2½ squares chocolate,
* unsweetened and*
* cut in small pieces*
Pinch of salt

Put corn syrup, 2 unbeaten egg yolks and chocolate in upper part of double boiler and cook until chocolate is melted and mixture is slightly thickened. Add gelatin which has been soaked for five minutes in cold water. When this is completely dissolved, remove from fire, cool, and add vanilla. Chill until partially congealed but not too set. Add stiffly beaten, sweetened and flavored egg whites. Last fold in whipped cream. Pile into baked pastry shell. Chill.

Mrs. Vic Varney

My sister Nancy who lives in Alexandria, is the artistic member of the family. She can paint, do original needlepoint, help put on a TV show for children's hospital, and think up lovely Williamsburg touches for her house. When we go to visit in Alexandria, we take the children sightseeing by day then sit up all night laughing and talking. Nancy is a good person to get recipes from because she likes quick ones. Cooking all day is not her idea of fun. This chocolate bar pie is an easy one that she likes.

ALMOND CHOCOLATE BAR PIE

1 almond Hershey bar, (9 ounce) ½ cup milk
22 marshmallows   1 cup whipping cream, whipped

Melt the chocolate bar, marshmallows and milk in the top of a double boiler. Chill. (You can add 1 teaspoon lemon juice and 1 teaspoon vanilla flavoring to cut the richness.) Fold in the whipped cream. Put in an uncooked graham cracker crust. This may be frozen, as it doesn't freeze hard. Or let set in the refrigerator for at least 6 hours.

Mrs. Roger Reinke
Alexandria, Virginia

An unusual chocolate pie is from Virginia. This is an uncooked mixture of butter, sugar, chocolate and eggs. It is light as a feather and reminds me of a remark one of the children made as he was licking the batter after I had made a cake. "I think the batter is better than the cake," he said. In the case of this pie, it certainly is. It would be a shame to cook anything as delicious as is this French Silk Chocolate Pie.

FRENCH SILK CHOCOLATE PIE

Cream 1 stick butter with ¾ cup sugar until the mixture is light and fluffy. Add to this 2 squares of unsweetened cooking chocolate, melted, and 1 teaspoon of vanilla and beat until smooth. Now add 2 eggs, one at a time, beating at least 3 minutes after each addition. The mixture should be light and creamy.

I have added one more thing. I add 1 teaspoon of lemon juice at the very last to cut the sweet taste and point up the chocolate. I think it really helps.

Pour in a baked 8 inch pie shell. Chill at least 3 hours before serving. Just before serving spread thickly with sweetened whipped cream. Then sprinkle it with shavings of bitter chocolate. With practice and a small sharp knife, you can shave off beautiful little curls of chocolate. This final touch of bitterness is another accent to this rich silky pie.

One of the gourmet cooks in the family was my Knoxville aunt, Mrs. Harry McDonald. When she made Rum Cream Pie for a party, everyone wanted the recipe.

RUM CREAM PIE

6 egg yolks	½ cup cold water
1 cup sugar	1½ cups heavy cream
1 tablespoon gelatin	¼ cup Jamaica rum

Beat the egg yolks until light, adding sugar slowly. Soak the gelatin in cold water. Put the gelatin and the water over low heat and let come to a boil. Pour it over the sugar and egg mixture, stirring briskly. Whip cream until it is stiff. Fold in above mixture. Add the rum and stir well. Cool, but do not allow to set. Pour into a cooked pastry shell, mound generously with more sweetened whipped cream and shave bitter chocolate curls over the top.

This is a thick pie and is prettiest in a spring form pan rather than a pie pan. If you use a pie dish, the large 10-inch size is best.

The late Mrs. Harry McDonald
Knoxville, Tennessee

MRS. FOWLER'S LEMON TARTS

½ cup butter	3 lemons (juice of 3;
6 eggs	grated rind of 2)
2 cups sugar	

Into a double boiler melt ½ cup butter. Add yolks of eggs well beaten, 2 cups sugar, lemon juice and grated rind. Cook until thick, then fold in whites which have been beaten until stiff. Put cooked mixture into prebaked pie shells. Serve with whipped cream on top.

Mrs. Hugh Maclellan

Rock City is a fascinating formation of rock on the brow of Lookout Mountain, with paths in and out of big boulders, a swinging bridge, an amazing view of valleys and mountains, and planted with ferns, wild flowers, rhododendron, mountain laurel, and every plant native to our area. In the 1920's when the late Garnet Carter bought the Fairyland area of the mountain top and began to divide it up for residential lots, it was not a tourist attraction at all.

He chose as the site for his own home a lot just to the left of the present Rock City Gardens, with a lovely view of the valley. Miss Frieda, his wife, wanted to save the area of the rock formations to develop a rock garden where she could plant wild flowers and ferns with paths of stepping stones. She was the former Frieda Uttermoellen, a concert pianist, who had given concerts with her father Herr Uttermoellen, a concert violinist, before her marriage to Mr. Carter.

At this time Garnet Carter was busy in several fields. He had one of the three original trading stamp companies in the United States (the other two being Sperry and Hutchinson, who later merged), and he was in the premium business. He also originated the idea of Tom Thumb golf courses and built the first one here, with cotton seed hulls dyed green for paths and special small sized golf clubs. He sold franchises all over the country, and fortunately sold the national franchise before the crash in 1929. There are hundreds of anecdotes about Garnet Carter that are still told by his friends.

Miss Frieda was busy working among the rocks, planting moss and fern at the entrance of the caves, masses of rhododendron and laurel. Soon people began to ask to come through her garden, and as the numbers increased, Mr. Garnet decided to charge an admission of 10 cents a person. He went through the whole Southland on every major highway and offered to paint farmers' barns with his "See Rock City" signs.

People came by the thousands from all over the country and they still do. Mrs. Carter was presented the Garden Club of America award for the excellence of her beautification, and when "Country Beautiful" published a book of the 38 most beautiful gardens of the United States, Rock City was included. It is now run by Garnet Carter's nephew, Ed Chapin III.

The most familiar part of Rock City to Chattanoogans is "High Falls" or "Lover's Leap," which you can see from the Ochs Highway extension up the mountain. Indian legend is that an Indian princess, Nacoochee, fell in love with a brave from an enemy tribe, Sautee. They married, much against the wishes of her father. In his rage, he threw the brave over the cliff, only to see his daughter fling herself after him. It was an Indian "Romeo and Juliet" story.

The Rock City Coffee Shop was for years the best place for mountain people to meet and have lunch. It is now remodeled and enlarged

"Lover's Leap" is a familiar landmark of Lookout Mountain and is
a part of Rock City Gardens.

as the Saddle Rock Inn, with a huge boulder that is shaped like a saddle, as an inside feature. Mrs. Don Gault, who was at the Gingerbread House at the Tom Thumb Golf Course, then the Coffee Shop, is now making the same wonderful chocolate pie for the Saddle Rock Inn.

ROCK CITY CHOCOLATE PIE

1½ cups sugar	*4 eggs, separated*
½ cup cocoa	*3 tablespoons butter*
2 rounded teaspoons cornstarch	*2 teaspoons vanilla*
Salt	*¼ teaspoon cream of tartar*
2 cups milk	*3 tablespoons sugar*

Beat the 4 egg yolks, then add the milk. Add this mixture to the 1½ cups sugar, the cocoa, cornstarch and salt which you mix in the top of a double boiler. Cook this over hot, not boiling, water. Stir constantly until thick. Add butter and vanilla. Cool the mixture. Pour into a baked pie shell. To make the meringue, beat the egg whites with the cream of tartar and the ¼ teaspoon salt until stiff. Add 3 tablespoons of sugar, sprinkling over the whites and continue beating until the whites look like whipped cream. Spread over chocolate pie and put in a 350 oven a few minutes to brown.

Mrs. Don Gault

Muffet Brock, as the wife of Senator Bill Brock, attends many important Washington affairs, and we are always asking her what she cooks in Washington that is good. Lots of people have gotten the recipe for an easy chocolate fudge pie that she makes. Here it is.

MUFFET'S FUDGE PIE

2 ounces unsweetened chocolate	*⅛ teaspoon salt*
¼ cup butter (½ stick)	*½ cup flour*
1 cup sugar	*1 teaspoon vanilla*
2 eggs, unbeaten	

Preheat the oven to 325 degrees. In a large saucepan melt the butter and chocolate over low heat until melted. Remove from heat and stir in the sugar, eggs, salt, flour, and vanilla. Spread in well buttered 7 inch pyrex pie pan. Bake at 325 degrees for about 30 minutes. Cool. Serve with shipped cream or ice cream.

Mrs. William E. Brock III

Chattanooga's skyline has changed many times over the years. Downtown 1973 is belted with freeways, and features new bank buildings, insurance buildings, and high rise apartments. Chattanooga is a manufacturing center for the Southeast, with an area population of 317,000.

The Buche de Noel is a Christmas tradition that can also be made as a chocolate log the rest of the year.

CHAPTER XIV

Desserts

The earliest Chattanooga cookbooks were the ones printed by various churches and the ones written by hand by individual cooks as their own collection of recipes. Almost all go into great detail when it comes to cakes and desserts, since it was taken for granted that not as many recipes for other courses were needed. In the Christ Church Cookbook a bit of Shelley is quoted, "We'll have custards for supper and an endless host of syllabubs and jellies and other such lady-like luxuries." The vogue was for custards, Spanish creams, Charlotte Russe, sherbets, ice cream, candy, and whipped cream on tipsy pudding.

Although fashions have changed, a delightful dessert to end the meal has not. Custards, ice creams, candy, whipped cream desserts all are a part of planning a menu that is civilized and offers a variety of taste sensations. Our personal favorites in this chapter are the Marchioness Pudding, pretty with whipped cream and cherries, and the Chocolate Log, which has made every Christmas for years.

Custard desserts have always been considered elegant and yet a very simple way to end a meal. Macaroon Pudding is very popular with boys and men ... it makes grown men remember their mothers' cooking, because this was a real favorite a generation ago. This is Dolly Berry's recipe, which she uses at parties for the W.C. Cartinhours.

MACAROON PUDDING

3 cups milk	1 tablespoon gelatin
4 eggs	1½ dozen macaroons
¾ cup sugar	1 teaspoon vanilla

Cream sugar in egg yolks, then add milk. Cook in a double boiler just as you would custard. Remove from stove when it will coat the back of a silver spoon, and add the gelatin, which you have already dissolved in ½ cup cold water. Cool. Beat the egg whites until stiff, and fold into the cooled custard. You may add a few almonds.

315

Line a ring mold with macaroon crumbs. Butter it first and it will stick better. Pour in the custard. Let it chill in the refrigerator. To serve, invert the mold and fill the center with whipped cream. Garnish with marschino cherries in the winter, and fresh strawberries or blueberries in the summer. This can be made in individual molds, and it can also be flavored with sherry.

Mrs. Dolly Berry

Catherine Laws (Mrs. Hiram III) makes a different macaroon pudding from any I know. She makes the boiled custard using marshmallows to give it body, she pours sherry on the macaroons, and spreads a lady finger layer with plum jelly. When chilled overnight in the refreigerator the layers combine flavors and you have a very old fashioned and delicate pudding.

ALMOND MACAROON PUDDING

Heat 4 cups of milk in a double boiler. Put 4 egg yolks in a bowl and beat in 8 tablespoons sugar. Pour the very hot milk over the egg and sugar mixture, mix, and put back in the double boiler on the stove. Add 15 marshmallows. Stir frequently and by the time the marshmallows have melted the custard should be thick enough. Flavor with 1 teaspoon vanilla.

In a pyrex loaf pan, place a layer of almond macaroons. Spoon 1 teaspoon medium sherry on each macaroon. Now split lady fingers and make a layer of lady fingers spread with a nice tart jelly. Sprinkle with chopped almonds, and then pour on half of the boiled custard. Repeat the whole procedure again. Refrigerate for about 24 hours to mellow. Serve in individual sherbet dishes, and top with whipped cream and a dash of nutmeg.

Mrs. Hiram Laws III

Some of our nicest specialties in Chattanooga are those that have been brought to us by our newcomers. Oga and Socrates Sabater fled Cuba in 1962 with only their clothes and their professions. Socrates is one of our talented young architects and Oga, an accountant, has taught Spanish at Senior Neighbors and now at G.P.S. Oga says that a great favorite in Cuba is Flan, or Spanish Custard. This is a baked custard dessert topped with caramel and fruit, especially delicious when served with Cuban expresso coffee.

FLAN OR SPANISH CUSTARD

2 cups scalded milk
4 egg yolks
1 egg white, beaten
4 tablespoons sugar
¼ teaspoon salt

1 teaspoon vanilla
Caramel:
½ cup sugar
1 tablespoon water

Mix sugar, egg yolks, egg white, salt and vanilla. Pour milk slowly over the misture and mix well. Make a caramel with the ½ cup sugar and the 1 tablespoon water. Spread into mold and let it harden. (Caramelize by heating this in a little skllet.)

Pour the mix into mold and place mold in pan with ½ inch water. Cook in the oven at 325 until you insert a knife in it and it comes out clean. Let cool to room temperature and then refrigerate for several hours. Before serving, turn out onto serving dish. Serve surrounded with sweetened fruit. This can also be made in individual molds.

Mrs. Socrates Sabater

Making a name for herself at Senior Neighbors was Mrs. Richard Dahlstrom, the dietitian who planned delicious hot lunches every day both for the senior citizens who gathered downtown and for those who were home bound and sent lunches through the Portable Meals program. Betty came to Signal Mountain with her husband, who is with Du Pont, and passed along this recipe for Soft Custard with Floating Island.

SOFT CUSTARD WITH FLOATING ISLAND

3 eggs or 6 egg yolks
3 tablespoons sugar
3 cups scalded milk

¼ teaspoon vanilla
Pinch of salt

Beat eggs and sugar together. Scald milk in top of double boiler, and pour gradually over egg mixture. Return to double boiler and stir constantly until custard begins to thicken, then occasionally until it forms a coating on the spoon. The water under the double boiler should simmer and not boil, because custard will curdle if eggs are cooked at too high a temperature. Add vanilla and salt when slightly cool.

3 egg whites
6 tablespoons powdered sugar

Pinch of salt
¼ teaspoon vanilla

Whip egg whites until stiff. Fold in salt, sugar, and vanilla. Pour custard into serving dishes and chill. The meringue may be browned slightly in an oven if desired.

Mrs. Richard Dahlstrom

On the screened porch, which is the best refrigerator at Christmas, is our Christmas dessert, the Chocolate Yule Log. I first saw this as an illustration in the "Gourmet Cookbook," a Mother's Day present long ago. It was beautiful ... a light chocolate roll filled with whipped cream and iced with mocha icing. The garnishes of icing from the pastry tube, the little chocolate twigs, the nuts on top make this so spectacular looking that we use it all year round ... a Lincoln log in February and chocolate log when we have twelve for dinner and need one dessert that will feed that many.

I have changed the recipe so that it scarcely resembles the original, but it is quickly made and a great favorite. For grownups, we sometimes flavor the icing with rum or brandy but our children don't like it, so at Christmas we just use the chocolate and coffee flavors. Don't let the long recipe scare you. One night Susan and I had to make six and had a fresh one in the oven every twenty minutes.

CHOCOLATE YULE LOG

6 egg whites	*1 teaspoon vanilla*
¼ teaspoon cream of tartar	*¼ cup cocoa*
½ cup sugar	*¼ cup flour*
6 egg yolks	*½ teaspoon salt*
½ cup sugar	

Beat the egg whites with the cream of tartar until stiff. Gradually add the ½ cup sugar and beat until stiff and glossy. In another bowl beat the egg yolks and gradually add the ½ cup sugar. Put in the vanilla. Sift dry ingredients and quickly fold into the yolk mixture. Fold in the egg whites.

Take a long cookie pan, about 10 by 15 inches, and fit into it a piece of foil. Grease the foil with oil. Pour in the batter and bake at 325 for 20 to 25 minutes. When done, turn out on cup towel, peel off foil, and roll up while warm just as you would jelly role. Let cool all rolled up.

WHIPPED CREAM FILLING

2 cups whipping cream	*1 teaspoon sugar*

First chill the beaters and small bowl of mixer in the freezer. This makes the cream whip faster and to a smoother texture. Whip the cream and sweeten it. Set aside to wait in the refrigerator until time to fill the roll.

MOCHA ICING

¼ cup butter	*3 cups sifted powdered sugar*
1 teaspoon instant coffee	*Pinch of salt*
3 tablespoons water	*1 tablespoon cocoa, sifted*
* (or rum or brandy)*	

Melt the instant coffee in the water. Sift the cocoa with the sugar. Blend all together in the mixer until fluffy. You may have to add more sugar to get the right consistency.

Unroll the chocolate roll and remove to a platter. Fill with the whipped cream and roll up again. Ice with the icing. If you want to, cut off one slice of the roll and break into three pieces. Roll up each of these to make mock twigs to garnish the iced roll. It is pretty, but not necessary to put some of the icing in a paper cone and run through a large star pastry tube to decorate the edges of the roll. Do sprinkle chopped pecans on the top...

An old Southern Christmas dessert, especially pretty with both red and green cherries mixed with the whipped cream and coconut is Marchioness Pudding. This comes from my husband's Mississippi family.

MARCHIONESS PUDDING

1 pint whipping cream	1 can coconut or,
whipped	1 package frozen
1 envelope gelatin dissolved	1 teaspoon vanilla
in ¼ cup cold milk	1 jar maraschino cherries,
2 egg whites beaten stiff	drained
1 cup sugar	

Whip the cream. Soften the gelatin in cold milk and heat until dissolved over hot water. Add sugar gradually to the egg whites until they are glossy. Gradually pour in the gelatin. Fold in the whipped cream, vanilla, coconut, and 1 jar maraschino cherries, drained and halved. Get out your prettiest crystal or silver dish, line with lady fingers, and pour in pudding.

Miss Jessie Thatcher got an old fashion sponge cake with rum sauce from Mrs. Emeline Hedges' cook over 30 years ago. All the Thatchers have loved it ever since. When dessert time came, it was brought to Mr. Hugh at the head of the table to be sliced, topped with the rum sauce in a separate bowl, and then served to each guest.

OLD FASHIONED SPONGE CAKE

This makes a large super melting cake. Be sure the cream of tartar is fresh.

Sift before measuring 1½ cup cake flour. Add ½ teaspoon baking powder and ¼ teaspoon salt. Re-sift 5 times with 1 cup sugar.

Beat until light 5 egg yolks. Gradually beat ½ cup sugar. Combine 1 tablespoon fresh lemon juice, and ¼ cup cold water. Add the flour mixture to the yolks in three parts, alternating with the liquid. Mix all well. Beat until foamy 5 egg whites. Add ¾ teaspoon cream of tartar. Beat until stiff but not dry. Fold in the flour mixture gently. Bake in a 10 inch tube pan in a 325 degree oven for 50 to 60 minutes. When you take it out, let stand for 3 to 4 minutes, then invert it.

RUM SAUCE

4 egg yolks, beaten	*1 pint milk*
1 teaspoon (rounded)	*3 tablespoons sugar*
cornstarch	

Cook in double boiler until thickened. When cool, add ½ pint whipping cream, whipped until stiff. Flavor well with rum. Serve over fresh homemade sponge cake.

Mrs. Hugh Lynn Thatcher

One day I bought myself a present ... eight old fashioned custard cups, white inside and brown out, made from the heavy sort of stoneware that keeps either very cold or very hot. How nice, I thought, to have custard or chocolate mousse on hand in the refrigerator for dessert. In classic French restaurants these desserts are very popular. If you order chocolate mousse, it comes in one of these little round brown pots with a swirl of whipped cream on top. The little pot is so cold and the mousse looks so good that everyone at the tables wishes they had ordered chocolate mousse, too.

Rachel Wilmot gave French cooking classes one year to benefit the Art Gallery. Among many elaborate recipes, she gave us a wonderful custard to try. Her baked custard is a little different, because it calls for more eggs than most and powdered sugar to keep it smooth. The secret is in slow cooking. If you have every had worm holes in your custard, it cooked too fast. If it curdles, it was put in the refrigerator while too hot.

These things have happend to us too, so we know. Sometimes after we have made angel food cake and have egg yolks left, we substitute 8 egg yolks for the 4 eggs, and although it is quite sturdy, it is very smooth and rich and the children like it.

POWDERED SUGAR BAKED CUSTARD

4 whole eggs	*¾ cup sifted powdered sugar*
(or 8 yolks)	*2 cups milk, scalded*
1 teaspoon lemon extract	*Pinch of salt*
(or vanilla)	

Beat the eggs together with the sugar and extract. Add gradually the scalded milk. Pour into individual baking cups. Put in a shallow pan with about ½ inch hot water. Bake in a 300 degree oven until done. They are done when they are firm except in the middle, which will firm up as they cool. Cool before putting in the refrigerator.

Mrs. Rachel Wilmot

The first time Mrs. Edward Signaigo tried the new cheesecake recipe her sister had sent her from California, I happened to drop by her house. After tasting the new recipe, I wrote it down and have been making it ever since. It is fool-proof and never falls, because it is not supposed to rise. This is very rich and creamy, and we judge all other cheesecakes by this one.

MRS. SIGNAIGO'S CHEESECAKE

Mix and line a 9 inch pie pan with the following:
1½ cups graham cracker crumbs ¼ cup sugar
¼ cup butter

Now mix the following cream cheese mixture until smooth and free from lumps:

12 ounces cream cheese	*4 eggs*
1 teaspoon vanilla	*½ cup sugar*

Pour this cheese mixture over the crust. Bake 25 minutes at 350 degrees. Remove and cool for about 15 minutes.

Spread the following mixture on the top:

8 ounces sour cream	*1 teaspoon vanilla*
3 tablespoons sugar	

Put back in the oven for five minutes. I forgot to say that when you are baking cheesecake, use the same rule as for a custard pie. Bake until it is fairly solid except for about an inch in the center. The remaining heat in the pie will take care of that. You don't want a cheesecake that is not firm.

Mrs. Edward Signaigo

My friend Patty Boyd (Mrs. Robert) made our cheesecake and loved it. Then one day she was having a big dinner party and needed a larger cake, and the thought came to her that this cheesecake would be good flavored with rum. She increased the proportions and added rum, and the dessert was such that one guest from out of town always begs her to make her rum cheesecake the next time he comes for a visit.

RUM CHEESECAKE

Crust:
3 cups graham cracker crumbs
1 stick butter, melted
½ cup sugar
Cheese mixture:
6 eggs
18 ounces cream cheese

¾ cup sugar
1 tablespoon rum (or to taste)
½ cup cream
Topping:
2 cups sour cream
6 tablespoons sugar
1 teaspoon vanilla

Combine the melted butter with the sugar and the crumbs and toss until light. Press along the sides and bottom of a 9 inch spring form pan. In the mixer soften the cream cheese and beat until smooth. Add the sugar, then the eggs, rum and cream. Pour into the crust and bake in 350 degree oven about 40 minutes or until it is set when a silver knife is inserted and comes out clean. Leave out of oven 10 minutes. This makes a huge cake about 2 inches high and will serve 10 or 12. Sometimes Patty grates chocolate across the top before serving to dress it up.

Mrs. Robert Boyd

On the Missionary Ridge site of the famous Colyar mansion, Dr. and Mrs. Deene Leventhal have built a delightful contemporary house that has been featured nationally. Mickey is not only a talented home-maker with an eye for art, design, and easy maintenance living, she is a real planner when it comes to either family meals or parties. She knows how to cook ahead and freeze, and managed a New Year's party for over a hundred all by herself. She prefers smaller dinner parties around the white fiberglass dining table with upholstered swivel chairs.

When Mickey and Deene go on trips to California, they usually come home with a new painting or two, and some new recipes. It was here she found her best cheese cake recipe. She has made it many times for parties, but this is the first time she has given it out. It needs a 10-inch spring form pan, and she says it is worth getting one for this cake.

MICKEY'S CALIFORNIA CHEESE CAKE

Crust:
1 large box vanilla wafers

1 stick melted butter

322

Roll the wafers into fine crumbs, mix with melted butter, and press into a 10 inch spring form pan, bottom and sides.

Cheese Filling:	*⅛ teaspoon salt*
2 pounds cream cheese	*4 eggs*
(4 packages 8-ounce)	*1 tablespoon lemon juice*
1 pint sour cream	*1 tablespoon vanilla flavoring*
1½ cups sugar	

Beat the eggs and sugar until thick. Cream the cream cheese and sour cream. Add eggs and sugar mixture. Add salt, vanilla flavoring, and lemon juice. Cream well. Pour into lined 10 inch spring form pan. Bake at 375 for 30 minutes. Cool 3 hours, then place in refrigerator over night. Next day remove from pan. Can be frozen. This cake is large, but is very creamy and light. It will serve 20.

Mrs. Deene Leventhall

The whole News-Free Press family was very proud when Carolyn Owens was named Miss Chattanooga several years ago, because her father, Ronald Owens, is foreman of the press room, and a good friend. Carolyn is a beautiful girl, and after she cut all the ribbons for grand openings, rode in parades and made public appearances for the city, she married and had children. In 1968 she decided to enter the Mrs. America contest and won the title "Mrs. Tennessee." She went to the pageant in Minneapolis and represented the state. She had to cook a foreign dinner, prepare a dinner for 6 on less than $10, cook a creative breakfast, arrange flowers, and in the camping contest she and her husband won first place. She is Mrs. Tennessee, and a talented homemaker. Sometimes for dessert she makes Vanilla Wafer Stack Cake.

VANILLA WAFER STACK CAKE

1 large box vanilla wafers	*4 tablespoons liquid chocolate*
2 cups whipping cream	*2 tablespoons sugar*

Whip the cream until light and fluffy. Add sugar and chocolate and dip vanilla wafers, one by one, into the cream and begin stacking. Make a round, square or oval cake. Let stand overnight in refrigerator, or make early in the morning for dinner party that evening. When sliced, it looks like many tiny layers of cake. The wafers soften to make a very interesting cake. This can be served with a scoop of chocolate ice cream.

Mrs. E.T. Shearer II
"Mrs. Tennessee"

In Chattanooga Miss Ruby Carter represents fine Southern cooking, delicate cakes, and genteel taste. She has catered informally for luncheons, open houses and teas, and has written several books of her recipes in longhand for family brides. She makes very delicate meringues, either to be served for dessert or in tiny bite size meringues for teas and coffees.

MISS RUBY'S MERINGUES

3 egg whites	1 teaspoon vinegar
1 cup sugar	½ teaspoon baking powder
1 teaspoon cold water	

Put egg whites in mixing bowl with the baking powder and beat at high speed until very stiff. Now begin to add the sifted sugar, 1 teaspoon at a time, beating constantly, and alternating with a few drops of the mixed liquid. Continue to beat until all the ingredients are used, adding the sugar last. Cover a cookie sheet with brown wrapping paper (or foil). Place a teaspoon of meringue on the paper and make a hollow in the center. Do not let them touch, as they spread. They may also be made into 8 dessert size meringue shells. Bake at 325 for 45 to 50 minutes. They are done when they are dry and you can lift them from the paper. They will be slightly brown. Fill with Strawberry Bavarian.

STRAWBERRY BAVARIAN

2 packages frozen strawberries, thawed and mashed	1 cup sugar (optional)
	1 tablespoon lemon juice
2 envelopes plain gelatin	2 cups whipping cream,
3 tablespoons cold water	whipped

Soak the gelatin in the cold water for 5 minutes and then dissolve over boiling water. The berries should be sweetened. If they are not, add 1 cup sugar, or however much needed to sweeten them. Add the lemon juice and the dissolved gelatin. Cool in refrigerator and when it begins to thicken, add the whipped cream. Place in a wet mold and keep in refrigerator until serving time. This will fill the centers of 8 dessert size or 24 tiny meringues.

Miss Ruby Carter

Farol Seretean (Mrs. M. B.), as wife of the President of Coronet Carpets, probably does as much business entertaining as anyone in town. Who would ever have dreamed that the tufted bedspreads that used to line the road from Chattanooga to Dalton would develop into the carpet center of the world, with about 75 carpet factories in the Dalton-Chattanooga area turning out everything from the most luxurious acrilan carpets to the hardiest indoor outdoor miracles. The Sereteans are hosts to business friends from all over the United States and Europe as well as film and TV friends from Hollywood. Buffet suppers are the easiest form of entertaining and when Jim Nabors visited them last year, they had apple cake for dessert.

APPLE CAKE

In a mixer place 1½ cups salad oil, 2 cups sugar, and 3 eggs. Sift together 3 cups sifted flour, 1 teaspoon salt, and 1 teaspoon soda. Add this slowly to the mixer and flavor with 1 teaspoon vanilla and 1 teaspoon lemon juice. Fold in 3 cups of chopped peeled apples (Winesaps preferred). Grease and flour a rectangular pan, and bake at 325 degrees for 1 hour.

GLAZE: Put in a saucepan 1 cup brown sugar, 1 stick butter or margarine, ½ cup sweet milk and 1 teaspoon vanilla. Cook 2½ minutes. Pour on hot cake. Cool in the pan. Slice in squares. Sometimes she does not glaze the cake, but just slices it

Mrs. M. B. Seretean

Our neighbor Meredith Bishop is a native of our region, having grown up in nearby Trenton, who lived in Oakland, California, nearly 20 years and then came back home. She paints portraits and landscapes for a hobby, was art editor for the Lookout Mountain Breeze, and has opened up our eyes to a world of art that we didn't know too much about. When her California friends come to visit, we enjoy fine dinners and good conversations. At one of these she served a pretty molded dessert of custard, chunks of angel food cake, and whipped cream.

MEREDITH'S COMPANY DESSERT

6 beaten egg yolks	1 tablespoon unflavored gelatin
¾ cup sugar	¼ cup water
¾ cup lemon juice	6 beaten egg whites
1½ tablespoons grated	¾ cup sugar
lemon peel	1 small angel food cake

Make custard in double boiler of egg yolks, sugar, lemon juice and peel. Remove from heat; add gelatin which has been soaked in ¼ cup water. Fold in whites which have been beaten with ¾ cup sugar. Tear cake into bite size pieces and fold into mixture. Place in oiled angel food cake pan or spring form pan. Chill. Ice with whipped cream.

Mrs. Hugh Dexter Bishop

Churning a freezer of ice cream late one summer afternoon takes fresh peaches, whipping cream, ice, salt, and some willing hands. Ellen adds ice while Roy turns.

Every summer there comes a hot sultry afternoon when we all get hungry for homemade freezer ice cream. Someone goes to the attic for the freezer, and I look to be sure we have enough whipping cream and some peaches.

There is always a sort of excitement that goes with freezing ice cream. I mix up the ice cream recipe, but from then on, there are all sorts of opinions about how the messy procedure will be carried out. The chunks of ice don't quite fit down into the sides of the freezer, and we haven't needed an ice pick in so long that we can't find it. One summer the head of the house got the hammer and had nice little chunks in no time. Then Susan went to the smokehouse to get the ice cream salt that we had left over from using on the driveway during the snow the winter before. It must have sat on the snow for awhile, because when Susan brought it, the bottom gave and the salt spilled.

But we did get started, and honestly, when you start to turn that crank, all sorts of memories come back to you. You remember all the times you have taken your turn and turned until your right shoulder felt as if it might come off. The younger children start to turn very fast and then slow up, counting every turn. The older boys who could do it easily, never seem to be home at the right time.

The peach ice cream, made by my Aunt Clara's recipe, was better even than I remember it. By the time the freezer got very hard to turn, and we brushed all the salty ice away to open it and take out the dasher, the children all had their spoons ready to lick. When we got it out one year, we tried a new trick. Instead of packing the ice cream to mellow until it was hard, we put the container in the freezer, which was a much easier way to ripen it.

After dinner we had not just one dish, but two. It was not too rich, just right. Roy kept getting another dish, then another. Everyone was so pleased with themselves that they began planning all the flavors of ice cream they would make next . . . vanilla, peppermint, strawberry.

AUNT CLARA'S PEACH ICE CREAM

2 cups fresh peaches	*3 whole eggs*
1½ to 3 cups sugar to taste	*2 cups whipping cream, whipped*
1 quart milk (including 1	*2 teaspoons vanilla*
large can evaporated milk)	

Puree the peaches or mash well with a fork. Let stand an hour or two with sugar to sweeten. Mix eggs, some sugar and milk. Fold in whipped cream and peaches and freeze in freezer.

When freezing, remember to fill the barrel about 1-3 full of ice, and then pour in a layer of ice cream salt. Pour more ice, then ice, more salt. Keep the freezer full of ice, but be careful that no salty water gets into the freezing container. When you have turned until hard, remove dasher, and pack tightly with ice and salt to ripen and harden. Or you can remove container to your own freezer. Serve when hard.

Mrs. Gene Ketner

AUNT CLARA'S PLAIN VANILLA

¾ cup sugar	3 eggs
1 quart milk (containing 1	1 pint cream, whipped
large can evaporated milk)	1 or 2 tablespoons vanilla

Combine ingredients and freeze as you would peach ice cream.

Mrs. Gene Ketner

MRS. DINGLE'S VANILLA ICE CREAM

3 cups cream, whipped	2 cups milk
5 eggs	1 teaspoon pure vanilla
1 cup sugar	

Whip cream, beat eggs, add sugar to cream and eggs, and add other ingredients. Freeze in old fashioned freezer.

Mrs. R. H. Dingle

Some of the 80,000 Federal troops stationed here in the Civil War liked Chattanooga and came back to live, such as Thomas Payne, Z. C. Patten and others.

Then in the 1880's Chattanooga experienced a land boom, because many people felt that with the new railroad from Cincinnati completed, Chattanooga would be the iron center of the South. We never got the advantageous freight rates, nor did the mines nearby prove as rich as at first thought, but many Northern investors came here at the time, prospered, and remained to found some of the leading Chattanooga families today. Most of them lived over on East Terrace. Captain Hiram Chamberlain, T. G. Montague, Henry Clay Evans, Will Lasley, and others built fine Victorian houses and set a standard of living new to Chattanooga.

Mrs. Griffin Martin, who was Rosalind Ewing and a granddaughter of Captain Chamberlain, remembers hearing about the receptions each family would have every year. These were usually in the late afternoon and almost always featured chicken salad, sandwiches, cookies, cakes, mints, and ices. There would be punch or coffee or champagne.

The Montagues later tore down the Victorian house and built an elaborate Italian one. Two daughters married Italian counts, and the festivities before these weddings were very elaborate.

Much later one of the most elaborate affairs in Chattanooga was hosted by the Walter Hensons, who had bought the Faxon house (now the Hunter Art Gallery). They had either Sherry's or Delmonico's from New York to come down in a private car, cater, and bring their staff. As each guest would come to the door, the English butler would ask the name and then in a loud resonant voice announce him. Will Shepherd, a great jokester, told the butler with a straight face, "The Duke of Ooltewah," (the Shepherd dairy farm was near there). The butler announced "The Duke of Ooltewah," in a booming voice, and the party laughed about it for weeks.

In these years a fancy ice cream or sherbet was accepted as the most elegant dessert. Sometimes it was served in fancy fluted cups, sometimes molded in bombes. It is still sensational when someone takes the time and trouble to turn a freezer of homemade ice cream. This is Mrs. Martin's homemade maple ice cream.

MAPLE ICE CREAM OR MOUSSE

1½ cups maple syrup   *1 pint heavy whipping cream*
4 eggs, separated

Beat the yolks until light and add the syrup slowly to them. Cook over a double boiler until thick, beating constantly. Let cool. Whip the cream and add to the maple custard. Put in a freezer and turn until about half frozen. Unpack and take off the top and add the egg whites, beaten to a stiff froth. Finish turning in the freezer until hard to turn. This was a specialty of Emma Wilson, former cook of the Martin family.

Mrs. Griffin Martin

A good dessert to have for a luncheon is the easy Biscuit Tortoni that Mrs. Richard Thatcher makes. She uses ice cream, which refreezes to a much smoother consistency than whipped cream, macaroon crumbs and sherry, and makes them in dainty fluted paper cups. These can be put in the freezer days in advance of a luncheon.

EASY BISCUIT TORTONI

For 8 servings, scoop out about 9 scoops of vanilla ice cream into the bowl of the mixer and stir until just soft enough to manage. Fold in ½ cup ground blanched almonds or macaroon crumbs. Stir in 3 tablespoons of sherry (more if it is dry sherry). Pour into individual paper cups. Sprinkle the tops with extra ground almonds or macaroons. Place in the freezer. Before serving, garnish the top with a maraschino cherry.

For a buffet party where you want a small dessert to pass and be eaten on the dinner plates, this is very convenient.

Mrs. Richard Thatcher

MOTHER'S TRICK TO MAKE BOUGHT ICE CREAM TASTE HOME MADE

1 cup mashed peaches, sweetened to taste	½ gallon vanilla ice cream
2 teaspoons almond flavoring	2 cups whipping cream, whipped

First mash the peaches with a fork and sugar. Add lemon juice if peaches need it. Next whip the cream and have it ready. Chill the large mixing bowl of an electric mixer. Put in the vanilla ice cream and mix quickly until mushy. Be careful that you don't mix too much, because you are losing precious air. This is why you whip the cream ......to add back the air you have lost. When just barely mushy enough, blend in the peaches and fold in the whipped cream. You can add more peaches if you want to. Repack the ice cream mixture in a plastic ice cream carton. Sometimes Mother packs it in individual white fluted paper cups. Return to the freezing section of the refrigerator.

Mrs. Roy McDonald

A creamy chocolate sauce that all Chattanooga likes on ice cream is Miss Gertrude's which is made with evaporated milk.

MISS GERTRUDE'S CHOCOLATE SAUCE

4 squares bitter chocolate	Pinch salt
½ cup boiling water	1 small can evaporated milk
2 cups granulated sugar	(7 ounces)
¼ stick butter	1½ teaspoons vanilla

In a double boiler, let the chocolate melt and the ½ cup of boiling water dissolve to a smooth paste. Add the granulated sugar and let cook until it dissolves. Add the butter, salt, milk, and vanilla and cook until everything is hot and the sauce of a nice consistency. Serve warm over ice cream or cake. This can be stored in the refrigerator in a jar ready to the heated and served anytime.

Miss Gertrude Oehmig

To serve Peaches Melba, you need vanilla ice cream, topped with either fresh or frozen peaches, with a raspberry sauce to go over it all.

RASPBERRY MELBA SAUCE

1 package frozen raspberries,   1½ teaspoons cornstarch
   thawed   1 tablespoon cold water
½ cup currant jelly

In a saucepan mash the raspberries and add the jelly. Bring to a boil and add the cornstarch which has been mixed with the cold water. Cook until clear, stirring constantly. Strain and cool.

Mrs. Roy McDonald

Estes Stephens comes from a family of good cooks, and her open houses, suppers for the convention of bankers who meet here, and buffets after the White Christmas service at church, are looked forward to events by her friends. One spectacular dessert that she makes combines tiny cream puffs with ice cream in a frozen dessert topped with chocolate sauce.

CREAM PUFF DESSERT

Heat to rolling boil in a saucepan 1 cup water and ½ cup butter. Stir in all at once 1 cup sifted all purpose flour. Stir vigorously on low heat until mixture leaves the sides of the pan and forms into a ball, about one minute. Remove from heat.

Beat in 4 eggs, one at a time. Beat until smooth and velvety. Drop in very small balls about the size of a quarter on an ungreased baking sheet. Bake until dry and golden brown in a 400 degree oven. They should be done in about 20 minutes. Let cool.

Take spring form pan and arrange layer of cream puffs solid across the bottom. Spread with softened ice cream. Alternate layers of cream puffs and ice cream, ending with a layer of cream puffs on top, about 3 layers in all. Freeze.

331

When ready to serve, unmold. Drizzle the top layer of cream puffs with either chocolate or butterscotch sauce. With pistachio or peppermint ice cream, chocolate sauce would be best; with butter pecan or almond ice cream, butterscotch sauce would be good.

Mrs. Gerry Stephens

At the Christmas tea planned by the Shepherd Hills Community Club, a delicious orange dessert proved to be a simple combination of orange juice, marshmallows, whipped cream and macaroons. Mrs. Jake Marshall brought it and here is how she did it.

ORANGE DESSERT

1 cup fresh strained orange juice	½ pound plain white marshmallows
1 pound almond macaroons	1 pint whipping cream, whipped

Put both in double boiler and melt marshmallows. Let cool and fold in 1 pint whipping cream, whipped. Crush 1 pound almond macaroons. Line bottom of deep dish with half of macaroons, pour in cream mixture and top with remaining half of macaroons. Cover closely and chill overnight. Do not stir or freeze.

Mrs. Jake Marshall

Dr. Park McCallie's family came to Chattanooga in the 1840's when McCallie Avenue was nothing but a buffalo trail leading out to Missionary Ridge. The diary of his father, Dr. Thomas Hooke McCallie, is a remarkable account of Chattanooga during the Civil War and afterward. Dr. Park is one of the founders of McCallie School and a leader in the Christian life of Chattanooga for ninety years.

His men's class at the First Presbyterian Church used to meet for dinner every Monday night with Miss Pearl Tatum in charge. Since this was a small dinner meeting they called themselves "the little men," and liked to get together, although many were 6 feet tall with huge appetites. Miss Pearl saw that they ate well and got the meat, gravy and potatoes they all loved. Their favorite dessert was a recipe of Mrs. James Fowle's, a custard sauce served over angel food or sponge cake. As a joke, one of them called it "yellow gravy" and the name stuck. Margaret Brown (Mrs. Scott) gave me this recipe.

CUSTARD SAUCE FOR "THE LITTLE MEN"

4 egg yolks	1 teaspoon vanilla
¾ cup sugar	½ pint whipping cream, whipped
½ cup water	
1 teaspoon almond flavoring	

Cook water and sugar until it spins a thread. Beat yolks til very light. Add the syrup gradually. Cook in double boiler until thick like custard. When cold, fold in the whipped cream and 1 teaspoon almond and 1 teaspoon vanilla. Serve over slices of angel food cake or orange sponge cake.

Mrs. Scott Brown

Any number of new ice creams can be made by folding in your favorite combination of ingredients. Jellis Moncure (Mrs. Richard) makes a quick ginger ice cream.

GINGER ICE CREAM

Let 1 quart of vanilla ice cream get soft but not melted. Stir in ½ cup crushed candied ginger and 3 or 4 tablespoons sherry. Refreeze. This can be refrozen in small white paper cups, but Jellis usually serves it in sherbet dishes.

Mrs. Richard Moncure

Anita Siskin Levine (Mrs. Lawrence) makes a chocolate mousse roll that is different from any that I have had. It is a chocolate sponge roll, spread with a chocolate mousse, rolled up and chilled. If you are hunting a glamorous chocolate dessert this is it.

CHOCOLATE MOUSSE ROLL

First make a mousse filling. In the top of a double boiler melt:

1½ cups semi-sweet   *¼ cup sugar and*
chocolate bits with   *¼ cup water*

While it melts, stir until smooth and free from lumps. Remove from heat and cool, stirring from time to time. When cool, add the yolks of 5 eggs, which have been beaten until thick and lemon colored, as for sponge cake. Stir in 2 teaspoons vanilla. Beat the 5 egg whites until stiff enough to hold a peak. Add the chocolate egg mixture to the whites and beat with a rotary beater just long enough to incorporate all the whites. Chill to spreading consistency in the refrigerator about 3 to 4 hours.

For the Roll: Sift together 3 times 6 tablespoons cake flour, 6 table-spoons cocoa, ¼ teaspoon salt, ¾ teaspoon baking powder. Separate 4 eggs, and beat whites until they form soft peaks. Fold in ¾ cup sugar, a tablespoon at a time. Now beat the 4 egg yolks until very thick and lemon colored.

333

Add 1 teaspoon vanilla and fold in the egg white and sugar meringue. Next, carefully fold in the dry ingredients. Grease a shallow jelly roll pan about 10 by 15. Line with greased waxed paper. Pour batter and spread out evenly. Bake in a hot oven 400 degrees for 13 minutes. Turn out on tea towel sprinkled with confectioner's sugar. Quickly cut off crisp edges of the cake. Roll up. Cool in rack.

Unroll and spread with the chocolate mousse. Roll up again. Chill in the refrigerator 1 hour before wrapping in foil and freezing. Before serving, thaw in refrigerator 2 or 3 hours and remember the roll slices better if it is left in the refrigerator until just before serving time.

Mrs. Lawrence Levine

Mrs. Mark Hays used to make a delicious Lemon Fluff dessert for her grandsons when they were young and spent the weekends with their grandparents. It is a favorite dessert of the Hays' family and aptly named . . . a cloud of lemon fluff with a graham cracker bottom and top.

Mark Hays is "Mr. R.C.A." in Chattanooga, and has been so successful that he has made the Chattanooga distributorship one of the largest in the country. With his enthusiasm, his wit, and his genial personality, he is a well-known and popular Chattanoogan, whose son, Mark Hays, Jr. and grandsons are following in the family tradition.

LEMON FLUFF

1 package lemon gelatin	1½ cups boiling water
9 tablespoons lemon juice	¼ cup sugar
1 large can evaporated milk	Vanilla wafer or Graham
(chill over night)	cracker crumbs

Dissolve gelatin in boiling water, add sugar and lemon juice — partially jell in refrigerator. Whip chilled milk in mixer and fold in gelatin mixture. Grease bottom of 8" x 12" x 2" Pyrex dish and cover with crumbs. Fill with the mixture, sprinkle remaining crumbs on the top, and refrigerate.

Mrs. Mark H. Hays, Sr.

Hot gingerbread on a winter's day was the specialty of Mrs. Don Gault when she ran first the Gingerbread House and later the coffee shop at Rock City.

One secret of the gingerbread was the old fashioned sorghum. This is sugar cane, which is fed into a mill which separates the juice from the pulp. The juice is boiled down in long flat copper sorghum pans by old time experts who know how thick it must get.... until it is rich caramel colored and sweet.

MRS. GAULT'S GINGERBREAD

1 cup sugar	½ teaspoon allspice
1 cup sorghum	1 teaspoon ginger
1 cup shortening	½ teaspoon cinnamon
3 eggs	½ teaspoon nutmeg
1 cup boiling water	3 cups flour
1 teaspoon soda	

Cream sugar and shortening together, then add sorghum and hot water with the soda in it. Add 3 eggs. Mix the spices and flour and stir well until blended. Pour into a rectangular pan which has been greased and floured, and bake at 350 until done.... about 40 minutes.

Mrs. Don Gault

All through this book there are recipes that people have taken to church for church suppers. Some churches have family suppers every Wednesday night, meeting early at six and ending about 7:30 so that the children can get home to study. Other churches have family dinners once a month. There are also rallies and homecomings.

Some people call the southeastern part of our country the Bible belt, and once when a New York friend flew into have lunch with us on Sunday after church, he said, "I find this all over the South. Your churches are to you what our clubs in the North are to us. People need to get together and you do it in your churches." We laughed, but told him we couldn't agree completely. It goes much deeper.

Chattanooga is certainly influenced by the Scotch Irish or the Anglo-Saxon tradition of emphasis on religious convictions and education. There are many churches in every part of town, and traffic is very heavy in Chattanooga just after noon on Sunday when everyone who has gone to church heads home. Whether Catholic, Protestant or Jewish, our faith is an important part of Chattanooga life.

I can only describe the sweetness that church has for me. When I hear and sing the familiar hymns and pray, I am worshipping God; when I listen to the words as the Bible is read, regardless of who is the minister, my heart is warmed. It either convicts me about some shortcoming, challenges my heart and mind, tells me something about my Lord that I had never noticed before, or gives me strength to go on. I find that I think more about Christian things when I am with other Christians. When I am seeking God's guidance, it is more probable that He can speak to me when I am in a prayerful mood.

Over the years as you grow to love family after family that you have been connected with either in Sunday School, church, the women's work, a Bible class, it is only natural that you love being together. The church suppers all over Chattanooga are an important part of our spiritual and social life.

It is a feeling that goes far deeper than any club; it is a fellowship of sinners and believers. It is natural when you get together, to have a meal, and when you take something to church, it is probably one of the best things you make.

There are many Chattanoogans, many good friends, who for various reasons, don't feel this way at all. The recipes in this book that people have given me as their "church specials" would be good at any picnic, or gathering of people when everyone is bringing something.

One of the favorite recipes out of the old Presbyterian Cookbook is Date Torte. Sometimes Jane Bowers (Mrs. Clayton) makes this for a luncheon dessert, and sometimes takes it to church suppers.

DATE TORTE

4 eggs	*1 pound dates*
1 cup sugar	*½ cup flour*
1 cup nuts, broken	*1 teaspoon baking powder*

Beat eggs slightly, add to sugar. Mix in flour and baking powder, stirring constantly. Cut nuts and dates into small pieces and beat into mixture thoroughly. Bake in a 350 degree oven in a layer cake pan. Bake about half hour until done and cut in squares. Serve with whipped cream.

Mrs. Clayton Bowers

Nearby Huntsville, Alabama, is even better known as the Rocket City, because of the space industry located there. Their work has brought many people from around the world to Huntsville, and as often happens when women gather, they exchange recipes. Nut cake is the specialty of Mrs. Werner von Braun, and was first printed in the "Huntsville Heritage Cookbook." This recipe was given to me by Kitty Crider of the Huntsville Times.

MRS. VON BRAUN'S NUT CAKE

8 eggs, separated	2 to 3 tablespoons rum
½ teaspoon cream of tartar	or brandy
½ cup sugar	1½ cups finely chopped pecans

Beat egg whites with cream of tartar until stiff shiny peaks form. Beat egg yolks with sugar until light and lemon colored; add rum. Pour over egg whites; sprinkle pecans on top. Gently fold mixtures together. Pour into 2 greased and floured 9 inch layer pans. Bake at 325 for 1 hour. Cool in pans; remove. Spread layers with Lemon Icing; decorate with pecan halves.

LEMON ICING

Mix 1½ cup confectioner's sugar with 3 to 4 tablespoons hot water. Add 2 tablespoons lemon juice and blend well.

Mrs. Werner von Braun

Raspberry mousse is an easy dessert when you have a package of frozen raspberries on hand and a cup of whipping cream.

RASPBERRY MOUSSE

1 box frozen raspberries	¼ cup cold water
½ pint heavy cream,	4 tablespoons sugar
whipped	2 teaspoons lemon juice
1 tablespoon unflavored gelatin	Dash of salt

Soften the gelatin in cold water. Drain the juice from the fruit and heat it. Add sugar and salt to hot liquid, then pour over gelatin. Stir until dissolved. When cool, add raspberries and lemon juice. When slightly thick, fold in the whipped cream. Chill. Serve on pieces of pound cake. Or pour into baked pastry shell and chill as a pie. This was brought back from Nippersink Lodge in Mentone, Alabama, by Mrs. Harry Stone.

The S and W Cafeteria has long been a popular place to get good Southern food and over the years almost everyone has developed favorites. One secretary who eats at the S and W often says she wishes she could have the recipe for the rice pudding with lemon sauce she orders every Friday. Rufus Sherrill, vice-president of the Charlotte, North Carolina chain that has cafeterias all over the Southeast, was a Chattanoogan for four years of school here, and sent their recipe.

S & W RICE PUDDING

Cook ½ cup raw rice in 2½ cups boiling water with ¾ teaspoon salt. When tender, remove from stove, drain and rinse thoroughly. (This is most important.) Place in a baking dish ½ cup seedless raisins, which have been soaked and dried, and the rice. In a separate bowl mix ¼ stick butter, melted, 4 fresh eggs, and 1¼ cups sugar. Cream butter, sugar and eggs well and add ½ teaspoon salt, ½ teaspoon vanilla extract, and ¼ teaspoon lemon extract. Add 2½ cups milk. Mix and pour the custard into the dish with the rice and raisins. Put the baking dish in a pan of water and bake in a 350 degree oven until done ......about 30 minutes. Serve cold with lemon sauce.

LEMON SAUCE

Cream together 4 tablespoons butter and 1½ cups sugar. Add 3 tablespoons cornstarch and mix well. Add ¾ cup cold water and cook over medium heat until thick. Stir in 3 slightly beaten egg yolks. Return to stove and cook a few minutes. Remove from stove and add the juice of 2 lemons, 1 teaspoon grated lemon rind, and a pinch of salt.

S and W Cafeterias
Rufus Sherrill

A very beautiful homemade candy was the Quick French Creams that General Foods served at a food conference. They looked like small balls not much larger than marbles, creamy chocolate rolled in finely chopped nuts. This is how they did it. They would be delicious on a tea table.

QUICK FRENCH CREAMS

1 package (8 squares)
  semi-sweet chocolate
1 cup sifted confectioner's
  sugar

1 egg, well beaten
1 tablespoon milk
1 cup finely chopped nuts

Partially melt chocolate over hot water. Remove from water; stir rapidly until entirely melted. Add sugar, egg and milk; beat only enough to blend. Chill until firm enough to handle.

Shape chocolate mixture into ½ inch balls, using 1 teaspoonful for each. Roll in chopped nuts. Makes about 5 dozen confections.

Miss Pat Kohl
General Foods Kitchens

Our favorite Christmas candy is pralines. These are smooth and rich with pecans, butter, brown sugar and cream. Jonathan is our champion praline maker and casually comes in the kitchen, rubs a copper saucepan well with butter so no crystals can form, measures out the sugar, syrup, butter, cream, sticks a candy thermometer in it, puts it on the stove and goes out in the playroom to watch TV.

During commercials he comes in to check, and with uncanny sense of timing, the pralines seem to come to an exact soft ball during a commercial. He adds the pecans and lets them cool a little. And when he has time, he drops the pralines onto a piece of foil stretched out the length of the counter. They dry and the texture is perfect. He made hundreds of pralines one year so that we gave them to neighbors, teachers, godparents, relatives, and had plenty left to have here at home. This was when he was 11 or 12. Now that he is older and his social life has picked up, he is too busy. It is also the best caramel icing you can put on a white cake.

CREAMY PRALINES

1 box yellow sugar
1 cup white sugar
¾ cup clear corn syrup
1 cup cream (no substitute)

½ stick butter
1 teaspoon vanilla
1½ cups chopped pecans

Butter a heavy saucepan. This will prevent the pralines from sugaring. Combine the sugar, syrup and cream. Cook slowly until it reaches a soft ball (238 degrees on a candy thermometer). Remove from stove. Add butter, pecans, and vanilla. Beat until creamy. Drop by soup spoons on waxed paper or aluminum foil.

I have found that this must be made on a clear day or night. If it is rainy, it will never get hard. We also wrap each praline individually in waxed paper; they keep better this way.

A specialty at the Shepherd Hills Christmas Tea one year was the creamy smooth Chocolate Caramel Candy that Mary Jo Lavecchia brought. She is a noted cook who loves to cook for her big family and her doctor husband.

CHOCOLATE CARAMEL CANDY

2 cups sugar	1¾ cup white corn syrup
2 tablespoons cocoa	Dash salt
1 stick real butter	2 cups pecans, chopped
1 pint whipping cream	3 or 4 teaspoons vanilla

Let cook slowly. Stir often. Cook about 1 hour and 20 minutes, or 248 degrees. Remove from fire. Add vanilla and pecans. Pour on greased cookie sheet (with sides). After cooling, cut and wrap pieces in foil.

Mrs. J. V. Lavecchia

The best divinity that we know is that made by Neva Boyd, who is more famous as a carver of exquisite birds. She makes it with corn syrup to keep it creamy and keeps it made to serve after dinner instead of dessert. She also told me that in case it ever gets sticky, you can run it in the oven (the separate pieces) and the candy will dry out. Anyone can make this with a candy thermometer, which is a wise investment that will pay for itself many times over.

MRS. BOYD'S DIVINITY

1st part:
3 cups sugar
1 cup clear corn syrup
1 cup water
Boil to 260 degrees

2nd part:
1 cup sugar
½ cup water
Boil to 238 degrees

3rd part:
3 egg whites
¾ pound pecans

Add the second part to the first part. Then slowly beat into the stiffly beaten egg whites. Add the chopped nuts. (You can also make plain divinity and top each piece with a pecan half.) Cool the candy mixture. Drop by teaspoons on waxed paper. Mrs. Boyd likes to keep this in the refrigerator because it mellows so well.

Mrs. J. H. Boyd

CHAPTER XV

Beverages

Almost every city has a Summertown, a place where several families gather in simple summer houses to escape the heat of summer. Summertown for Chattanooga today is undoubtedly the lake, for all you have to do is drive across Chickamauga Dam on a Saturday or Sunday to see thousands of people seeking the sun and water.

Summertown for old Chattanooga was a spot on Walden's Ridge that centered around Mabbitt Springs. Before the Civil War a New Yorker, Mabbitt, heard about the healing waters of the spring, bought 400 acres around it, and brought his ailing son hoping for a cure. He built a two story log cabin and left after several years. During the cholera epidemic in Chattanooga in 1873, Judge D. M. Key and his family, and his brother Summerfield Key refugeed to the log cabin, which was run as a boarding house. That next summer they bought lots and built two cabins. In the yellow fever epidemic of 1878, these same families came back, joined by many others.

The late Creed Bates, who was up on all this history, said that from the '80's on, more and more families came and spent every summer, and the residents made a sort of Chattanooga directory. There were Smartts, Davenports, Gillespies, Pattens, Bates, Williams, Kruesis, Sharps, Poindexters, Strangs, Eugene Bryans, Luptons, Probascos, Ochs, Averys, Fergers, Robbins, Friersons, Brocks, Longs, Viers, Priors, Henry Bryans, Thompsons, and others.

Mary Willingham says that her father used to drink the waters of the spring for his stomach trouble, and that now doctors say that what probably helped him was the relaxed way of life and the walk to the spring. The water of Mabbitt Spring is the sort called "iron water" by old timers, and I tasted it only once. The spring itself is beautiful as you walk down in a sort of glen, and generations of children have hunted crawfish, played on the mountain rocks, courted, and whiled away pleasant summers.

Summertown, for all these people is not just a place......it is a spirit, a way of life. It is simple houses with unpretentious furniture, delicious dinners and picnics shared with good friends, it is company

A *Summertown picnic is long tables of fried chicken, barbecue, casseroles, homemade cakes and watermelon.*

and games, long walks, houseparties, Sundays at the Little Brown Church where Miss Ellen Poindexter taught.

It seems to be very far from town, because the only road up Signal Mountain for years was the "W" which means just what it sounds like, a W-road placed sideways up a steep mountain. Miss Ellen remembers once driving her mother, Mrs. L. J. Sharp, up the "W" when they ran into unexpected ice. Mr. Charlie James, the developer of Signal Mountain, and his chauffeur came by in time to chop the ice on the corners so the horse could get up without slipping. It was an 8 hour trip.

Some of the original families still live in Summertown, but now on a year round basis. With good roads, it is only 20 minutes from town and quite close to the booming town of Signal Mountain. Many of the old summer houses have been remodeled by young people who find it an ideal place to raise families.

But no one who ever had a part in the old Summertown will ever forget the delightful picnics on the 4th of July and Labor Day. Creed Bates always brought his homemade cider, there were huge crocks of lemonade, and Mary Ruth Bryan (Mrs. Eugene) boiled coffee almost all day to be sure there would be enough and that it would be strong enough.

Everyone brought stuffed eggs, sandwiches, fried chicken and more fried chicken, potato salad. Miss Louise Lupton (Mrs. Allen) usually brought a big wooden bowl or tray of fresh sliced fruit. Windy Willingham made the barbecue, chopped in small pieces to go on buns. There were sliced tomatoes, sliced cucumbers, sliced onions. The last thing down the line was an array of homemade cakes. Mary Ruth Bryan and Toots Thompson (Mrs. T. C.) always cut the cake, and I can almost hear Toots, with her twinkling brown eyes, say, "Now you've got to taste this caramel cake. I've tasted the icing, and it's wonderful."

Then everyone would eat under big old trees, enjoy each other, introduce new friends, admire new babies, and just talk. This was Summertown, a very real part of Chattanooga.

Summertime means picnics and visiting cousins, and these grand-daughters of the Winborn Willinghams enjoy fried chicken and stuffed eggs just the way their parents and grandparents did when they were young.

I'm including Creed Bates' recipe for making cider. Apple trees have always produced bountifully on Signal Mountain, and Creed has always made the best cider in town. He makes it and puts it in jugs, using a corn cob as a stopper. His lovely old house burned in 1968, and he rebuilt it with logs from his own land, hand hewn by an Appalachian craftsman. As the retired principal at Chattanooga High School, beloved by generations of Chattanoogans, and one whose very presence on the platform at City High gets a standing ovation, his friends number in the thousands.

Any one of them who drop in on him for a visit, is treated to a glass of sweet, tangy apple juice, ripened to the exact degree by the pro himself.

SUMMERTOWN CIDER

Creed Bates Said, "The nectar of the gods is the elixir of the fruit of fruits . . .the apple!"

For making fresh cider, note a few ground rules.
1. Keep the mill clean, including washing good immediately after using.

2. Mix the varieties of apples used. Old Virginia Winesaps are tops.

3. Cider can be made from the time apples come in during the summer on through the season, but fall is the cider season.

Making:

Gather apples, cut out the decayed places, wash, rinse and drain. Then grind. If you have a small mill with wooden tubs, it is difficult to use mellow apples. With a large press using burlap cloths, mellow apples give good results. After filling the tub with ground apples, place in position to press, letting juice run into large container. Strain the juice through a white cloth or filter paper. Place in jugs and put in the refrigerator. Even better, if you have a wooden keg or a barrel, let the cider remain in this container overnight. Then "rack off" (pour off the top liquid, leaving the sediment in the bottom) and place in jugs, keeping always in a cool place. If left in warm temperature, cider ferments quickly. Cider in the refrigerator, if racked off every few days, will stay fresh much longer. But friends and neighbors will usually solve this turning-into-vinegar problem.

In getting this cider procedure down, Creed consulted with W. L. Brinkley of Signal Mountain, whom the horticulturists at U.T. say knows more about apple culture than anyone around.

The late Creed Bates

346

A refreshing summer punch is a lemon and grapefruit version with ginger ale. This is a recipe of Mrs. John Chambliss.

SUMMER PUNCH

1 large bottle ginger ale
2 cans frozen lemonade
(diluted as instructed)

2 cans unsweetened grapefruit
juice (diluted as instructed)

Mix the lemonade and grapefruit juice and add the ginger ale last. Serve over crushed ice.

The late Mrs. John Chambliss

Every once in a while we print a recipe in the column that everyone in town immediately tries and loves. We first heard about Tea Tang and Twist when it was served at Senior Neighbors here. They all thought that the hot spicy Russian tea they were drinking was the best they had ever had. Actually it is a combination of instant tea, instant orange drink, instant lemonade, plus powdered cloves, powdered cinnamon and sugar. Once you make up the dry mix, you add one spoon per cup and add boiling water.

One friend says she was visiting in Nashville and on a brisk day had walked to a friend's house, out of breath and famished. In a few minutes she was having a hot cup of Tea Tang and Twist and says it was so elegant, she never plans to be without the mixture in a jar in her own kitchen! This mixture will fill a 2 pound coffee can or apothecary jar, so you could halve the recipe for a smaller amount.

INSTANT RUSSIAN TEA

1 cup instant tea (2 ounce jar)
1 cup orange Tang
2 packages instant lemonade

½ teaspoon ground cloves
1 teaspoon ground cinnamon
1½ cups sugar (optional)

Mix all together to form a dry mix. This will about fill a 2 pound coffee can. To make a cup of Russian tea, put 1 heaping spoon to each coffee cup and finish filling with boiling water. Sweeten to taste, if you leave out the sugar.

For large groups, boil water in a 36 cup coffee maker. When boiling, add ½ of the mixture. This is a very easy way to serve Russian Tea to a crowd.

347

Dalton, Georgia, is a pleasant town about 30 miles south of Chattanooga on the way to Atlanta. Like Chattanooga, this was Indian country until the 1830s when settlers came in. During the Civil War, Gen. Joe Johnston wintered his troops in Dalton one year.

The first lady of Dalton was undoubtedly Mrs. B.J. Bandy. During the depression Mr. and Mrs. Bandy were running a country store and when their large credit business could not pay, they owed their suppliers $20,000. They were determined to get out of debt, and thought of Mrs. Catherine Evans Whitener who made hand-tufted bedspreads. The Bandys wondered if there would be a market nationally for these bedspreads. B.J. Bandy worked as a telegrapher with the Southern Railroad in addition to running the store, so he got his wife a pass to Washington and New York so she could try to sell large quantities of the bedspreads.

She sat up all night on the day coach, got to Washington, and walked with her suitcases to the first store, Woodward and Lothrop. She explained to the buyer that she had never tried to sell anything before, and he smiled kindly and said he knew! He ordered 400 spreads at $4 a spread, which meant she was doubling her money. She says she got on the train immediately before he could change his mind, and headed for Baltimore where she sold 200 more to Hotchschild and Kohns. She says she was so excited she didn't even go on to New York, but came back home to hire the people to tuft those 600 bedspreads.

They set up a shop in a tin building on Thornton Avenue and figured out how to stamp the spreads and get them tufted. On other trips with the railroad passes, she sold Macy's, and the other big stores of the East. She says she just prayed the bedspread business would last long enough to pay the $20,000.

When the minimum wage laws were passed, everyone thought the tufted bedspread business was over, but machines were invented, and the Bandy's bedspread factory grew beyond their greatest expectation. With all the improvements, the tufted carpet industry grew to be a much bigger thing for North Georgia than the bedspreads. The Bandys, who had been leaders from the beginning, have interests in several of the largest carpet companies. Her son, B. J. Bandy Jr., is vice president of Coronet Industries, one of the largest; her daughter, Mrs. Joseph McCutchen, is the wife of the Chairman of the Boards of J. and C. Carpet Company and Universal Carpets of Ellijay.

To drive through Dalton with Mrs. Bandy and have her point out first one and then another of the 75 carpet mills, the new bank building, the Dalton Junior College, the Vann House whose restoration she led,

Mrs. B. J. Bandy pioneered the huge carpet business in Dalton when during the depression she sold the first tufted bedspreads to the large Eastern market. She was widely interested in civic and charitable projects and hosted many teas for such worthy causes as the hospital or the restoration of the Vann House.

was an experience. No one around her could fail to catch the enthusiasm, the drive, the character, and the warm grace of a lady who had an important part in the industrial revolution of our region.

Her gracious home on Thornton Avenue hosted her garden club, teas for the Whitfield-Murray County Historical Association, and the many other groups she was interested in. She played bridge almost every day, was a trustee of Dalton Junior College, and was vitally interested in The Hamilton Memorial Hospital where her family built a wing for intensive care in memory of Mr. Bandy and of Chrissie McCutchen, her granddaughter who was killed in an automobile accident at the University of Georgia.

Mrs. Bandy gave me her Russian Tea recipe which she served many times at home.

MRS. BANDY'S RUSSIAN TEA

Juice of 3 lemons	*2 quarts weak tea*
Juice of 3 oranges	*2 cups sugar*
1 medium sized can pineapple	*1 cup boiling water*
juice	*4 tablespoons whole cloves*

Make the tea weak and amber colored. Cover the lemon and orange rinds with water and let boil a few minutes. Strain and add 2 cups sugar to the hot water. Pour 1 cup boiling water over 4 level tablespoons of whole cloves. Cover and let steep fifteen minutes. Mix the fruit juices, tea, sugar, syrup, and strained clove water and stir. This can be made ahead and heated before serving. This will serve 16 people.

The late Mrs. B. J. Bandy
Dalton, Georgia

For a summer tea or coffee, sometimes it seems too complicated to ask guests whether they would like tea, coffee, or a Coke. A popular and pretty way to solve the problem is with a coffee punch bowl.

PLANTATION COFFEE PUNCH

½ cup sugar	*5 cups milk*
¼ cup instant coffee	*1 pint vanilla or*
Dash salt	*coffee ice cream*
1 teaspoon vanilla	*Whipped cream*

Combine all ingredients except ice cream and whipped cream. Stir until sugar dissolves. Chill until serving time. Then ladle ice cream, by large spoonfuls into punch bowl, pour coffee mixture over. Top with puffs of whipped cream and sprinkle with a little nutmeg. Serves 12.

Mrs. William Bennett

With box lunches of fried chicken at the Chambliss farm, Mary Rozendale served a pink punch in tall glasses full of crushed ice. This is a glorified tea, delicious with a meal as well as at a reception in punch cups. Nearly everyone had re-fills at the picnic. It is unusual because it is not sweet, using part soda water and part ginger ale.

MARY ROZENDALE'S PINK PUNCH

7 cups strong tea, hot
6 cups sugar
   Steep these together 5
   minutes to melt sugar
6 cups orange juice
2 cups lemon juice

4 cups pineapple juice
2 boxes frozen red raspberries
   boiled in 4 cups of
   water and strained
2 quarts soda water
4 quarts ginger ale

While the tea is steeping with the sugar, boil the raspberries and let simmer a few minutes to get all the flavor out of the berries. Strain through a fine strainer and cool. When the tea is cold, add all the fruit juice. At the very last, before serving, mix the chilled soda water and the chilled ginger ale with the cold fruit juice and tea. Serve over lots of crushed ice. This makes between 3 and 4 gallons and will serve about 50 or 60. It is just as good in tall glasses instead of iced tea at a summer luncheon or outdoor party.

Mrs. G. Rozendale

At the Christmas open house of the H. Clay Evans Johnson's, the dining room was filled with all sorts of good things to eat as well as a large bowl of eggnog at one end of the table and another of a claret red punch at the other. The punch recipe is delicious . . .not too sweet.

KRIS KRINGLE PUNCH

6 cups chilled cranberry juice
3 cups chilled bottled
   apple juice
¾ cup chilled lemon juice
   (fresh)

1½ cups chilled orange
   juice (frozen)
2 bottles ginger ale
   (1 pint 12 ounce size)

Combine all juices in punch bowl. Just before serving, pour in ginger ale. Stir well. Garnish with ice ring. Makes 4½ quarts or about 28

At Cravens House, the herb garden is a favorite place with the different textures of thyme, parsley, sage, chive against the old brick walk and white fencing.

servings. For Christmas we make three double batches of this.

Ice Ring: Half fill a ring mold with cold water and freeze until solid. Arrange one or more of the following fruits in a design over the surface of the ice: red and green maraschino cherries, mandarin orange segments, pineapple chunks, lemon or lime slices. Cover with water and freeze. To unmold, dip in warm water until loosened. (We use cherries and lime and lemon slices ... very thin.) Let float in punch bowl.

Mrs. H. Clay Evans Johnson

This was served at the Craven's House tea one year.

CRAVEN'S HOUSE MULLED CIDER

1 gallon cider	*1 cinnamon stick*
1 quart pineapple juice	*3 cloves*
1 quart orange juice	*Juice of 1 lemon*

Scrape and score the cinnamon stick before putting in. Combine the cider and all the juices. The mulled part of this is very mild, with just 1 cinnamon stick and 3 cloves. It can be served hot or cold. At Christmas it could be served in a punch bowl surrounded by holly and garnished with dainty slivers of lemon and orange slices.

CHAPTER XVI

Memorable Dinners

Ice Storm Meals

I suppose our family will never forget the night the trees fell down on Lookout Mountain in March 1960. We had a freak ice storm, with zero and below zero weather, no heat or electricity for a week, and for the first time we found ourselves in the middle of a disaster area, with military patrols on every road.

Calamities are always sudden and unexpected, which is just as well, and you generally think of them happening to someone else. None of us had any idea on Wednesday afternoon that the ice that was forming on all the trees would work the havoc that it finally did. Our power and our heat went off about three. We figured it might be several hours before it came back on, so we got out candles to have ready and decided on a gay dinner in the living room....hamburgers cooked over the fire. I have never cooked in the fireplace before, but my husband assured me that with a large iron skillet and plenty f wood, the possibilities were unlimited. Then we had the idea of boiling water in a large covered pot so we could make tea and coffee.

Our first meal was a makeshift temporary thing. We didn't set up a table, but passed trays around to everyone. Some of the boys ate even before the blessing, and jumped up every few minutes to watch the trees as they were falling. This was getting to be quite an eerie thing. First we would hear an awful crack; then in a few seconds it would be followed by a thunderous crash as the tall pines, bearing their unbearable load of ice gave up and fell. The strange thing was to hear no howling wind. The air was still, and unbelievably quiet, emphasizing the thunderous fall of these tree warriors as they lay down and died.

Some of the trees were topped, others came up by the roots. It was a very strange thing to be able to do nothing but stand and watch something we had never seen before. As the temperature suddenly dropped, the heavy ice formed on the trees, and we were in an ice storm.

It was interesting, too, to see how differently the different children reacted to it. We have two who wanted to go out and inspect each

When ice forms on the trees of Lookout Mountain, it makes an icy sort of fairyland . . .very beautiful. But in 1960, the ice storm came suddenly and turned the mountains into a disaster area with zero weather and no power for a week.

tree as it fell, as well as to "look" and see if the fallen electrical wires were live. The other two were very calm, with that "whatever will be, will be" philosophy that characterizes Calvinists. One of these boys went to get a Cub Scout book of camping songs, and we sat in front of the fire and sang, rubbing three year old Franklin's back and singing "Oh, Susannah," "She'll Be Coming Around the Mountain," "I've Been Working on the Railroad," and "Swing Low, Sweet Chariot." Did you know, for instance, that "Polly Wolly Doodle" has a verse that goes, "Behind the barn, down on my knees, I thought I heard a chicken sneeze. He sneezed so hard with the whooping cough, he sneezed his head and tail right off." This seemed terribly funny at the time.

We found out that Jonathan, our first grader then, was the most patriotic. He insisted on "My Country 'Tis of Thee," "America the Beautiful," and "The Star-Spangled Banner." Franklin wanted all the hymns, so we sang those, and with "Amazing Grace" and "Rock of Ages" we had sung every song we knew. By then it was nine, and the head of the house, who had been nervously going from window to window, assured us that every tree in the yard had fallen. For lack of anything else to do, we decided to go to bed.

Layering and bundling were two principles that were well known to Chattanooga pioneers. I now believe that if you dress in enough layers of clothes, you can withstand any temperature. I thought of Miss Ellen Poindexter who said that having a sister on winter nights in Chattanooga 70 years ago was a real advantage, because two people bundled together under lots of cover can be much more snug and warm. The family paired off so that each bed had twice the usual amount of cover ....about four blankets and a comfort or sleeping bag. The house was beginning to get chilly, but we all slept soundly, waking only to the occasional crack of another tree giving up. Susan was our year-old baby who slept in her snowsuit and did fine.

The next morning the fire felt unusually welcome, and we started the old custom of wearing several layers of clothes. I wore four sweaters and three skirts and was not cold. By this time, we pulled the draperies across the windows in the living room, tacked blankets and shower curtains over the doors, moved Susan's baby bed to the living room, and the living room became exactly that......a real family living room. By keeping the fire going, even in zero weather, we had a temperature of 40 or 50 degrees in this room. With the prospect of being a week or more without power (not a power line or phone line on the mountain was standing), we got more organized, set up a table with a cloth for meals, bought more candles, and started living more like people.

Outside the desolation was so complete, we could not believe it. It looked as if Lookout Mountain had been systematically bombed. For the first time we were in a real distress area. Our neighbors had had trees fall on their houses and rip gutters. We heard of a friend who had a tree fall through the roof and into the dining room.

Our curiosity was hampered by the lack of a phone, so the older boys, Kinch and Roy, then 12 and 10, got out and began checking on the neighbors. I began to realize why people used to visit more than they do now . . . they were curious and had to find out the news.

By Thursday night we were beginning to settle down and get used to the situation. To keep our pipes from freezing, we left a trickle of water running in them. The kitchen was icy by this time, with Coca-Colas freezing on the counter, but by keeping a slight trickle of water coming through the pipes, our water didn't freeze.

One by one the mountain families began to leave, either to stay in the hotels and motels or with relatives or friends in town. Actually we had plenty of wood and coal to keep the fireplaces going. And we also had our grandmother living with us for a couple of years then. She was 86 and begged not to leave. Her small room was originally our study with a fireplace in it. Because the room was small, the fireplace kept this room warmer than any place in the house. So the thought of leaving never occured to me. Not until practically everyone else in the neighborhood did. Then I was miserably sorry for myself. Imagine, I thought, having to wash dishes and raise a baby under such terrible conditions!

In my dark mood I mentioned to my husband that everyone seemed better cared for than I. This was not exactly the thing to have said. He pointed out that central heating is a comparatively recent thing, although our area has been inhabited by men, women and even babies for hundreds of years. He looked at Susan, who did seem to be having a grand time, and pointed out that her eyes were bright and happy and her cheeks rosy. She wore some coveralls and a snowsuit of Byrd cloth (made to withstand the Artic), with a toboggan cap on her head, and seemed to feel the same way dogs and horses do in cold crisp weather. Then he pointed out that it was a wonderful time to explore the intricacies of fireplace cooking. I had no choice.

And from that moment I began to enjoy in some ways the experience of seeing if I could match the achievements of Chattanooga women three or four generations ago, who managed to live graciously and raise their families without benefit of electricity, telephones, and instant stoves.

357

My first meal cooking over an open fire was an easy one. Not many disastrous things can happen to a skillet full of hamburgers. But you do learn right away to manage the fire so that the logs make a flat surface on top for the skillet and also the ever important kettle of boiling water. Just learning to do this made me feel so clever, that it was with real pride that I saw the family relishing those hamburgers.

The kettle of water was kept either on the fire or on some hot coals at the side all day, and we became great coffee and tea drinkers. When I asked a friend once how she managed to paint a difficult room, she said she just had another cup of coffee every hour or two, and it gave her courage to go on! This was the situation and we made constant coffee for friends, for work crews, and for ourselves.

Actually, pan broiling over the fire has the same principles as on the stove. First you want to sear the meat, or brown it quickly. This takes a good flame on top of the fire. If you have let the fire go down for the hot coals, you can get the brief flame you need by putting a few twigs on the fire. These flame up, sear the meat, and then die down so it will cook slowly. But always the high heat section is on top of the fire.

The part of the fire that cooks at moderate speed, I discovered, are the red coals on the bottom. These I raked to the front, and put the skillet (covered, so the ashes didn't get in the meat,) on them to cook gently. At either side of our fire were the ashes, and a pan of food put in these, will simmer the tiniest bit and keep hot. As soon as I began to learn about all these places we began to eat very well, indeed.

In preparing a meal, you have to do all the setting and arranging first, because once you begin cooking, you don't dare leave it, or at least I didn't. We also found that camping gets old fast. Cans of lunch-meat and sandwiches served just any old way in a living room may be necessary but not satisfying. For a meal, I got out a tablecloth, candlesticks, napkins, and fixed a vase of green leaves. That began to lift our spirits. And since we had absolutely no heat in the rest of the house (except Grandmama's room), I began warming all the plates and cups by putting them just inside the fireplace fender. This was the ideal place for warming the baby food, too.

FIREPLACE MENUS

One night we had a feast. We had steak, potatoes wrapped in foil and baked in the ashes, an avocado and lettuce salad, bread and tea. The Eskimos eat lots of meat and fat to keep them going, and we reasoned that we needed it, too. But I do think a cold crisp salad with a good dressing points up the meat. About the tea, we found that if we made a pot and had it on the table, it was not only better than individual cups, but very convenient to keep talking and reaching for another refill. One day for lunch we had chili that had simmered a long time on the red coals. It was wonderful.

Another night we had pork chops, French green beans cooked in consomme, fried potatoes, fruit salad and coffee. First I seared the meat on top of the fire in the big iron skillet and let it cook for a few minutes over a flame that was a couple of inches high. Then I transferred it to the red coals to finish cooking. Meanwhile I put the consomme in a copper pan and brought it to a boil with the green beans. They just went on cooking fast because there was no room on the coals. The potatoes were cooking on the top and took longer than on the stove. When I had the logs level and stable, I had room for the water and two other pans, but everything needed constant attention.

One dinner was a tenderloin of pork. Another meal was smothered chicken tenderly cooked on the coals. We planned to do barbecued chicken, but the electricity came on before we got around to it. I learned that your pans need to be heavy ones. Aluminum and stainless steel are not nearly as good as heavy iron or copper. Our copper pans lined with tin did fine, and polished up later.

For breakfast we had sausage, scrambled eggs, or something similar. Cold fruit such as bananas and grapefruit were good, as was cereal. My failures at fireplace cooking seemed always to have to do with bread. I always ended up with something burned. I would certainly never have been interested in fireplace cooking if I had not been driven to it, but after a week, we found out all sorts of things. We humans adjust remarkably fast, and can do what we have to. We can all say we never ate better.

One night when the sun had gone down on the western side of the mountain, and darkness had enveloped the icy trees and yards in our part of the world, we sat in front of the fire. In one corner of the living room Susan was alseep in her baby bed, warm in her snowsuit and Olympic hat; in another the hamsters, moved to a warm place for the duration, were making those annoying ratlike sounds as they played in their cage; and the birds, now covered, had settled down for the night. Grandmama was tucked in her room, frail, but warm under a mountain of cover. The boys were down, too. Papa (since we were pioneers) and I sat in our chairs and read by a kerosene lamp and watched the fire.

As we listened to the sweet whistles and hums a good fire makes as it sings, we relaxed and thought. Bone-tired physically, we completely relaxed, and my thoughts surprised even me. Life with no tensions and no pressure makes for a contemplative life. I thought of early Chattanoogans. I thought of the fire and how often we had to put on another log. Proverbs classes a fire as one of the four things that can never be satisfied ...... the more you give it, the more it demands and devours.

I thought, too, the way values had sifted down in the last week, to their proper level. My first thoughts had been of what we were going to eat, and how to keep everybody warm. These primitive needs taken care of, I relaxed and the material things of this world were not given another consideration.

I thought of the most important things human creatures can think about, with a peace and clarity that I hadn't had for a long time. God's definite plan for the ages is a wondrous pondering. I thought about the great doctrines of faith, of redemption, of grace, and thought through everything that I knew about them. I thought about the covenant keeping God that we have, and how faithful He has been and is. That night, quiet and restful as it was, I felt my soul strengthened, and I realized how blessed were the men who built our country. Their growing up years were hard in the way that builds character. And when the day was done, they read and talked. Coming to this country for religious freedom, many were God fearing spiritual men who took the evening hours for reading, teaching their children, and thinking.

I thought, too, of the point passed along by a friend . . . that we know what it is to be without electrical power. Our appliances can't function as they were meant to because the power is cut off. Suppose God ever withdrew His power from on high, how awful would be that darkness and how helpless we would be! How comforting to know that "nothing can separate us from the love of God which is in Christ Jesus."

Why don't I contemplate these things in an unhurried way more often, I wondered. Could it be that the constant noise of TVs, radios, phones, washers, dryers and dishwashers dulls our sensitivities? The constant pressure is to go, go, go . . . chauffeuring the children to all manner of worthwhile things like brace tightening appointments, scouts, music, and all the other lessons; garden clubs, book clubs and all the other clubs. All this racing builds up tensions in nice people that they can't throw off in an hour or two. And when we sit down at night, no wonder we read silly magazines, mediocre books, and hypnotize ourselves in front of TV. It is difficult to think at all, much less deep thoughts.

The power was finally restored. The lights came on, the house got warm, the stove worked, and again I was expected to do a hundred things well. The phone rang very few minutes in a house so warm we were all lazy!

One night soon after, three-year-old Franklin, having been put to bed, called out, "Mother, I like quietness, don't you?"

"Then be quiet and you'll have it," I answered.

"But the big boys got so much radio-ness in their room, I can't hear the quietness," he reasoned.

I'm glad we live today. But the week of the ice storm taught us lessons that I hope we don't forget. I hope I remember the important values and the trivial ones. The week that our mountains were without power, phone, car, meetings, appointments, and noise, the meals were main events.

A Family Barbecue

When a family from the Carolinas moves anywhere else in the world, one of the fond memories of home seems always to be summertime barbecues when friends and relatives gather for delicious roasted pork and all the good things that go with it. These happy and festive barbecues have signified family celebrations all over the South for hundreds of years. There are many variations on the barbecue sauce, and in South Carolina you might have rice with the pork, while in North Carolina you would eat potatoes, but the feeling is always the same.

A barbecue calls for lots of people with ties either of blood or friendship, huge platters of food that seem never to run out, a smattering of all age groups from the toddlers of the family to the elders, with everything in between from teenagers who bring their dates to out-of-town visitors.

When the Jim Glascocks went to North Carolina years ago to visit all Sarah's Bryan kin, there was a big barbecue in their honor. They enjoyed it so much, Jim went down to the master barbecuer, a Mr. Wooten, to learn the fine art of roasting pork. Since then at family celebrations here, Jim plans weeks ahead and takes his boys to the woods to cut a hickory.

They barbecue a whole pig the day before, with help from all twelve children, their cousins, and friends. How can you describe the sweet tangy smoke that gets in everyone's eyes when the breeze shifts, the drama of seeing a whole hog spread out on the wire mesh over the ashes, the busy sorting, of waiting, putting on another log, scooping up hot coals to go under the pork, seeing that the pork gets doused with vinegar from time to time.

In the kitchen, the girls of the family and their cook, Mrs. Lessie Siner, are preparing the rest of the menu. The whole menu is keyed to the fact that pork is fat and needs things to complement it........

362

One good way to see Lookout Mountain and Chattanooga, if you are a tourist or on a convention, is to ride the "Tennesseer." In this picture Mrs. James Glascock poses with her children, Gus, Chris, Battle, Tommy, Anne, Monica, Tim, Paul, Lucille, Bill, Henry, and Jimmy.

boiled potatoes, cold sliced cucumbers, cold sliced tomatoes, sliced onions, lots of slaw with a dressing of only salt, pepper and vinegar, and hundreds of baked corn pones which Lessie bakes in the oven.

This recipe for barbecue is simple and different, and so delicious that the people who love it judge all other barbecues by it. I asked how you know when you have put in enough salt, pepper, and vinegar.

The Glascocks say that there are official tasters in the family. Sarah and Jim taste the pork until they think it is right; then they put it under refrigeration. Sometimes her mother, Mrs. Henry Bryan will come by and taste and add a little more vinegar. Then her father will come in, taste, and decide to cut the fat a little with more vinegar. Her brother Bill tastes and adds a speck more to suit him. The real pro is her aunt, Miss Sarah Fletcher Bryan of Tarboro. When she is here, she tastes and pronounces, "This is almost as good as Wooten's," or "This is really as good as Wooten's," or sometimes, "This is even better than Wooten's!" Then they know it is really good.

EDGECOMBE COUNTY BARBECUED PORK

First construct a grill 4 by 6 feet. It should be 18 inches high above the heat (18 inch tile plumbing pipes can be used to support it). Near the grill should be a separate fireplace where a hickory fire should be burning all day. The coals from the fire should be shoveled under the grill to provide a slow smoky heat under the meat.

The best meat is a whole hog from 100 to 135 pounds. The hog should be thoroughly cleaned and de-haired, as usually delivered by provision companies. Place the hog, stomach side down, for the first hour or two of cooking, until that side is well seared. Keep a garden hose or bucket of water handy in case the dripping grease drips down and catches the carcass on fire. After the underside has seared, turn the carcass over, leaving the open cavity upward. This cavity will collect grease and juices from the cooking meat, and can be used to baste the pork. It will require about 12 hours of slow cooking to thoroughly cook the meat and render most of the fat.

During the last two hours of cooking, pure apple cider vinegar should be used to baste every 10 or 15 minutes. When the meat draws from the bone, and the bones can be separated easily, the cooking is over. Remove the meat from the grill, debone, and chop the entire remainder, including the "whistle." (This refers, of course, to the old saying that everything goes in except the whistle.)

Season to taste with pure apple cider vinegar, freshly ground red pod pepper, and salt. More vinegar will be required than you might think. The important points of the recipe are the use of hickory coals only, cooking the entire animal; the slow cooking, (this should not be speeded up to less than 12 hours), and the use of no other sauce than pure apple cider vinegar and freshly ground red pod pepper and salt. Serve hot and eat hearty. This serves about 100.

The James Glascocks

364

CORN PONE TO SERVE WITH BARBECUE

Pour corn meal into a large bowl with enough salt to season it. Pour over this, boiling water, and stir to make a stiff batter. Let cool enough to handle and shape small corn pones with your hands. Lessie's are very small so they can be picked up and eaten easily...not much bigger than silver dollars, about 2 or 3 inch pones. These are placed on a baking sheet and baked until done in a hot oven. They should be slightly browned and pretty. The oven should be about 425 or 450.

Mrs. Lessie Siner

SLAW FOR BARBECUE

Chop up plenty of cabbage and a few chopped carrots for color. Season with salt, vinegar, and celery seed. Do not add oil or mayonnaise to this slaw, because the pork will be slightly greasy, and this tart slaw will complement it better if seasoned only with salt and vinegar.

Mrs. James Glascock

The International Set

In the spring of 1966, we had an All-American dinner for a group of foreign visitors to Chattanooga. I can't think when our whole family had such fun ... planning all the courses to come from different regions of the United States, making flags, and picking up the house so it would be neat enough for guests. By the time we began eating one course after another, we had many funny things happen.

First of all, the guests were the Junior Executive Group of the Experiment in International Living. The whole purpose of the Experiment is that people from different nations can understand one another best by living together in a family situation. A tour of all the sight seeing places can never teach you the heart of a country as well as knowing a family, meeting their friends, sharing their meals, joining in their worship, going to school with the children, and being a part of the family activities and discussions.

This is the way Humberto Chavez, an architect from Mexico City, came to live with us for three weeks, this is the way we met the others of the group, Frabizio Cerruti from Italy, Lief Backman from Sweden, and Franz Wurth, Marthe Zaech, and Sylvia Balmer from Switzerland.

We began to think how much we would like to have the whole group for a meal, as we got to know them and learn about their homes. We thought about a picnic, but Humberto insisted that he wanted his friends to come here. "My best times in America have been at this table with this family. I want my friends to know all the children," he said. So invite them we did.

Planning the menu was the most fun. We thought of having a soup first, the main course, and a dessert. Then we kept thinking up more things. Having several courses is not much more trouble, really. When I finally thought everything up, I got out a piece of monogrammed notepaper, and wrote out the menu to put on the table for the guests. This is the way it read.

AMERICAN DINNER FOR THE EXPERIMENT
IN INTERNATIONAL LIVING

Florida Watermelon Wedge
Clam Soup ... Williamsburg, Virginia
Tossed Green Salad ... Palo Alto, California
Chicken in Wine ... New Orleans, Louisiana
Alabama Creamed Hominy
Lady Peas ... Charleston, South Carolina
Tennessee Hot Biscuits
Texas Pickled Okra
Blackberry Jelly ... Sewanee, Tennessee
Orange Marmalade ... Lookout Mountain, Tennessee
Artichoke Relish ... South Carolina

Black Bottom Pie ... Savannah, Georgia
Mississippi Black Coffee
Kansas City Mints

I really didn't know where the mints had come from until I asked Susan to look on the box.

Another idea was from Williamsburg. On a visit with Mrs. Carlisle Hummelsine, whose husband is president of Williamsburg, she told me that when the King and Queen of Thailand came and wanted to visit an American home, she hurried around and found a small flag of Thailand to go at one end of the table; then she put an American flag at the other end. If this is the custom at diplomatic dinners, I thought we would do the same thing. We didn't think of it in time to get the flags, so we made them by looking in the World Book Encyclopedia. The flags of Mexico, Italy, Sweden and Switzerland were colored with Susan's crayons, put on little poles and stuck in some blocks that Ellen had. They flew proudly at one end with the Stars and Stripes at the other.

Our oval table actually seats 8 or 10, but that night 14 of us gathered from all over the world, and squeezed around without being too crowded. The first course was a narrow wedge of cold watermelon, and for place plates we used the Cincinnati plates with eagles. This was the first time Ellen had ever had watermelon as a first course, and she began eating delightedly before the blessing was asked. Our Swiss friends wished us "Bon appetit."

The boys alternated taking out the courses, and two took off the watermelon and put the dishes in the dishwasher. They began carrying in the cups of soup until I didn't trust them. We used the set of French Limoges given us by a friend in California who had switched to contemporary. In Switzerland, Franz told us, the boys learn to cook, too. He approved the soup and agreed that the soup is better when the vegetables are sauteed first.

When we got to the salad course, I brought it in and tossed it at the table as we had learned in California. Fabrizio says they do it exactly the same way in Milan...salt, pepper, vinegar, oil...except they use more salt. We think this must make Jonathan part Italian since he tosses a fine salad, but a bit salty. About this time, Ellen got down out of her high chair and walked around the table two or three times. She didn't turn her chair over until later.

Earlier in the day, our cook turned up her nose at having hominy and said why didn't we have rice. I assured her that hominy would be new to them, and besides, it goes alll the way back to the Indians. I was right. They did like it with all the butter and cream. The Swiss were fascinated with tiny lady peas from Charleston, as well as the way they were seasoned with streaked meat. The chicken was rich and tender, with plenty of sauce to go over the hominy.

Hot buttered biscuits seem to go over in any language, although Humberto had suggested hoecakes. He agrees with our children that they ought to be a national specialty!

The Black Bottom Pie was one that we found in Savannah one spring. It is different from the other we have made over the years. This has a chocolate crust, is very light and tender, and is the recipe I plan to use the rest of my life. Lief, from Sweden, liked this pie and had two pieces.

Ellen went to bed after the chicken course but the rest of us stayed to the end. At one point. Jonathan (our teenager of 13), got carried away with himself and began speaking English with a thick French accent until Humberto and I gave him the eye to behave. But all the Exums felt richer in our new friendships. We are interested in things we hadn't thought about before...the school in Switzerland where Marthe is a secretary, the country all around Stockholm, the growth of industry in Italy, as well as Italian politics. Kinch and Roy asked Franz all about military service in Switzerland since they were 17 and 18.

We were most partial, though, to Mexico, because Humberto had become a part of our family. We will never think of Mexico again without thinking of the family of Humberto Chavez who has been host to many foreign Experimenters who come to Mexico, and we will never see pictures of the beautiful buildings of Mexico without thinking of our architect friend and of his hopes and dreams.

Never again will we feel that we don't have the necessary room to entertain house guests. Big families can move over and switch things around so that everyone can be included. Guests need privacy, but the family can double up. The most important thing is not to make company of people, not to plan too many exhausting side trips, or to feel that you just have to sit and talk. Ten year old Franklin said, "This is the best thing we have ever done!" and he said it five times at least.

Here are the recipes for our American dinner. The soup, chicken, hominy, lady peas, and pie were fixed ahead of time. You can probably improve the menu by substituting some of your own specialties. This was lots of fun.

CLAM SOUP
(Williamsburg, Virginia)

Take 3 slices of bacon, dice into small squares with a sharp knife, and begin sauteeing over medium heat in a saucepan. Dice 1 onion and 2 ribs of celery. Add to the pan. When soft, pour off any excess grease if there is any. Now add 1 can of chicken broth, 1 can water, 1 bottle of clam juice, and 1 can tomatoes (303 size.) Let this simmer on the back of the stove. You may have to add water from time to time, depending on how much boils away. I chopped about ½ cup parsley and added to this. The last half hour I added 1 large potato, cut up in small cubes, and because I was afraid I needed more liquid, added more water. Let cook until the potatoes are soft.

At this point, taste for seasoning. I tasted and decided to add a squirt of lemon juice, some black pepper, some salt, and a dash of Tabasco. It tasted very good. At the last I opened 1 can of whole clams, chopped them myself, and added to the mixture.

The secret of this soup is that you need something besides water and vegetables and clams. The broth adds just the amount of delicate strength that you need, as does the clam juice.

CHICKEN IN WINE WITH MUSHROOMS

Take 1 cut up fryer and wash well. Dry. Season with salt, pepper, paprika and Accent. Put 1 tablespoon butter and 1 tablespoon oil and melt in a heavy skillet. Saute the chicken until nicely brown. In the meantime dice two medium onions and 1 clove of garlic. Remove the chicken from the skillet and add the onion and garlic. When it is soft but not burned, return the chicken to the skillet. Add 1 square inch of ham, chopped fine (use bacon if you don't have ham,) some chopped parsley, a bay leaf, and a good pinch of powdered thyme. Now add about one-third cup of red wine. Cover the skillet and let cook slowly either in the oven or on top of the stove for about an hour. Along with the chicken juices you should have plenty of gravy. At the last add a can of mushrooms.

When making this in large quantities, I have found you can do all the sauteeing in the skillet, then move to a roasting pan lined with foil. Cover the top with foil. I have done this many hours ahead. About an hour and a half before serving, put in a 350 oven or even slower. There is no wine taste in this because you use so little. You can even substitute water and have a delicious creole smothered chicken.

Creamed hominy we originally got from Fannie Warren, one of the most famous cateresses Chattanooga has ever had. She helped us with a large brunch once and she promised that it would be the best thing we had. She was right. She put it in a heavy pan with cream and butter and let it cook gently for an hour until the cream had cooked down and was thick. To this day we have been doing hominy this way for buffets.

CREAMED HOMINY

Get a large size can of white hominy (2½ can) and drain off the liquid. Put it in a heavy saucepan. Pour in ½ cup whipping cream and ½ stick butter, a little salt and pepper and a dash of Tabasco. This must simmer slowly for about an hour until the cream has turned to a thick sauce. For a large group double or triple the recipe, since 1 large can will serve about 6.

Before serving, butter a round mixing bowl. Pack the hominy into this. Unmold onto a platter and sprinkle the top with chopped parsley.

The late Mrs. Fannie Warren

BLACK BOTTOM PIE

Chocolate Cookie crust:
4 tablespoons melted butter   *1¼ cups ground chocolate wafers*

Roll out the cookies with a rolling pin. Mix with the butter and press into a pyrex 9 inch pie pan. Put in slow oven 5 minutes to set, or put in refrigerator to set.

Pie Filling:
2 cups milk   *1 teaspoon vanilla*
½ cup and 4 tablespoons sugar   *1¼ tablespoons plain*
1¼ tablespoons cornstarch   *gelatin soaked in*
4 eggs, separated   *¼ cup cold water*
1½ ounces chocolate   *2 or 3 tablespoons rum*

Put milk in double boiler. Combine ½ cup sugar, cornstarch, and egg yolks. Add to the milk. Cook and stir until custard coats the spoon.

370

A Black Bottom Pie is a combination of a chocolate crust, chocolate custard, an airy layer of creamy rum, and a topping of whipped cream ... a dessert for high and festive occasions.

Remove 1 cup of the custard and add it to the chocolate and vanilla flavoring. Pour into the chocolate cookie crust. Add gelatin to the remaining custard. Cool. Add rum. Beat the egg whites, adding 4 tablespoons sugar slowly. When stiff but not dry, fold in the gelatin custard mix. Pile on top of the gelatin custard in the crust. Set in refrigerator at least 8 or 10 hours. Decorate with whipped cream and shaved chocolate.

The Pirate's House, Savannah, Georgia

A Tennessee Hunt Breakfast

One of the most distinguished hunt breakfasts is a menu Katherine Brooks had at a family brunch before her son Howard left for Vietnam. This was not the sort of hunt breakfast you have after a fox hunt. This was a hunt breakfast in the best sense of the word ... a hearty meal featuring the doves that the men and boys of the Brooks family had gotten on their hunts since dove season opened in the fall.

This was such a late breakfast it was almost lunch. First they had dove smothered in orange juice and wine the way their cook, Katherine Brown, fixes them, garlic cheese grits, a creamed egg casserole from Columbia, Tennessee, curried fruit, sliced country ham, some unusual homemade biscuits, lots of hot coffee, and for dessert, fudgecake squares and applesauce squares. I suppose they had to have dessert, because by the time they had eaten through this brunch, it must have been nearly afternoon.

Katherine says she was inspired to have a brunch because the party she enjoyed the most at a wedding in Middle Tennessee the year before, was a big brunch in a lovely big old home. This part of Tennessee is famous for its hospitality and for the good things they have to eat. She had had turkey hash served on a hominy ring, the egg casserole, curried fruit, country ham, whole wheat biscuits, and tea cakes. For her own brunch, she substituted dove for the turkey hash, garlic cheese grits for the hominy, egg biscuits for the whole wheat ones. The brunch was a real banquet according to all the family who were there, and Howard must have felt very properly sent off with the pride and best wishes of a big family and lots of friends. Now that he is safely home, it is nice to remember.

These recipes are so unusual that we have given them out many times since Katherine first gave them to me.

Many wives of hunting men have trouble with dove, because they dry out. These are first wrapped in bacon and smothered in orange juice, sherry, and chicken broth. Everyone has good luck with these.

POTTED DOVE

Clean, wash, and dry whole doves. 25 or 30 dove will feed 8 or 10 people. Season the dove with tenderizer, salt, and pepper. Wrap each dove in bacon and stick a toothpick through to hold. In a roaster, put a big piece of heavy duty foil (big enough to fold over the top later and seal). Now pour over the dove 3 tablespoons Worcestershire sauce, 1 tablespoon butter, 1 small can of orange juice concentrate plus 3 cans of water, 1 can chicken broth, ½ cup cooking sherry, and 1 teaspoon Kitchen Bouquet. Now pull up foil and seal top.

Roast covered in a 325 oven for 1 hour. The last 10 minutes, take the foil off the top and turn up the heat so the bacon will crisp. Mallard Ducks can be fixed this way, too.

With the drippings, make the gravy. Take about 3 tablespoons flour, and mix with enough cold water to make a paste. Add gradually to the hot liquid. Strain the gravy and add ½ cup more sherry. Taste. You may want to add salt or pepper. Glaze the doves with a small amount of gravy. Arrange on platter garnished with parsley.

Mrs. Katherine Brown

This recipe for grits has spread all over town, and it has become a popular addition to ham and turkey buffets.

GARLIC CHEESE GRITS

1 cup grits
3½ cups water
1 teaspoon salt
1 stick butter

1 package garlic cheese
2 eggs
Plus enough milk to make
   1 cup

Cook the grits according to directions. When done, add the butter and garlic cheese. Now measure 2 eggs in a measuring cup and fill up with milk. Beat together and add to the grits. Pour into a buttered casserole and bake at 350 for 30 to 35 minutes until set.

Mrs. Howard Brooks

MIDDLE TENNESSEE CREAMED EGGS

This recipe is different, because the hard cooked eggs are grated and then put in a cream sauce.

12 eggs
3 cups milk
6 tablespoons butter
6 tablespoons flour

Salt and cayenne pepper
to taste
Worchestershire sauce to taste

Hard boil the eggs. Put in cold water, and when cool, shell. Put the eggs through a potato ricer or grate them. Now make a medium cream sauce by melting the butter, adding the flour, and when the roux is made, gradually add the milk, beating so that there are no lumps. A small pastry whip is fine to keep it smooth. Season to taste. Add the eggs. Taste again to be sure. Now put in a long rectangular pyrex casserole and bake 20 minutes at 325 degrees.

Mrs. Howard Brooks

Cleveland parties are very gala, whether a luau, a hunt supper or a dinner dance. This is a dinner dance scene at the D.S. Stuart's Hardwick Farm with Duke Ellington as the attraction.

Cleveland

Chattanoogans with Cleveland friends love to drive north 30 miles on the interstate freeway toward Knoxville, look out over the rolling country and the horse farms of the Johnstons and Mayfields, and visit in a delightful town known for its handsome homes and imaginative parties.

Cleveland developed about the same time as Chattanooga, and in a history of Bradley County edited by Colonel James Corn, there is an account from an English visitor who was amazed by the activity as the small town got started. "There is a spirit of enterprise ... and the tavern keeper, the trader, the doctor, the lawyer, all build to allure others to settle near them."

As the years passed, Cleveland became a stove center, with three large stove companies who ship their ranges and heaters all over the world. The Hardwick and Stuart families have the Hardwick Stove Comany; the Rymers have Magic Chef; whose stock is bought and sold on the New York Stock Exchange; the Browns have the Brown Stove Company. These families have been close friends and neighbors for generations, and have all contributed to Cleveland's reputation as a town of energetic delightful people who take pride in their businesses and in their homes.

If you are ever invited to a luau given by the D.S. Stuarts at Hardwick Farm, you will probably never forget it. Joe Corn Stuart can organize parties and see them through with her own original flair whether it is a four day houseparty for 44 adults at the farm one summer, or her own daughter Harris' wedding and reception at the big house there.

Joe likes to have a luau as a summer party in honor of a visitor or distinguished event. She arranges long low tables under the trees at Hardwick Farm made from either standard doors stacked on concrete blocks or wide planks put on low saw horses. The table tops are covered with canna leaves.

The menu is made up of specialties that can all be eaten with your hands. She usually has Suckling Pig, Chicken Breast Steamed in Corn Shucks, Shrimp Marinated with Soy Sauce and Butter, and Steamed in Shells, Fresh Fruit Served in Watermelon Halves, Chinese Egg Rolls, Barbecued Ribs, Baked Sweet Potatoes and Corn Roasted in the Oven. There are Japanese lanterns hanging in the trees, and guests are invited to wear "island dress," which can mean anything from shorts to simple summer dresses and muumuus.

One summer day of the luau, the rain came down in torrents, and Jo wondered what to do with 400 guests invited for dinner. They decided to clean out the three greenhouses of all the plants, put hay on the floors and Japanese lanterns from the ceilings, and she says it was the best luau ever, with special island music piped in from the stero.

In Cleveland a luau will be authentic, imaginative, colorful and as much like the real thing on Wakiki as Joe can remember. She will order or make leis for the honored guests, make everyone eat with their hands, and the tables will be tropical beauties.

Guests will mingle unde the big trees and a full moon, there will be much talking and laughing with the same informal summer feeling that you would have at a barbecue. But the Japanese lanterns, the Hawaiian food, and the music will be South Seas style and fun. "Someday we are going to have real Hawaiian music," she says, and she will.

Jo may have cooked for days ahead, and every detail will be perfect, but the party will have the relaxed fun that every Cleveland party seems to have for Chattanooga visitors. Jo gave me the following recipes which could be used for large scale or small luaus.

CHICKEN AND CORN LAUAUS

8 chicken breasts, small size	Salt and pepper
½ pound butter	1 tablespoon Worchestershire sauce
½ to 1 clove garlic	1 tablespoon grated onion

Brown the chicken breasts in butter on top of the stove.

Make a paste of the above ingredients. Cover each breast with a generous helping of the paste and wrap in spinach leaves. Remove the ear of corn from the corn husk, and place a chicken breast inside the husk in its place. Squeeze lemon juice over the chicken and pull the corn husks over it, securing the end of the husk by using a "twistem" to tie it. Steam 2 or 3 hours in a covered steamer or bake in oven at 250 degrees for 2 to 3 hours.

378

The ears of corn which were shucked, should be cleaned of corn silks and put in a roasting pan. These bake at 350 degrees until brown on all sides. Turn occasionally as they brown. Serve with melted butter or brush on melted butter before serving. Everything is eaten with the fingers at a luau.

MARINATED SHRIMP

Marinate shrimp unshelled and uncooked in a sauce made of 1 part butter and 1 part soy sauce at least 24 hours. Bake in the same container until done at about 350 degrees. When the shrimp turn pinkish white, they are done.

CHINESE EGG ROLL

1 can 7-ounce crabmeat
1 cup ground veal
2 tablespoons melted butter
1 cup celery, finely chopped
½ cup water chestnuts, chopped

½ cup spring onion, chopped (stems and all)
2 teaspoons salt
1 teaspoon sugar
1½ tablespoons peanut butter

Brown the veal in the butter. Mix in all the other ingredients. Roll out the egg dough and cut in squares or circles as you desire. Place a dab of filling on each to make a packet, sealing the edges. Fry in deep fat until golden brown.

EGG DOUGH

2 cups flour
¼ cup shortening
4 egg yolks

3 tablespoons water
1 teaspoon salt

Cut the shortening into the flour and salt and mix as pastry.

FRESH FRUIT IN WATERMELON HALF

Marinate as many kinds of fresh fruit as available overnight in a classic French vinegar and oil dressing. Cut a watermelon in half and scoop out melon for use in salad. Fill with marinated fruit and sprinkle with grated coconut and raisins.

Mrs. D.S. Stuart, Jr.
Cleveland, Tennessee

The Tom Moores enjoy cooking everything from Sunday morning omelets to the fanciest French recipes Tom can read about, to outdoor grilling on their terrace.

Gourmet Dinner For Eight

It is a memorable dinner when the host is an inspired cook and gourmet, and wants an audience of friends for a new dinner menu. Tom Moore, when in a cooking mood, might make Sunday morning omelets for Sarah and their five sons. Or he might make a fabulous stew from the Escoffier cookbook, or he might just plan an elegant dinner beginning with Oysters Rockefeller, followed by Caesar Salad, then Broiled Chicken Vanderbilt, a Wild Rice Mold with Mushrooms and Artichokes, Hot Rolls, Strawberries Romanoff for dessert, and coffee. When the host is also the cook, there is a contagious sort of enthusiasm about having dinner and enjoying good food. Everything is seasoned perfectly. It is an occasion to be remembered.

TOM MOORE'S OYSTERS ROCKEFELLER

32 oysters on the half shell
2 packages frozen
   spinach souffle
1 bunch green onions
1 bunch parsley
1 green pepper
2 stalks green celery
¼ pound butter
Fine bread crumbs

3 tablespoons
   Worcestershire sauce
1 teaspoon anchovy paste
Tabasco sauce
2 ounces annisette
Paprika
Salt
Grated Parmesan cheese

Cook the spinach souffle according to the directions on the package. Open the oysters, being sure to cut the muscle underneath. (You can use oysters, that have already been shelled and a supply of old oyster shells that you have saved.) Place 4 oysters in shells on each of 8 small pie pans filled with rock salt. Chop very finely the onions, parsley, green pepper and celery. Saute in butter.

When the spinach is still slightly undercooked, remove from the tin into a large saucepan, and stir in the sauteed vegetables. Add Worcestershire sauce, several drops of Tabasco, annisette, paprika, and a scant teaspoon of salt. If the resulting mixture is too dry or stiff, add soft butter and stir. Cover each oyster with the mixture. Dust lightly with bread crumbs and Parmesan cheese. Bake in hot oven (425) until brown. Serve hot on pie plates.

BROILED CHICKEN VANDERBILT

4 broilers, split	Garlic
1 onion, sliced	Lemon juice
1 carrot, sliced	Salt, pepper, paprika
2 cups water	Butter
1 cup sauterne	1 tablespoon flour

Simmer necks, giblets, onions and carrots in water until tender. Add wine and strain. Chop giblets fine. Rub chickens with a cut clove of garlic and sprinkle with salt, pepper, paprika, and a little lemon juice. Place skin side up in a shallow pan, brush with butter, and place under broiler. Baste frequently with wine sauce and turn occasionally. When chickens are tender and brown, (30 minutes), remove from pan. Thicken remaining sauce with the flour and a little Beau Monde seasoning. Add chopped giblets, cook until thickened, and pour over chickens.

WILD RICE MOLD

1 cup wild rice	1 quart boiling water
2 teaspoons salt	4 tablespoons butter

Pick over and wash rice. Cook in double boiler until tender, about 45 minutes. Add salt and mix with rice. Put in a buttered ring mold, place in a pan half filled with boiling water, and bake in moderate oven (350) for 25 to 30 minutes.

CAESAR SALAD

Lettuce	¼ cup lemon juice
2 cups fried bread croutons	2 tablespoons anchovies,
1½ cups olive oil,	cut and drained
garlic flavored	2 eggs
¼ cup Worcestershire sauce	Grated Parmesan cheese
¼ cup wine vinegar	Freshly ground pepper
Salt	
1 teaspoon dry mustard	

Fry croutons which have been soaked in a little olive oil well ahead of time. In a large salad bowl, place lettuce (Romaine may be added). Sprinkle with salt, pepper and mustard; add croutons and toss. Pour oil, Worcestershire sauce, vinegar, lemon juice, and toss. Add anchovies and cheese and toss. Drop in eggs, which have been coddled for 1½ minutes. Toss and blend thoroughly. Serve immediately.

MUSHROOMS AND ARTICHOKES

1 can French artichokes	*6 tablespoons butter*
1 pound fresh mushrooms	*Salt, pepper*
½ grated onion	

Drain artichokes; cut in halves. Saute mushrooms and onions in butter for 3 minutes. Add artichokes and seasonings. Cover and simmer 10 minutes. Fill center of rice ring.

STRAWBERRIES ROMANOFF

2 quarts strawberries,	*Juice of 1 lemon*
* sugared*	*2 ounces Cointreau*
1 pint vanilla ice cream	*1 ounce Bacardi Rum*
1 cup whipping cream,	
* whipped*	

Whip cream and fold into ice cream. Add lemon juice, Cointreau and rum, and pour over the whole chilled strawberries. (From the Church of the Good Shepherd Cookbook.)

Tom Moore, Jr.

Teen Age Cateresses

It is a memorable dinner when you sit down to gourmet food that has been prepared by a young pair of cateresses in Chattanooga, 13 year old cousins Sue Ferguson and Dottie Allison. The Dottie and Sue Catering Company began when their grandparents, the James R. Hedges, offered to pay them to come cook Thursday night dinner for them. The girls liked to cook anyway, and this was a chance to earn some pin money.

With great enthusiasm they began planning delightful meals, reading Gourmet magazine, looking at cookbooks. One night they had a Ground Beef Stroganoff with Noodles, Minted Green Peas, a Green Salad, Hard Rolls, and a French Peach Cake. Another night they made Seafood in Patty Shells, French Green Beans with Almonds, an Avocado Salad with French Dressing, and a dessert called Lemon Squares. Another night they tried one of their grandmother's specialties, Chicken and Orange.

One day their Mama Dot said, "You girls are getting so good, you should go in the business." Right away they got on the phone and called the various Hedges family and friends to announce their newest service, and they have been busy ever since. They first do the grocery shopping, then they cook the dinner, serve it, and clean up the kitchen.

They have been brought up on delicious food, and no recipe seems too difficult. They make Hollandaise sauce, biscuits, lard leg of lamb with both lemon peel and garlic. They are very strict with each other about doing things "right," and consult, criticize, giggle, and praise each other the way all cousins do. Now they are cooking memorable dinners for their various aunts, cousins, and friends, who are delighted to find such attractive professional cateresses. The recipes for their memorable meal follows.

384

SEAFOOD IN CHAFING DISH

1 can mushroom soup
1 can frozen shrimp soup
2 cans King crab meat
  (drained and picked over)
1½ pounds shrimp,
  cooked and shelled
2 cans sliced mushrooms

1 pint canned oysters,
  drained
2 cups thick cream sauce
½ can chicken stock
½ onion, grated
1 rib celery, grated
½ cup sherry

Make the cream sauce using 2 cups milk, 6 tablespoons butter and 6 tablespoons flour. Cook in a double boiler over low heat for a long time so there is no flour taste. Add the chicken stock. Stir while adding the mushroom soup and the shrimp soup. Add the seafood and the mushrooms, the grated celery and onion which you have sauteed. Add the sherry last. Now taste to see that the seasoning is correct. Be sure it has enough salt and pepper and whatever else you think it needs. When it is very hot, it is ready to serve in patty shells. You can buy frozen patty shells and have them baked and ready.

MINTED PEAS

Use frozen peas and cook according to instructions. Put fresh mint leaves in the water as it boils. When they are tender, take the leaves out, since they will turn dark. Add some real butter and about 3 fresh mint leaves for each serving as a garnish. Be sure and taste to see that the salt and pepper are right.

LEMON SQUARES

1 cup flour
½ cup butter

¼ teaspoon salt
¼ cup powdered sugar

Mix just as you would a pie crust (cut in) and press in a greased pan with your fingers. Use an 8 by 8 inch pan. (If you want to double the recipe use a 9 by 13 inch pan.) Bake at 350 degrees for 20 to 25 minutes. Check in 15 minutes because it may get done quicker.

Beat 2 eggs and add 1 cup sugar, 3 tablespoons lemon juice, ½ teaspoon baking powder, and the grated rind of 2 lemons. Pour over the crust and bake 25 minutes at 350 degrees.

Dottie Allison and Sue Ferguson

*When your grandfather has a birthday, blowing out the candles is a
family affair. Susan and Roy sing "Happy Birthday" while my father,
Roy McDonald, holds Ellen on his lap.*

When Father Was 65

There are all sorts of ways to have parties. The usual way is to take a week or two out of your life and completely clean the house, worry about the menu, and agonize over where everyone will sit and how to cook the food, arrange the flowers, and polish all the silver. When you realize that all this is added to the everyday things like washing, ironing and feeding your family you can understand why people don't have parties more often.

Recently I came upon an easier way to entertain and it involves mostly your own attitude. Very few of us are perfectionists . . . we had rather have a warm, hospitable homey party than a spotless house and be tired. I have found out that you can have almost any kind of party with only one day's actual work if you concentrate on the food and use two or three tricks to make the house look festive.

The day after Thanksgiving 1966 was my father's 65th birthday, and we decided to surprise him by asking a few friends for dinner . . . the list actually grew until somehow we had invited 80 people to come to our house for dinner. In the fall we had put plastic around the screened porch, which gave us another room when we had a heater in it. I counted up the chairs and stairsteps and figured some people could just sit on the floor. I did the shopping on Wednesday, planning Ham, Baked Apricots, Green Beans, Creamed Hominy, Tossed Green Salad, Hot Buttered Biscuits, Coffee and Iced Tea, and for dessert, Orange Cake and $100 Brownies passed on trays.

I don't know how to explain this, but if you have the feeling that everything is going to work out fine, and if you are calm and in a good humor, it is fantastic the good fortune that usually comes your way. If you worry about all the wrong things that might happen, sometimes they do. Even when things don't work out so well, being calm and happy is a much better frame of mind from which to work out some ingenious solutions.

Thanksgiving afternoon we baked the hams so they would slice easily the next day. We had polished the brass some that week and arranged Magnolia leaves in the fireplaces. I can't describe what this does for a house...to have greenery in the fireplaces, or in large vases, and to have containers of philodendron or fern gives any house or apartment a gracious dignity in my eyes. People never go into a corner to see if it is dusted, but if a house is picked up and there are touches of green, then it is plenty festive enough for friends.

The day of the party we had excellent help. Belle and Elmer Pettyjohn came, as did Annie Lewis. We had a wonderful time that day putting everything together and things began getting done. (We went from the sublime to the ridiculous the day after Christmas when we had a buffet supper for fifty teenagers with no help at all!)

About noon I went to borrow a rectangular pyrex dish for the apricots from a friend. I was amazed...she had not only the dish and an extra tray, but a huge clear plastic bowl for the salad. At the beauty shop another friend offered a screen to go in the kitchen and separate the work area from the end people would have to walk through. Another offered wrought iron candle stands with hurricane shades to light the steps outside. I came home laden with bounty.

We were a little behind making the clothes line art show of newpaper clippings and old pictures, when my cousin arrived and offered to help. Mother came in time to help with the salad making, as did my aunt. Things worked together, just as I knew they would. My small kitchen had never cooked for so many, but everything got done. My husband sliced ham with the electric knife until he was sure we could feed an army.

It really seemed a miracle, but about an hour before the guests arrived, we were finished. If I had it to do over again, I would have worked the day ahead as well, but it would have spoiled Thanksgiving, and it had been a busy week. It couldn't have turned out any better if we had planned and worried.

I have helped with some parties when the hostess was upset and nervous. If she couldn't find the right can opener or spoon of knife, she would go into a long tirade about how nothing was ever in the right place. Or if time were slipping up and things were not getting done, the atmosphere in the kitchen would get dark, the help would get sullen, and the desperateness of the situation would be awful.

From experience I have learned that the more desperate the situation, the more important for the one in charge to be optimistic and happy. So what if dinner is late or the silver doesn't get polished, or something doesn't get done. You just make the best of it. You want to have a good time yourself.

What few people realize is that the very air of a house is charged with the feelings of the hostess. If she is upset, the air is actually cold, people can't think of anything to say, they can't relax. There is another thing that I hardly understand. If you have created a party and if you are slightly breathless, because it came together rather quickly and spontaneously, then sometimes there is a warm feeling in the air, everyone seems unusually glad to see each other, and it is a better party than if you had scientifically strung out the planning for a week or two.

But we will never forget this birthday party. My father was surprised, people did find a place to sit, but because there were so many and because everyone wanted to see the old pictures, souvenirs and clippings, they mingled the way all good parties should. I think we did finally run out of hot buttered buscuits, but we had made 300, so we didn't run out until the very last. There were silly presents, poems, some front pages of the News-Free Press with fake headlines put in for the event. It was a memorable dinner for someone we love.

HOW I DISCOVERED CREMATED HAM

The afternoon before the dinner, we put in the hams to bake for the party and decided to get a coat of white paint on the new Williamsburg fence out by the herb garden. It was a beautiful day. I didn't worry about the ham because the directions on the wrapper called for 15 minutes to the pound. We wanted it cooked about 30 minutes to the pound, so I had put it in an open roasting pan in a slow oven. I didn't plan to look at it for hours.

Later that afternoon Susan came out to say that the ham was burning. I paid no attention, because it hadn't been in long enough. An hour later I went into the house and found out she was right. The oven had kicked on to a higher speed and the ham was really very well done. The shank bone would have lifted right out if I had pulled. But we like ham overdone or cremated. It dries out and takes on a sweet taste and a tenderness that is a cross between a regular ham and a country ham. We mixed up a brown sugar glaze with about 1 cup brown sugar, 1 teaspoon mustard, and enough orange juice to make a paste. I glazed it and let it cool, then put it on the back porch until the next day. The other two hams we baked for the party the usual way . . . just until done, then glazed them.

The next day when we sliced them, the cremated ham was the more tender, sweet, and succulent. It was almost a Charles Lamb and the roasted pig discovery. One uncle who tasted this ham, called later to find out what kind I had bought; he declared it was a cross between a regular ham and an old fashioned country ham. I realized that I had treated it to my own sort of curing and smoking. Smokehouses all over the South were built for the very purpose of drying out a ham. It makes it tender and sweet.

Ever since our big party we have been nearly cremating our hams. These tender sweet slices served with biscuits are very popular.

Good ham always calls for hot buttered biscuits, and we figured out a way to make hundreds ahead of time on a sort of brown and serve theory. At the last minute, you have only to run several pans of buttered biscuits in the oven and as soon as they brown, you pass them hot. This is a good thing to know in large groups.

HOMEMADE BISCUITS TO BROWN AND SERVE

First get a 2 pound bag of self rising flour. Sift this into a large bowl and cut in 1½ cups shortening or lard. This is your ready mix. Put about 2 cups of the mix (but don't stop to measure), in a small bowl and add enough milk to make a biscuit dough that will come away from the sides of the bowl. Turn out on floured pastry cloth, knead 7 or 8 times, roll out and cut biscuits to put on the pan.

If you are having a party or large group, repeat making the dough until you have 3 or 4 biscuits for each person. About an hour (or two hours if it suits you better), before dinner put the biscuits in a 450 degree oven and let bake until they are definitely risen but not brown. Take out of the oven and butter each while hot.

You won't believe this, but set the tray aside on an unused counter covered with a newspaper. Do all your biscuits this way. Right before you want to serve them, run in the oven to brown . . . 3 or 4 minutes. You can have all your biscuits hot and buttered at the same time, and they taste fine. People seem so grateful to get them already buttered.

BAIRD'S ICED TEA

½ gallon strong tea
1 small can frozen lemonade,
undiluted

Sugar to taste
(½ to 1 cup)
2 bottles (10 ounce)
ginger ale

Sweeten the tea. Add the frozen lemonade. At the very last add the ginger ale. When you are doubling this, you can add 3 bottles of ginger ale and 1 of soda water. This adds a dryness that is refreshing.

Be sure to make enough of this. I have always run out.

Miss Baird McClure

Thanksgiving

When Thanksgiving comes each year, we order the turkey, invite all the family, bustle around with all the fixing of food, polishing the house, and arranging big vases of fall leaves. And we try to talk to the children occasionally about being thankful.

It is a hard thing to feel thankful in the midst of great bounty. Like a child at Christmas with too many nice things, I turn on the stove, dial my mother's number, put away the groceries, and adjust the thermostat so the heat will be right, as a matter of course. And I forget the week of the ice storm on our mountain years ago when we had none of these things.

One year just before Thanksgiving my husband was sick; Kinch wrote from Vietnam that his jungle rot was worse and that in one awful battle, he had been one of the two survivors in his unit; the bottom burner of the oven burnt out; Susan got a strange virus that made her stomach and head ache; a sock got stuck in the washing machine so that it overflowed on the floor that had just been fixed; and life was almost unbelievable. One night when everyone had gone to bed, I felt so low that I fixed myself some tea and just on an impulse made a list of all the things I was thankful for . . . it took two pages! I didn't tell a soul, but it did help.

As life evens out for all of us, we have good years and bad. Like all families, we have our faults and our failings. We have had big happy Thanksgivings here, inviting both family and any friends or strangers who might be eating alone. Other years have been quieter, with an empty place or two, a son away from home, or a grandmother who has died. Yet the kitchen is our mainstay. There will always be a turkey and the old fashioned fixings that cannot be improved on, and we will gather around the piano to sing first "Come Ye Thankful People, Come," "We Gather Together to Ask the Lord's Blessing," and "America." The last year my grandmother was with us, Franklin said, "Did you hear Mama sing America by heart? And she's 86!"

All over Chattanooga Thanksgiving is a sweet family time, a time to gather in and be together. We serve our big dinner buffet style on the sideboard. The big turkey will be tender and good, sliced on a platter. The dressing is an old Mississippi one made with both cornbread and white bread, sauteed onions and celery, both raw eggs and hard boiled eggs, and some turkey broth. It is baked in a long pyrex baking dish, because with so many people, it is easier to serve in squares.

Congealed cranberry salad makes a pretty touch of red. Broccoli and Hollandaise sauce go well with the turkey, along with Belle Pettyjohn's special Sweet Potato Casserole, and a big bowl of rice for the turkey gravy. And Annie or I make croissants.

For dessert there is either Ambrosia, cold with lots of oranges and fresh pineapples, or little Chess Pies and coffee. This is Thanksgiving, the day we count our blessings and give thanks—the most memorable dinner of all.

ROAST TURKEY

First thaw the turkey and wash it well inside and out. Pat dry and rub all over with butter, then salt, Accent, and a little white pepper. I stick a rib of celery and a small onion in the body cavity. The turkey can be stuffed, but we fix the stuffing separately.

Preheat the oven to 425 degrees. We have experimented with many ways of roasting turkey, from the low heat, baste frequently method, to the newer tent method. Always looking for ways to save time, and because this is the quickest and just as good, we use the high heat method.

In a roaster place a long strip of heavy foil. Put the turkey on this, breast side up. With a little extra foil cover the wing tips. Now wrap the turkey up, not tightly, but with a loose drug store wrap. Put the turkey in the 425 oven and for a 12 to 15 pound turkey, allow about 15 minutes to the pound. Your only problem here is that you might overcook it, and it won't slice as pretty if it falls off the bones. 45 minutes before you think it will be done, uncover the turkey so that the top can brown. You might brush with butter.

You know when a turkey is done by watching the thigh, the last part to get done. Poke it with a fork. If it feels tender and if the juice that runs out is clear, the turkey is done.

At Thanksgiving aim to have the turkey out of the oven an hour before dinner. You can cover it with foil and it will keep warm. As with any roasted meat, it needs a little while for the juices to be absorbed into the meat. If cut immediately after coming out of the oven, the juices will spurt out and you will lose them.

HOW TO MAKE GIBLET GRAVY

Wash the neck and the giblets. Put in a saucepan with water, a piece of celery, a small onion, and salt and pepper. Boil til tender. Take out the giblets and strain broth. Chop up the liver and gizzard fine. In a pan make a roux with 2 tablespoons butter and 2 tablespoons flour. Gradually add the liquid from the giblets and stir so it is very smooth. You can taste and add paprika to give color, some chopped parsley, and maybe more salt. Add the chopped giblets and you have your gravy.

DRESSING FOR CHICKEN OR TURKEY

5 cups corn bread,
   crumbled
1 cup light bread,
   torn in small pieces
2 onions, chopped

1 cup celery, chopped
2 raw eggs
2 hard boiled eggs
2 eggs, beaten
Salt and pepper to taste

First you will need some broth that the hen has cooked in or that can be found inside the foil that the turkey has roasted in. You can use chicken broth from a can.

Soften the bread crumbs with the broth and add 2 beaten eggs. Saute the chopped onions and celery in a little butter until soft. Add this to the bread mixture and grated hard boiled eggs. Add about 1 teaspoon salt and a little pepper and taste. Some people like thyme or sage in dressing, but we like it plain.

I can't be specific about the amount of broth you will need, but go light. You want a wet dressing, but not soupy. Put in a greased baking dish and bake at 350 for 30 to 40 minutes. Double this recipe for a turkey.

BELLE'S CREAMED SWEET POTATOES

Pick out about 6 sweet potatoes that are medium sized. Put in water to cover and boil with the skins on until tender. When done, peel, and put in bowl to mix. Let the mixer mash them until smooth. Add 1 teaspoon salt, the juice and grated peel of 1 orange, the juice and grated peel of ½ lemon, 2 eggs, ½ stick butter, ½ teaspoon cinnamon and a dash of nutmeg. Now sweeten to taste with brown sugar. Drain a small can of crushed pineapple and add the pineapple to the potatoes.

If the potatoes are too stiff, thin down with a little sweet milk. They should be thick enough to mound slightly, but not stiff. At the last add ½ cup chopped pecans, and put in a buttered casserole. Top with marshmallows. Before serving, bake in a 350 oven until sweet potatoes are hot and the marshmallows slightly brown, about 20 or 30 minutes.

Mrs. Elmer Pettyjohn

MOLDED CRANBERRY SALAD WITH COCA-COLA

1 package orange gelatin
1 cup boiling water
1 envelope plain gelatin
½ cup cold water
1 large can whole
  cranberry sauce
1 can crushed pineapple

1 tablespoon lemon juice
1 tablespoon grated
  orange rind
1 cup pecans, broken
1 bottle Coca-Cola
  (6 ounces)

Dissolve the orange gelatin in boiling water. Add the cranberry sauce to the hot mixture and mix well until the sauce is soft and blended. Add the plain gelatin which has first been dissolved in the cold water. Remove from stove and add the pineapple, lemon juice, orange rind, nuts, and finally the Coca-cola. Pour into a mold and put in the refrigerator.

This recipe was one of Winnie Holmes' ideas with the lemon juice and orange rind added by us.

The late Miss Winnie Holmes

ANNIE'S AMBROSIA

12 oranges
1 fresh pineapple
  (or 1 can crushed)

½ package frozen coconut
½ cup to 1 cup sugar
Juice of 1 lemon

Peel oranges and cut in sections. Save the remaining part of the orange and crush with an orange juice squeezer to get the juice.

394

Sweeten with sugar. Use 1 cup of sugar if you are using a fresh pineapple. If you are using a can of pineapple, it has already been sweetened, so just use ½ cup sugar for the oranges. Add the coconut and the juice of a lemon. Put in the refrigerator in a plastic covered container to mellow. This is better if made a day ahead, and will keep several days for whoever is in the mood for a light dessert.

Mrs. Annie Lewis

This is Chattanooga. As you drive down any of our mountains on a fall day, curve after curve, the sun plays on the leaves, the sky is a crisp blue and white against the vivid landscape. The huge gray rocks and ledges have a timeless quality and a strength. The Tennessee River and Chickamauga Dam are beautiful from the neights, and the city in the valley below is a busy place. There are old buildings and new buildings, freeways carrying cars and trucks across town. There is progress everywhere.

From almost any spot in town, you can look up and see the surrounding mountains, standing majestically and watchfully. They change with the seasons. The same pleasant roads that are almost fairylike with white dogwood in the spring, grow cool and green all summer, brilliant orange and red in the fall, and sometimes icy with their beauty in the winter.

They are always with us, and to those of us born here, they are a part of us. We know the shape of Lookout, Elder, Signal and the ridges. We have welcomed the very sight of the hills of home when returning from a trip. If we stay away too long, they are magnets drawing us back. We have mourned quietly at the foot of a mountain as we have gathered at funerals and returned our loved ones to the ground from whence they came.

We are big people and little people; we come from many backgrounds and traditions. No one group of people is Chattanooga. We are Greek wedding feasts, Hungarian bakeries; we are church suppers and Bar Mitzvah receptions. We have eaten everything from beef heart in the lean years, country ham and oysters for a President, hoecakes at home, fried chicken on the lake, and cider in Summertown. Whether we are children still in school, busy homemakers, or tired workers home from our jobs, we enjoy gathering in for the simple southern food that we like best.

It is our people who make Chattanooga cooking the very special thing that is, to those of us who love it, and who live here in the shadow of the mountains.

RECIPE INDEX

INDEX

INDEX

403

INDEX

INDEX

INDEX

INDEX